Z in Practice

BCS Practitioner Series

Series editor: Ray Welland

Z in Practice

Rosalind Barden
Susan Stepney
David Cooper

Logica Cambridge Ltd

Prentice Hall
New York   London   Toronto   Sydney   Tokyo   Singapore

First published 1994 by
Prentice Hall International (UK) Limited
Campus 400, Maylands Avenue
Hemel Hempstead
Hertfordshire, HP2 7EZ
A division of
Simon & Schuster International Group

Printed and bound in Great Britain

Library of Congress Cataloging-in-Publication Data

Barden, Rosalind, 1959–
    Z in practice / Rosalind Barden, Susan Stepney, David Cooper.
        p.   cm. — (BCS practitioner series)
    Includes bibliographical references and index.
    ISBN 0-13-124934-7
    1. Z (Computer program language)   I. Stepney, Susan, 1958.
II. Cooper, David, 1958–   .   III. Title   IV. Series.
QA76.73.72B37   1994
005.1′.2—dc20   94–30571
                                                        CIP

British Library Cataloguing in Publication Data

A catalogue record for this book is available from
the British Library
ISBN 0-13-124934-7

---

1   2   3   4   5   98   97   96   95   94

Contents

V Appendices   329

Series Editorial Preface

The aim of the BCS Practitioner Series is to produce books which are relevant for practising computer professionals across the whole spectrum of information technology activities. We want to encourage practitioners to share their practical experience of methods and applications with fellow professionals. We also seek to disseminate information in a form which is suitable for the practitioner who often has only limited time to read widely within a new subject area or to assimilate research findings.

The role of the BCS is to provide advice on the suitability of books for the series, via the editorial panel and to provide a pool of potential authors upon which we can draw. Our objective is that this series will reinforce the drive within the BCS to increase professional standards in IT. The other partners in this venture, Prentice Hall, provide the publishing expertise and international marketing capabilities of a leading publisher in the computing field.

The response when we set up the series was extremely encouraging. However, the success of the series depends on there being practitioners who want to learn as well as those who feel they have something to offer! The series is under continual development and we are always looking for ideas for new topics and feedback on how to further improve the usefulness of the series. If you are interested in writing for the series then please contact us.

The need for formal methods of software development is becoming more widely accepted and this is an excellent practical book about Z. This book is written by practitioners; it discusses how Z is used to solve real problems and gives practical advice on how Z should be used. There are case studies to illustrate the use of Z and guidance on using Z within a project, including management issues. This is the book for the practitioner wanting to find out about the current practice of formal methods.

Ray Welland
Computing Science Department, University of Glasgow

xi

Editorial panel members

Frank Bott (UCW, Aberystwyth), Dermot Browne (KPMG Management Consulting), Nic Holt (ICL), Trevor King (Praxis Systems Plc), Tom Lake (GLOSSA), Kathy Spurr (Analysis and Design Consultants), Mario Wolczko (University of Manchester).

Preface

There are many books available that provide an introduction to Z and its underlying mathematics. There are also a number of short industrial courses and higher education modules that teach students about the basic mathematical ideas of Z. What is missing is a book aimed at people who have understood the basics of the language and now wish to become *users* of Z. This book does just that.

Z users may be those who have to write a specification, or they may be 'advanced' readers who need to work from Z specifications, such as reviewers, evaluators, assessors, designers, and programmers.

This book contains plenty of examples of using Z. The examples chosen reflect the fact that not everyone who uses Z specifications has a computer science background. While we address some typical computer science problems we also examine some everyday areas such as games. Our aim is to present example problems that are readily understood.

Many published case studies present solutions to problems without indicating why that particular approach has been taken. Throughout the specifications in this book we have woven commentary on the techniques of Z specification that we are using. These are collected together in a glossary which allows the interested reader to follow links into the case studies to see the techniques in the context of problem solving. These glossary entries vary in complexity, and many are based on our experience of the questions that people often ask on industrial short courses.

The majority of the book is technical, although the early chapters address the more managerial issues of using Z within an organisation. These will be of interest to team leaders who are managing groups of Z specifiers as well as to technical readers.

The typical technical reader will have studied Z to some extent, perhaps by having attended a short industrial course or an introductory higher education course, or by having read an introductory text on Z. The material should also be suitable for people who are familiar with other model-oriented formal specification languages who do not need an introduction to the mathematics involved but want a description of how Z specifications are written.

Although this book contains a glossary and a notation guide it is not a reference manual for the notation. It does not introduce the basic mathematics. It is a practical book of helpful hints and explanations about using Z given in the context of problem solving and specifications.

Text in the book

There are different kinds of text in this book

- the Z itself (the 'mathematical text')
- the explanatory 'accompanying text', which (should) occur in any Z specification, motivating the mathematics and relating it to the real world entities described
- pedagogical notes.

We use a stylistic convention to distinguish these kinds of text. The accompanying text is interleaved with the Z in the usual manner. The notes are set in a smaller typeface with an indented key identifying phrase, thus

> ▷ *key phrase*
> A pedagogical note explaining why the given approach was taken, or why an apparently better approach was not taken, or explaining a more unusual use of the notation.

Appendix B is a comprehensive glossary and cross reference, which should help with finding the information given in these notes. It consists of an alphabetical list of key phrases. Each section consists of a short definition of its key phrase, and list of references to the pages where that phrase occurs, accompanied by a short description of its context. The glossary entry corresponding to the above note would appear as

> **key phrase**
> A key phrase is used in each pedagogical note to indicate the content of the note and as a cross reference entry in the glossary. The cross reference entry includes a note of the section in which the glossary reference appears, provided as an aide-mémoire for anyone who knows they have seen the point illustrated *somewhere*.
>
> page xiv: Preface: explanation of glossary structure

Towards the end of the glossary we collect together various discussion points that appear throughout the text. Finally, a list of symbols and their names appears at the end of the glossary.

The notation

We have used the definitions and mathematical toolkit of [Spivey 1992], the *de facto* standard for Z. In this book it is referred to as the *sample toolkit* . At the time of writing, a Z standard is being prepared for submission to the British Standards Institute (BSI) and the International Standards Organisation (ISO) [Brien & Nicholls 1992]. The glossary includes some notes of anticipated changes.

Structure of the book

This book need not be read in a linear order. As indicated above various readers may find different sections relevant. Below we give an outline of what appears in each chapter to enable readers to select those which are appropriate.

In **Part I** (Chapters 1–7) we describe various methods that can be used in conjunction with the Z notation for specifying a variety of systems. Chapter 1 sets the scene, giving advice for newcomers to Z, managers, project leaders and specifiers, including some of the management issues involved in using Z on a project. In Chapter 2 we discuss the components necessary in any method: structure, process and fluency. Chapter 3 explains the Established Strategy for writing Z specifications in a 'state and operations' style. An alternative method used for writing security specifications is described in Chapter 4. An overview of other approaches that can be used with Z is given in Chapter 5. In Chapter 6 we discuss ways of checking that a specification is 'correct'. Chapter 7 suggests questions to consider when putting together an appropriate method for using Z.

In **Part II** (Chapters 8–13) we present five case studies. Our aim is to show Z being used to specify realistic problems. Each case study concentrates on illustrating particular aspects of Z. First in Chapter 8 we describe our 'house style' for the specifications in the book.

In Chapter 9 we examine the familiar computer science problem of counting words within a document and producing frequency tables. We start with a simplistic specification which takes a 'lateral' view of what a word might be. We then specify the solution in increasingly complex ways, finishing with an implementation-oriented specification based on Unix. Our aim is to show that a problem can be solved at varying levels of abstraction. We wish to encourage you to pick the most abstract specification appropriate for your needs.

In Chapter 10 we illustrate how the schema calculus, in particular schema conjunction and disjunction, can be used to structure a specification, here of a space flight company. (Further use of schemas is covered in Chapter 23.)

Structuring specifications is looked at in a different way in Chapter 11. We use Entity Relationship Diagrams to break down the problem and guide the structure of the specification of a video hire shop. We concentrate on operations such as checking that a borrower is old enough to hire a given film, rather than on the mechanics of borrowing and returning videos. Such operations have been described elsewhere in specifications of book-lending libraries, including [King & Sørensen 1989], [Diller 1990], [Potter *et al.* 1991] and [Wordsworth 1992].

The techniques of precondition calculation and promotion are used in Chapter 12. The way in which preconditions are calculated is described in some detail, whereas the use of promotion is just illustrated. For a full explanation of promotion you should read Chapter 19.

Chapter 13 provides solutions to the Tower of Hanoi problem. The main aim of this chapter is to illustrate the process of refinement. As this book is primarily about specification, we do not show a full transformation towards code. Rather we show how a more concrete solution refines the abstract view and give the required proofs.

This part contains the largest specifications in the book. Subsequent chapters look at smaller problems to illustrate various useful points.

In **Part III** (Chapters 14–19) we look at some common Z styles that have been found to be useful, and that you can use or adapt for your own purposes.

Abstraction is a desirable property of specifications. A specification that is too concrete includes unnecessary details that makes it difficult to read, and may also include premature design or implementation decisions that are better left until later. An abstract specification, on the other hand, includes only the essentials of the problem eschewing clutter and deferring design decisions to a later, more appropriate, time. Abstraction is notoriously difficult to define, so we have sidestepped the problem by providing some examples of abstraction in Chapter 14, pointing out where the temptations to be more concrete have been avoided.

Next we discuss various modelling choices. In Chapter 15 we present the same small specification using two different models (using sets and using functions) and discuss their advantages and disadvantages. Chapter 16 contrasts various styles of defining sets.

In Z sequences are functions, which are relations, which are sets. Chapter 17 describes how this means that specifications can sometimes be simplified by using set operations where, at first sight, they might not seem applicable.

If examples are always presented using one particular style there is the danger that such a style might be assumed to be the only one possible. The treatment of errors is one such case since the Established Strategy of disjoining error handling with the 'correct' operation is the one presented most often. In Chapter 18 we contrast this approach with an alternative way of describing error cases.

In Chapter 19 we explain the technique of promotion, a style for structuring specifications that can lead to clear and compact descriptions.

In **Part IV** (Chapters 20–26) we look at some of the less common aspects of Z. Our aim is to explain the use of those symbols that are often ignored or given only a glance in introductory texts. We illustrate some uses for them.

Free types often cause difficulties, especially in their recursive form. Chapter 20 illustrates the various forms of free types and their uses. We end on a note of caution with an example of a tree specification. At first it appears that this is the classical application of a recursive free type, but a different model proves to be more appropriate for specifying the required operations.

Bags are an underused part of Z, but at times they are useful. In Chapter 21 we illustrate some cases where bags are applicable.

Next, in Chapter 22, we look at axiomatic descriptions. Not every specification uses schemas and the example of the four function calculator contrasts a specification using schemas with one that does not. This chapter also includes a discussion of the different ways of under-specifying.

Having shown how sometimes schemas are not necessary, in Chapter 23 we move on to examine the many uses of schemas that are possible. This extends Chapter 10 by illustrating other parts of the schema calculus, the use of schemas as predicates, and the way in which one can quantify over schemas.

Chapter 24 provides explanation of other parts of the notation. Here we look at restrictions on relations, generic definitions and the usefulness of **disjoint** and **partition**. We then go on to explain θ and μ, which often cause confusion.

Chapter 25 has a discussion on toolkits, and we provide a real number toolkit as an illustration of how toolkits may be devised. In Chapter 26 we look back over the book and ahead to the future of Z.

Finally, **Part V** contains a variety of appendices. Appendix A describes the extensions to the sample mathematical toolkit that we have used in the main text of the book. Appendix B is a glossary as described earlier. Appendix C contains a list of all the references mentioned in the book.

Acknowledgements

Many people have contributed in a number of ways to this book, commenting on various drafts, suggesting examples for specification, and discussing approaches to specification. Our thanks to you all.

In particular, the file system examples in sections 16.3 and 20.6 are based on the work of Trevor King, and we are grateful to him for permission to use them. The example in section 24.2 is used with the permission of Ian Stewart. The example used in Chapter 11 was suggested by Andy Gravell, and that of Chapter 13 is a problem set by Neville Dean to his students.

We would also like to thank the following people who helped in other ways: Jardine Barrington-Cook, Tony Boswell, Stephen Brien, Neville Dean, Tim Denvir, Andy Gravell, Hans-Martin Hörcher, Iain Houston, Debi Kearney, Haim Kilov, Steve King, Trevor King, Kevin Lano, John McDermid, Fiona Polack, Jo Primrose, Julian Rose, Paul Smith, Roger Stokes, Sam Valentine, John Wordsworth and Nick Youd.

Our thanks also to Aldus (for IntelliDraw), Donald Knuth (for TeX), Leslie Lamport (for LaTeX), Ed Sznyter of LaTeX-help@stanford.edu (for help with LaTeX macros), Mike Spivey (for $f$uzz), and Paul King (for `oz.sty`), without whom this book would have looked very different.

The quadrilaterals example of sections 23.6 and 24.6.4 is based on the work in [Stepney *et al.* 1992]. Some of the other examples have been developed from those presented in Logica's course on Z specification—we are grateful to all those participants of the courses who have helped to make these examples more interesting and, above all, less error prone.

Much of this work was carried out as part of the ZIP project, which was an IED initiative, project number IED4/1/1639. The part-funding by the United Kingdom's Department of Trade and Industry is gratefully acknowledged.

Finally, thanks are due to our employers, Logica UK Limited, for providing the backing that allowed us to produce the book.

Rosalind Barden
Susan Stepney
David Cooper
Cambridge, England
August 1994

Part I

Using Z

Chapter 1

Welcome to Z Newcomers

In which advice is given to the newcomer to Z, whether manager, project leader or specifier.

1.1   Introduction

Over there on the horizon is the completed Z project, with well-structured abstract Z specifications, carefully discharged proof obligations, and a neat path of refinements from initial requirements analysis to delivered code. The project was on time and on budget, and all the experienced Z specifiers, designers and programmers in your team are well pleased with the result. Just now you have a team who think Z is the sound of sleeping, no project plan that has even a mention of refinement, and a blank sheet of paper entitled 'Specification'. What should you do?

The task of the manager starting up a Z project is to create a plan of how to reach there from here. In order to obtain well-structured Z specifications, the plan must include decision points on what to specify in Z and what to specify some other way. It must include solutions to the problem of team inexperience and explain how Z is to work with existing company practices.

In this chapter we look at these areas, and explain the decisions that must be made, and the information on which these decisions must be based.

1.2   Why a Z project?

The first question that must be answered is *what is the objective of using Z on this project?* The whole structure of the project plan depends on the answer. Some possible objectives are

- to learn about Z technically
- to learn how Z projects can be managed
- to have better communications with the client
- to have better communications between members of the development team
- to have better documentation for subsequent use by maintainers
- to have better design (for example because design of this system is tricky and we are in danger of implementing too soon just to have something we think we can handle)
- to satisfy a client requirement (because the client has specifically asked for Z to be used)
- to analyse properties of the system early in the life-cycle (for example, security or safety properties).

If your objective is to learn Z, you need lots of different small areas to try out different styles of Z, a budget for training, and time to consolidate findings. If, on the other hand, you need to have a provably secure system design, you may use Z during the design phase only and you may buy theorem proving tools.

Having identified and written down your objectives you are in a position to decide where in the life-cycle you will apply Z. Without an explicit objective it is easy just to use Z for its own sake. Z specifications can be produced without a lot of thought and subsequently left unused. It would be easy to draw the erroneous conclusion from such a project that Z was just a difficult-to-learn notation that delivers few benefits.

1.3   Obtaining support

Before you start your use of Z, you need to have already convinced senior management of its benefits. And you need to be prepared to withstand pressures from above, and from within your own team, to move on from the specification directly to code production. All concerned must be made aware that the shape of the project life-cycle alters when Z is used. More time is spent in the early phases, and the first code appears much later on than usual, but there is often less rework and fewer errors.

Educating management about Z is described in [Cooper 1990]. Managers need to be given sufficient information to enable them to make decisions about the use of formal methods. Senior managers do not tend to become involved in technical issues, but they do need information about the benefits, costs and risks. While there is not as much published evidence available as we would like, the number of success stories from Z users is growing.

1.4   Where can Z be used in the life-cycle? ·

In this section we summarise the things that can be *done* with Z. In the next section we discuss how to gain specific *benefits* by using Z.

1.4.1   Things to do with Z

Specifying functionality

Specifying functionality is the most obvious use of Z. In the most popular form, some schemas are defined and drawn together to specify the *state* of the system to be built. The state schema includes sufficient information for all of the required behaviour of the system to be described by changes to this state. It does not necessarily include everything that appears as the state in the eventual implementation. The behaviour of the system is specified by operation schemas that act on all, or part, of the state. Often these operation schemas are structured to express the different behaviour under successful completion of the operation and under 'error' conditions. This approach is explained in more detail in Chapter 3.

Other styles can be used; for example, stateless applicative style, rather like an algebraic specification. For an example see Chapter 22.

Whichever style is used, the idea is to describe what the proposed system does in terms of its *actions*.

Building a model of the subject area (thinking tool)

In direct contrast to the use of Z described above, it is possible to model the *subject area* rather than the *system* in question. This is used as a vehicle for discussing the purpose of the system and the sorts of things it has to handle. It builds up a *theory* of the subject area rather than a specification of a particular system.

The sophistication of such a theory can range from something as simple as studying 'sortedness' prior to writing the specification of a sorted list (section 23.7.1), through a model of a general grammar and investigations of the properties of various specific grammar recognisers before specifying the 'front end' of a compiler, all the way to something as complex as studying the definition of 'security' before developing a secure operating system (section 4.2.1).

Specifying properties

A functional specification describes how the proposed system behaves. Specifying properties, however, puts certain *constraints* on aspects of the system. These may limit the possible behaviour of the system significantly in certain areas, while leaving other areas completely unconstrained. A common example is to specify certain safety properties, such as 'the reactor temperature must remain below $maxTemp\,°\mathrm{C}$', while leaving the functionality aspects largely unspecified.

In order to have a base upon which to specify properties, a general system is defined, with a largely unconstrained behaviour. Constraints are then specified, limiting the system to behave in a manner consistent with some property required, such as safety or integrity. Chapter 4 discusses such an approach to secure system specification.

1.4.2   Things to do with your Z once you've produced it

Proving properties of a specification

Specifiers are obliged to prove certain 'reasonableness' properties of any Z specifications they write. For example, a specifier may wish to prove that an operation on a state is *total*: that it always has a specified behaviour, that its precondition is *true*. It is also wise to show that any generic constants are uniquely defined (section 24.3).

One style of writing state-based Z specifications is to include only *sufficient* conditions to ensure the required behaviour—further redundant constraints are omitted. It is useful to express some of these redundant, but important, constraints as *theorems*, and prove that they are indeed implied by the system model. For example, a control system may be required to maintain two values within certain constraints.

$$
\begin{array}{|l}
\hline
\_SafeState _____ \\
reactorTemp, coolantTemp : \mathbb{N} \\
\hline
reactorTemp \leq 2000 \\
reactorTemp - coolantTemp \geq 100 \\
\hline
\end{array}
$$

An additional property, redundant but useful to check understanding, is that the reactor temperature must be greater than the coolant temperature. A suitable theorem states that if *SafeState* holds then it is possible to deduce that *reactorTemp* exceeds *coolantTemp*.

$$SafeState \vdash reactorTemp > coolantTemp$$

This approach can be used to express a desired property of a state-and-operations style specification, and to prove that this property follows from the specification.

An alternative style of writing state-based Z specifications is to put some of the redundant information into the predicate, which can make the specification more readable since more consequences are made explicit. In this case is is necessary to show that the extra conditions are indeed redundant and not contradictory. This requires a proof that there is at least one assignment of variables in a state schema that satisfies the predicate (that such a state is not impossible) and for each operation that it can be performed from at least one 'before' state (that its precondition is not always *false*).

Proving conformance between two specifications

In moving from an abstract specification towards code, we produce *refinements* of the specification. These are more concrete versions of the specification in which certain properties are preserved. If one Z specification is claimed to be a refinement of another, there is an obligation to prove that this is true. These *proof obligations* can be expressed in Z, and Z can be used to document the steps in an informal proof. Z does not have a syntax for proof, but work to rectify this situation is continuing, see for example [Woodcock & Brien 1992]. We look at an example of refinement in Chapter 13.

Animating the model

Z is not an executable notation. Nonetheless many Z specifications (of functionality or models of the subject area) can be translated in a fairly straightforward way into an executable language, such as Prolog. This allows a specification to be 'run'. Such a translation cannot, in general, be done automatically. This is because Z is such an expressive notation that it is possible to describe systems for which no execution is possible. Nonetheless a combination of automatic translation and translation by hand can result in an effective executable model, which can be used to help validate the specification. See section 6.3 for more discussion.

Test conditions

A Z specification states facts about the system in a clear manner making it possible to use the Z to generate information about the code, for example, to spot end conditions that the code must accommodate. These can be used to generate test cases.

From a specification of behaviour it is possible to devise test data to test all the different sorts of behaviour of the system. This allows *black box testing*, where the outputs resulting from given inputs are checked without looking at the internal details of the design or code. The accurate behaviour specification also allows the correct results to be calculated before any design proceeds. Non-deterministic specifications allow *classes* of allowable results to be calculated.

Data for *white box testing*, where the internal details of the code are exposed to scrutiny, is probably better generated from the code; although Z specifications can contain implementation detail, there is no accepted way of highlighting this in the specification.

1.5   Specific benefits

Different benefits can be gained from different uses of Z. Broadly the benefits are

- project management visibility

- reviews, walk-throughs, testing
- improving design
- clarifying and capturing requirements.

1.5.1   Project management visibility

A project manager may have difficulty in seeing the progress made on a project. Expenditure, in terms of effort and cost, can usually be tracked easily; judging technical achievement is not so straightforward. Although the production of specification documents does not guarantee technical achievement, the presence of Z specifications is particularly strong because simplifications and deferred decisions are made more obvious and are hard to overlook.

Specifications of the subject area can usefully document progress in the early stages of a project, showing that useful work is being done when there is a danger that project managers may push staff into initial system specification too early.

A formal proof is an irrefutable demonstration that a correct (that is, *meaning-preserving*) design step has been taken (Chapter 6). Completed proofs can be used to indicate progress through the design process. A proof demonstrates that a design step preserves functionality; it does not demonstrate that the design step is *good*.

1.5.2   Review, walk-through, testing

Formal reviews and walk-throughs need some form of documentation to act as the material for review. In the early stages of design a Z specification can act as a clear statement of the design so far. It is more useful than many design notations for a formal review because it is unambiguous, and errors can be identified more objectively.

At times a specification is complex, and understanding the full richness of its behaviour may be hard. Its behaviour under certain constraints, for example, end conditions, can be deduced as a property of the specification. These 'partial behaviour properties' can be used in review to understand and check a complex behaviour.

Later in the design process a functional specification can be used in a review as the specification against which program code can be compared. The formal statement of the relationship between specification and implementation (or even its proof) can be used to structure an informal review of a design step. See section 13.5.1 for an example of such a formal relationship. It offers an objective, documented account of what the design step *is*, although it does not document the rationale behind the step.

1.5.3   Improving design

Z functional specifications can be used as the (sole) means of documenting the *design process*. This does not mean that only schemas and other formal text is used—Z specifications should always consist of a mixture of mathematics and explanatory accompanying text (including informal diagrams). A specification with more mathematics than text probably has too little explanation—difficult mathematics or a complex relationship between the real world and the model could well result in a ratio as high as 9 parts text to 1 part mathematics. As an example, the specification of the video shop given in Chapter 11 has a ratio of about 3:2 text to mathematics (counted as number of lines of text to number of lines of mathematics).

These specifications may be used to document the process of design by specifying progressively more concrete representations of the system. At a low level it becomes more effective to express system description in a programming language; the last level of Z then becomes the module specification for the coding process.

Designers can use the functional specification to express their design ideas at an abstract level, rather than dropping down to pseudo-code. Z has the benefit that it is able to express the behaviour accurately (unlike, say, a data flow diagram). This sometimes acts negatively, because the broad architectural ideas can be lost in detail.

From a functional specification of the correct behaviour of an operation in Z, it is possible to calculate the precondition of the correct operation (Chapter 12). That is the conditions under which the operation does or does not work correctly can be calculated, and hence the errors that must be addressed are identified. The designer can be sure that all possible error conditions have been considered.

A subject area model can act as a guide for the designer at various points in the development. Generally this occurs where the developer is swamped by new concepts or design options, and 'can't see the wood for the trees'. A subject area model puts some structure on the information, and helps the developer to gain insight into the domain and hence the design.

Proof can help the process of design. In writing down the proof obligation for one specification to be the refinement of another, the relationship between the variables of the two specifications must be formally documented. This can serve as a record of the design decisions taken at this step in the development. The correctness of design steps can be assured through proof. A proof obligation may be discharged with varying degrees of rigour: sketch proof, informal proof, formal partial proof, or fully formal proof (see sections 4.3.3 and 6.2 for discussion of these). Even an informal sketch proof significantly increases confidence in the correctness of a design step. It is important to keep the concept of proof in perspective. If the design step is fully proved it shows that the lower level specification is a *correct* implementation of the higher level. It does not show that it is a *good* design step (for example, that it leads to an efficient implementation). Neither does it say anything about the *validity* of the higher level specification—if this is wrong, a 'formally proved' implementation still does not do what the client wants.

Proof is expensive, but lack of proof may turn out to be even more costly.

1.5.4   Requirements capture

If the client and the developer have different backgrounds discussing possible requirements is a difficult task because there is no shared understanding of concepts. Formalising some of the key ideas being discussed leads to a well-defined terminology resulting in a more productive dialogue that helps to enhance understanding.

It is often easier to agree with the client some important properties that must hold, rather than a functional system that achieves some goals. This is especially true when the client is concerned about some aspects (for example, safety) and less concerned about others (for example, user interface). In addition clients' requirements are often couched at many levels of abstraction, from high level abstract requirements to low level implementation constraints. In order to maintain a uniform level of abstraction in the top level system model, without missing some of the client's requirements, some of the requirements can be farmed out to properties.

A top level specification is written after some discussions with the client in an effort to understand what the client requires. It is likely that such a specification includes in it many properties specifically stated by the client. In order to gain confidence that the specification does indeed capture the client's requirements, additional properties may be introduced and proved. These additional properties, which in general have not been explicitly asked for by the client, can be given to the client for checking. If they are indeed properties the client expected it is likely that the specification accurately reflects the client's desires. If they are unexpected (and unwanted), they can be used to guide the improvement of the specification.

A client may not understand Z, and so requirements capture discussions centred around a Z specification may not be fruitful. An animation of the specification can allow the client to 'play' with the specification as it grows. This may prompt clients to investigate their requirements more deeply. Requirements capture is by nature iterative. An animated model is an effective way of closing the loop back to the customer. Making use of a formal model as the basis of the animation has the benefit that the intuitive feel obtained from running the animator can be investigated fully within the formal model. If the client does understand the formal Z model, animation can nevertheless help the client and the developers more rapidly to obtain an intuitive grasp of the system.

1.6   Working with other approaches

Much effort has been devoted to developing ways of using formal methods with object oriented notations. In section 5.3 we look at this topic and illustrate it with a small example.

Formal methods can usefully be combined with a structured method. See for example [Barden *et al.* 1992], which gives an indication of the structured methods with which Z has been used. For model-oriented notations such as Z, a method that is based around information structures is likely to fit well. The use of Z with SSADM and with Yourdon is discussed in sections 5.2.1 and 5.2.2.

In Chapter 11 we use Entity Relation Diagrams in a case study, to help to structure the Z specification of a database for a video hire shop.

One approach is to use a structured method to break the problem down into subsystems and then specify each of these formally. [Nash 1990] describes a specification of a large system. The task is broken down into a number of subsystems, each of which is specified in Z in a separate document. The full specification includes another document that shows how the various components combine to form the complete system description.

Another example of breaking down a problem into smaller modules is that given in [Garlan & Delisle 1990]. Their underlying approach is to focus on models that can serve as reusable components. The aim is to find regularities across the system and to abstract away from them. Making the specification modular helps to ameliorate configuration problems.

The Z technique of *promotion* (Chapter 19) helps to modularise a specification.

Project managers who wish to gain experience of Z without committing to it wholeheartedly are well-advised to incorporate some use of Z within a project primarily using a structured method. The Z can be used as a support, but the main configuration control and project documentation are supplied by the structured method.

1.7   Achieving abstract thought

As with any notation, using Z does not guarantee good specifications. Benefits can be achieved only if Z is used well. Indeed Z is a tool that encourages and assists certain modes of thought, but it is those modes of thought that give most of the benefits, not the notation. It is possible to use other notations (for example, pure logic, natural language) in a way inspired by Z and achieve (nearly) the same results. On the other hand Z can be used as a baroque assembly language with devastating results on costs and time-scales.

Abstraction means focusing on essentials, whilst neglecting irrelevant details. It is notoriously hard to define, and achieving it is largely a matter of experience. A good Z specification captures the right level of abstraction, neither too low, mired in confusing details, nor too high and too far removed from reality (though this latter case is rarely a problem for newcomers). The examples given in this book point out the principles of abstraction, and working through these examples can be used as a training aid.

In putting together a team for a Z project, it helps if experts in abstraction (not necessarily in Z) are included. They may be used to extract high level requirements from a wealth of detail, or to choose a data model appropriate for a range of uses.

1.8   Costs and time-scales

Hard figures directly comparing a system built in a traditional manner with an equivalent system built using Z are difficult to find. It is generally accepted that the overall shape of a development changes when a formal method such as Z is used. Z both allows and forces the developer to spend more time than is traditional doing requirements analysis and design. Misunderstandings and confusion are harder to hide in an unambiguous language, and so developers are able to spend more time early in the life-cycle resolving these issues. (But we are *not* saying it is impossible to make mistakes in Z!) In the early stages clear thinking about the system is promoted. Thus, more time is spent *really* understanding the system. Since the specification is given in a precise formal notation errors can be spotted more readily. [Nix & Collins 1988] report that errors are introduced in a more uniform manner when using Z, and are thus easier to unearth. Work early on is repaid later through reduced effort in implementation and maintenance.

[Houston & King 1991] report on a development in which the use of Z led to more errors being discovered in the early parts of the development, with a 9% improvement in productivity overall. Additionally, in the first eight months after software release, the parts of the code originally specified in Z had around 40% as many errors as did the parts not specified in Z.

Specifying the functional behaviour of a system is one of the first things new Z practitioners learn; indeed, it is often the only thing they learn. It is a use of Z that is most easily constrained and guided by company standards. For many straight-forward systems specified at a low level of abstraction the difference between a good specification and a bad one is small. Therefore, the cost in staff training and the risk of rejection is small.

Such a use of Z is likely to produce large quantities of reasonably straightforward Z. Tool support is discussed in section 1.10.

1.9   Training and the use of consultants

Many universities offer some training in formal methods as part of their computer science degree and diploma courses. This means that often new entrants to the computing profession have some knowledge of formal methods. Various institutions and companies offer one-week training courses in Z that provide a sound introduction to the notation and give some experience of using Z.

Sending people on courses is highly desirable. Immersing oneself in the notation for a week is an excellent way to learn it. A good teacher answering questions and guiding the course participants imparts an understanding that a book, however well written, never can. Choose a course that is practically based. When learning it is important to be able to try out new ideas straight away; a course has the advantage that the teacher is there to assist.

No matter how good a course is, there is a learning period when the new techniques are set into the context of a real project and the working practices of a company. We recommend that specifiers have access to expert advice during this period. It is best if the project team includes an expert. The expert can guide the team in correct and appropriate use of the Z notation, and in achieving a suitable level of abstraction. If you cannot have an expert directly involved, then you should try to ensure that there is an expert available who can help you out on an occasional basis.

1.10   What tools to use

Tools to support Z are becoming available, and are steadily being taken up. A summary of Z tools may be found in [Parker 1991] and in [Steggles & Hulance 1994]. Many people still write their formal specifications without recourse to tools. Most people are glad of support for the special symbols, and those who have used type checkers appreciate them.

Tool support is not necessarily the answer to problems of producing good formal specifications. Tools are not a substitute for thinking. You should beware of rushing to push your specification through a tool, when what is really required is deeper and clearer thought. Specification is a cerebral activity and may best be done with pencil and paper in the early stages. In later stages, especially when the specification is growing, tool support is essential for catching 'silly' errors and maintaining the specification, allowing you to focus your time on the real problems.

Tools for Z offer various options, such as

- *type setting:* help with special fonts and layout of Z structures such as schema boxes
- *syntactic checking:* tests to ensure that mistakes in the syntax are avoided, for example, missing brackets, incorrect formulations of set comprehensions
- *cross referencing and navigation:* support for moving around a specification and finding declarations
- *schema expansion:* support for expanding schema inclusions

- *type checking:* tests that no statements involve clashes of types such as asserting that an integer belongs to a set of letters
- *theorem checking and proving:* assistance with checking the details of simple proofs and proving simple lemmas
- *animation:* options showing through example inputs how the eventual system may behave
- *code generation:* ability to generate some code from some formal specifications.

A good type setting package is indispensable. Only the smallest of specifications can reasonably be presented in manuscript, and if your font support is inadequate you will soon find document production frustrating. A good package not only offers you the necessary symbols ($\rightarrowtail$, $\oplus$, $\mathbb{Z}$ and so on), but also provides automatic support for setting out the various boxes, such as schema boxes and axiomatic descriptions.

Experience on projects suggests that type checking is useful, as it helps to iron out many silly errors. Any reasonable size specification benefits from being checked for type clashes. This process also reveals any variables that are used and not declared, as well as those that are used incorrectly. This book has been type checked, a process that revealed errors missed by human reviewers.

Proof, undertaken properly, is an involved and often tedious process. This means that it is easy to make slips. Proof assistants can ameliorate the proof process by checking the work that has been done, and also by proving simple lemmas. Machines will never be able to prove *every* theorem, but there is no point in reproducing a proof that has been done many times before and can be regurgitated by a machine.

1.11   What Z doesn't give you

Although Z gives a notation in which formal (mathematical) reasoning can take place, its use does not guarantee a 100% correct system. Errors can occur at the early stages, when the developer (and sometimes the client) is trying to understand what the client wants. No specification method can guarantee that the system you are designing is the one that your client had in mind, however, with formal specification you are more likely to achieve success. Experience shows that the use of formal methods leads the specification team to ask many questions of the client, as a result of trying to formalise what may appear as rather 'woolly' requirements.

Errors can occur during the design of the system, although this can be made less likely by using proof and machine checking. Errors can also occur when incorporating existing code into a system, such as low level utilities, device drivers and the operating system. Z can help you to produce fault-free software, but it is not a panacea.

Z should not be seen as a replacement for more traditional approaches to system development, such as the use of structured methods. Z should be seen as a tool to be used where appropriate. We give a small example of using the two together in Chapter 11.

Chapter 2

Structure, Process, Fluency

In which the characteristics of 'method' are discussed.

2.1   Is Z a method?

Authors often reach for their dictionaries in answer to such a question. We are no exception. [Chambers 1972] defines 'method' as follows

method *n.* the mode or rule of accomplishing an end: orderly procedure: manner: orderly arrangement: classification: system, rule: manner of performance: an instructional book systematically arranged.

Many so-called 'formal *methods*', including Z, are nothing of the sort. The sample toolkit describes the notation for Z, together with laws that govern the manner in which the aspects of the language behave. It is an invaluable reference manual that most Z specifiers keep by their sides. At the time of writing, a Z Standard is being prepared. (For information about the standard and the sample toolkit, the reader is referred to the preface.) Neither of these publications provide a *method* in the sense defined above.

We present an overview of different approaches to using Z in this part of the book, to serve as an introductory guide and survey for those who are looking for assistance with developing their Z specifications. Below we discuss the components that go towards making up a method. The remaining chapters in this part review the known approaches to Z and relate them to the components of a method.

2.2 Three ingredients of a method

2.2.1 Structure

Structure is that part of method concerned with 'orderly arrangement and classification'.

A simple system can be understood as a whole. But for any realistically sized system, a specifier needs to structure the specification in such a way that it can be understood in parts. Approaches that help to gain an initial understanding can also lead specifiers to a good structure for the eventual specification. [Woodcock 1989] shows how Z's schema language can be used to help structure a specification. [Morgan & Sufrin 1993] show how the technique of promotion can be used to partition the system specification into local and global concerns (see Chapter 19 for an explanation of this technique). Even so a survey of Z users [Barden *et al.* 1992] showed that many specifiers feel the need for additional support for structuring their specifications.

Two approaches that can help with understanding and structuring a Z specification of a large system are structured analysis (discussed in section 5.2) and object orientation (discussed in section 5.3).

2.2.2 Process

Process is the aspect of method concerned with 'orderly procedure or manner'. A process provides users with a staged approach to specification development; a refinement process assists with steering the abstract specification towards code. Details of each stage in the process are provided and there are checkpoints to assist with monitoring. An approach based around the ideas of state based specifications with operations has been largely developed at the Programming Research Group at the University of Oxford (PRG), and introduced into industry, notably at IBM United Kingdom Laboratories Ltd at Hursley Park for use on the CICS system. We have dubbed this 'the Established Strategy'. This describes an approach to systems specification (see Chapter 3 for more details) and also the production of the system design with its refinement to code.

An approach for developing Z specifications of secure systems has been developed principally by the Government Communications Headquarters, and is described in Chapter 4. Other organisations have begun to develop processes, and we provide summaries of these in Chapter 5.

An iterative approach to specification development is needed, although often processes are presented as 'one-pass'. [Guindon 1990] reports experiments showing that the focus of software designers' attention does not follow a fixed path, but makes opportunist shifts as insight is gained into various aspects of the problem. [Worden 1991] argues that the process of refinement of a specification equally does not follow a smooth path from abstraction to code, but that the designer moves back and forth as if moving along a 'saw-tooth' until the refinement is eventually reached. The same argument is readily applied to the process of producing a fairly abstract specification from a highly abstract partial description given by the abstract state and global variables. Review stages are an important part of this iteration.

The order of the final presentation of the specification may differ from they order in which it was constructed as part of the development process. Certain items may be introduced as the specification is written (for example, reports from operations and global variables), but these may well be presented all together at the beginning of a specification document. It is important to realise the distinction between presentation and production. Do not expect the specifications you read to tell the development story, and do not present your specifications in the order that you first wrote them!

2.2.3   Fluency

Fluency addresses the 'manner of performance' aspects of method. Fluency in Z is comparable with fluency in any other language. The user is able to express ideas clearly without stumbling, constructions are neat, and the meaning is apparent to anyone else conversant in the language. Good use is made of the language and the appropriate notation is used.

Many introductory texts for Z encourage users in their first take-up of the language. Such books usually concentrate on explaining the notation and Z's features are illustrated through the use of small examples. These books play a valuable rôle in providing users with an explanation of the notation. For example, [Lightfoot 1991] and [Imperato 1991] provide an introduction to the principal parts of the Z notation, [Woodcock & Loomes 1988], [Diller 1990] and [McMorran & Powell 1993] introduce the mathematics of Z and include some small case studies. [Potter *et al.* 1991] and [Wordsworth 1992], as well as providing an introduction to the notation, also describe the Established Strategy for writing Z specifications.

For the more experienced user there are some brief guides for enhancing one's facility with the notation. [Gravell 1991] describes some guide-lines for writing a good Z specification (for example, 'prefer clarity to brevity', 'choose the state to simplify the description of the operations'). [Macdonald 1991] gives useful tips about writing succinct and readable Z. There are a number of published case studies about Z. These do not provide the reader with any direct instruction about Z, but by studying them the reader can learn from the style adopted by the authors. Notable amongst such case studies is the collection [Hayes 1993b].

Notice that most of the texts mentioned in this section are not exclusively concerned with fluency; they may include some pointers to process and structure.

2.3   Putting it all together

To write a good Z specification, you need a method that is characterised by the following

- a way of structuring the specification
- a process that provides steps to follow and checkpoints in building the specification
- fluency with the notation, to ensure that the eventual specification is written clearly and concisely.

We have not dealt with the aspect of method covering 'the mode or rule of accomplishing an end: system, rule'. Although 'process' can give steps through which a development should go, it is not appropriate to give a *rule* applicable to all Z projects, because they vary so widely.

Chapter 3

The Established Strategy

In which an established strategy for building Z specifications is described.

3.1 Introduction

The Established Strategy covers the whole cycle of development from specification through to code; here the parts relating to specification only are examined.

The method documented here is distilled from [Wordsworth 1989a], [Wordsworth 1989b] and [Woodcock & Davies 1994]. This approach is followed, to varying degrees, in [King & Sørensen 1989], [Blyth 1990], [King 1990a], [Houston & Wordsworth 1990], [Mundy & Wordsworth 1990] and [Potter *et al.* 1991].

The specification describes the user's functional requirements and is a basis for developing the system. Understanding the requirements is achieved by producing a formal description of the system and discussing this with the users.

3.2 What should a specification contain?

The specification is presented in the following order

- the given sets and global constants for the specification, together with an informal description of their significance
- a schema that describes the abstract state, if the state is complex different parts should be determined in separate schemas, then combined using the schema calculus
- a schema that describes the initial state of the system, accompanied by a proof that such a state exists
- schemas that describe the abstract operations on the state, written without regard to errors

- descriptions of the preconditions of these partial operations, the preconditions should be made explicit in the operation schemas
- schemas that describe the error conditions
- a summary of the operations, typically based on the schemas that describe the partial operations and the error cases
- information to assist the reader of the specification, for example, a cross reference list of schema names.

Ensuring that each of these components is included in the specification is part of the process of constructing specifications, as outlined in the following section.

3.3 Constructing specifications

3.3.1 Preliminary analysis

First the requirements are analysed to identify the important parts of the problem; these are described by sets and constants. Some of the sets are not related to others, and some have a structure, for example, ordered lists.

3.3.2 Recording the given sets and global constants

The first items to appear in the specification are a record of the given sets that are to be used as types, and the global variables for the specification, together with some explanation of their purpose. Ensuring these are right is part of the process of modelling the requirements at the appropriate level of abstraction.

3.3.3 Application-oriented theory

Often some special purpose theory has to be developed when writing specifications. Since the theory is important for the specification, it is placed here—after the global declarations, and before the description of the state. (For an example of application-oriented theory see section 20.6.3.)

3.3.4 Describing the abstract state

Next, the abstract state is described using one or more schemas. The state schema should be kept brief and include only those declarations that are necessary to construct the model of the specification.

```
┌─ AbstractState ─────────────────────────────────────────────
│ declaration for abstract state
├─────────────────────────
│ predicate for abstract state
└─────────────────────────────────────────────────────────────
```

3.3.5   The initial state

A schema that describes the initial state of the system is given, and a proof is given that such a state exists. Creation of the initial state is regarded as an operation, the result of which is the initial state.

$$InitialAbstractState \,\hat{=}\, [\,AbstractState' \mid predicate\ for\ initial\ state\,]$$

The theorem that has to be proved is

$$\vdash \exists\,AbstractState' \bullet InitialAbstractState$$

▷ *proof obligation*
Specifiers often provide an initial state of the system. It is prudent to verify that this really is a legitimate state of the system.

Typically, the predicate for the abstract state supplies an assignment of particular values to the variables. In such a case the proof reduces to demonstrating that these satisfy the properties of the abstract state.

3.3.6   Specifying the successful case of the operations

Each operation is specified, ignoring any error conditions. These partial operations are described using schemas of the form

```
┌─ AbstractOperation ─────────────────────────────────────────
│ ΔAbstractState
│ Inputs
│ Outputs
├─────────────────────────
│ predicate for the abstract operation
└─────────────────────────────────────────────────────────────
```

The predicate relates the input and output variables, and the initial and final states.

3.3.7   Preconditions

The preconditions of the partial operations are calculated. The precondition schema of an operation is formed by hiding all the output and final state variables. This is done using existential quantification.

$$\boxed{\begin{array}{l} \_\,PreAbstractOperation\,_____ \\ AbstractState \\ Inputs \\ \hline \exists\,AbstractState';\ Outputs \bullet \\ \quad\quad \text{predicate for the abstract operation} \end{array}}$$

This predicate part is simplified (see Chapter 10 for an example calculation of a precondition). The description of the abstract operation is checked to ensure that its precondition is explicit in the operation's predicate; if not the operation definition is modified to make it so.

It is helpful to provide a summary of the preconditions of these successful case partial operations. This assists in the description of the error cases and forms the basis for the complete operation table (see later).

3.3.8   Schemas describing error cases

Normally we wish to build complete interfaces so that systems can handle any input and provide sensible results. The preconditions tell us where to start in describing the errors, but discussion with the user is essential to ensure that the errors are handled in the appropriate way. If the precondition of an operation is a conjunction of two predicates

$$p \wedge q$$

there are three possible error conditions

- $\neg\,p \wedge q$
- $p \wedge \neg\,q$
- $\neg\,p \wedge \neg\,q$

It would suffice to describe the case where $\neg\,(p \wedge q)$, but this may not provide a sufficiently detailed description of the system's behaviour in the event of errors occurring. (See section 10.5 for an example of error schemas.)

It is important to understand the user's requirements in each of these error conditions, and to document those requirements. A schema describing each requirement should be specified.

3.3.9   Making the operations total

The partial operations that describe the successful cases and the various errors are combined to give a total description. This is usually achieved using schema disjunction.

$$TotalAbstractOperation \;\hat{=}\; AbstractOperation$$
$$\lor\; Error_1$$
$$\lor\; Error_2$$
$$\lor\; \ldots$$

The use of disjunction may lead to non-determinism in the operation interface in deciding which of several possible error conditions to report if more than one occurs simultaneously.

▷ *non-determinism*
  Such non-determinism can be helpful as it leaves more options available to the implementor, however, any non-determinism should be documented at this point.

Finally, a table is produced that shows the inputs for and precondition of each partial operation.

Operation	Inputs	Precondition
$AbstractOperation_1$	$Inputs_1$	Predicate of pre $AbstractOperation_1$
$AbstractOperation_2$	$Inputs_2$	Predicate of pre $AbstractOperation_2$
...	...	...

3.3.10   Assisting the reader

Once the specification has been constructed, further detail can be added to assist the reader. A cross reference of schema names, and possibly other variables, can be provided. This gives details of where an item is first defined and where it is used. For a longer specification an overview can be provided, to give the aim and direction of the specification. This helps to give the reader a context for the specification.

3.4   Reviewing the specification

Once the specification has been written, it is reviewed. The reviewers should not have been involved in writing the specification but should understand Z well. They come to the review prepared, having read the specification thoroughly. Once the reviewers are happy with a document, they sign it to show they agree that the specification is 'correct'. The check list below, based on those given in [Wordsworth 1989a] and [Wordsworth 1992], is useful for that review.

Tools can be used to assist in configuration control of the specification as it passes through review and revision stages.

In general

The first question to be considered is whether the specification has been understood by the reviewers. No review can take place if this is not the case. Next it is necessary to ask whether the specification captures the requirements; if it does not then there is little point in pursuing the rest of the review.

The following questions are aimed at establishing in what ways the specification can be improved.

Informal text

- Is the technical vocabulary in the informal part consistently used, and does it accord with that usually found in this subject area?
- Are charts, diagrams and listings used to good effect?
- Is the informal text easy to read?

The relation of the informal text to the formal text

- Is the balance between the formal and the informal text satisfactory? (There is often too much formal and not enough informal text.)
- Is the vocabulary of the informal text reflected in the names used in the formal text?
- Does the informal text give convincing examples of the way the interface might be used?

The formal text

Tools should be used to check that the specification is free of syntax and type errors.

- Is the model appropriate?
  - are the state items few in number?
  - has the schema calculus been used to good effect in presenting the model?
  - are the state's predicates short, easily understood, and few in number?
  - are the operations easily understood?
  - are all the invariants on the state documented?
  - are the operations in the interface total, and, if not, are the preconditions well documented?
  - are the proofs simple, and do they add confidence?
- Does the formal text demonstrate understanding of all the aspects of the operations?

- Does the formal text overspecify the requirements by making decisions that are not justified?

The relation of the formal text to the informal text

It is important that the formal and informal parts of the specification agree with one another. It may be the case that the formal text reveals information which is missing in the informal description. Such areas should be identified.

3.5   Discussion

The Established Strategy for constructing Z specifications helps to structure the specification to an extent. For example, it encourages the description of the successful case of operations first, followed by calculation of preconditions, and thence to specification of exceptions.

It is mainly a process. It provides steps which should be performed to produce a specification. Some guidance is given on structuring the specification document, and the state and operations style used by the Established Strategy provides a way of structuring the specification itself. The steps involved in this approach represent both the order used to present the finished specification, and the order in which the specification is developed. The development process may well involve one or more iterations, as unhappy consequences discovered later may require the model that was developed earlier to be modified.

Chapter 4

Security Properties

In which an approach to specifying secure systems is explored.

4.1 Introduction

The style described in this chapter is rather different from that of the Established Strategy (Chapter 3), because of the requirement for proof. The proofs needed are not the usual refinement ones but proofs that a particular property, of being secure, holds. This method was developed to help prove that a specification exhibits a set of desired properties. Although it is particularly suitable for proving *security* properties, it can be used for other properties described by a formal model.

Here we confine ourselves to providing an overview of the method; for a detailed description of the approach and for a worked example the reader is referred to [CESG 1991].

4.2 The method

The approach uses an abstract *security model*, which defines the security policy, and an *FTLS* (Formal Top Level Specification), which defines the actual operations on the system. A proof is needed to show that these operations satisfy the security policy; the aim is a single, clear proposition to be proved.

The method, described below, is summarised in figure 4.1.

4.2.1 The security model

The abstract security model is generic, and has as parameters such things as Object, User, Classification, and Data. It has the following components

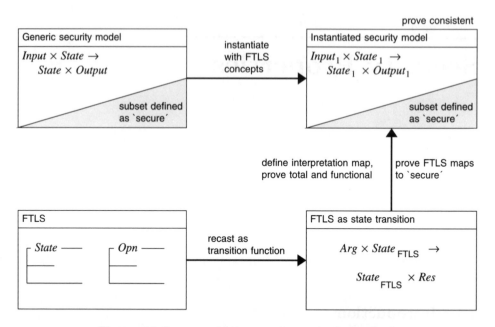

Figure 4.1 Summary of the security properties method.

- a generic definition of the system's *State*, *Input*, and *Output*
- a generic definition of the abstract *System*, in terms of a (total) state transition function (and possibly other components, such as a dominance relation on Classification)

$$\_\_\ System[\ldots]_____$$

$trans : Input \times State \longrightarrow State \times Output$
$dominance : Classification \longleftrightarrow Classification$

$\ldots$

predicates relating to general systems

- a security policy, as an extra constraint on the abstract system.

$secure : \mathbb{P}\ System[\ldots]$

predicates relating to security

The security policy includes such things as a *clearance property* (saying that users cannot receive outputs that they are not cleared to receive) and *information flow properties* (that objects with low classification are not affected by, and hence cannot deduce the existence of, objects or inputs of higher classification). This policy *defines* what is meant by security in the system. It is written at a high level of abstraction with the aim of easing its validation against the informal security requirements.

There is a choice to be made between putting predicates into the schema *System* or into the axiomatic definition *secure*. *System* is intended to model all those things that are to be regarded as systems, some of which may be insecure. Things not modelled by *System* are not within the scope of concern at all, whereas things modelled by *System* but not by *secure* are regarded as being of interest, but not secure. The extra predicates defining *secure* could instead be placed in *System*, thus limiting the universe of discourse to only the secure systems.

It is generally better to place in *System* those structured aspects that make the system the kind being studied, and put into *secure* those aspects that make it a secure system. For example, that data is marked with a classification is a property of all systems under study, so this property should go in *System*, but that highly classified data should not leak information to lowly classified data is what makes it secure, and so this property should go in *secure*.

A state transition function, rather than a more conventional collection of operations defined using schemas, is used for the following reasons

- it is easier to express the requirement that the state transitions be deterministic (functional, only one result allowed) and total (defined for all inputs and states)

- with schemas, it is only an implicit convention that there are no other operations allowed, but for secure systems we need a formulation in which any behaviour not specified is forbidden

- machine-assisted proofs about functions are easier than proofs that need to manipulate schemas, given the current proof technology.

▷ *non-determinism*
Although non-determinism can be useful in many cases, it causes us problems when specifying secure systems, particularly when endeavouring to prove security properties. Thus, we avoid it.

4.2.2   The FTLS

The lower level FTLS looks more like a conventional Z 'state and operations' specification. This has the advantage that the operations can be split up into *SecureSuccess* and *SecureFailure* components, and combined using disjunction to give a total operation. Since the FTLS needs to be related to the security model, these operations eventually need to be recast as a state transition function. This can be done in a relatively mechanical fashion, but is rather involved, so needs explanation. Let $State_{FTLS}$ be the FTLS state schema. Let operation Op_i have argument of type ARG_i and result of type RES_i (these could be given sets, or schemas).

$$
\begin{array}{|l}
\hline
\_\ Op_i _____ \\
\Delta State_{FTLS} \\
arg? : ARG_i \\
res! : RES_i \\
\hline
\end{array}
$$

Group together all the argument and result types from all the operations, using a free type definition.

$$
ARG ::= arg_i \langle\!\langle ARG_i \rangle\!\rangle \mid arg_j \langle\!\langle ARG_j \rangle\!\rangle \mid \ldots
$$
$$
RES ::= res_i \langle\!\langle RES_i \rangle\!\rangle \mid res_j \langle\!\langle RES_j \rangle\!\rangle \mid \ldots
$$

Define a general state transition schema.

$$
\begin{array}{|l}
\hline
\_\ Transition _____ \\
a : ARG \\
s, s' : State_{FTLS} \\
r : RES \\
\hline
\end{array}
$$

For each operation, define a schema to set up the relevant state transition, setting the values of the state transition to those in the operation.

$$
\begin{array}{|l}
\hline
\_\ TransOp_i _____ \\
Op_i \\
Transition \\
\hline
a = arg_i\ arg? \\
s = \theta State_{FTLS} \\
s' = \theta State'_{FTLS} \\
r = res_i\ res! \\
\hline
\end{array}
$$

▷ *schema binding*
$\theta State_{FTLS}$ gives the binding of the values of $State_{FTLS}$ to its variables, which we then set as the values of the operations as required.
▷ *schema decoration*
Normally subscripts at the end of schema names act as decorations, however, in the secure properties style they are used routinely as labels.

Form a schema that joins together all these transitions, hiding the operation declarations, leaving only the state transition declarations.

$$
TransOp \;\hat{=}\; (TransOp_i \upharpoonright Transition) \vee (TransOp_j \upharpoonright Transition) \vee \ldots
$$

▷ *schema projection*
The schema projection operator $\upharpoonright$ hides all the components in the $TransOp_i$ schema except those that are also components of the $Transition$ schema. Hence it hides all the components of Op_i.

Finally, convert this into a function

$$trans_{FTLS} : ARG \times State_{FTLS} \longrightarrow State_{FTLS} \times RES$$
$$trans_{FTLS} = \{\ TransOp \bullet (a, s) \mapsto (s', r)\ \}$$

Note that $trans_{FTLS}$ is required to be total (and functional). A proof is needed to establish this.

▷ *proof obligation*
    For secure system specification, many of the proof obligations must be formally discharged.

4.2.3   Instantiating the security model

The generic security model is instantiated using concepts from the FTLS. For example, generic Objects might be instantiated in terms of FTLS Files and Applications. A justification needs to be given that each of these instantiations is reasonable. This justification is necessarily informal.

An instantiated system and instantiated secure system are just the generic abstract system and generic abstract secure system with these instantiations. Such instantiated objects are indicated by a subscript I, for example, $System_I$.

4.2.4   The interpretation functions

Various interpretation functions need to be defined. These give the mapping from the components of the FTLS (its state, inputs, outputs, and state transition function as constructed from the operations) to the corresponding concepts in the instantiated security model.

$$iState : State_{FTLS} \longrightarrow State_I$$
$$iInput : ARG \longrightarrow Input_I$$
$$iOutput : RES \longrightarrow Output_I$$

$$\ldots$$

$$itrans : ((ARG \times State_{FTLS}) \longrightarrow (State_{FTLS} \times RES))$$
$$\longrightarrow ((Input_I \times State_I) \longrightarrow (State_I \times Output_I))$$
$$\forall\, a : ARG;\ s, s' : State_{FTLS};\ r : RES \bullet$$
$$itrans\{\ TransOp \bullet (a, s) \mapsto (s', r)\ \} =$$
$$\{\ TransOp \bullet (iInput\ a, iState\ s) \mapsto (iState\ s', iOutput\ r)\ \}$$

Again, the justification for the reasonableness of these interpretation functions is necessarily informal. One good criterion (though it is neither necessary nor sufficient) is that the interpretation functions be injective (one-to-one). Thus nothing that might potentially be compromising security at the FTLS level is lost (and hence overlooked) when interpreted at the security model level.

The *interpretation* is then the unique instantiated system that matches the FTLS under the interpretation function

$$\begin{array}{l} interpretation : System_I \\ \hline interpretation = (\,\mu\,System_I\,| \\ \qquad trans = itrans\ trans_{FTLS} \\ \qquad \wedge\ dominance = \ldots \\ \qquad \wedge\ \text{any other components of}\ System_I\,) \end{array}$$

▷ *definite description*
A mu-expression is used to ensure that the *interpretation* is unique.
▷ *proof obligation*
There is a proof obligation here, to show that the interpretation is indeed unique, that is that the mu-expression can be satisfied.

4.2.5   A secure FTLS

An FTLS is *secure* if it obeys the security policy under the interpretation

$$\vdash interpretation \in secure_I$$

4.3   Proof

4.3.1   Totality and determinism

Proofs are needed to demonstrate that the various transition and interpretation functions are indeed functions and are total.

4.3.2   Consistency, and conservative extension

Since it is possible to prove anything, including the security property, of an inconsistent specification, it is important to prove the specification is consistent. This is not possible in general, but it is possible if the restriction that only *conservative extensions* are used is imposed, and hence such a style is recommended by the method.

A conservative extension is one in which every model of the specification up to the point of the extension is also a model of the specification after the extension. This means that new objects can be introduced and defined, but previously defined objects cannot have extra constraints put on them (because otherwise a model of the old specification that did not satisfy this new, stronger, constraint would no longer be a model of the new specification).

▷ *axiomatic description*
   Such a style is not too restrictive. In general, it is probably a bad idea to structure
   any specification along the lines of 'This is x, a number. Here is another 500 pages of
   specification. Oh, and by the way, $x < 3$'.

4.3.3   Security, and formal partial proof

The proof that the FTLS is secure boils down to proving the theorem stated in
section 4.2.5. If it is infeasible, because of time or budget restrictions, to complete
a full formal proof of this theorem, the method advocates the technique of *formal
partial proof* to gain a satisfactory level of assurance. Instead of proving the goal as
it stands, it is proved under certain assumptions or *hypotheses*. These hypotheses
need to be chosen using the following criteria

- to ease the proof of the goal
- to be plausible
- not to be too difficult to prove in their turn.

There are tradeoffs in this choice. The idea in the partial proof approach is at each
stage to prove the most implausible or problematic hypothesis (using the technique
recursively, if necessary) until all the remaining hypotheses are obvious enough to
give the required degree of assurance. The more assurance required of the system,
the more 'obvious' the remaining hypotheses have to be.

   For example, assume it is possible to prove the goal under some hypotheses

$$H_1, H_2, \ldots, H_k \vdash goal$$

Then, without loss of generality, assume that hypothesis H_1 is the most implausible.
So prove this one next, possibly under some new assumptions.

$$h_{11}, h_{12}, \ldots, h_{1j} \vdash H_1$$

This means that

$$h_{11}, h_{12}, \ldots, h_{1j}, H_2, \ldots, H_k \vdash goal$$

If all these hypotheses are obvious enough for the required level of assurance, stop.
Otherwise, choose the most implausible one, and prove it. And so on.

   The key to successful use of this technique is to choose sensible hypotheses that
ease the proof process. To start with, the number of hypotheses will probably grow
quite quickly, but eventually they should be simple enough that they can be proved
without introducing new ones.

▷ *proof*
   What is important about this approach is that it demonstrates that proof is not an 'all or
   nothing' technique. By structuring the proof process using a series of hypotheses, only as
   much proof as is necessary to reach a required degree of assurance need be done.

4.4   Summary

The approach to specifying and proving a secure system described above can be summarised as

1. construct a generic security model and its security policy
2. construct an FTLS
3. propose and justify an instantiation of the security model, using FTLS concepts
4. mechanically recast the FTLS into a state transition function
5. propose and justify interpretation functions from the FTLS to the instantiated security model
6. prove the totality and functionality of the state transition functions and interpretation functions
7. prove the consistency of the specifications (aided by using a conservative extension style)
8. prove the security property holds for the FTLS under the interpretation, to an appropriate level of assurance.

4.5   Concluding remarks

As with the Established Strategy (Chapter 3), this method is mainly a description of a process through which a specifier should step in order to produce a proven-secure specification. It does provide some structure in the state and operations part, which also need to be translated into state transition functions.

Owing to the style restrictions used to make proof more tractable, little use is made of schemas, which might suggest that the fluency required is not as great as in a more general systems case. Given the alternative uses of notation adopted, the fluency must be at least as great as in, say, the established strategy.

Chapter 5

Other Approaches to Z Specification

In which other approaches to structuring Z specifications are investigated, and Object-Z is explored.

5.1 Opening remarks

In the previous two chapters we looked at two well-documented approaches to Z specification. This chapter aims to give a flavour of other approaches, and to provide references to sources of further information.

5.2 Z and structured methods

Structured methods provide a process for analysing a system and for structuring it into smaller subsystems. Structured methods are based on informal text and diagrams, are typically well documented, and offer a methodical process. Many organisations already use structured methods with Z. The ZIP survey [Barden *et al.* 1992] discovered instances of Z being used with a variety of structured methods.

Several groups are working on producing a well-defined integration of Z with a structured method, where the method provides the process and the Z provides the formalism (and, additionally, increases the opportunity for mechanical verification of the structured analysis).

5.2.1 Structured methods projects

The SAZ project investigated how to combine Z with SSADM version 4 [Polack *et al.* 1993], [Polack *et al.* 1994], [Mander *et al.* 1994]. The SAZ method is used after the requirements specification module of SSADM, to guide the development of a Z specification from the outcome of the SSADM analysis. The Z specification is guided by the systems analysis, rather than being exclusively derived from it, in order that the process of formalisation can help detect errors and omissions in the informal analysis. SAZ recommends that the formalisation be focused on the most critical or complex areas of the system.

[Semmens & Allen 1991] describe a method of using Z and Yourdon together to produce a specification. The Entity Relationship model is used as the basis for developing a formal model of the system state. An Entity Relationship Diagram provides a clear picture of the structure and relationships of a system; the corresponding Z provides a formal basis, and can be used to capture further constraints that are not easily expressed on a diagram. Processes in the data flow diagram in the Yourdon model are mapped onto operation schemas in the Z model.

Other work in this area includes: [Bryant 1990] a report of a structured and Formal Methods workshop; [Giovanni & Iachini 1990] on Z and HOOD, and [Hee *et al.* 1991] on Z and Petri nets.

5.2.2   Rôle of structured methods

Structured methods themselves provide a process for writing specifications. The work that has looked at how to integrate Z into such processes has concentrated on slotting Z in at a specific point. Typically the approach is to use the structured method to provide an overall structure of the system and then use Z within this framework. Thus these approaches can mainly be assigned to the 'structural' side of 'method'. The relatively routine translation into Z used by this approach does not demand a higher than average fluency.

There is a tension when combining a structured analysis method with Z. If the form of the Z is kept close to the informal analysis, it tends to result in a verbose and cluttered specification that lacks the elegance that is essential for understanding. But a more concise and elegant form of the Z is further removed from the informal analysis, and it is less clear that the correspondence between the two forms is correct. It is important that Z and any accompanying structured method being used should each be applied where they can benefit the development process most. For example, [Draper 1993] describes a way of developing and proving secure systems that uses both Z and SSADM. SSADM is used in the requirements specification and design stages, while Z is used to formalise the requirements, and as a basis for the formal proof of security. The Z corresponds closely to the SSADM, but it is not produced by some merely mechanical translation. Components may be removed or added to the specification, in order to make the Z form more appropriate for its task.

5.3   Z and object orientation

Object orientation is a way of structuring software [Meyer 1988], [Booch 1994], and promises many benefits, including that of *reuse*. An *object* can be thought of as something that encapsulates a piece of state together with some behaviour (the operations that access and modify that state). Objects provide a way to structure a system specification by partitioning an otherwise global state space into meaningful chunks. In addition objects are instances of *classes*, which are arranged in *inheritance* hierarchies. Classes can inherit properties from their parents, as well as defining new state and behaviour of their own. Inheritance is an abstraction mechanism that can be used to structure a specification. Properties of similar classes are described once, in the specification of a common superclass, and hence complex classes can be specified incrementally. It is being recognised that the further structuring concept of a *framework* is necessary for object oriented system specification. A framework describes how various objects work together to make a system. (See, for example, [Helm *et al.* 1990], [Johnson 1992], [MacLean *et al.* 1994]).

Object oriented concepts can be used to provide a structure for Z specifications. Reuse provides the further benefits that existing class specifications can be reused in new contexts, and any associated proofs (for example, of refinement) may also be reusable. [Hammond 1994] describes how to produce a Z specification from a Shlaer-Mellor object oriented analysis.

Z can be used to specify state and behaviour, however Z provides no construct to group operations on a particular state, to apply these operations to different instances, to inherit these properties, or to specify frameworks. Following Wegner's classification [Wegner 1987a], [Wegner 1987b], we might say that Z is object *based*—it supports objects—but it is not object *oriented*—it does not support classes or inheritance. [Hall 1990], [Hall 1994] describe conventions that can be used to make a Z specification have a more object oriented structure (see section 24.6.4 for a small example).

Some object based uses of Z, and many object oriented extensions to Z being developed that include support for classes and inheritance, are described in [Stepney *et al.* 1992] and [Lano & Haughton 1994]. Of all these, Object-Z [Carrington *et al.* 1990], [Duke & Duke 1990a], [Duke & Duke 1990b], [Duke *et al.* 1990], [Duke *et al.* 1991], [Rose 1992], is probably the most mature and the best known, because of the size of the research team developing it, and the many case studies that have been published. (See section 5.3.2 for a small example of Object-Z.)

5.3.1   Discussion

Some extra fluency is needed with the object oriented languages, because they all provide additional constructs for defining classes, and some for composing objects into systems. The object based variants use plain Z, but in an idiosyncratic manner.

Most of these object oriented approaches to Z offer plenty of help with structure as objects can be used to split up a system's state space, and inheritance to build up complexity. They offer little help with the process; they all implicitly assume the use of some existing object oriented analysis and design process.

An object oriented approach makes it possible to write clear, abstract specifications of classes and inheritance hierarchies that are readily comprehensible. Framework specifications (the way in which the various objects are composed in a particular system) can be expressed, but be aware that this is still an active research area in object orientation. Also be warned that these object oriented variants have a long way to go before they can match the maturity of Z in language stability, formal semantics, and tool support. Nonetheless they offer promise in the areas of structuring specifications of large, complex systems, and for reusing specifications and proofs.

5.3.2   Object-Z example

Problem Statement. Consider a specification of a simple bank account, which has an owner and a current balance (which may be negative, to add a small element of realism). There are three operations: crediting the account with an amount, debiting it, and querying the balance. There is a limit on the number of debit operations allowed per day.

This could be specified as an Object-Z class.

$$
\begin{array}{l}
\hline
\quad BankAccount \\[-2pt]
\hline
owner : Owner \\
openingBalance : \mathbb{Z} \\
debitLimit : \mathbb{N}_1 \\
\hline
balance : \mathbb{Z} \\
debitDate : \text{seq } Date \\
\hline
\forall\, d : Date \bullet \\
\qquad \#(debitDate \upharpoonright \{d\}) \leq debitLimit \\
\hline
\quad INIT \\
\hline
balance = openingBalance \\
debitDate = \langle\,\rangle \\
\hline
\end{array}
$$

Credit _____
$\Delta(balance)$
$amount? : \mathbb{N}$

$balance' = balance + amount?$

Debit _____
$\Delta(balance, debitDate)$
$amount? : \mathbb{N}$
$today? : Date$

$balance' = balance - amount?$
$debitDate' = debitDate \frown \langle today? \rangle$

Query _____
$amount! : \mathbb{Z}$

$amount! = balance$

The various components of the class definition are described below.

Constants These may be different for each instance of the class, but do not change during the lifetime of an object. *owner*, *openingBalance* and *debitLimit* are constants. Note that *Owner* could be a previously defined class, an ordinary schema or a given set.

State The unnamed schema defines the state, and any state invariant. The state invariant is assumed to hold both before and after any operation. In this case, the state consists of the current balance, and a sequence of dates on which debits were performed. The state invariant requires that no date appears more than a limited number of times in the sequence.

Initial state The INIT schema specifies the initial state of the object. Here, the balance is the opening balance, and no debit transactions have occurred. Notice that the components are not primed.

Operations The Δ list gives all those state components that can change during the operation; all the others remain the same. In this case, the credit operation increases the balance by the given amount, leaving the transaction list unchanged. The debit operation decreases the balance, and adds today's date to the transaction list. Note that the state invariant ensures that the debit operation does not occur more than *debitLimit* times per day. The query operation returns the current balance, leaving the state unchanged.

Class specifications can be inherited.

> **Problem statement.** Consider, for example, a bank account that pays interest on the balance, but charges for debits, only accepts cred-

its above a minimum amount, and requires a minimum balance to be maintained.

```
┌─ InterestAccount ──────────────────────────────────────
│ BankAccount[redef Debit]
│ ┌───────────────────────────────────────
│ │ interestRate : ℕ
│ │ minCredit : ℕ₁
│ │ debitCharge : ℕ₁
│ │ minBalance : ℕ₁
│ ├───────────────────────────────────────
│ │ interestRate ≥ 100
│
│ ┌───────────────────────────────────────
│ │ balance ≥ minBalance
│
│ ┌─ Credit ─────────────────────────────
│ │ amount? ≥ minCredit
│
│ ┌─ Debit ──────────────────────────────
│ │ Δ(balance, debitDate)
│ │ amount? : ℕ
│ │ today? : Date
│ ├──────────────────────────────────────
│ │ balance' = balance − amount? − debitCharge
│ │ debitDate' = debitDate ⌢ ⟨today?⟩
│
│ ┌─ addInterest ────────────────────────
│ │ Δ(balance)
│ ├──────────────────────────────────────
│ │ balance' = balance * interestRate div 100
```

This illustrates the following Object-Z features

Inheritance *InterestAccount* inherits the state and operations of *BankAccount*. The debit operation is to be redefined.

Adding constants *InterestAccount* has constants in addition to the ones inherited. These describe the interest rate, the minimum amount that can be credited, the charge for a debit operation, and the required minimum balance. There is a constraint on *interestRate*, it must be at least 100, corresponding to a percentage increase greater than zero. (Note that in a more realistic system, these would more likely be state variables, and have operations available to change their values.)

Adding a state invariant There is a new component to the state invariant: the requirement that the balance must not fall below a minimum amount is conjoined with the state invariant inherited from *BankAccount*.

Modifying an operation The credit operation has a new constraint about the amount: this is conjoined with the predicate from the operation inherited from *BankAccount*.

Redefining an operation The debit operation is redefined to include the charge. This definition replaces the operation from *BankAccount*.

Adding an operation The operation to add interest is a new operation available to instances of *InterestAccount*.

This brief overview merely gives a flavour of the extensions to Z that Object-Z provides. Full Object-Z has many more facilities, for example, for accessing objects' operations, for composing classes, for promoting operations from individual objects to aggregates, and for specifying constraints on the order of operations using temporal logic.

5.4   Applicative-style specification

Although the form of the specification does not necessarily dictate the eventual form of the program that is derived from it, if you plan to use an applicative implementation language to implement your system it helps if the specification is written in a similar style.

Note: we avoid using the word 'functional' to describe this style, since it may lead to confusion with the term 'functional specification', which is usually understood to mean a specification of a system's functionality.

An example of reorganising a specification into a more applicative style is given by [Mitchell *et al.* 1991], in which the flexitime specification of [Hayes 1993a] is used as an example.

[Delisle & Garlan 1990] describes how they use Z to gain an insight into the system architecture of an oscilloscope. Their approach is an applicative one; complex functions are broken down into a composition of simpler ones, each of which describes part of the oscilloscope from a user's view point. The specification is fairly abstract, which helps to avoid the complexities that might occur at a lower level. For example, a model of time as a ticking clock suffices.

In section 9.3 we show how a word counting function may be specified in an applicative style.

5.5   An aside on specifying hardware

We have already cited some of the many published uses of Z being used to develop hardware. [Gerhart 1990] suggests some reasons for this preponderance of hardware specifications: hardware may be an area where there are the best returns for using formal methods, techniques already exist for checking circuit designs, and hardware designers are accustomed to using mathematical techniques.

There are many papers on the use of Z for the development of the floating point unit of the T800 transputer chip such as [Shepherd & Wilson 1989], [inmos], [May 1990], and [Barrett 1989]. The development of the chip proceeded in three main phases. First, a high level specification of the chip's behaviour was produced in Z. Then this was translated, using mathematical techniques, into a description of how the chip would perform the operations. Finally, the commands in these procedures were translated into the low level micro-instructions that control the individual components of the chip. Using formal techniques the initial design of the floating point unit resulted in significant time savings, and the formally specified parts of the hardware worked first time. Much of the process of producing the floating point unit was concerned with the refinement aspects and the proof of the refinement.

Other sources of information on hardware specifications include: [Smith & Duke 1989], an Object-Z specification involving a substantial amount of proof; [Bowen 1987a], [Bowen 1987b], microprocessor instruction sets; [Kemp 1988a], [Kemp 1988b], the Viper microprocessor; and [West *et al.* 1992], a pedestrian operated traffic signal ('pelican crossing').

5.6   Concluding remarks

In order to use Z successfully you must know 'why' you are doing so, 'what' you will use it for, and 'how' you will do so. The 'why' and the 'what' need to be considered carefully and decisions taken. These will help you to decide how you will use Z, but these matters are not independent of each other. The decision of what you will use Z for relies on there being appropriate methods to support the 'how' of Z's application.

Z in its raw state is not a method. Nonetheless the various approaches to Z specification that have been developed provide considerable help for Z users. None of the approaches provides *the* method for Z, rather each offers assistance with aspects of the structure–process–fluency view. Your choice of approach depends on the particular requirements of your project and the project team's initial knowledge of Z and other techniques.

Better techniques for integrating Z with various structuring techniques are being developed. Tool support for Z and extensions to it are improving, which in turn is leading to a greater take-up of Z. We believe that the object oriented approaches to Z exhibit particular promise, and we look forward to the development of more rigorous underpinnings for them, as well as larger examples of their use.

Chapter 6

Validation

In which the validation techniques of proof and animation are explored.

6.1 Introduction

Validation and *verification* are two different processes that can be used to check whether a specification is 'correct' in some sense. These terms can be defined as follows [Cohen *et al.* 1986, page 97]

- *verification* involves rigorous, formally justifiable proofs; for example, that a design satisfies a specification or that a specification is internally consistent (that is non-vacuous)

- *validation* involves convincing demonstrations of the soundness of conjectures; for example, that a formal specification 'captures' a system requirement or that an implementation is acceptable to the customer.

This chapter looks at techniques of validation.

A specification is a mathematical model of part of the real world. Properties of this model can be formally derived and verified, but to show that these are also properties of the real world requires validation. Dijkstra's well-known aphorism, *program testing can be used to show the presence of bugs, but never to show their absence* [Dijkstra 1979, page 44], applies equally to specification validation.

In section 6.2 we describe how proof fits into the specification process, and in section 6.3 we describe the validation technique of *animation*.

6.2 Using proof

There is a common misconception that formal methods are entirely concerned with proof. This is not so. There is significant benefit to be gained simply from *writing* a specification using a formal notation such as Z. Nonetheless, proof does have a rôle to play within a Z specification.

There are two levels of proof involved with formal specification. The first, and most common, is proof at the specification level. This can involve

- calculating the precondition of an operation to check that it is feasible, or that it provides a total interface (for example, see section 12.2.4)

- checking that the predicate of a schema is consistent, usually this involves calculating the precondition (for example, see section 12.2.4) as the precondition will be false if there is an inconsistency

- ensuring that a specification statement does not contain any surprises. For example, it is a good idea to check that any use of implication, $\Rightarrow$, behaves as desired

- showing that a desired property of the specification is correct (for an example, see section 23.3.2).

The second level of proof involves demonstrating that the refinement of a specification towards code is correct. We must show that we do not introduce inconsistencies or changes in behaviour as we refine the specification. (Chapter 13 provides a case study of refinement and its associated proofs.)

Using the first level of proof adds to the level of assurance that the specification is correct within itself. Proof is an involved, and thus expensive, process. How much is undertaken depends on how important it is that the specification contains no mistakes. Proof can be performed to various levels of rigour. Often an informal justification is provided (section 20.5 has an example). A fully formal proof gives a much higher level of confidence in the specification, but is also much more expensive. The effort needed to prove a specification formally is far greater than that for writing it. The cost of avoiding errors must be balanced against the cost of producing the proofs, in order to decide how much proof to undertake. The technique of formal partial proof (section 4.3.3) can be used to balance assurance against cost.

One reason that proof is so expensive currently is because of the dearth of proof tools that can assist with proof checking and proving of simple lemmas. As these tools are improved, specifiers will be able to make better use of proof.

6.3   Animation

It is impossible, even in principle, to prove the correctness of a specification against the *informal* requirements. Proof can be performed only on something that is represented as a mathematical model. We need a way to determine whether this model has correctly modelled everything of importance. We need to *validate* the specification.

There are a variety of ways of exploring and validating a specification. For example, desired properties of the specification may be stated as theorems, and proved. The dynamic properties of a specification are particularly difficult to deduce from a static written description. Animation is an appropriate technique for exploring these dynamic properties, through a translation of the specification into an executable language. Indeed, animation is mandated as a validation technique in the UK Ministry of Defence's Interim Standard 00-55 [MoD 1991], concerned with safety critical software.

Animation involves translating a specification into some executable language, and running it for various interesting scenarios. In general, specifications are not executable. So some manipulation may be necessary to state the specification in an executable form before it can be translated. (For an argument that non-executability is a desirable, or even necessary, property, see [Hayes & Jones 1991].) Even if a specification were executable, it is unlikely that the whole animation could be generated automatically: the aim is to explore how a specification relates to the real world, and this linking information is not contained in the specification (at best, it may be hinted at by the names given to some of the components).

6.3.1   Why

Animation is valuable in the following areas

Testing Mistakes in the specification, either owing to errors in the mathematics, or to errors in the requirements capture process, may be made apparent by animation.

Requirements capture Animation may expose unforeseen emergent properties of a specification that correctly captures the stated requirements. If these properties are not desirable, then the stated requirements fail to capture what is really wanted, and have to be modified. Alternatively, if these properties are desirable, they may be formalised as theorems.

Confidence Animation can provide more confidence that the specification does correctly capture the requirements, both for the specifiers and for clients who experiment with the animation.

The increased confidence and understanding animation provides makes specification animation a worthwhile validation exercise.

6.3.2   What

One area where animation is valuable is for applications that have important non-functional requirements, such as security properties. It can be used for real time requirements, provided that time is simulated too. A specification for such an application may be written in a highly abstract manner in order to capture these requirements (for example, a security policy model, as in Chapter 4), and as such it can be difficult to relate it to the real world; animation can help. Alternatively, if the specification is written in a more concrete fashion, as a behavioural specification written in terms of state-and-operations, it can be difficult to determine if the non-functional requirements have been captured properly; again animation can help here.

Another appropriate area is when a specification has become large, and difficult to comprehend as a whole, so that it is difficult to obtain a feel for the overall structure. An animation can provide a valuable alternative view of the specification, aiding understanding.

6.3.3   How

Translating the specification and providing a user interface are two distinct parts to animation. What executable language should be used? High level languages, such as a logic language like Prolog [Clocksin & Mellish 1987], [Sterling & Shapiro 1986], or a functional language like Miranda [Turner 1986] or ML [Wikström 1987], seem appropriate target languages for translating Z predicates. Smalltalk [Goldberg & Robson 1983], [Goldberg 1984], or another object oriented language, seems an appropriate choice for implementing the user interface to an animation. [Diller 1990] gives an overview of animating Z using Miranda or Prolog. [Johnson & Sanders 1990] explains how to translate Z into a Miranda-like language. [West & Eaglestone 1989] discusses approaches to animating Z in Prolog, and [West *et al.* 1992] uses these techniques to animate the Z specification of a Pelican crossing.

Below, one particular experience of using each of Prolog and Smalltalk to translate the whole of the same specification is described.

Prolog

An early account of animating a Z specification using Prolog is given in [Stepney & Lord 1987]. There, a medium-sized Z specification was hand-translated into Prolog, and a simple user interface was also written. The hand-translation involved writing predicates to handle Z constructs such as sets, including relations and functions, and toolkit operations, then performing an almost line-for-line translation of the Z schemas into their Prolog counterparts. Sequencing information was also included; if a requested operation's precondition was false, rather than just saying 'no', other operations were tried in order to make it true (since this was the whole point of the system being specified). More effort was spent on writing the user interface than in translating the Z specification itself. This was partly because the user interface was not formally specified, and so was slower to write and debug, and partly because the mismatch between the language and the 'graphical' interface (Prolog being used to generate VT100 control codes for block graphics characters!) This effort was well-spent, although the graphics were crude they were sufficient to make understandable what was happening. More importantly, users could interact directly with the animation, and watch the consequences of their requests appearing on the screen.

The advantages of this animation were quite substantial. The specifiers became happier that they had captured the requirements correctly in Z, and the clients were satisfied that requirements that had been captured really were those wanted. Also, the clients found that they could subsequently understand the Z itself much better.

Other work has looked at automatic translation of Z specifications into Prolog [Dick et al. 1990]. Automation is valuable, since it reduces possible transcription errors. Effort has been spent on performing valid optimisations of the resulting Prolog, since naïve automatic translations can often result in highly inefficient (of order n factorial) generate-and-test algorithms. But sequencing operations and building a sensible user interface still has to be done by hand. (The system described in [Dick et al. 1990] requires the user to type Prolog queries, and hence to know the translation from Z.)

Smalltalk

The same specification as described in [Stepney & Lord 1987] was also animated in Smalltalk [Mearns 1989, private communication]. The support in Smalltalk for the user interface meant that this aspect was straightforward, however, the translation of the Z specification itself was more complicated.

The experiences with animation described above suggest that a hybrid approach to specification animation should be pursued. Use a (semi-)automatic translation of Z to Prolog for the specification part, and link that in with a special-purpose object oriented component for the user interface.

6.3.4   When

Animating Z is a technique still in its infancy, and there is no commercially available tool support. Hence any animation still needs to be done manually, which can be costly. As noted above, the effort needed to animate a specification may equal that of writing it.

As in the case of proof (section 6.2), it is wise to consider whether the benefits justify the cost in your particular project. For example, if the project is particularly critical for any reason, so that the specification requires thorough validation, then animation is particularly valuable.

Chapter 7

Putting Together Your Method

In which the difficulty of defining a suitable method is revealed.

7.1 Introduction

The preceding chapters discussed a number of 'methods' for using Z on projects. It is not possible to point to one particular method and say that *it* is the perfect method for *all* projects. Instead, you have to decide which of the styles of writing Z you will use, what form of verification and validation you will use, and to what depth in your project you will use Z, amongst other management aspects.

7.2 Questions to be considered

In putting together a method for a particular project, you must decide on the three elements of a method: structure, process and fluency. Of course, the use of Z may only be a small part of a larger development method for the whole project. To fit Z in, you must consider three key factors

What is the objective of using Z on the project? What is to be achieved, and how is success to be determined?

For example, the project may have a specific objective to educate its staff on Z techniques, or produce a piece of software *guaranteed* to work, or understand a particularly difficult client requirement.

Under what constraints will the project work? These may include money, time, skilled personnel, client requirements (the client may have specifically asked for Z).

Where are the key risks? These include risks to the project success, in particular to the use of Z.

Examples are: a lack of detail in the requirements specification, uncertainty in the viability of proof tools, client resistance to formal methods.

The answers to these three questions drive your choice of what structure to adopt, what development process to follow, and the level of fluency required from your staff.

7.3   Aspects to consider for a Z project

How does Z fit into the overall development process?

- as the primary means of specifying the system?
- as 'annotation' for a structured method?
- by reusing already-existing components?
- post hoc specification of a system already in existence?
- as overall structuring for a number of subsystems?
- in the development of application-oriented theory? (it may be appropriate to develop some Z to capture the results of domain analysis).

What is being specified?

- a requirements description
- a system specification
- a set of module specifications
- an aspect of the problem domain
- other.

How is the specification to be structured?

- the Established Strategy, consisting of a state schema and operation schemas (see Chapter 3)
- a top level system, constrained by desirable properties, and an Established Strategy lower level specification, together with a proof of correspondence (see Chapter 4)
- the use of object oriented extensions (see section 5.3)
- other.

What approach to validation and verification is to be adopted?

- reviewing work: Fagan inspections [Fagan 1986], walk-throughs
- animation (see section 6.3)
- proof: sketch, informal, formal partial, fully formal (see Chapter 6)
- other.

Will you aim to specify reusable components?

- If parts of this system are expected to be used on other projects later, effort must be expended to ensure that the specification is general enough. The use of Z's generic features may be useful here.

- If the system reuses existing components, then specifying their abstract behaviour may help to determine whether they are the right components to be reused. Specifying their detailed behaviour may not be useful.

What is the appropriate level of abstraction?

For any use of Z the correct level of abstraction must be decided. It is not always true that a high level of abstraction is good; module specifications, for example, should be close enough to code to have captured the major design decisions. It is true, however, that the most common failing with Z specifications is insufficient abstraction.

Based on the answers to these questions, you need to design a project-specific *development process*. This should identify the places in the development where you intend to use Z, the way in which you will use the Z at each of these places, and any specific requirements these decisions place on the project, such as training, consultancy or tool acquisition.

Part II

Case Studies

Chapter 8

House Style

In which the conventions we use for the specifications are stated.

8.1 The need for a style

It is a good idea to have a house style for your Z specifications. A consistent style helps people to read others' work, and can ease the reuse of parts of a specification within another. Using a tool may enforce a style, and certain quality standards may well mandate adherence to a certain style.

House styles can cover a variety of aspects, including

- naming conventions
- layout of the mathematics
- accompanying text
- Z style conventions
- document structure
- cross referencing and index conventions
- layout of proofs
- statement of proof obligations.

We illustrate a number of different ways of writing Z specifications in this book, so we have not set a standard for that aspect. We have adopted a common approach to naming items in the specification, and also to the way that we declare schemas, and various other conventions, which is described below.

We recommend that you adopt a common presentation strategy for your project. As an absolute minimum, everyone on a team should follow the same naming conventions, as this aids readability of the specification. We also recommend you follow various widely accepted 'standard' conventions, such as the use of Δ, Ξ,

? and !, and the Sample Toolkit defined in [Spivey 1992, Chapter 4], wherever possible.

8.2   Naming conventions

8.2.1   Given set and generic parameter names

We write given set names in upper case, for example

$$[BOOK, PERSON]$$

We usually accompany such a declaration by some explanatory text that documents the intended usage of each given set.

It is possible to think of given sets as the generic parameters of a whole specification. So generic parameters of schemas and axiomatic descriptions are similarly written in upper case.

If more motivation is required for each given set then we declare each of them individually, with the surrounding text explaining their rôle, thus

Some discussion of *BOOK* ...

$$[BOOK]$$

Some discussion of *PERSON* ...

$$[PERSON]$$

We use singular, rather than plural, nouns for the names. A declaration like

$$book : BOOKS$$

looks messy, because it says that '*book* is a *BOOKS*'.

We use the conventional symbol $\mathbb{Z}$ for the given set of integers.

8.2.2   Schema names

We start schema names with an upper case letter, and use further capitals to distinguish separate words, or abbreviations. For example

$$LibrarySystem \mathrel{\widehat{=}} [\dots]$$

We feel that underscores in names make a specification look too much like a computer program, and so we do not use them.

We use *OK* as part of a schema name when we wish to indicate that we are describing the successful case. For example

$$HireCar \mathrel{\widehat{=}} (HireCarOK \wedge Success) \vee (NoLicence \wedge Fail) \vee \dots$$

8.2.3 Delta and Xi convention

We follow the convention of using the initial letters Δ and Ξ to indicate operation schemas that respectively do, and do not, change the state. For a schema S, ΔS always means $S \wedge S'$ and ΞS always means $[\Delta S \mid \theta S' = \theta S]$. Where additional information is included in a delta schema, we call it ΔSx where x indicates the additional information. Similarly for a xi schema.

8.2.4 Variable names

We start variable names with a lower case letter, but use capitals to distinguish separate words, or abbreviations. Again, we do not use underscores in the name. For example

$\quad myBook, yourBook : BOOK$

In general, we try to avoid distinguishing variables from types by relying on the case only, such as in $book : BOOK$. Using a name such as $aBook : BOOK$ is one way round this problem.

We try to use intuitively meaningful variable names, but avoid ambiguous names. For example, the name $newBook$ can be confusing as a variable name for adding a book to a database when describing the error condition of trying to add a book that already exists to the database. A name like $inputBook$ would be better. We also try to use compound nouns for sets and functions wherever possible, for example $hand : \text{seq } CARD$ rather than $cards : \text{seq } CARD$.

If we wish to distinguish a number of instances of items with integer labels, we use subscripts rather than putting the number in the name. For example

$\quad a_1, a_2, \ldots, a_n$

is preferred to

$\quad a1, a2, \ldots, an$

because the use of subscripts looks less like a programming language.

We follow the convention of using the decoration $'$ to indicate 'after' state variables, and the decorations $?$ and $!$ to indicate input and output variables. Because of this convention, variable names such as $in?$ and $out!$ provide no more 'meaning'; we try to avoid them.

We use the conventional symbol $\mathbb{N}$ for the set of natural numbers, a subset of $\mathbb{Z}$.

8.2.5   Abbreviation definition names

We follow the same rules for abbreviation definition names as for the expression that they are defining. For example

$maxNumber == 10$

$time == \mathbb{N}$

$compositeNumber == \{\, i, j : \mathbb{N} \setminus \{0, 1\} \bullet i * j \,\}$

$TEMPERATURE == \mathbb{Z}$

$POSITION == \mathbb{Z} \times \mathbb{Z}$

8.2.6   Free type names

A free type definition is a way of introducing a given set, together with some additional information. So we name free types in upper case. The branch names are injective functions, so we follow the convention for variables when naming them.

Care should be taken with the intuitive meaning associated with the name given to the accompanying injections. For example, consider

$EXTENDNAT ::= plainNat \langle\!\langle \mathbb{N} \rangle\!\rangle \mid error$

The name *plainNat* conveys the intended meaning of the injection better than, say, *nat*.

8.3   Layout of mathematics

8.3.1   Schema declarations

We put included schemas before simple declarations, with Δ and then Ξ versions first. The same order is used wherever that group of declarations occurs. If we have components that are included merely to make the specification simpler, with values derived from the values of other components, we put them last and leave a little gap, as a visual cue.

```
┌─ ForExample ─────────────────────────────
│ Δ Weather
│ Ξ Country
│ forecaster : PERSON
│
│ derived : ℕ
└──────────────────────────────────────────
```

8.3.2 Predicates

We place the parts of the predicate that describe preconditions in a schema operation before those that describe the postcondition.

We put disjuncts on separate lines, and put the disjunction symbol at the start of the second line, or on a line by itself, to draw attention to it.

8.3.3 Parentheses

We try to keep the use of parentheses to the minimum required to make the meaning clear. In particular, we use parentheses in function application in exceptional circumstances only, where their absence would be confusing.

8.4   Z style conventions

8.4.1 Maplet notation

The maplet notation $x \mapsto y$ is synonymous with the ordered pair notation (x, y). We use the former where the ordered pair represents an element of a relation (including functions, sequences and bags) and the latter for a 'plain' ordered pair.

So, for example, if we had declarations like

$$
\begin{array}{|l}
r : X \times Y \leftrightarrow A \times B \\
f : X \twoheadrightarrow Y \twoheadrightarrow A \times B
\end{array}
$$

then we would write expressions like

$$((x, y) \mapsto (a, b)) \in r$$
$$f\, x = \{y_1 \mapsto (a_1, b_1), y_2 \mapsto (a_2, b_2)\}$$

and *not* like

$$((x, y), (a, b)) \in r$$
$$(x \mapsto y, a \mapsto b) \in r$$
$$f\, x = \{(y_1, (a_1, b_1)), (y_2, (a_2, b_2))\}$$
$$f\, x = \{(y_1, a_1 \mapsto b_1), (y_2, a_2 \mapsto b_2)\}$$

8.4.2 Function overriding

We use override $\oplus$ to *update* a function (to change what an existing member of its domain maps to), but we use set union $\cup$ to *extend* a function's domain.

For example, consider

$$f = \{a \mapsto x, b \mapsto y\}$$
$$s = \{a \mapsto w\}$$
$$t = \{c \mapsto z\}$$

If we want to update f by changing what a maps to, we write $f \oplus s$. On the other hand, if we want to add a new maplet to f, extending its domain to include c, we write $f \cup t$, thus drawing attention to the extended domain.

8.4.3   Abbreviation definitions

We use abbreviation definitions wherever possible. For example, we write

$$upper == 65 \mathbin{..} 90$$

rather than the equivalent axiomatic description

$$\begin{array}{|l}
upper_0 : \mathbb{P}\,\mathbb{N} \\ \hline
upper_0 = 65 \mathbin{..} 90
\end{array}$$

The abbreviation definition is more concise, and offers the reassurance that it will not be further constrained elsewhere in the specification, for example, in something like

$$\begin{array}{|l} upper_0 = 68 \mathbin{..} 85 \end{array}$$

Axiomatic definitions can be used to define functions by using lambda-expressions. If it might be a little difficult for the reader to deduce the type of the result of such a function, we include the information in the accompanying text. For example

$divisors : \mathbb{N}_1 \longrightarrow \mathbb{P}_1\,\mathbb{N}_1$ is a function that takes a positive integer k and returns the non-empty set of its divisors

$$divisors == (\lambda\, k : \mathbb{N}_1 \bullet \{m, n : \mathbb{N}_1 \mid m * n = k \bullet m\})$$

8.5   Accompanying text

8.5.1   Mathematics within the text

In-line mathematics often appears in the natural language description of the specification. This is useful for explaining the mathematics 'proper'. We try to ensure that this mathematics is not split across a line in a way that makes it difficult to read. So unless the mathematical expression is short, we tend to place it on a line of its own.

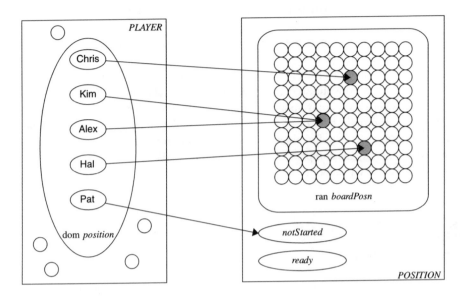

Figure 8.1 An example of a diagram in our house style.

8.5.2   Diagram conventions

Diagrams can be a powerful form of explanatory material; we use some simple ones to help explain some of the concepts we are describing. We have adopted a few conventions in their style, to make them more readily understandable without recourse to a long caption.

We draw given sets (including the base type of a free type) and constructed types (for example, $\mathbb{P}\,X$, or $A \times B$) as rectangular boxes. We draw the ranges of free type injections as boxes with rounded corners, and other sets as ellipses enclosing the relevant elements. We draw single elements as small ellipses, sometimes labelled with the element's name. We use arrows to link the relevant elements of relations and functions. For an example see figure 8.1.

8.5.3   Illustrative examples

Examples, either textual or diagrammatic, can be very helpful for explaining concepts. We try to choose representative examples that do not accidentally have more properties than the concept being explained. For example, when we use a diagram to illustrate a partial function (figure 17.4), we make sure that it is neither total, nor injective, nor surjective.

8.6   Cross reference and index conventions

As explained in the Preface, we have provided a glossary in appendix B as a means for finding entries in the text.

Rather than have a cross reference of declarations at the end of each specification, we have a consolidated index at the back of the book. This helps to find definitions where particular specifications are scattered throughout the book.

We index the definition of any term that is used elsewhere in the specification: given sets, axiomatic definitions, abbreviation definitions, schemas, and schema state components (as *component*; *SchemaName*). We do not index nonce-words defined in glossary asides.

8.7   Proofs

8.7.1   Proof layout

We provide all proofs with explanation of how the deductions are made. We indicate the end of a short argument by an open box □, and the end of a larger, multi-page argument, by a filled box, ■.

8.7.2   Proof obligations

There are many places in a specification where it is not obvious that the mathematics presented captures the desired properties. For example, a set comprehension may be used to specify a total function, but it might not be obvious that the set of pairs written down is either total, or functional. At such times, there is a proof obligation needed to justify the specification. Often an informal argument is sufficient justification, but sometimes a fuller, more formal, proof may be needed.

Some of the cases where we need to provide justifications are outlined below. Other cases are noted as they occur (see the cross references under 'proof obligation' in the glossary).

Implication

Whenever we use an implication we need to demonstrate that there are no unexpected outcomes from the definition.

If the antecedents do not overlap (there is never more than one that is true), and they cover all eventualities (they are never all false), the justification is trivial, since one and only one of them is true.

If some antecedents do overlap (more than one can be true), we need to show that the consequents are compatible, otherwise the specification is unsatisfiable.

If the antecedents do not cover all the possibilities (if they may sometimes all be false) then the consequent is allowed to be anything (since *false ⇒ anything*). We need to justify that this is not a problem.

We recommend using implication only in the first manner (no overlapping, exhaustive antecedents).

Applying partial functions

If a partial function is being applied to an element, we may need to show that the element is in its domain.

Functions and set union

Whenever a function is modified using set union (for example, when following our house style and adding a new maplet) we need to justify that functionality has been preserved. Usually this reduces to the observation that the maplet does not overlap the domain, the use of the following law [Spivey 1992, page 102]

$$\text{dom } q \cap \text{dom } r = \varnothing \Rightarrow q \oplus r = q \cup r$$

and the observation that $q \oplus r$ is a function if both q and r are functions.

If the function has stricter properties, for example injectivity, then the preservation of those properties must also be demonstrated.

Cardinality

Whenever # is used to find the size of a set, we need to show that the set it is applied to is finite. To assist with this we sometimes use $\mathbb{F}$ and $\rightarrowtail\!\!\!\!\rightarrow$ in declarations, to avoid unexpected infinities.

Chapter 9

A Word Counting Utility

In which a word counting utility is specified in increasing detail.

9.1 Word count

Problem statement. Count the number of words in a document. Words contain letters but no other characters.

The problem is stated only vaguely. What is a 'word'? Does a word containing an apostrophe count as one or two words? Should 'a' and 'antidisestablishmentarianism' be given the same weight?

9.1.1 Number of spaces

Often the *reason* for counting words is to get an estimate of a document's size. So, as a first approximation, it is probably sufficient to count the number of spaces, since that is usually roughly the same as the number of words.

We use a given set for characters

$$[CHAR]$$

and define the set of space characters

$$whiteSpace : \mathbb{P}\ CHAR$$

Defining *whiteSpace* to be a set of characters, rather than a single character, enables us to include tabs and newlines, punctuation, and other non-letters, as spaces if we want to.

▷ *axiomatic description*
The definition of *whiteSpace* is loose, it provides no information as to the possible elements of *whiteSpace*. This kind of loose definition can be convenient.

62

A document is a sequence of characters.

$$document == \mathrm{seq}\ CHAR$$

The word count is the number of space characters in the document.

$$wordCount_1 : document \longrightarrow \mathbb{N}$$
$$\forall d : document \bullet wordCount_1\ d = \#(d \upharpoonright whiteSpace)$$

▷ *sequence, filtering*
  $(d \upharpoonright whiteSpace)$ is a sequence containing only the *whiteSpace* characters of d.

Notice that the eventual definition of *whiteSpace* is important. If we decide that an apostrophe is a space character, then a sequence of characters such as *user's* is counted as two words.

▷ *accompanying text*
  It is important to think about the consequences of what you are specifying and note them down in this manner.

9.1.2 A more sophisticated word count

Suppose that we *do* want an exact count of the number of words in the file. (Maybe we are a publishing house paying authors by the word, and don't want to pay for lines full of space characters!) First, we need a clearer idea of what a word is. We take it to be a non-empty sequence of characters that does not have any spaces in it. Assuming that all characters are either spaces or word characters, we have

$$word == \mathrm{seq}_1(CHAR \setminus whiteSpace)$$

This is a necessary but not sufficient condition for a word. It does not stop a part of a word, for example 'xampl', being picked out as a word. So *wordCount$_2$* below splits the sequence at space characters (and nowhere else), and thus counts only whole words. (A similar approach is used later, in the 'blue pencil' problem of section 14.2.)

$$wordCount_2 : document \longrightarrow \mathbb{N}$$
$$wordCount_2\langle\,\rangle = 0$$
$$\forall sp : whiteSpace;\ l, r : \mathrm{seq}\ CHAR \bullet$$
$$wordCount_2(l \frown \langle sp \rangle \frown r) = wordCount_2\ l + wordCount_2\ r$$
$$\forall w : word \bullet wordCount_2\ w = 1$$

▷ *concatenation*
  Here we see that concatenation can be used to 'split up' a sequence as well as to join smaller sequences together.

9.2   Word frequencies

Problem statement. Find how many times each word appears in a document. Produce a list of those words and their frequencies, sorted by frequency.

A full word is a *word* surrounded by spaces, however, there are the cases of a word appearing at the beginning of a document with no preceding space, or at the end with no following space. Also, a document may consist of a single word not surrounded by spaces, or even be empty. We add a space character to the beginning and end of each document, so that we do not need to consider these as special cases.

The *lexicon* is the set of full words appearing in a document.

$$
\begin{array}{|l}
lexicon : document \longrightarrow \mathbb{P}\, word \\
\hline
\forall\, d, sd : document;\ sp : whiteSpace \mid sd = \langle sp \rangle \frown d \frown \langle \tilde{sp} \rangle \bullet \\
\quad lexicon\ d = \{\, w : word;\ sp_1, sp_2 : whiteSpace \mid \\
\qquad\qquad \langle sp_1 \rangle \frown w \frown \langle sp_2 \rangle\ \text{in}\ sd \bullet w \,\}
\end{array}
$$

▷ *in*
The predicate in the set comprehension gives us that $\langle sp_1 \rangle \frown w \frown \langle sp_2 \rangle$ is a contiguous part of *sd*.

▷ *set comprehension*
We need the constructing term w because of the two variables sp_1 and sp_2 that appear in the declaration part. We could instead introduce them using a quantifier, and avoid the need for a constructing term.

$$
\begin{array}{|l}
lexicon_1 : document \longrightarrow \mathbb{P}\, word \\
\hline
\forall\, d, sd : document;\ sp : whiteSpace \mid sd = \langle sp \rangle \frown d \frown \langle sp \rangle \bullet \\
\quad lexicon_1\ d = \{\, w : word \mid (\exists\, sp_1, sp_2 : whiteSpace \bullet \\
\qquad\qquad \langle sp_1 \rangle \frown w \frown \langle sp_2 \rangle\ \text{in}\ sd\,) \,\}
\end{array}
$$

Now that we can identify words we can convert our document into a sequence of the words it contains. Once we have separated the words in this way we can count how often each different word appears.

The sequence of words formed from a document is a sequence of sequences of characters. If this is collapsed into a simple sequence of characters, it contains all the non-space characters in the same order as does the document. In addition, each element of the word sequence is a word in the lexicon.

$$
\begin{array}{|l}
wordSeq : document \longrightarrow \text{seq}\, word \\
\hline
\forall\, d : document;\ s : \text{seq}\, word \bullet \\
\quad (wordSeq\ d = s) \Leftrightarrow \\
\qquad ((d \upharpoonright whiteSpace = \frown/\,s) \wedge (\text{ran}\, s = lexicon\ d\,))
\end{array}
$$

▷ *total function*
When declaring a total function it is wise to be sure that it really is total. Given any
sequence of characters it should be possible to remove the spaces from it, provided we have
stated what happens if there are no spaces. We have achieved this by stating what the
output looks like, without specifying how to operate upon an input.

▷ *toolkit*
↾, the anti-filter function, is defined in our extension to the sample toolkit, appendix A.8.
$d \upharpoonright whiteSpace$ is a sequence containing only those characters of d that are not in the set
whiteSpace.

▷ *concatenation, distributed*
$^\frown / s$ collapses the sequence of sequences s into a single sequence with the order of the
elements in the original sequences being preserved.

We can now produce a word frequency and a total word count. The word frequency
is a bag of words formed from the word sequence, so the bag count gives the number
of times the word appears in the document.

$$\begin{array}{|l}
\hline
wordFreq : document \longrightarrow \text{bag } word \\
\hline
\forall d : document \bullet wordFreq\ d = items(wordSeq\ d) \\
\end{array}$$

The total number of words is given by the total number of elements in the bag.

$$\begin{array}{|l}
\hline
wordCount_3 : document \longrightarrow \mathbb{N} \\
\hline
\forall d : document \bullet wordCount_3\ d = sizebag(wordFreq\ d) \\
\end{array}$$

▷ *toolkit*
The *sizebag* function is defined in our extension to the sample toolkit, in appendix A.9.

The final step is to produce a list of words sorted by the frequency of each word.
We arbitrarily choose to put the least common word at the start of the sequence.

$$\begin{array}{|l}
\hline
sortedFreq_1 : document \longrightarrow \text{iseq}(word \times \mathbb{N}_1) \\
\hline
\forall d : document;\ s : \text{iseq}(word \times \mathbb{N}_1);\ b : \text{bag } word\ | \\
\quad\quad s = sortedFreq_1\ d \\
\quad\quad \wedge\ b = wordFreq\ d \bullet \\
\quad (\forall i,j : \text{dom } s\ |\ i < j \bullet b(first(s\ i)) \leq b(first(s\ j))) \\
\quad \wedge \text{ran } s = b \\
\end{array}$$

▷ *sequence, injective*
We use an injective sequence in order to exclude the possibility of duplicate elements in
the result.

▷ *projection function*
The use of *first* here extracts the words from the pairs of words and their frequencies.

▷ *bag*
The range of *SortedFreq₁* is a set of pairs of words with their frequencies. This is nothing
more than a bag; indeed it is precisely the bag that is produced by *wordFreq*.

9.3   Word frequencies with a Unix pipeline

We now consider the classic word frequency problem as set by Jon Bentley [Bentley *et al.* 1986] as part of his *Literate Programming* column.

> **Problem statement.** Given a text file and an integer k, print the k most common words in the file (and the number of their occurrences) in decreasing frequency.

In the same article, Don Knuth contributed a solution in the form of a sophisticated 'literate program', whereas Doug McIlroy went to the opposite extreme and gave the following concise six stage Unix pipeline solution:

```
tr -cs A-Za-z '\012'   \
    | tr A-Z a-z       \
    | sort             \
    | uniq -c          \
    | sort -rn         \
    | sed ${1}q
```

Of course, this solution is understandable only to those people who are familiar with the relevant Unix commands (and there are an awful lot to know!) In order to have such a short, neat specification of this problem in Z, each of the pipe stages would have to be fully specified. In this section, we give such a specification of each stage, and hence a post hoc specification of the word frequency problem.

Specifying bits of Unix is a popular pastime; see, for example, [Morgan & Sufrin 1993] and [Bowen 1989].

9.3.1   A look ahead at the solution

The solution we give here involves specifying a series of functions, each of which corresponds to a stage in the Unix pipe. First, we summarise the solution, to give an overview.

1. $tr\_cs(upper \frown lower, nl)$
   Convert non-alphabetic characters to newlines, and collapse multiple newlines into one. This puts all 'words' on a line by themselves, with no blanks.

2. $tr(upper, lower)$
   Convert upper case to lower case.

3. *sort chop*
   Chop the stream into lines (words). Sort the words in alphabetic order. So all the words in the stream are in alphabetical order, occurring the same number of times as in the original stream.

4. $uniq\_c$
   Replace consecutive occurrences of word by the word and a count of the

number of times it occurred. This gives a sequence of $\langle count, word \rangle$ lines, sorted in alphabetical order of the words.

5. *sort_rn*
   Sort this sequence numerically by the count, in reverse order. This gives a sequence of $\langle count, word \rangle$ lines, in decreasing order of occurrence.

6. *uhead k*
   Take the first k lines of this sequence, giving the required result.

9.3.2   Characters

Unix uses the ascii character set. For this problem we identify the newline character explicitly.

$$char == 0 \,.. \, 127$$

$$nl == 10$$

▷ *number range*
  We have now given a definition for characters, where previously we used a given set. Here
  we need a convenient way of describing the upper and lower case letters, and picking out
  particular characters. This could still be done without introducing numbers, but as the
  ascii representation of numbers is well known, it seems artificial to ignore it.

Sets identifying the upper and lower case alphabetic characters are needed.

$$upper == 65 \,.. \, 90$$

$$lower == 97 \,.. \, 122$$

9.3.3   Cutting the stream into lines

Each stage in the pipeline is a Unix filter. In Unix, filters' input and output are usually considered as uninterpreted streams of characters (this is why the pipe components can be glued together so easily).

$$stream == \text{seq } char$$

$$stream_1 == \text{seq}_1 \, char$$

On occasion it is convenient to think of the stream as a (possibly empty) sequence of lines. A line is a sequence of characters that contains no newline, except for one at the end.

$$line == \{ \, l : \text{seq}(char \setminus \{nl\}) \bullet l \,\widehat{}\, \langle nl \rangle \, \}$$

▷ *set comprehension*
  Note how the constructing term is doing some of the work of defining *line*.

The function *chop* converts a stream into the corresponding sequence of lines. Since the stream need not be terminated with a newline, one may have to be added.

$$\begin{array}{|l}
chop : stream \longrightarrow \text{seq } line \\
\hline
\forall s : stream \bullet \\
\qquad \frown/(chop\ s) = \textbf{if } last\ s = nl \textbf{ then } s \textbf{ else } s \frown \langle nl \rangle
\end{array}$$

▷ concatenation, distributed
  chop s cuts *s* up into a sequence of lines, and then $\frown/(chop\ s)$ glues them back together again into a single line.

The predicate says that concatenating the lines back together gives the original stream if it ended with a newline, otherwise it gives the stream with a newline added. So no other characters are added or removed. There is no need for a predicate to ensure that individual lines end in newlines and do not contain other newlines since that is an implicit predicate given by the use of *line*.

   Note: this is not exactly the way Unix does things, because it does not add an extra newline at the end. Our formulation simplifies the following discussion. If Unix filters were being specified 'properly', the definitions of *line* and *chop* would need to be modified.

9.3.4   tr: translating characters

Changing non-alphabetic characters to newlines

The first stage in the pipeline solution is `tr -cs A-Za-z '\012'`. This translates all non-alphabetic characters into newlines (the `-c`, or complement, option translates every character *not* in the first argument, here all the alphabetic characters, into the second argument, here a newline, expressed as octal character 012) and collapses multiple newlines into a single newline (the `-s` option). The following Z specification separates these two functions. The function tr_s collapses multiple consecutive occurrences of its argument to single occurrences. For example

$$tr\_s\ b\langle a, a, a, b, b, b, c, c, d, e, e, a, b, b \rangle = \langle a, a, a, b, c, c, d, e, e, a, b \rangle$$

▷ accompanying text
  Providing examples such as this one can help to explain a concept to a reader.

$$\begin{array}{|l}
tr\_s : char \longrightarrow stream \longrightarrow stream \\
\hline
\forall c : char;\ s : stream \mid s \in monoSeq_1\ \{c\} \bullet tr\_s\ c\ s = \langle c \rangle \\
\forall c : char;\ s : stream \mid c \notin \text{ran } s \bullet tr\_s\ c\ s = s \\
\forall c : char;\ s, t : stream_1 \mid last\ s \neq c \lor head\ t \neq c \bullet \\
\qquad tr\_s\ c\ (s \frown t) = (tr\_s\ c\ s) \frown (tr\_s\ c\ t)
\end{array}$$

▷ *naming convention*
The function name *tr_s* does not follow our house style (Chapter 8). There we derided underscores, because they made the specification look too much like a programming language. Hence underscores are entirely appropriate in this context, and emphasise the connection with the existing Unix syntax.

▷ *curried function*
tr_s creates a family of functions in which, for any given character c, multiple occurences of c are removed from the first stream in forming the second.

▷ *toolkit*
$monoSeq_1$, the set of non-empty sequences of a single element, is defined in our extension to the sample toolkit, appendix A.8.

This recursive definition has two base cases. A *stream* consisting of only *cs* is translated to a single c; a *stream* containing no *cs* (which case includes the empty stream) is unchanged. The recursive step splits the stream into two parts, not between two *cs*, and translates each part.

The function *tr_c* translates all characters *not* in its first argument pattern into its second argument, and leaves the others unchanged.

$$\begin{array}{|l}
tr\_c : (\mathbb{P}\, char \times char) \longrightarrow stream \longrightarrow stream \\
\hline
\forall\, patt : \mathbb{P}\, char;\ c : char;\ s : stream;\ i : \mathbb{N} \mid i \in 1\,..\,\#s \bullet \\
\quad tr\_c(patt, c)s\, i = \textbf{if } s\, i \notin patt \textbf{ then } c \textbf{ else } s\, i
\end{array}$$

▷ *number range*
The constraint on i could also be written $i \in \text{dom}\, s$. We prefer the use of number range, since it better indicates the intended use of i to range over the index of the sequence s.

▷ *if then else*
Usually we would prefer a more 'positive' formulation of the predicate, as

$$tr\_c(patt, c)s\, i = \textbf{if } s\, i \in patt \textbf{ then } s\, i \textbf{ else } c$$

This corresponds to the description 'the function *tr_c* leaves all characters in its first argument pattern unchanged, and translates the others into its second argument'. In this case we choose the 'negative' form, to correspond more closely to the Unix description.

▷ *implicit definition*
Here is an equivalent recursive definition of *tr_c*. This demonstrates that recursive definitions are not always superior!

$$\begin{array}{|l}
tr\_c_1 : (\mathbb{P}\, char \times char) \longrightarrow stream \longrightarrow stream \\
\hline
\forall\, patt : \mathbb{P}\, char;\ c : char \bullet \\
\quad tr\_c_1(patt, c)\langle\,\rangle = \langle\,\rangle \\
\quad \wedge\ (\forall\, d : char \mid d \notin patt \bullet tr\_c_1(patt, c)\langle d \rangle = \langle c \rangle\,) \\
\quad \wedge\ (\forall\, d : char \mid d \in patt \bullet tr\_c_1(patt, c)\langle d \rangle = \langle d \rangle\,) \\
\quad \wedge\ (\forall\, s, t : \text{seq}\, char \bullet tr\_c_1(patt, c)(s \,\frown\, t) = \\
\qquad tr\_c_1(patt, c)s \,\frown\, tr\_c_1(patt, c)t\,)
\end{array}$$

The combination of translating and collapsing is given by

$$\begin{array}{|l}
tr\_cs : (\mathbb{P}\, char \times char) \longrightarrow stream \longrightarrow stream \\
\hline
\forall\, patt : \mathbb{P}\, char;\ c : char;\ s : stream \bullet \\
\quad tr\_cs(patt, c)s = tr\_s\, c(tr\_c(patt, c)s)
\end{array}$$

Translating all non-upper and lower case to single newlines is

$$tr\_cs(upper \cup lower, nl)$$

Lower casing

The next stage in the pipeline solution is **tr A-Z a-z**, which translates upper case to lower case.

The function *tr* converts characters in its first argument pattern to the corresponding characters in its second argument pattern. It leaves other characters unchanged. (We ignore here what happens if the second sequence is shorter than the first.)

$$tr : (\text{seq}_1 \ char \times \text{seq}_1 \ char) \nrightarrow stream \longrightarrow stream$$

$$\forall from, to : \text{seq}_1 \ char; \ s : stream; \ i : \mathbb{N} \mid \#from \leq \#to \wedge i \in 1..\#s \bullet$$
$$(\exists k : 1..\#from \mid s \, i = from \, k \bullet tr(from, to)s \, i = to \, k)$$
$$\vee$$
$$(s \, i \notin \text{ran} \, from \wedge tr(from, to)s \, i = s \, i)$$

Sequences that identify the upper and lower case alphabetic characters are

$$upperseq, lowerseq : \text{iseq} \ char$$

$$upperseq = squash(\text{id} \ char \rhd upper)$$
$$lowerseq = squash(\text{id} \ char \rhd lower)$$

▷ *identity relation*
  id *char* is the identity relation instantiated for characters, so is the relation that maps every character (represented by a number) to itself.
▷ *restriction, range*
  We restrict this relation to just those that are upper (or lower) case letters, each mapping to itself.
▷ *squash*
  We now squash this relation down to a sequence, so that we have '1' mapping to 'A' (or 'a'), and so on.

Translating upper to lower case is then

$$tr(upperseq, lowerseq)$$

9.3.5   sort: sorting into order

The next stage in the pipeline solution is **sort**, which sorts the lines into alphabetic order. Later on we find **sort -rn**, which sorts the lines into reverse (**-r**) numeric (**-n**) order. The distinction between numbers and words is necessary, because an ascii-order based sort of numbers would give 1, 10, 100, ..., 2, 20, ...

The full Unix **sort** filter is rather complicated, since it can sort on multiple fields, delimited by user definable characters. Here, however, sorting from the beginning of the line, either as a string or as a number, is all that is required.

The relation *before* defines an 'alphabetical order' on sequences of characters in terms of their ascii order.

$$\_\,before\,\_ : \text{seq } char \leftrightarrow \text{seq } char$$
$$\forall s : \text{seq } char \bullet \langle\,\rangle \text{ } before \text{ } s$$
$$\forall s, t : \text{seq}_1 char \mid head \text{ } s < head \text{ } t \bullet s \text{ } before \text{ } t$$
$$\forall s, t : \text{seq}_1 char \mid head \text{ } s = head \text{ } t \bullet s \text{ } before \text{ } t \Leftrightarrow (tail \text{ } s) \text{ } before(tail \text{ } t)$$

Using this definition, the function *sort*, which sorts lines according to ascii order, can be defined.

$$sort : \text{seq } line \longrightarrow \text{seq } line$$
$$\forall l : \text{seq } line \bullet$$
$$\qquad items(sort \text{ } l) = items \text{ } l$$
$$\qquad \wedge \text{ } sort \text{ } l \in \{\, l : \text{seq } line; \text{ } n : \mathbb{N} \mid n \in 1 \mathinner{\ldotp\ldotp} \#l - 1$$
$$\qquad\qquad\qquad\qquad \wedge (l \text{ } n) \text{ } before(l(n+1)) \bullet l \,\}$$

▷ *bag operations*
  items(*sort l*) creates a bag containing the entries in the sequence *sort l*. So here we are saying that the entries in the original and the sorted sequences are the same.

The first predicate ensures the same lines occur in the sorted as in the unsorted sequence, and the second predicate ensures that they are sorted in the required order.

Before being able to sort in (reverse) numerical order, we need a way of interpreting a line (a string of characters) as a number. Here we consider only natural numbers consisting of digits; the full Unix sort can cope with minus signs and decimal points, too.

$$digit == 48 \mathinner{\ldotp\ldotp} 57$$
$$zero == 48$$
$$space == 32$$

$$strToNum : line \longrightarrow \mathbb{Z}$$
$$strToNum \langle\,\rangle = 0$$
$$\forall l : \text{seq } digit; \text{ } d : digit \bullet$$
$$\qquad strToNum(l \mathbin{^\frown} \langle d \rangle) = 10 * strToNum \text{ } l + d - zero$$
$$\forall l : line; \text{ } c : char \setminus digit; \text{ } i : \mathbb{N} \mid c = l(i+1) \bullet$$
$$\qquad strToNum \text{ } l = strToNum((1 \mathinner{\ldotp\ldotp} i) \upharpoonright l)$$

Any line consisting only of digits is converted to a number in the usual way: the final digit is peeled off the sequence and converted to a number (by subtracting the ascii value of the digit 0) and then added to 10 times the converted value of the remaining digits.

If the line contains a non-digit character, converting the line to a number is the same as converting the shorter line up to but not including the non-digit character. Notice that we do not have to say that c is the first non-digit in the line. The other cases in the recursive definition apply only once all the non-digit charaters have been removed.

$$
\begin{array}{|l}
\hline
sort\_rn : \text{seq } line \longrightarrow \text{seq } line \\
\hline
\forall\, l : \text{seq } line \, \bullet \\
\quad items(sort\_rn\ l) = items\ l \\
\quad \wedge\ sort\_rn\ l \in \{\, l : \text{seq } line;\ n : \mathbb{N} \mid n \in 1\,..\,\#l - 1 \\
\qquad\qquad\qquad\quad \wedge\ strToNum(l\ n) \geq strToNum(l(n+1)) \bullet l \,\} \\
\hline
\end{array}
$$

9.3.6   uniq: removing multiple copies

The next stage in the pipeline solution is uniq -c. This collapses multiple consecutive copies of a line into a single line prepended with a count of the number of times the line occurred.

No counting

First, we define the function $uniq$, which replaces multiple consecutive occurrences of an element in a sequence by a single occurrence, but with no count. This can be defined generically, then used with sequences of any type.

$$
\begin{array}{|l}
\hline
[X]\!=\!=\!= \\
\hline
uniq : \text{seq } X \longrightarrow \text{seq } X \\
\hline
uniq\langle\,\rangle = \langle\,\rangle \\
\forall\, x : X;\ s : monoSeq_1\ X \mid \text{ran } s = \{x\} \bullet uniq\ s = \langle x \rangle \\
\forall\, s, t : \text{seq}_1\ X \mid last\ s \neq head\ t \bullet uniq(s \frown t) = uniq\ s \frown uniq\ t \\
\hline
\end{array}
$$

  ▷ *generic constant*
  This definition of $uniq$ is generic; it can be used with any type of sequence.
  ▷ *range*
  Taking the range of a sequence gives a set of the elements in the sequence. Saying it is the singleton set $\{x\}$ says that the sequence consists entirely of xs.

The three lines of the predicate ensure that

1. $uniq$ has no effect on the empty sequence.

2. $uniq$ transforms a sequence consisting of identical elements (possibly only a singleton) into a singleton sequence.

3. The recursive part of the definition ensures that the sequence can be split into two subsequences only if their last and first elements are different. Hence the sequence is recursively split until eventually only sequences consisting entirely of the same element are left, when the base predicate can be applied.

▷ *recursive definition*
Rather than the recursive step splitting the sequence into two subsequences, the definition could have been written less abstractly by splitting the sequence into its *head* and *tail*

$$
\begin{array}{|l}
\hline\hline
[X] \\
\hline
uniq_1 : \text{seq } X \longrightarrow \text{seq } X \\
\hline
uniq_1 \langle\,\rangle = \langle\,\rangle \\
\forall x : X \bullet uniq_1 \langle x \rangle = \langle x \rangle \\
\forall x : X;\ s : \text{seq } X \bullet uniq_1 (\langle x, x \rangle \frown s) = uniq_1 (\langle x \rangle \frown s) \\
\forall x, y : X;\ s : \text{seq } X \mid x \neq y \bullet uniq_1 (\langle x, y \rangle \frown s) = \langle x \rangle \frown uniq_1 (\langle y \rangle \frown s) \\
\hline
\end{array}
$$

or into its *front* and *last*

$$
\begin{array}{|l}
\hline\hline
[X] \\
\hline
uniq_2 : \text{seq } X \longrightarrow \text{seq } X \\
\hline
uniq_2 \langle\,\rangle = \langle\,\rangle \\
\forall x : X \bullet uniq_2 \langle x \rangle = \langle x \rangle \\
\forall x : X;\ s : \text{seq } X \bullet uniq_2 (s \frown \langle x, x \rangle) = uniq_2 (s \frown \langle x \rangle) \\
\forall x, y : X;\ s : \text{seq } X \mid x \neq y \bullet uniq_2 (s \frown \langle y, x \rangle) = uniq_2 (s \frown \langle y \rangle) \frown \langle x \rangle \\
\hline
\end{array}
$$

▷ *implementation bias*
It is often better, if possible, to define the recursion in terms of two concatenated sequences, rather than in terms of an element and a sequence. This is because such a specification style has less bias towards a seemingly sequential form (walking along the sequence, in one direction or the other).

Counting multiple copies

The count of the number of duplicates can be added by prepending the line with a string version of the count.

$$
\begin{array}{|l}
\hline
numToStr : \mathbb{Z} \longrightarrow \text{seq } char \\
\hline
\forall n : \mathbb{N} \bullet numToStr\ n = \\
\quad \textbf{if } n < 10 \textbf{ then } \langle n + zero \rangle \\
\qquad \textbf{else } numToStr(n \textbf{ div } 10) \frown \langle n \textbf{ mod } 10 + zero \rangle \\
\end{array}
$$

$$
\begin{array}{|l}
\hline
uniq\_c : \text{seq } line \longrightarrow \text{seq } line \\
\hline
uniq\_c \langle\,\rangle = \langle\,\rangle \\
\forall l : line;\ s : monoSeq_1\ line \mid \text{ran } s = \{l\} \bullet \\
\quad uniq\_c\ s = \langle numToStr(\#s) \frown \langle space \rangle \frown l \rangle \\
\forall s, t : seq_1\ line \mid last\ s \neq head\ t \bullet uniq\_c(s \frown t) = uniq\_c\ s \frown uniq\_c\ t \\
\end{array}
$$

We include a space after the number count, to separate it from the following 'word', which might well start with a digit itself.

9.3.7   head: the first few lines

The last stage in the pipeline solution is `sed ${1}q`, which prints out the first k lines, as supplied by the parameter, and then quits. In its general form, `sed` is rather complicated, but in this case it has the same effect as another, much simpler, Unix command: `head`.

The function *uhead* takes a sequence of lines and a number k, and returns the first k lines. If there are fewer than k lines, the whole sequence is returned.

$$\begin{array}{|l}
uhead : \mathbb{N} \longrightarrow \text{seq } line \longrightarrow \text{seq } line \\
\hline
\forall l : \text{seq } line;\ k : \mathbb{N} \bullet uhead\ k\ l = (1 \mathbin{..} k) \vartriangleleft l
\end{array}$$

▷ *restriction, domain*
  The restriction ($\vartriangleleft$) of the domain of l to the first k entries picks out the items in which we are interested.
▷ *curried function*
  The use of a curried function in the definition of *uhead* allows partial application.
▷ *lambda-expression*
  The definition could be written using lambda-expressions as

$$uhead_1 == (\lambda k : \mathbb{N} \bullet (\lambda l : \text{seq } line \bullet (1 \mathbin{..} k) \vartriangleleft l))$$

If the function were not curried, so that $uhead_2 : \mathbb{N} \times \text{seq } line \longrightarrow \text{seq } line$, only a single lambda-expression would be necessary

$$uhead_2 == (\lambda k : \mathbb{N};\ l : \text{seq } line \bullet (1 \mathbin{..} k) \vartriangleleft l)$$

9.3.8   The complete solution

Putting all this together, by applying the relevant functions one after another, we obtain the solution to the word frequency as

$$\begin{array}{|l}
sortedFreq_2 : \mathbb{N} \longrightarrow stream \longrightarrow \text{seq } line \\
\hline
\forall k : \mathbb{N};\ s : stream \bullet \\
\quad sortedFreq_2\ k\ s = \\
\qquad ((uhead\ k)\circ \\
\qquad sort\_rn\circ \\
\qquad uniq\_c\circ \\
\qquad sort \circ chop \circ \\
\qquad tr(upperseq, lowerseq)\circ \\
\qquad tr\_cs(upper \cup lower, nl))s
\end{array}$$

▷ *backward relational composition*
This definition uses backward relational composition, which is suited to composing functions (as here).
▷ *relational composition*
If you prefer your functions written the other way around (which looks more like the pipeline, too) you could use relational composition

$$
\begin{array}{|l}
sortedFreq_3 : \mathbb{N} \longrightarrow stream \longrightarrow \text{seq } line \\
\hline
\forall\, k : \mathbb{N};\ s : stream \bullet \\
\quad sortedFreq_3\ k\ s = \\
\qquad (\ tr\_cs(upper \cup lower,\, nl)\ \mathbin{\raise.5ex\hbox{\tiny 9}} \\
\qquad tr(upperseq,\, lowerseq)\ \mathbin{\raise.5ex\hbox{\tiny 9}} \\
\qquad chop\ \mathbin{\raise.5ex\hbox{\tiny 9}}\ sort\ \mathbin{\raise.5ex\hbox{\tiny 9}} \\
\qquad uniq\_c\ \mathbin{\raise.5ex\hbox{\tiny 9}} \\
\qquad sort\_rn\ \mathbin{\raise.5ex\hbox{\tiny 9}} \\
\qquad uhead\ k\ )s
\end{array}
$$

This (unsurprisingly!) looks almost the same as the original Unix solution.

9.4   Concluding remarks

Each of the different definitions of word count and word frequency above is valid. They are simply at different levels of abstraction. Which one is used depends upon the functionality required. If a rough measure of the number of words is all that is needed then $wordCount_1$, which counts the number of space characters, is fine. If the exact number of words is needed then $wordCount_2$ is a good description of the function. The third version $wordCount_3$ also provides an exact count of the number of words, but the method of describing it is less simple than $wordCount_2$; it makes sense to describe the operation this way only if the word frequency function $sortedFreq_1$ is also needed.

$sortedFreq_2$ gives yet another approach by reusing existing components instead of specifying from scratch. Some of these specifications seem a bit heavy handed in this context as the Z functions that specify the two **tr** filters could be combined into one fairly simple function (but even here it is not specified in full), and *sort* is far too general for this problem.

So would it be 'better' to simplify them? It depends on what happens next. The power of the Unix filters comes from the fact that they are small pieces that can easily be reused, slotting together to form new solutions. Are you going to reuse your specification? If so, make it general for reuse; if not, simplify as much as possible.

In either case, this is a potentially useful way of breaking a complex problem down into a sequence of simple (to understand, at least) stages. Granted, the complete solution looks rather explicit and algorithmic. But each stage in the pipe can have a suitably non-algorithmic specification. In this particular example, the problem itself is rather messy and poorly defined anyway, since we have no clear definition of a 'word'. A rather arbitrary decision has been made here, but changes are easily made by altering the appropriate stages in the pipe, rather than the whole specification.

Chapter 10

Rôles in Space

In which a spaceflight booking system is specified, and schema conjunction and disjunction are examined.

10.1 An aperçu of the client's requirements

Ventures Unlimited into Space (VENUS) offers space flights to every imaginable destination. Using new improved TARDIS technology, travellers can forget the drudgery of long haul flights. Indeed, some flights arrive before they depart! VENUS is looking for a computer based booking system that will allow it to record information about its flights, including

- the route details
- the launch and touch down sites
- the days on which the service is offered
- the number of seats of each class available
- the kind of spacecraft
- the local departure time.

The system should be able to determine the local arrival times of each flight from the speed of the spacecraft, route details, and knowledge about the movement of heavenly bodies. All times, except the local arrival and departure times, are given in GMT (Galactic Mean Time).

VENUS offer reduced fares for juveniles (aged two to 12 Terran years), and infants (under two years) travel for free, provided that they do not occupy a seat.

VENUS staff should be able to delete flights from the booking system, print out a passenger list for any flight, check the total number of seats booked, and find out whether there are any spare seats on a flight. The price of a VENUS space flight is calculated from the day of travel and various of the flight details (such as the kind of spacecraft and the route). Discounts are often available for combination tickets (the 'see the universe' combined ticket is increasingly popular), and for block bookings on the same flight.

Travel agents who sell VENUS flights must be able to access the booking system to make and cancel bookings. They should be able to discover the arrival and departure times of flights at a given space port on a particular date, the price of a flight, the total number of seats booked, and whether there are any spare seats on a flight. For security reasons, agents should not be given access to the details of the passenger list.

10.2   Basic types

In this section we define the basic types we use in the VENUS specification: given sets, free types and schema types.

10.2.1   Given sets

The system is accessed by users, travel agents and space companies, who are interested in flight numbers, places, price of flights, arrival and departure times, days of travel, kind of spacecraft and class of seat. We model aspects of time using integers; for the other parts we introduce given sets. We will deal with the details of passengers shortly.

$$[AGENT, CLASS, CRAFT, DATE, DAY, PLACE, PRICE, SPACECO]$$

▷ *readability*
Where there are many sets to give at once, it helps if these are stated in alphabetical order. A reader looking back to the declaration will be able to spot whether a particular set is included, or not, more quickly than if the names are arranged randomly.
▷ *overspecification*
Although we know that prices are numbers in the real world, we have no need of arithmetic operations on price for this specification. Therefore, modelling price as, say, natural numbers would be overspecification.
▷ *overspecification*
It would also be tempting to define the days using a free type such as

$$DAY_0 ::= sun \mid mon \mid tues \mid wed \mid thur \mid fri \mid sat$$

but it is not necessary as for this level of specification we have no need to know about particular days. (Indeed, most planets do not have 7-day weeks.) Likewise, there is no point in specifying particular classes of seat as the information is never used.

In summary, these given sets are used to represent the following

AGENT	travel agents who access the booking system
CLASS	the different classes of seating on board a space craft
CRAFT	the kind of space craft
DATE	particular dates on which flights run
DAY	the days of the week
PLACE	the departure and destination points
PRICE	the price of a seat
SPACECO	space companies who access the booking system

▷ *accompanying text*
It is good practice to document the intended usage of the given sets. Using meaningful variable names is a good start, but a few words explaining how the given set is used helps both reader and writer of the specification.

10.2.2 Dates and times

We introduce sets to describe times. *GMT* is the galactic mean time, which represents the number of galactic minutes relative to an arbitrary zero time.

$$GMT == \mathbb{Z}$$

We use *minute* to represent the number of galactic minutes since the most recent local 'midnight'.

$$minute == \mathbb{N}$$

▷ *abbreviation definition*
We need to test whether a particular time is before or after any other time, and we need to find the duration between two times. Thus it makes sense to model times as numbers, and to introduce special names for them. This allows us to record in the accompanying text our intentions for their use.

There are three distinct concepts of time that are used in booking a flight:

- *time of departure*, an instant in time
- *day of the week*, an accounting concept to help explain why there is a flight from Tau Ceti to Epsilon Eridani at weekly intervals
- *date*, an interval of time, used because customers often have a fixed date on which they wish to travel, but not necessarily a fixed time.

Days and dates are local to a place, because they relate to intervals of times between midnight and midnight. Therefore, given a global time and a *PLACE*, we can find the *DAY* and the *DATE* on which that *GMT* falls in that *PLACE*. Similarly, given a global time and a *PLACE* we can find the local time (in minutes past local midnight).

$$localDay : GMT \times PLACE \longrightarrow DAY$$
$$localDate : GMT \times PLACE \longrightarrow DATE$$
$$localTime : GMT \times PLACE \longrightarrow minute$$

▷ *abstraction*
As far as this specification is concerned, the declarations of these functions suffices. We do not need to know any further details of these functions, and thus do not provide them. This helps to prevent the abstract specification from becoming cluttered.

▷ *loose specification*
The definitions of *localDay*, *localDate* and *localTime* are all *loose*. All we know of them is their declarations. In a more detailed specification information needs to be provided about how to calculate these functions. For a specification written using the Established Strategy, such details would typically be included as part of the *application oriented theory* section.

10.2.3   Flight details

We describe those details of a flight necessary to support the description of the operations. A flight is characterised by its departure time (including the date), the route (start and destination locations), the available seating, and the kind of spacecraft.

```
┌─ Flight ─────────────────────────────────────────
│  depart : GMT
│  start, dest : PLACE
│  seating : bag CLASS
│  craft : CRAFT
├──────────────────────────────────────────────────
│  start ≠ dest
└──────────────────────────────────────────────────
```

▷ *bag*
When we first wrote this specification, we defined *seating* as $seating_0 : CLASS \nrightarrow \mathbb{N}_1$. When we reviewed the specification we noticed that this is a bag. Making this change meant we could specify a number of the operations involving seating using the bag operators. Do be aware that you may, on occasion, be using bags without realising it!

▷ *bag*
Our use of bag *CLASS* prevents pairs like *steerage* ↦ 0 from being an element of *seating*. Using a bag makes later descriptions neater, so there is a good reason for it as far as the specification is concerned. Moreover, if the client did want to be able to detect that some flights had no seats of a particular class, we could write a definition that would report this. For example

```
┌─ ReportAllocations ──────────────────────────────
│  ...
│  class? : CLASS
│  noOfClass! : N
├──────────────────────────────────────────────────
│  noOfClass! = seating ♯ class?
└──────────────────────────────────────────────────
```

The predicate states that VENUS does not have 'trips around the bay'; you cannot finish where you started on a single flight.

▷ *accompanying text*
It is good practice to write down the consequences of the way in which the system has been specified.

10.2.4   Kinds of passenger

VENUS recognises that different kinds of passenger have different nutritional requirements. For example, although Solarians eat almost anything, inhabitants of
the Vega system require their food to be cellulose-based. Passengers from Alpha
Geminorum prefer a sugar-only diet, whilst those from Betelguese have a taboo
against any foods coloured pink, but VENUS does not intend to charge passengers
differently on this basis.

The age of the passenger does affect the price charged for the seat. There are
three age groups

- infants travel for free, but do not merit a seat
- juveniles receive a discount
- adults pay the full fare.

We describe these three groups using a disjoint union free type.

$$[INFANT, JUVENILE, ADULT]$$

$$PASSENGER ::= infant\langle\!\langle INFANT\rangle\!\rangle$$
$$| \quad juvenile\langle\!\langle JUVENILE\rangle\!\rangle$$
$$| \quad adult\langle\!\langle ADULT\rangle\!\rangle$$

▷ *free type, disjoint union*
   This approach has the advantage that functions applicable to only one branch can be
   defined on that branch, and the correct use of the function can be checked by a tool.
   Alternatively we can use *PASSENGER* in declarations where we do not need to distinguish
   between *INFANT*, *JUVENILE* and *ADULT*.

10.3   The state

In this section we define the overall state of the spaceline reservation system, in
terms of the schedule, the bookings and the booking system users.

10.3.1   Schedule

We must restrict the state to include only those flights that have been scheduled
by VENUS. We introduce a given set *FID* to label them. This labelling also allows
us to distinguish otherwise identical flights (identical craft scheduled for a given
route and time).

$$[FID]$$

We also have a requirement to be able to calculate the duration of a flight from its
details. The duration depends on the particular flight, not just the route, because
the start and destination planets move with respect to each other.

The price of a flight depends on details of the route, the class of ticket, and the kind of passenger. VENUS has special arrangements so that if you book a series of flights, the total price is less than if you booked each of the individual ones separately. For example, in a 'see the universe' ticket many flights are reserved for the one (relatively) cheap price. Equally, there are discounts for block bookings on a flight. Bearing this in mind we need not introduce the notion of a return ticket, since a return ticket is just a special case of booking a series of flights.

  ▷ *abstraction*
  Here we realise that a number of apparently unrelated concepts can be regarded as special cases of a single, more general concept. Usually return tickets, series flights (one person on a series of linked flights) and block bookings (many people on one flight) are treated as three separate cases. But viewing them all as special cases of a general idea (a set of bookings) simplifies the specification, and the implementation.

To allow for prices varying with the number of seats booked at once, we calculate the price for a set of tickets.

```
┌─ Schedule ─────────────────────────────────────────────
│ flight : FID ⇸ Flight
│ duration : FID ⇸ ℤ
│ price : ℙ(FID × bag CLASS) ⇸ PRICE
│─────────────────────────────────────────────────────────
│ dom duration = dom flight
│ dom price ⊆ ℙ{ f : dom flight; b : bag CLASS | b ⊑ (flight f).seating }
```

The predicate constrains prices to be defined only for possible sets of seats: ones on existing flights and not overflowing the capacity. It does not, however, require all possible combinations of prices to be defined, or say how the price might be calculated.

We choose to map *duration* to ℤ rather than to ℕ to allow flights using TARDIS technology to have a duration less than zero.

  ▷ *relation, binary*
  Notice that we use a set of pairs as the domain of *price*. We could have written this as

  $$price : (FID \leftrightarrow bag\ CLASS) \nrightarrow PRICE$$

  We have chosen to use the set form, however, because we feel it better expresses what *price* is: the price of a set of tickets. We do, however, take the domain of this set later.
  ▷ *power set*
  Note that a power set can be used to construct an expression in a predicate, as well as in a declaration.
  ▷ *loose specification*
  As it stands the definition of *duration* is *loose*, because there are many functions that could satisfy its declaration. We can tighten the specification a little if we know that there is a special class of vehicles called *tardis*, which are the only vehicles able to arrive no later than they started.

  | *tardis* : *CRAFT*

Adding the constraint

$$duration (\!|\{\, f : FID \mid (\textit{flight } f).craft \neq tardis \,\}|\!) \subseteq \mathbb{N}_1$$

would say that the duration of flights for all non-tardis craft is a positive number of minutes. This would still leaves the definition of *duration* loose, but not quite as loose as before!

10.3.2   Bookings

The booking system keeps track of the seat bookings. We introduce the given set *BID* to identify the bookings.

$$[BID]$$

passenger maps the booking id to the relevant passenger, *seat* maps the id to the bag of seats booked, and *onFlight* records the relevant flight.

Booking
$passenger : BID \rightarrow\!\!\!\!\rightarrow PASSENGER$
$seat : BID \rightarrow\!\!\!\!\rightarrow \text{bag } CLASS$
$onFlight : BID \rightarrow\!\!\!\!\rightarrow FID$

$\text{dom } passenger = \text{dom } seat = \text{dom } onFlight$

A bag of seats is used because passengers may require more than one seat. An additional seat for a 'cello may be needed, or a block of seats may be required for a stretcher case. Multiple seats often need to be adjacent (for the stretcher case, for example). This suggests that there are further requirements concerning seat allocation that would need to be raised with the client.

10.3.3   Users of the booking system

Travel agents and space companies may access the booking system.

$$User \,\widehat{=}\, [\, agent : \mathbb{P}\, AGENT; \; spaceCo : \mathbb{P}\, SPACECO \,]$$

▷ *design decision*
   We make a design decision by forcing separate identifiers for two groups, using different types, even though they might physically be represented by the same person or office.
▷ *thinking ahead*
   We are not restricting access to the booking system to just one space company, our client VENUS, but allowing access to any user who the system recognises as a space company. This general case allows additional companies to use the system, but does not mean they have to.
▷ *thinking ahead*
   Why have we bothered to specify the details of the users within a schema? There is nothing in the requirements about changing the set of users, so it would be legitimate to provide the information with global variables. However, it seems prudent to allow for this sort of change in client requirements.

▷ *abstraction*
   User is a short schema, with no constraints. Should schemas like this be used? A balance
   needs to be found. Too many such schemas makes life difficult for the reader who must
   try to recall what each means. Nonetheless keeping them separate helps to make obvious
   the various constituent parts of the whole system as well as permitting separate access to
   them without needing to affect the remainder of the system.

▷ *schema*
   When a schema is very short, as in *User*, it looks neater to use a horizontal definition.

10.3.4   The complete booking system model

The complete state of the booking system, called *Venus* to flatter our client, is built
up from the individual state components. There is also a derived function *alloc*,
which returns the bag of seats already allocated on a given flight, and a predicate
that puts further 'global' constraints on the state components. We describe the
predicate parts of the schema in more detail below it.

$$
\begin{array}{l}
\underline{\;Venus\;} \\
Booking \\
Schedule \\
User \\
alloc : FID \twoheadrightarrow \text{bag } CLASS \\
\hline
\text{dom } alloc = \text{dom } flight \\
\forall f : \text{dom } flight \bullet \\
\qquad alloc\, f = \biguplus(\,(\text{dom}(passenger \rhd \text{ran } infant) \cap \\
\qquad\qquad\qquad (onFlight^\sim(\!|\{f\}|\!))) \lhd seat\,) \\
\qquad \wedge\ alloc\, f \sqsubseteq (flight\, f).seating
\end{array}
$$

▷ *schema inclusion*
   This use of schema inclusion in *Venus* is a common approach to specifying a state, in
   which separately specified aspects are combined, along with some additional predicates
   that further constrain the state.

▷ *house style*
   We leave a small gap before the declaration of *alloc*, to act as a visual cue; *alloc* is a derived
   function, introduced for later convenience, not a fundamental component of the system.

The predicate part

$$
alloc\, f = \biguplus(\,(\text{dom}(passenger \rhd \text{ran } infant) \cap \\
(onFlight^\sim(\!|\{f\}|\!))) \lhd seat\,)
$$

defines the utility function *alloc*, which returns the bag of seats booked on a given
flight. Infant bookings are not included, since infants are not allocated a seat.

▷ *anti-restriction, range*
   passenger ▷ ran *infant* restricts the *passenger* function to non-infants; taking the domain
   gives the set of non-infant *BID*s.

▷ *relational image*
onFlight~ is the relational inverse of the *onFlight* function; it relates *FID*s to *BID*s. Taking the relational image of the single flight of interest, $onFlight^{\sim}(\!|\{f\}|\!)$ gives the set of *BID*s for that flight. This set of *BID*s could also be written as $\mathrm{dom}(onFlight \rhd \{f\})$.

▷ *restriction, domain*
Taking the intersection of the two sets of *BID*s gives the *BID*s of non-infant passengers on the flight; domain restricting *seat* to this set results in a mapping from the *BID*s of just the relevant passengers to their bag of seats.

▷ *toolkit*
⨄ is distributed bag union, defined in our extension to the sample toolkit, appendix A.10. It combines all the bags in the range to give the total bag of seats allocated on that flight.

The predicate part

$$alloc\,f \sqsubseteq (flight\,f).seating$$

requires that on any flight the allocated seats are a sub-bag of the available seats; no overbooking is permitted. (It costs too much to accommodate overbooked passengers in the grossly expensive space-port hotels.)

▷ *bag operations*
The inclusion of this predicate in the state definition simplifies the specification of the operations to book seats. They do not have to include an explicit check that there is enough space available, since the existence of this predicate in the 'after' state ensures it.

10.4   Initial state of the space flight system

The initial state is given by the following schema.

```
┌─ InitVenus ─────────────────────────────────────────────
│  Venus'
│ ────────────────────
│  passenger' = ∅
│  duration' = ∅
└──────────────────────────────────────────────────────────
```

▷ *initial state*
Often an initial state is given in which all the sets involved are empty. In this example we have no operations that add users to the system, so we say nothing about them here. A full specification would cover those operations, too.

▷ *proof obligation*
It is good practice to demonstrate that an initial state of the system can exist. The informal argument given below is typical of those presented when absolute rigour is not demanded.

We are obliged to show that such an initial state can exist, that is, to show

$$\vdash \exists\, Venus' \bullet InitVenus$$

▷ *theorem*
We express as a theorem the requirement that an initial state exists. We are obliged to prove this theorem.

We show that the values for *InitVenus* satisfy the state invariant of *Venus'*.

- The types of the variables must be of the correct type; this follows directly from the declaration of the variables through the inclusion of *Venus'*.

- The functions *passenger'* and *duration'* must satisfy their declarations when set to the empty set. This they do, because the empty set is always a valid partial function.

- The other functions defined in *Booking'* and *Schedule'* must satisfy their declarations and definitions. This they can do, if they are taken to be empty functions.

- The extra conditions in *Venus'* also follow. *alloc'* = ∅ satisfies its definition. Also, *passenger'* = ∅ and hence dom *passenger'* = ∅, so the universal quantifier ranges over the empty set, and is therefore always true.

10.5   Approach to operation specification

The approach we take to specifying the operations is to consider partial requirements one at a time, and then build up a complete operation description from these individual fragments.

Typically we have the successful case where the operation does as it should, which is described as a list of conjuncts, each item of which corresponds to a separate part of the operation description. Each of these parts has an associated exception, which is described by a disjunct.

This leads to an operation structure like

$$FullOp \mathrel{\hat=} (PartOneOK \wedge PartTwoOK \wedge PartThreeOK)$$
$$\vee\ PartOneError$$
$$\vee\ PartTwoError$$
$$\vee\ PartThreeError$$

These part descriptions of the operations are guided by the following list of required operations. (The last column indicates which operations are available to travel agents (a), and which to the space company (s).)

enquiry	*SeatPrice*	a
	Spare	a,s
	DepTimes	a
	ArrTimes	a
	NumberBooked	a,s
	PassengerList	s
update	*AddBooking*	a
	DeleteBooking	a
	AddFlight	s
	DeleteFlight	s

Once we have the operations specified, we depart slightly from the Established Strategy by building an extra layer on top, specifying who may carry out what operation. In other words we are taking a rôle model view of the system operations—organising the specification around the various rôles that can be played.

This leads to a structure like

$$AllOp \,\hat{=}\, ActorOne \wedge (FullOpA \vee FullOpB \vee FullOpC)$$
$$\vee\ ActorTwo \wedge (FullOpC \vee FullOpD \vee FullOpE)$$
$$\vee\ ActorThree \wedge (FullOpA \vee FullOpD \vee FullOpF)$$

This structure means that all the permitted operations are gathered together in one place. Some consequences of adopting it are discussed in section 10.9.4.

> ▷ house style
> There are other formulations that can be used here, for example, the Established Strategy (Chapter 3). Choice of an appropriate style may be included in your own house style.

10.6 Flight details

Many of the operations defined below have as input a flight $f? : FID$ and need to check that this refers to a known flight. We separate out this common check here, and include it where needed.

Although this schema itself does not change the state of the booking system, it is used in conjunction with schemas that do; hence it includes $\Delta\,Venus$ rather than $\Xi\,Venus$.

```
┌─ KnownFlight ──────────────────────────────────
│ Δ Venus
│ f? : FID
├────────────────────────────────────────────────
│ f? ∈ dom flight
└────────────────────────────────────────────────
```

A flight is unknown if it is not in the domain of the *flight* function. As we will use this schema as an error condition, we ensure the booking system is unchanged in such a case.

```
┌─ NotFlight ────────────────────────────────────
│ Ξ Venus
│ f? : FID
├────────────────────────────────────────────────
│ f? ∉ dom flight
└────────────────────────────────────────────────
```

10.7 Enquiry operations

Enquiry operations do not change the state of the *Venus* booking system.

10.7.1   Finding the price of a group of seats

In order to find out the price of a bag of seats we must examine the flight details record. The input is the details of the ticket required: a set of flight ids with the bag of seats required on that flight. The output is the price for this ticket.

```
┌─ SeatPriceOK ─────────────────────────────────────────
│ Ξ Venus
│ ticket? : ℙ(FID × bag CLASS)
│ price! : PRICE
├───────────────────────────────────────────────────────
│ ticket? ∈ dom price
│ price! = price ticket?
└───────────────────────────────────────────────────────
```

If the details in *ticket?* are not recognised by the system, this is an error.

```
┌─ NotSeat ─────────────────────────────────────────────
│ Ξ Venus
│ ticket? : ℙ(FID × bag CLASS)
│ price! : PRICE
├───────────────────────────────────────────────────────
│ ticket? ∉ dom price
└───────────────────────────────────────────────────────
```

So the complete *SeatPrice* enquiry is

$$SeatPrice \mathrel{\widehat{=}} SeatPriceOK$$
$$\lor NotSeat$$

▷ *schema disjunction*
  We use ∨ in the definition of *SeatPrice* to show the alternative behaviours; the operation
  may be successful or error conditions may arise.

10.7.2   Number of spare seats

To find out the total number of spare seats on a flight, we define the following enquiry

```
┌─ SpareOK ─────────────────────────────────────────────
│ Ξ Venus
│ f? : FID
│ spare! : bag CLASS
├───────────────────────────────────────────────────────
│ spare! = (flight f?).seating ⊎ alloc f?
└───────────────────────────────────────────────────────
```

▷ *bag operations*
  spare! is found by taking the difference of the bags that record how many seats there are
  and how many have already been allocated.

The complete description of checking the capacity requires a known flight, otherwise it is in error.

$$Spare \triangleq (SpareOK \land KnownFlight)$$
$$\lor NotFlight$$

10.7.3 Departure times

We need to be able to list the flights departing from a particular port on a given date. We produce the relevant flight numbers and their departure times, in local time for that spaceport.

$$
\begin{array}{l}
\_\_\_ DepTimes _____ \\
\Xi Venus \\
date? : DATE \\
port? : PLACE \\
dep! : FID \nrightarrow minute \\
_____ \\
dep! = \{\, f : \mathrm{dom}\, flight;\ Flight\ | \\
\qquad \theta Flight = flight\, f \\
\qquad \land\ start = port? \\
\qquad \land\ localDate(depart, start) = date?\ \bullet \\
\qquad\qquad f \mapsto localTime(depart, port?)\,\} \\
\end{array}
$$

▷ *schema in set comprehension*
The schema *Flight* is being used as a declaration in the set comprehension; this makes all its components available, and so we do not need to use component selection to access the individual parameters.

▷ *schema binding*
In the expression $\theta Flight = flight\, f$ we are ensuring that the bindings of values to variables in the *Flight* schema are the correct ones for the flight in question.

▷ *design decision*
We are taking a design decision here about what information would be useful to return in reply to this query. There is no requirement to provide the departure times; it is our decision that this information might be useful.

10.7.4 Arrival times

To calculate the list of arrival times we need to add the duration of the flight (calculated using the function *duration*, section 10.3.1) to the departure time, having first converted the departure time to our absolute reference of GMT. We then check to see if this arrival time is on the required date.

```
 ___ ArrTimes _____
| Ξ Venus
| date? : DATE
| port? : PLACE
| arrival! : FID ↦ minute
|_____
| arrival! = { f : dom flight; Flight; arr : GMT |
|                 θ Flight = flight f
|                 ∧ dest = port?
|                 ∧ arr = depart + duration f
|                 ∧ localDate( arr, dest) = date? •
|                       f ↦ localTime( arr, port?) }
|_____
```

▷ *readability*
In order to make the specification clearer, we introduce the local variable *arr*. This means that we write *depart + duration f* for the time taken for the flight once only.

10.7.5   Number of bookings on a flight

To find out the number of bookings on a flight we define the following enquiry

```
 ___ NumberBookedOK _____
| Ξ Venus
| f? : FID
| n! : ℕ
|_____
| n! = sizebag( alloc f?)
|_____
```

▷ *design decision*
Here we have interpreted 'number booked' to mean the number of seats taken. Infants may travel for free provided they do not occupy a seat, so infants are excluded from the calculation of *alloc* in *Venus*.
▷ *toolkit*
sizebag is defined in our extension to the sample toolkit, appendix A.9. It gives the total number of items in the bag.

The successful operation further requires that the flight be known.

$$NumberBooked \; \hat{=} \; (NumberBookedOK \wedge KnownFlight)$$
$$\vee \; NotFlight$$

10.7.6   Passenger list

A passenger list for a particular flight may be required. The flight is input, and there is no change to the booking system. A list of passengers is obtained by examining the *onFlight* function to determine the bookings on the flight, then using these bookings to extract the details from *passenger*.

__ *PassengerListOK* _____

Ξ *Venus*

$f? : FID$

$who! : \mathbb{P}\,PASSENGER$

_____

$who! = passenger\,(\!|\mathrm{dom}(\mathit{onFlight} \rhd \{f?\})\!|)$

▷ *relational image*

$\mathit{onFlight} \rhd \{f?\}$ restricts the *onFlight* function to just the flight of interest. Taking its domain yields the set of relevant *BIDs*. The relational image of this set through the *passenger* function gives the corresponding set of *PASSENGERs*. Using the same form for the set of relevant *BIDs* as in the predicate for *Venus* itself, this could instead be written

$$who! = passenger\,(\!|\mathit{onFlight}^{\sim}\,(\!|\{f?\}\!|)\!|)$$

The successful operation also requires that the flight be known.

$$PassengerList \,\hat{=}\, (PassengerListOK \land KnownFlight)$$
$$\lor\, NotFlight$$

10.8   Update operations

Update operations can change the state of the *Venus* booking system. Some operations change only the *Booking* components, others change only the *Schedule* components. Hence the following two schemas are useful.

$$\Delta VenusBooking \,\hat{=}\, [\,\Delta Venus;\, \Xi Schedule;\, \Xi User\,]$$
$$\Delta VenusSchedule \,\hat{=}\, [\,\Delta Venus;\, \Xi Booking;\, \Xi User\,]$$

▷ Δ *convention*

The Δ convention is being used to implicitly declare the schema Δ *Venus* as $[\,Venus;\, Venus'\,]$. The convention is not being used to declare Δ *VenusBooking* or Δ *VenusSchedule*; the Δ in their names is a visual cue to indicate that these schemas have before and after states that differ, but are not operations (operation names usually do not have a Δ).

10.8.1   Making a booking

Successful addition of a booking to the booking system happens when there is still room on the flight. The operation creates a booking identifier. The (partial) operation that describes this is

```
┌─ AddBookingOK ─────────────────────────────────
│ Δ VenusBooking
│ c? : bag CLASS
│ p? : PASSENGER
│ f? : FID
│ b! : BID
├─────────────────────────────────────────────────
│ b! ∉ dom passenger
│ passenger' = passenger ∪ {b! ↦ p?}
│ seat' = seat ∪ {b! ↦ c?}
│ onFlight' = onFlight ∪ {b! ↦ f?}
└─────────────────────────────────────────────────
```

Note that there is no explicit check that there are enough seats of the right class available; the predicate defining *alloc'* in *Venus'* enforces it.

The error case of no spare seats in this class is covered by the *ClassFull* error schema.

```
┌─ ClassFull ────────────────────────────────────
│ Ξ Venus
│ f? : FID
│ c? : bag CLASS
├─────────────────────────────────────────────────
│ ¬ (c? ⊑ (flight f?).seating ⊎ alloc f?)
└─────────────────────────────────────────────────
```

▷ *bag operations*
The predicate is satisfied if the requested bag of seats is not a sub-bag of the unallocated seats.

Successful booking is prevented if there are no free seats of the desired class (*ClassFull*), or the flight is not known (*NotFlight*).

Now we can give the complete description of adding a booking to the booking system.

$$AddBooking \;\widehat{=}\; (AddBookingOK \wedge KnownFlight)$$
$$\vee\; ClassFull$$
$$\vee\; NotFlight$$

10.8.2   Deleting a booking

In deleting a booking we check that the booking is known to the system and then remove it.

```
┌─ DeleteBookingOK ──────────────────────────────────
│ Δ VenusBooking
│ b? : BID
├──────────────────────────────────────────────────
│ b? ∈ dom passenger
│ passenger' = {b?} ⊲ passenger
│ seat' = {b?} ⊲ seat
│ onFlight' = {b?} ⊲ onFlight
└──────────────────────────────────────────────────
```

Since *b?* is in the domain of *passenger*, and not in the domain of *passenger'*, the predicate in *Booking* ensures that it is also in the domains of *seat* and *onFlight*, and also not in the domains of *seat'* and *onFlight'*. We cannot omit the predicates for *seat'* and *onFlight'*, however, since *Booking* merely determines their domains. Here we need to say more. The whole of the *seat* and *onFlight* mappings are unchanged, except at *b?*.

It is an error if the booking does not exist.

```
┌─ NotBooked ────────────────────────────────────────
│ Ξ Venus
│ b? : BID
├──────────────────────────────────────────────────
│ b? ∉ dom passenger
└──────────────────────────────────────────────────
```

The complete description of deleting a booking from the booking system is given by

$$DeleteBooking \mathrel{\widehat{=}} DeleteBookingOK$$
$$\lor\ NotBooked$$

10.8.3   Adding a flight to the booking system

The following schema describes the operation of adding new route information.

```
┌─ AddFlightOK ──────────────────────────────────────
│ Δ VenusSchedule
│ flt? : Flight
│ f? : FID
├──────────────────────────────────────────────────
│ f? ∉ dom flight
│ flight' = flight ∪ {f? ↦ flt?}
│ {f?} ⊲ duration' = duration
│ (dom price) ⊲ price' = price
│ ∀ ticket : dom(price' \ price) • f? ∈ dom ticket
└──────────────────────────────────────────────────
```

Although *duration* is loosely defined, adding a new flight should not change the durations of the existing flights. Hence removing all reference to the new flight from *duration'* should recover *duration*.

Adding a new flight also requires changing the *price* component to include prices for tickets on this flight. Since we have said nothing about what these prices are, we can say little about what must be changed. In a similar manner to the way we updated *duration*, we can say that the old prices do not change. This is more subtle than before, since *price* works in terms of sets of flights, some of which may be old and some new. So we say that *price'* includes all the old *price* information: *price'* responds in the same way that *price* did when asked about any set of flights that does not include the new flight. We also say that not too much new information has been added: all the new price information includes the new flight.

> ▷ *relation, binary*
> *price' \ price* gives the new part of the *price* mapping, taking its domain gives the set of new sets of (*flight*, *seats*) pairs. So *ticket* ranges over the new sets of pairs. But a set of pairs is a relation. So taking its domain gives the flights in the set. We require at least one of these to be the new flight *f?*, in order that not 'too much' information be added by the operation.

It is an error if the flight number already exists.

$$AddFlight \cong AddFlightOK$$
$$\lor [\, \Xi\, Venus;\, f? : FID \mid f? \in \text{dom}\, flight\,]$$

> ▷ *schema, unnamed*
> We do not need to express elsewhere that the flight number already exists, so we define this within an unnamed schema. Because the schema has no name we have no means of referring to it elsewhere, and so it cannot be reused in another context.

10.8.4   Deleting a flight from the booking system

Following our usual style, we first deal with the mechanics of cancelling a flight and then deal with the exceptions afterwards. To cancel a flight we check that it has no bookings, and remove it from the booking system.

DeleteFlightOK
$\Delta\, VenusSchedule$
$f? : FID$

$f? \notin \text{ran}\, onFlight$
$flight' = \{f?\} \lhd flight$
$duration' = \{f?\} \lhd duration$
$price' = (\text{dom}\, price') \lhd price$
$\forall\, ticket : \text{dom}(price \setminus price') \bullet f? \in \text{dom}\, ticket$

Deleting a flight also requires removing occurrence of it in the *price* component, making sure not to remove any more information than is necessary. The remaining prices do not change. So *price* would respond in the same way as does *price'* when asked about flights not including the deleted flight.

> ▷ *design decision*
> Here we need to make a design decision about whether a flight with bookings may be deleted. We assume not. Note that this does not mean that we necessarily finish up with an unfriendly interface, since the system could, on discovering existing bookings, enter into a procedure for transferring them to alternative flights or alerting agents that the bookings should be reassigned, or whatever. Z specifies the meaning of operations, not how they should be sequenced in the implementation.

It is an error if the flight has some bookings.

```
┌─ HasBooking ─────────────────────────────
│ Ξ Venus
│ f? : FID
├──────────────────────────────
│ f? ∈ ran onFlight
└──────────────────────────────
```

It is an error if the flight number does not exist. We can now give a complete description of cancelling a flight.

$$DeleteFlight \mathrel{\widehat{=}} (DeleteFlightOK \land KnownFlight)$$
$$\lor\ HasBooking$$
$$\lor\ NotFlight$$

10.9 Collected operations

We now turn our attention to access rights for the operations defined above.

10.9.1 Travel agent operations

We have a requirement that only some operations are available to travel agents. We set up schemas that check that the user is a travel agent entitled to access the booking system.

We define travel agent updates, enquiries and non-agent operations. Travel agents updates can change only the *Booking* component of the booking system, all other components are unchanged.

$$AgentUpdate \mathrel{\widehat{=}} [\, \Delta VenusBooking;\ a? : AGENT \mid a? \in agent\,]$$

Travel agent enquiries leave the whole booking system unchanged

$$AgentEnq \mathrel{\widehat{=}} [\, \Xi Venus;\ a? : AGENT \mid a? \in agent\,]$$

A non-agent operation is used as an error condition, and so leaves the booking system unchanged.

$$NotAgent \; \widehat{=} \; [\, \Xi\, Venus;\; a? : AGENT \mid a? \notin agent\,]$$

Travel agents may make enquiries about seat prices, spare seats, departure and arrival times, and the number of seats booked on a flight. They may update the booking system by adding and deleting bookings.

$$
\begin{aligned}
AgentOp \; \widehat{=} \; &AgentEnq \wedge (SeatPrice \vee Spare \vee ArrTimes \\
&\qquad\qquad \vee DepTimes \vee NumberBooked) \\
&\vee\, AgentUpdate \wedge (AddBooking \vee DeleteBooking) \\
&\vee\, NotAgent
\end{aligned}
$$

10.9.2   Space company operations

Space companies may perform only some operations. We define space company updates, enquiries and non-space company operations. Space company updates may change only the *Schedule* components of the booking system, all other components are unchanged. As a consequence of this requirement, the space company's ability to delete some flights is restricted. (See the discussion in the glossary entry in section 10.8.4.)

A legitimate space company operation acts on the booking system with a user known as a member of *SpaceCo*.

$$SpaceCoUpdate \; \widehat{=} \; [\, \Delta\, VenusSchedule;\; sc? : SPACECO \mid sc? \in spaceCo\,]$$

Space company enquiries leave the whole booking system unchanged.

$$SpaceCoEnq \; \widehat{=} \; [\, \Xi\, Venus;\; sc? : SPACECO \mid sc? \in spaceCo\,]$$

A non-company operation is used as an error condition, and so preserves the booking system.

$$NotSpaceCo \; \widehat{=} \; [\, \Xi\, Venus;\; sc? : SPACECO \mid sc? \notin spaceCo\,]$$

Space companies can query the booking system to find out the number of spare seats on a flight, the number of bookings on a flight, or a passenger list. They can update the booking system by adding or deleting a flight.

$$
\begin{aligned}
SpaceCoOp \; \widehat{=} \; &SpaceCoEnq \wedge (Spare \vee NumberBooked \vee PassengerList) \\
&\vee\, SpaceCoUpdate \wedge (AddFlight \vee DeleteFlight) \\
&\vee\, NotSpaceCo
\end{aligned}
$$

10.9.3   Venus operations

All the operations on the *Venus* booking system are either agent operations or space company operations.

$$VenusOp \ \widehat{=}\ AgentOp \lor SpaceCoOp$$

This concludes the specification of the VENUS booking system.

10.9.4   Unwanted inputs and outputs

Gathering together the operations to form *AgentOp*, *SpaceCoOp* and *VenusOp* in this way has the advantage of making clear exactly what are the operations, and what are only partial definitions made merely for ease of specification.

This structure does have a drawback, however. Because the various operations are joined in this manner, the result has all the components of the individual operations, in particular, all the input and output components. This poses two problems.

Firstly, if the signatures of the operations are not compatible, for example, if one uses $x? : X$ where another uses $x? : Y$, the schemas cannot be combined. In the small *Venus* example, we ensured this did not happen by using a consistent naming convention. In a larger specification with more operations it might be necessary to rename some components before combining the operation schemas.

Secondly, what do these extra components imply for an implementation based on the specification? We would like to be able to interpret *AgentOp* as being either a *SeatPrice* enquiry, or a *Spare* seat enquiry, or ..., with only those inputs and outputs that are available to the selected sub-operation being available. We can choose to adopt this as an extra *convention*; however, an implementation that did make use of the other components could still be a valid refinement. Since the specification does not determine the components' values, an implementation could give these components *any* (type-correct) value, posing a potential security loophole. This is also a problem with the pure established strategy style—extra 'Trojan Horse' operations could be added during refinement, without affecting the correctness arguments. If security is an issue, then use a more sophisticated approach such as that described in Chapter 4, which is designed so that a correct refinement cannot add operations or outputs. [Jacob 1991] discusses the tension between refinement to preserve functionality, and refinement to preserve security (essentially, a lack of functionality!)

10.10   Concluding remarks

Throughout this case study we have exploited the power of the schema calculus. This allows us to break each operation into small, separate requirements. We apply that tactic to specification of the state and the operations. Each operation is built up from partial descriptions of the manner in which the operation works. This has the following benefits

- the operations are broken into small parts that are more readily understood
- extensive reuse of schemas becomes possible, which
  - draws attention to the common factors between operations
  - makes clear the differences between operations
  - reduces the work of both the writer and the reader of the specification.

We use a structure that is slightly different from the Established Strategy in order to highlight precisely what operations are available to which users. This leads to a structure that more clearly exposes the operations, but requires an extra convention to cope with unwanted components.

Chapter 11

Structuring a Video Shop

In which an Entity Relationship Diagram is used to help structure a specification.

11.1 The requirement

A video shop has video club members who may hire videos, and staff who are responsible for recording the transactions.

Members may hire videos, provided that they are old enough. For this reason the shop needs to record their date of birth. It also records members' addresses, so that appropriate action may be taken in the event of a video not being returned. Staff may also hire videos.

Videos are classified on the shelves according to subject, for example, horror or comedy. Each video is assigned a hire charge, depending on its current popularity and how recently it has been released. There are only a few different charges that apply at any given time.

11.2 Entity Relationship Diagrams

The stated requirements suggest a fairly standard 'state plus operations' style of specification. In such a case it is important to capture the 'right' state, one that supports the specification of the operations in a natural manner. How can we go about structuring this state?

Entity Relationship (ER) Modelling provides one technique for describing the structure of data. ER models are expressed using ER diagrams, which show the entities and how they are related, including information about optionality and cardinality of those relationships. ER modelling is used, for example, as part of SSADM [SSADM 1986], [SSADM 1990].

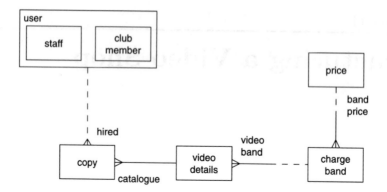

Figure 11.1 An Entity Relationship Diagram for the video shop.

The ER modelling concepts can be a useful starting point for structuring a Z specification, too, as we show here. An ER diagram consists of boxes and lines. The boxes show the types of the entities, and the lines show how instances of these types are related. A dotted line denotes an optional relation, whereas a solid line denotes a compulsory relation. A crow's foot on the line denotes a one-to-many relation.

An ER diagram that shows the structure of the video shop hiring system is shown in figure 11.1. (Here we are using ER diagrams to assist the understanding of the problem and writing of the Z specification. We are not concerned with translating ER diagrams into Z directly.)

The individual video cassettes that are hired out are the **copies**; there may be many copies of the 'same' video, and the relation **catalogue** captures this.

The people involved in the video shop are either **staff** or **club members** (customers). These two types are indicated on the diagram by the nested boxes. Since *staff may also hire videos*, the **hire** relation from **copy** goes to **user**.

The notion of **charge bands** captures the requirement that *there are only a few different charges that may apply at any given time*. Every video must have some unique charge associated with it. Some charge bands may not apply to any video, whereas others apply to many videos. All these conditions are captured by the line between **video details** and **charge band**, which says that every video detail is related to a single charge band (solid line from **video details**, no crow's foot on **charge band**) whereas a charge band may optionally be related to several videos (dotted line from **charge band**, crow's foot on **video details**).

Hire charges tend to vary with factors such as how recently the video was released and whether it is in the 'top 50'. A good way of dealing with this is to keep a record of which video is in which band and a separate record of how much each band costs. This allows the videos to be moved between bands (when they enter the 'top 50', say, or fall from favour) and automatically be assigned the appropriate price. Likewise the hire charges can be revised without the need to see which videos are in which band. The relation **band price** captures this idea.

11.3 Expressing the model in Z

Having used the ER method to determine the important entities and relationships in the model of the video shop, we next need to express these in Z.

The entity types (boxes) can be modelled by Z sets. Where the entities are simple (for example, **copy**), they can be modelled by Z's given sets. If we want a richer description for some entities (for example, **video**), we can use schema types or Cartesian products.

ER diagrams represent subtyping by nested boxes (for example, **club member** and **staff** are subtypes of **user**). Z does not support sub*typing*, only sub*setting*. So entity subtypes are represented as Z subsets, and are not Z types. If we really needed the entity subtypes to be Z types, we could use a free type to construct a disjoint union (see Chapter 20).

The relationships between the entities are Z relations or functions, depending on whether they are many-to-many or many-to-one respectively. An important point to note is that compulsory relations are compulsory only between the entities in the current state (given by the state schema), not between all possible entities (given by the type), so they do not quite correspond to total functions in Z.

We can use the ER diagram to help us to partition the global state into meaningful substates. In this case, we choose to put the information about users into *UserBase*, the information about the catalogue of copies and videos into *Stock*, and pricing information into *PriceBase*, as shown in figure 11.2.

This partitioning cuts across some of the relationships between the components. For example, the *hired* relation between copies and users straddles *UserBase* and *Stock*. We have to choose where to put these relationships, and how to define the constraints on their ranges and domains. In the *Venus* booking system, Chapter 10, which also has a global state made up of components, we choose to put the relationships in one of the substates, and express the constraints at the global level of the full *Venus* booking system. Here we take a different approach. We include the relation in *both* substates, and express the relevant domain or range constraint in the substate schema that has the relevant 'end' of the relation. When we combine the substates into the global state, the two relations become identified. For example, the constraint on the domain of *hired* appears in *Stock*, and that on its range in *UserBase*. This relieves the global state of the clutter of 'housekeeping' constraints.

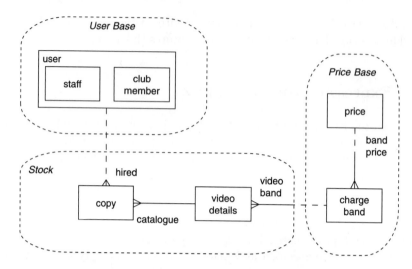

Figure 11.2 Partitioning the video shop state.

11.4   The entities

11.4.1   Videos

A video has a title, a subject by which we can classify it, and a certificate from the film censors. A video is a composite type; we model it using a schema. We need know nothing about the internal details of subjects and titles.

$$[SUBJECT, TITLE]$$

We need to know a video's certificate in order to check who may hire different videos.

$$CERT ::= exempt \mid uCert \mid pg \mid twelve \mid fifteen \mid eighteen$$

▷ *free type, enumerated*
The names introduced in an enumerated type represent instances of the type being defined. Two elements of *CERT* are thus *pg* and *eighteen*. The names of the elements must start with a letter, so we cannot use '12' as a name. If access to the numerical operations was needed then there could be a branch such as

$$\ldots \mid cert \langle\!\langle \{12, 15, 18\} \rangle\!\rangle \mid \ldots$$

▷ *readability*
When we originally wrote this specification, we used *u* for the name of the free type branch representing U certificate videos. Later on, we found ourselves getting confused, because we often read *u* as a variable identifying a user. So we renamed the branch *uCert*.

We use a schema to describe the details of the type *Video*.

```
┌─ Video ────────────────────────────────────
│ title : TITLE
│ subject : SUBJECT
│ cert : CERT
└────────────────────────────────────────────
```

▷ schema as type
  Video defines the set of all possible combinations of *title*, *subject*, and *cert*, not just the
  set of those videos that exist. A perfectly valid element of type *Video* is one with *title* =
  The Texas Chainsaw Massacre, *subject* = *Comedy* and *cert* = *uCert*.

11.4.2 Users

We need to record the name, address and date of birth of each user. We need the
date of birth to check the age entitlement to hire videos. We introduce given sets
for names, addresses and dates (used to record dates of birth, release dates for
films, and current dates).

[*NAME, ADDRESS, DATE*]

The video shop records the name, date of birth and address of each user.

```
┌─ User ─────────────────────────────────────
│ name : NAME
│ dob : DATE
│ address : ADDRESS
└────────────────────────────────────────────
```

We need to find someone's current age, given the date of birth and today's date,
in order to determine whether they are permitted to hire a video with a particular
certificate. We model *age* as a natural number, representing the age in years, since
this is what is important for hiring the various certificates.

$$age == \mathbb{N}$$

We introduce a function to calculate the age

$$ageToday : DATE \times DATE \longrightarrow age$$

We intend that the first *DATE* is today's date and the second *DATE* is the date
of birth.

▷ accompanying text
  Where a function applies to pairs of items of the same type and no defining information
  is given to specify what role each is playing, then it is a good idea to record this in the
  natural language description of the function.

▷ *loose specification*
We choose to add no further constraint on *ageToday* at this point. Defining it would be complicated, and would add little to our understanding of the system. We would have to define it eventually, though, unless we were to find a suitable reusable library function in our implementation. (Its suitability for reuse would have to be determined from its definition, which might well be informal.)

11.4.3   Copy

As the video shop may contain more than one copy of a given video, we identify the copies and set up a catalogue that records which copy represents which video. Copy identities are modelled using a simple given set.

[*COPY*]

11.4.4   Charge band

A video shop charges people for hiring the videos. To allow hire charges in a band to vary, we introduce given sets for the charge bands and the prices.

[*BAND*, *PRICE*]

11.5   The video shop hiring system

The video shop hiring system consists of sets of the various entities, and the relationships between them. The state schema can also have 'derived' sets; convenient shorthand names for certain interesting sets (such as the domain or range of one of the relations).

11.5.1   Hiring data

The *UserBase* schema defines the users of the video shop and which videos they have on hire.

The video shop *users* are a subset of all possible *Users*, and the *staff* and *members* are further subsets. The nested boxes in the ER diagram say that staff and club members are disjoint sets of entities; the Z says they partition the *user* set.

The function *hired* notes which copies are on hire to which user; all the copies that are on hire are on hire to valid users.

```
┌─ UserBase ──────────────────────────────────────────────
│  user, staff, member : ℙ User
│  hired : COPY ⤖ User
│ ─────────────────────────────────────────────────────────
│  ⟨staff, member⟩ partition user
│  ran hired ⊆ user
└──────────────────────────────────────────────────────────
```

▷ *partition*
The expression ⟨*staff*, *member*⟩ partition *user* ensures that the staff and the members are distinct groups of users. An alternative way to force such a distinction is given in the space flight system where different types are used (see the *User* schema on page 103).

11.5.2   Stock

The copies actually in stock are given by the set *inStock*.

The *catalogue* maps copies to the video details, defined by the schema *Video*. Every copy in stock has an entry in this catalogue, and hence the domain of *catalogue* is *inStock*.

The function *hired* is as in *UserBase*; all the hired videos are part of the *inStock*. The function *VideoBand*, used in *PriceBase*, maps videos to their price band; all videos in the catalogue have an associated price band.

```
┌─ Stock ─────────────────────────────────────────────────
│  inStock : ℙ COPY
│  catalogue : COPY ⤖ Video
│  hired : COPY ⤖ User
│  videoBand : Video ⤖ BAND
│ ─────────────────────────────────────────────────────────
│  dom catalogue = inStock
│  ran catalogue ⊆ dom videoBand
│  dom hired ⊆ inStock
└──────────────────────────────────────────────────────────
```

▷ *declarations, circular*
It would be convenient to be able to declare the *catalogue* as a total function from *inStock*

$$catalogue : inStock \longrightarrow Video$$

and dispense with the associated predicate. Unfortunately, this is not allowed. *inStock* is declared in this schema, and a declaration must not make reference to itself in this manner. Thus, we declare *catalogue* as above, and point out in the predicate part the extra information about its domain.

▷ *over specification*
We require all videos in the catalogue to have an associated price band, but we also allow videos not in stock to have a price band. (That is, we require ran *catalogue* ⊆ dom *videoBand* rather than ran *catalogue* = dom *videoBand*.) Avoiding an overspecification of the domain of *videoBand* may help the implementor, and may make for a more usable system.

11.5.3   Price base

The *PriceBase* schema specifies the pricing data. Note that we do not have to specify explicitly the set of allowed bands, just that all those actually used by the videos do have an associated price.

The derived function *price* uses the banding information to calculate the price of a video.

$$
\begin{array}{|l}
\hline
\;\textit{PriceBase} \underline{\hspace{6cm}} \\
\quad videoBand : Video \nrightarrow BAND \\
\quad bandPrice : BAND \nrightarrow PRICE \\
\quad price : Video \nrightarrow PRICE \\
\hline
\quad \mathrm{ran}\ videoBand \subseteq \mathrm{dom}\ bandPrice \\
\quad price = videoBand \ \mathbin{\fatsemi}\ bandPrice \\
\hline
\end{array}
$$

11.5.4   Video shop

The full *VideoShop* hiring system includes the *UserBase*, *Stock* and *PriceBase* components of the state, which overlap on *hired* and *videoBand*.

We introduce two new state components: *today*, to record today's date, needed to calculate a user's age from their date of birth, and *mayHire*, to record which videos a user may hire (depending in a complicated manner on their age and the certificate of the video). The final part of the predicate expresses the constraint that all the copies on hire are hired to users who are old enough.

$$
\begin{array}{|l}
\hline
\;\textit{VideoShop} \underline{\hspace{6cm}} \\
\quad UserBase \\
\quad Stock \\
\quad PriceBase \\
\quad today : DATE \\
\quad \_\,mayHire\,\_ : User \leftrightarrow Video \\
\hline
\quad (\_\,mayHire\,\_) = \{\, u : user;\ v : \mathrm{ran}\ catalogue;\ a : age \mid \\
\qquad\qquad a = ageToday(today, u.dob) \\
\qquad\qquad \wedge\ (a \geq 18 \\
\qquad\qquad\qquad \vee\ v.cert \in \{\,exempt, uCert, pg\,\} \\
\qquad\qquad\qquad \vee\ (a \geq 12 \wedge v.cert = twelve) \\
\qquad\qquad\qquad \vee\ (a \geq 15 \wedge v.cert = fifteen)\,) \\
\qquad\quad \bullet\ u \mapsto v \,\} \\
\quad (\forall\, c : \mathrm{dom}\ hired \bullet (hired\ c)\,mayHire(catalogue\ c)\,) \\
\hline
\end{array}
$$

The ER diagram is clearly easier to read and is more compact than the corresponding Z. As such it is a useful addition to the Z specification to help readers gain an overview. However, the ER diagram does not capture the important constraints on which user may hire which video, as described in the predicate defining *mayHire*. The ER diagram and the Z are complementary, benefiting from being used together.

11.6 Operations on the hiring system

We now have the the relevant data structures defined, and can start defining the various operations that go to making up a video shop. These operations correspond to manipulating entities (for example, adding a new video to the stock) and manipulating relationships (for example, hiring a video).

We describe only hiring a video and adding a new video. Other operations such as returning a video, removing a worn out copy, and adding and removing users, would also have to be defined for a full system.

11.6.1 Hiring a video

Hiring a video requires a member of staff (to perform the hire and take the money), a user hiring the video, and a copy of the video to be hired. The price of the hire is output, and the *hired* function updated appropriately.

$$\Delta\, VideoShopHire \,\widehat{=}\, \Xi\, VideoShop \setminus (hired, hired') \wedge \Delta\, VideoShop$$

▷ Δ *convention*
We use a Δ as part of the name of the $\Delta\,VideoShopHire$ schema, to indicate a changed state. We use the Δ convention for $\Delta\,VideoShop$, where ΔS is a conventional shorthand for $[\,S, S'\,]$.
▷ Ξ *convention*
By convention, ΞS is shorthand for $[\,S, S' \mid \theta S = \theta S'\,]$, a before and after state with the values of all the components unchanged.
▷ *schema hiding*
Hiding a particular before and after component in $\Xi S \setminus (x, x')$ gives a before and after state that does not have x or x', but still has all the other components, unchanged.
▷ *schema, updating a single component*
Conjoining this with ΔS reintroduces the declaration of x and x', and any predicates involving them, but does not include the predicate $x' = x$. Hence $\Xi S \setminus (x, x') \wedge \Delta S$ is a schema describing a before and after state of S that includes all the constraints on S and S', and in addition has all the components, except x, unchanged.
   Note that Ξ is merely a character forming part of the schema name that has a conventional meaning. It is not a schema operator. Hence it is incorrect to write $\Xi(S \setminus (x))$.

So the definition of the successful hire operation is

```
┌─ HireOK ────────────────────────────────────────
│ Δ VideoShopHire
│ s?, u? : User
│ c? : COPY
│ price! : PRICE
├──────────────────────────────────────────────────
│ s? ∈ staff
│
│ u? ∈ user
│
│ c? ∉ dom hired
│
│ hired' = hired ∪ {c? ↦ u?}
│
│ price! = price(catalogue c?)
│
│ u? mayHire catalogue c?
└──────────────────────────────────────────────────
```

▷ *redundancy*
Strictly, the *mayHire* check is redundant, since if the user is not permitted to hire the
video, the *hired'* component would not satisfy the constraint linking *hired* and *mayHire*
in the after state. However, it is helpful to have some such redundant information, rather
than make the reader deduce every consequence of a specification. Its presence also helps
when identifying possible error cases.

It is helpful to highlight in the accompanying text that certain predicates are redundant.
In more complicated cases, a precondition calculation may be used to demonstrate that
the predicate is redundant, rather than contradictory.

The error cases can be found by considering the criteria for success one at a time:
$s?$ is not a staff member, $u?$ is not a user, $c?$ has already been hired, or $u?$ may
not hire the video (because they are too young for the certificate).

$$REPORT ::= notStaff \mid notUser \mid alreadyHired \mid tooYoung \mid ok$$

$s?$ is not a staff member is described by

```
┌─ NotStaff ──────────────────────────────────────
│ Ξ VideoShop
│ s? : User
│ report! : REPORT
├──────────────────────────────────────────────────
│ s? ∉ staff
│ report! = notStaff
└──────────────────────────────────────────────────
```

$u?$ is not a user is described by

```
┌─ NotUser ───────────────────────────────────────
│ Ξ VideoShop
│ u? : User
│ report! : REPORT
├──────────────────────────────────────────────────
│ u? ∉ user
│ report! = notUser
└──────────────────────────────────────────────────
```

$c?$ is already hired out is described by

```
┌─ AlreadyHired ──────────────────────────────────
│ ΞVideoShop
│ c? : COPY
│ report! : REPORT
├──────────────────────────────────────────────────
│ c? ∈ dom hired
│ report! = alreadyHired
└──────────────────────────────────────────────────
```

$u?$ is too young to hire $c?$ is described by

```
┌─ TooYoung ──────────────────────────────────────
│ ΞVideoShop
│ u? : User
│ c? : COPY
│ report! : REPORT
├──────────────────────────────────────────────────
│ ¬ (u? mayHire catalogue c?)
│ report! = tooYoung
└──────────────────────────────────────────────────
```

The definition of the complete hire operation is

$$Hire \ \widehat{=} \ (HireOK \wedge [\,report! : REPORT \mid report! = ok\,])$$
$$\vee \ NotStaff$$
$$\vee \ NotUser$$
$$\vee \ AlreadyHired$$
$$\vee \ TooYoung$$

11.6.2   Updating today's date

One component of the *VideoShop* is today's date, needed to calculate a user's age from their date of birth. This date needs to change. (The operation may be implemented as some sort of batch process that runs every midnight.)

$$\Delta VideoShopToday \ \widehat{=} \ \Xi VideoShop \setminus (today, today') \wedge \Delta VideoShop$$

We could define a function like $tomorrow : DATE \longrightarrow DATE$, but that might be a bit restrictive, requiring the operation to be performed multiple times after a holiday, for example. Instead, we input the new required date.

```
┌─ TodayUpdate ───────────────────────────────────
│ ΔVideoShopToday
│ d? : DATE
├──────────────────────────────────────────────────
│ d? = today'
└──────────────────────────────────────────────────
```

This is a total operation, with no error cases.

11.6.3   Adding a new video to the stock

To add a new video to the stock of the shop, we must supply a new copy number for it and then assign the video together with its number to *inStock*. We choose here to introduce a new copy only if its price band is known. Adding a video to the price base is defined in a separate operation (not given here). A user friendly implementation could combine these operations where necessary.

$$\Delta VideoShopAdd \,\hat{=}\, [\, \Delta Stock; \,\Xi UserBase; \,\Xi PriceBase \,]$$

The inclusion of $\Xi UserBase$ ensures the *hired* component of $\Delta Stock$ remains unchanged. Likewise, the inclusion of $\Xi PriceBase$ ensures the *videoBand* component of $\Delta Stock$ remains unchanged. Hence only the *catalogue* and *inStock* components may change, as required.

```
┌─ AddVideoOK ──────────────────────────────
│ ΔVideoShopAdd
│ v? : Video
│ c? : COPY
├────────────────────────────────────────────
│ c? ∉ inStock
│ v? ∈ dom videoBand
│ inStock' = inStock ∪ {c?}
│ catalogue' = catalogue ∪ {c? ↦ v?}
└────────────────────────────────────────────
```

▷ *proof obligation*

We use our house style of adding a new element to a function with a union. Since this definition does not explicitly ensure that $c? \notin \text{dom } catalogue$, there is an obligation to show that the set union operation maintains functionality.

It is legitimate to apply union to *catalogue* since we have checked that $c? \notin inStock$ and we know that $\text{dom } catalogue = inStock$. Hence $c? \notin \text{dom } catalogue$, so functionality is preserved.

▷ *schema as type*

Here we see a schema used as a type: we take as input $v?$ with type *Video*. If we did not have this input, we could enter the details of the video separately.

```
┌─ AddVideoOK₁ ─────────────────────────────
│ ΔVideoShopAdd
│ title? : TITLE
│ subject? : SUBJECT
│ cert? : CERT
│ c? : COPY
├────────────────────────────────────────────
│ c? ∉ inStock
│ inStock' = inStock ∪ {c?}
│ let video == ( μ Video | title = title?
│                     ∧ subject = subject?
│                     ∧ cert = cert? ) •
│        catalogue' = catalogue ∪ {c? ↦ video}
└────────────────────────────────────────────
```

This is far more awkward to read than the definition using schema types.

▷ *let*

The **let** expression introduces a local definition in which the name *video* is given to the value that satisfies the definite description. This is then used to update the catalogue.

▷ *definite description*

The expression involving the μ selects the unique video that has the title, subject and certificate matching the inputs. It is being used to construct a particular binding.

The definition of *AddVideo* includes error cases; we omit the full definition.

11.6.4   Other operations

Instead of using Ξ schemas, some query operations can be expressed as a function that takes a *VideoShop* and other input parameters, and returns the items of interest.

For example, suppose the shop wants to provide a list of the titles of all the films it stocks of a particular certificate.

$$listByCertificate == (\ \lambda\ VideoShop;\ c : CERT \bullet$$
$$\{\ Video \mid \theta\ Video \in \text{ran } catalogue \wedge c = cert \bullet title\ \})$$

▷ *lambda-expression*

The lambda-expression here takes as arguments a *VideoShop* and a certificate, and returns an appropriate set of titles obtained from the videos in the shop's catalogue.

The same query expressed as a schema operation is

$$
\begin{array}{l}
\underline{\ ListByCertificate\ }\\
\Xi\,VideoShop\\
c? : CERT\\
list! : \mathbb{P}\ TITLE\\
\hline
list! = \{\ v : \text{ran } catalogue \mid c? = v.cert \bullet v.title\ \}
\end{array}
$$

We can define a function that returns a set of all the titles of films in a particular category.

$$listByCategory == (\ \lambda\ VideoShop;\ s : SUBJECT \bullet$$
$$\{\ Video \mid \theta\ Video \in \text{ran } catalogue \wedge s = subject \bullet title\ \})$$

To find out how many copies of a video the shop has, we restrict *catalogue* to that particular video and then take the cardinality.

$$howManyCopies == (\ \lambda\ VideoShop;\ v : Video \bullet \#(catalogue \rhd \{v\}))$$

▷ *proof obligation*

The cardinality operator # may be used only on finite sets.

The cardinality operator is being correctly applied to a finite set, if we have an initial version of *VideoShop* in which *catalogue* is empty. The operation that changes *catalogue*, *AddVideo*, adds videos one at a time, so the catalogue remains finite. Hence the particular part of it that we have selected is also finite.

If we wish to know which copy identities correspond to the video in question we can ask

$$whatCopies == (\lambda\; VideoShop;\; v : Video \bullet \mathrm{dom}(catalogue \rhd \{v\}))$$

11.7   Concluding remarks

In this specification we use an ER diagram to assist with structuring the specification. Not only does ER modelling help the specifier to understand the problem, presented as part of the specification it helps to provide the reader with an overview of the underlying model.

We use the ER diagram to help us partition the state. Where this partitioning cuts across a relationship, we choose to duplicate the relation definition in each substate schema, which allows us to express the domain constraint in one, and the range constraint in the other.

We have also used schemas as types, allowing a number of related components to be packaged together and handled as a single entity, simplifying some of the definitions. Often it is possible to put constraints on the allowed values of the components in the predicate part of the schema. However, in cases such as the videos it would be impossible to do this in practice (in theory we could list every real combination). The consequence of this is that any allocation of values to the schema components becomes possible. The way to overcome this is to have a set that represents the allowable assignments of values to variables, as we have done here with the *catalogue* function. Schemas as types are explored in more detail in section 23.2.

We have also shown how a query operation may be expressed as a function that takes the current state of the system as an argument, rather than as a Ξ schema operation.

The video example is picked up again in section 17.3, where a film buff's video encyclopaedia is specified.

Chapter 12

Promoting Snakes and Ladders

In which the game of Snakes and Ladders is specified, precondition calculation is discovered and operation promotion is explored.

12.1 Problem statement

There is a board game called *Snakes and Ladders*[1]. The game is played on a board of one hundred squares laid out in a ten by ten arrangement, numbered from 1 to 100. Snakes and ladders are drawn on the board. Each ladder has its foot in a square and its top in a higher-numbered one. Each snake has its head in a square and its tail in a lower-numbered one. No square has the end of both a snake and a ladder.

The game is played by between two and six players who move counters on the board according to the throw of a fair die that is numbered from 1 to 6. The players take it in turns to play. Throwing a six qualifies a player to take an extra turn.

In order to start play a player must take turns until a six is thrown. Once this is achieved, the player throws the die again immediately, and moves to the square corresponding to the number shown on this second throw of the die. Each subsequent move consists of a die throw and a move forward by the number of squares shown. Landing on the foot of a ladder means the player 'climbs' up the ladder to its top. Contrariwise landing on the head of a snake means the player 'slips' down the snake to its tail.

The players play in turn, moving their counters according to the throw of the die and the movements dictated by the snakes and ladders. The winner is the first to reach the hundredth square by an exact throw (if a player is on, say, 98 and throws, say, 5, then no move can occur).

---

[1] In the USA the same game is known as *Chutes and Ladders*.

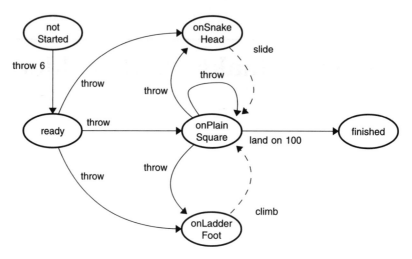

Figure 12.1 A state transition diagram summarising a player's moves.

The possible states of an individual player can be sketched informally in a state transition diagram (figure 12.1).

12.2   The schema specification

12.2.1   Description of state

The board may be modelled as a set of numbers. For an abstract specification we do not need to know how the squares are arranged. Squares may be defined as a set of numbers.

$firstSquare == 1$

$lastSquare == 100$

$square == firstSquare .. lastSquare$

▷ *abbreviation definition*
  We have introduced constants, rather than using the numbers 1 and 100 directly in the specification. It is good practice to give constants names.

There are two special cases we need to take into account: when a player has not started, and when a player is ready to start (that is, has thrown a six) but has yet to move onto the board. We create some special values, and combine them with *squares* using a free type as a disjoint union.

$POSITION ::= notStarted$
$\qquad\quad |\ \ ready$
$\qquad\quad |\ \ boardPosn \langle\!\langle square \rangle\!\rangle$

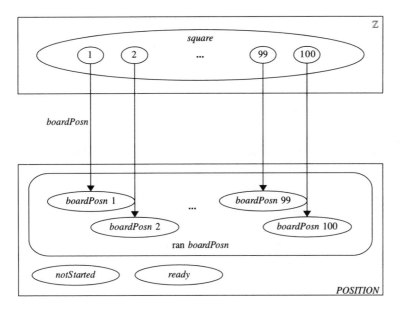

Figure 12.2 The free type *POSITION*.

▷ *free type, disjoint union*
  Later on we describe the position of players as a function that relates players to *POSITION*.
  If we had *POSITION* as simply the numbers involved, we would need to treat differently
  the cases in which a player has not yet entered the main part of the game, yet these players
  have to take their turns along with the players on the board. The free type formulation
  allows us to have just a single function. This use of free types is valuable in allowing
  'disjoint types' to be united for use in a specification.

▷ *free type, disjoint union*
  It is important to give the injection a meaningful name. Later on when we want to access
  the position that relates to a given square we use *boardPosn*. We need this to convey some
  meaning. See figure 12.2, which shows how *boardPosn* works.

We also define a function that is useful later on.

$$whichSquare : POSITION \nrightarrow \mathbb{N}$$
$$\text{dom } whichSquare = POSITION \setminus \{notStarted\}$$
$$whichSquare\ ready = 0$$
$$\forall p : \text{ran } boardPosn \bullet whichSquare\ p = boardPosn^{\sim}\ p$$

▷ *free type, disjoint union*
  As we often access the information about the square from a given position, it is useful to
  give the inverse of the injection a meaningful name. This idea is suggested by [Macdonald
  1991]. In the definition of *whichSquare* we have extended this definition slightly in order
  to simplify things later on.

The die can show any number from 1 to 6 and may be modelled as a set using an abbreviation definition.

$lowestScore == 1$

$highestScore == 6$

$die == lowestScore .. highestScore$

▷ *abbreviation definition*
  die may now be used as shorthand for 1 .. 6. Using an abbreviation definition has advantages over straightforward use of the numbers.
  – It is clearer to the reader of the specification.
  – In declaring $x : die$, x is automatically an element of *lowestScore .. highestScore*.
  – It reduces the likelihood of using the numbers inappropriately; the writer is constantly reminded of the intention of the definition.

We need a type to specify the players, but we do not need to know anything about them so we can simply use a given set

$[PLAYER]$

As the players of the game have a given order, it is natural to model the players as a sequence of *PLAYER*. Each player has a position on the board. A player may only be on one square at a time, but there is nothing to stop two players being on the same square. It makes sense to model the position of the players as a function. Because of the way in which *POSITION* has been defined we know that each player in the game must be at some *POSITION*, even if it is *notStarted* or *ready* (see figure 12.3).

At any given time there is always one player whose turn it is. We choose this player to be the first in the sequence and we alter the sequence after each turn to move the next player to the front. We call the sequence of players *player*.

▷ *design decision*
  Starting at the first position in the sequence of players is a design decision. The initial arrangement of the players in the sequence is not covered here.

We also name a sequence *place* to record the order in which players finish. As players complete the game we remove them from the *player* sequence and add them to the end of the *place* sequence. There must always be at least two and at most six people involved in the game, even if some of them have finished. The number of players in the game is constant.

$minPlayers == 2$

$maxPlayers == 6$

$numberOfPlayers : minPlayers .. maxPlayers$

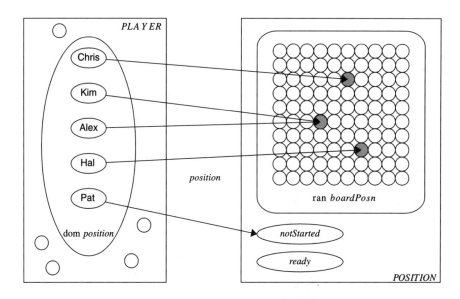

Figure 12.3 The *position* function mapping *PLAYER*s to *POSITION*s.

The players who have finished and achieved a place cannot still be playing. The current player is always the first player in the sequence, unless they have all finished. The players for whom we record a position are the same as those who are still playing or who have finished. The state of the game is thus described by

$$
\begin{array}{l}
\underline{\quad Game \underline{\hspace{10cm}}} \\
\hspace{0.5cm} player, place : \mathrm{iseq}\, PLAYER \\
\hspace{0.5cm} position : PLAYER \nrightarrow POSITION \\
\hspace{0.5cm} currentPlayer : PLAYER \\
\rule{10cm}{0.4pt} \\
\hspace{0.5cm} (player \neq \langle\rangle) \Leftrightarrow (currentPlayer = head\ player) \\
\hspace{0.5cm} \#\,player + \#place = numberOfPlayers \\
\hspace{0.5cm} \langle \mathrm{ran}\, player, \mathrm{ran}\, place \rangle\ \mathbf{partition}\ (\mathrm{dom}\, position)
\end{array}
$$

It is legitimate to apply $\#$ to *player*; we know it is finite since it is a sequence.

▷ *sequence, injective*
   We use iseq to declare *player* and *place*. This means that there can be no duplicates in either of these sequences. That is, one player cannot appear twice in the sequence of players, nor can any player have more than one position in the place sequence.

▷ *sequence operations*
   head player takes the first entry from the sequence, which is the current player according to our model.

▷ *partition*
   $\langle \mathrm{ran}\, player, \mathrm{ran}\, place \rangle$ **partition** $(\mathrm{dom}\, position)$ says that together the players in the two

sequences make up all the players who are allowed to have positions in the game, and that a player cannot be currently playing and finished at the same time.

12.2.2   Initialisation

At the start of the game all players are in the *notStarted* state, and so none has been *placed*.

```
┌─ InitGame ─────────────────────────────────
│ Game′
│ ─────────────────────────────────────────
│ place′ = ⟨ ⟩
│ ∀ p : ran player′ • position′ p = notStarted
```

Applying the function *position′* to *p* is in order since we have drawn *p* from ran *player′* and it follows from the state invariant that ran *player′* ⊆ dom *position′*.

▷ *initial state*
  Following our house style, we specify the initial state as the outcome of an operation. The initial state is created from 'thin air'.

12.2.3   Making a move

We now define the common parts of operations that change the state of the game. There is always a throw of the die, and the players involved in a particular game never alter (although their individual positions might).

```
┌─ ΔGameMove ─────────────────────────────────
│ ΔGame
│ throw? : die
│ ─────────────────────────────────────────
│ ran(player′ ⌢ place′) = ran(player ⌢ place)
```

▷ Δ *convention*
  Where convenient, additional information common to all operations can be included in the schema used to indicate a change of state. We use the Δ convention when we include ΔGame, and include the Δ character in the name of the schema we intend to include in state-changing operations.

Ladders move a player 'up' and snakes move a player 'down'. We observe that at an abstract level there is no difference between a ladder and a snake: they both map a square to another square. So we use a single concept to capture both snakes and ladders, which we call 'slide'.

No square has more than one start or end of a slide, and the last square has neither the start nor end of a slide. We model the slides as a function. This function is a partial injection, since a square contains at most one end of a slide.

$$\begin{array}{|l}
\hline
slide : square \rightarrowtail square \\
\hline
\text{disjoint} \; \langle \text{dom } slide, \text{ran } slide, \{ lastSquare \} \rangle \\
\end{array}$$

▷ *disjoint*

Another way of saying

$$\text{disjoint} \; \langle \text{dom } slide, \text{ran } slide, \{ lastSquare \} \rangle$$

is to expand it out into three statements

$$\text{dom } slide \cap \text{ran } slide = \varnothing$$
$$\text{dom } slide \cap \{ lastSquare \} = \varnothing$$
$$\text{ran } slide \cap \{ lastSquare \} = \varnothing$$

This shows the advantage of using disjoint once there are more than two sets to consider.

▷ *abstraction*

If we find we need to distinguish snakes and ladders as separate concepts (for example, to say they are represented differently on the board) we could define

$$\begin{array}{|l}
\hline
ladder, snake : square \rightarrowtail square \\
\hline
\langle ladder, snake \rangle \; \text{partition } slide \\
\forall\, l : \text{dom } ladder \bullet ladder\ l > l \\
\forall\, s : \text{dom } snake \bullet snake\ s < s \\
\end{array}$$

A player not having started is given by

$$\begin{array}{|l}
\hline
\_\,StartOfGame \underline{\hspace{7cm}} \\
\Delta\, GameMove \\
\hline
player \neq \langle\,\rangle \\
position\ currentPlayer = notStarted \\
\hline
\end{array}$$

We include $\Delta\,GameMove$ here since it enables us to introduce the variable *throw?* when we include *StartOfGame* in other schemas. Now either players throw the highest score, or they don't. These cases are considered separately. Throwing the highest score allows the player to move to the *ready* state.

$$\begin{array}{|l}
\hline
\_\,StartMove \underline{\hspace{7cm}} \\
StartOfGame \\
\hline
throw? = highestScore \\
position' = position \oplus \{ currentPlayer \mapsto ready \} \\
\hline
\end{array}$$

If the player does not throw the highest score, the positions of the players remain unchanged.

$$\begin{array}{|l}
\hline
\_\,NoStartMove \underline{\hspace{7cm}} \\
StartOfGame \\
\hline
throw? \neq highestScore \\
position' = position \\
\hline
\end{array}$$

We now turn our attention to the main part of the game. In the general case play can occur if there are still some players in the game.

MainMove
$\Delta\,GameMove$
$newPosn! : \mathbb{N}$

$position\ currentPlayer \in \mathrm{dom}\ whichSquare$
$newPosn! = whichSquare(position\ currentPlayer) + throw?$
$player \neq \langle\rangle$

---

newPosn is the place on the board to which a player attempts to move after throwing the die. If the result of the move is not the start of a slide, a player moves forward by the number of places thrown on the die. Landing on the start of a slide may cause a further movement to its end. Further, it may be impossible to make any move because it is past the end of the board (this is why *newPosn!* is declared as a member of $\mathbb{N}$ rather than as a member of *square*, since it may be greater than *lastSquare*).

Most moves are quite straightforward. The die is thrown and the current player moves forward by the number of squares shown on the die.

PlainMove
MainMove

$newPosn! \in square \setminus (\mathrm{dom}\ slide \cup \{lastSquare\})$
$position' = position \oplus \{currentPlayer \mapsto boardPosn\ newPosn!\}$

▷ set difference
$newPosn! \in square \setminus (\mathrm{dom}\ slide \cup \{lastSquare\})$ is a shorter way of saying that

$newPosn! \in square$
$\wedge\ newPosn! \notin \mathrm{dom}\ slide$
$\wedge\ newPosn! \neq lastSquare$

The following cases describe moves that are not 'plain'

- the number on the die would take the player past the last square (the player is near the end of the game but has thrown too high a number to finish)
- the player would land on the start of a slide
- the player would land exactly on the last square and therefore complete the game.

We examine these cases in turn. If the number on the die would take the player past the last square, no move occurs.

NoMove
MainMove

$newPosn! > lastSquare$
$position' = position$

If the player lands on a square that is the start of a slide, the player moves to the end of the slide.

```
┌─ SlideMove ────────────────────────────────────────────
│ MainMove
├────────────────────────────────────────────────────────
│ newPosn! ∈ dom slide
│ position′ = position ⊕
│      {currentPlayer ↦ boardPosn(slide newPosn!)}
└────────────────────────────────────────────────────────
```

Landing on the last square means that a player is removed from the board. (Adding them to the *place* sequence is covered later.)

```
┌─ WinMove ──────────────────────────────────────────────
│ MainMove
├────────────────────────────────────────────────────────
│ newPosn! = lastSquare
│ position′ = {currentPlayer} ◁ position
└────────────────────────────────────────────────────────
```

12.2.4   Precondition calculation

Below we show the steps taken to calculate the precondition of one operation, *SlideMove*. We select this as being reasonably representative of the operations. The preconditions of all the different move operations are presented in a table later, but we do not show all the calculations.

The purpose of a precondition calculation is to check that an operation is valid. There must be at least one before state in which the operation is applicable. If there is an inconsistency in the definition, the precondition is *false*, and hence there are no appropriate before states. If the precondition is *true* then the operation is applicable to any before state, that is, it is a total operation.

A specification written in the Established Strategy style includes only a list of preconditions, not the details of the actual calculations, unless there is something particularly tricky involved in the derivation. In such a case, the derivation can be relegated to an appendix, so as not to disturb the flow of the specification. We include a derivation here for pedagogical reasons.

In a precondition calculation the aim is to determine what must be true of the before state and the operation inputs to achieve a satisfactory outcome. This is done by hiding the output and after variables.

Step 1: expand pre *SlideMove*

We restate *SlideMove*, existentially quantifying all the after variables (decorated with a dash) and output variables (decorated with a !). In doing this we expand some of the schemas involved in the original *SlideMove*, to reveal the after variables included implicitly.

$$preSlideMove \mathrel{\hat{=}} \text{pre } SlideMove$$

▷ *precondition calculation*
  The use of 'pre' is a feature of the Z notation used to indicate that this is the precondition of the operation schema *SlideMove*.
▷ *schema*
  We define *preSlideMove*, as above, since Z does not permit the use of schema operators in the names of schemas.

---
preSlideMove
Game
throw? : die
─────────────────
$\exists\, player', place' : \text{iseq } PLAYER;\ position' : PLAYER \nrightarrow POSITION;$
$\quad currentPlayer' : PLAYER;\ newPosn! : \mathbb{N} \bullet$

$newPosn! \in \text{dom } slide$

$\wedge\ position' = position \oplus$
$\quad \{currentPlayer \mapsto boardPosn(slide\ newPosn!)\}$

$\wedge\ position\ currentPlayer \in \text{dom } whichSquare$

$\wedge\ newPosn! = whichSquare(position\ currentPlayer) + throw?$

$\wedge\ player \neq \langle\rangle$

$\wedge\ \text{ran}(player'\ \widehat{}\ place') = \text{ran}(player\ \widehat{}\ place)$

$\wedge\ (player' \neq \langle\rangle) \Leftrightarrow (currentPlayer' = head\ player')$

$\wedge\ \#player' + \#place' = numberOfPlayers$

$\wedge\ \langle\text{ran } player', \text{ran } place'\rangle \text{ partition } (\text{dom } position')$

Step 2: eliminate *newPosn!*

We simplify the predicate, by using the *one point rule* to eliminate *newPosn!*

$\exists\, player', place' : \text{iseq } PLAYER;\ position' : PLAYER \nrightarrow POSITION;$
$\quad currentPlayer' : PLAYER \bullet$

$whichSquare(position\ currentPlayer) + throw? \in \text{dom } slide$

$\wedge\ position' = position \oplus \{currentPlayer \mapsto$
$\quad boardPosn(slide(whichSquare(position\ currentPlayer) + throw?))\}$

$\wedge\ position\ currentPlayer \in \text{dom } whichSquare$

$\wedge\ player \neq \langle\rangle$

$\wedge\ \text{ran}(player'\ \widehat{}\ place') = \text{ran}(player\ \widehat{}\ place)$

$\wedge\ (player' \neq \langle\rangle) \Leftrightarrow (currentPlayer' = head\ player')$

$\wedge \, \# \, player' + \# place' = numberOfPlayers$

$\wedge \, \langle \mathrm{ran} \, player', \mathrm{ran} \, place' \rangle \, \mathsf{partition} \, (\mathrm{dom} \, position')$

Step 3: eliminate *position'*

We eliminate *position'*, using the one-point rule, by substituting the expression for *position'* into the **partition** expression, to give

$\exists \, player', place' : \mathrm{iseq} \, PLAYER; \; currentPlayer' : PLAYER \bullet$

  $whichSquare(position \; currentPlayer) + throw? \in \mathrm{dom} \, slide$

  $\wedge \, position \; currentPlayer \in \mathrm{dom} \, whichSquare$

  $\wedge \, player \neq \langle \, \rangle$

  $\wedge \, \mathrm{ran}(player' \,^\frown place') = \mathrm{ran}(player \,^\frown place)$

  $\wedge \, (player' \neq \langle \, \rangle) \Leftrightarrow (currentPlayer' = head \; player')$

  $\wedge \, \# \, player' + \# place' = numberOfPlayers$

  $\wedge \, \langle \mathrm{ran} \, player', \mathrm{ran} \, place' \rangle \, \mathsf{partition}$

    $\mathrm{dom}(position \oplus \{ currentPlayer \mapsto$

      $boardPosn(slide(whichSquare(position \; currentPlayer)$

      $+ throw?)) \})$

Step 4: simplify

We simplify the expression for $\mathrm{dom}(position \ldots)$, using rules from [Spivey 1992].

$\mathrm{dom}(position \oplus \{ currentPlayer \mapsto X \})$

  $= \mathrm{dom} \, position \cup \mathrm{dom} \{ currentPlayer \mapsto X \}$ [Spivey, page 102]

  $= \mathrm{dom} \, position \cup \{ currentPlayer \}$ [Spivey, page 96]

$\square$

This gives

$\exists \, player', place' : \mathrm{iseq} \, PLAYER; \; currentPlayer' : PLAYER \bullet$

  $whichSquare(position \; currentPlayer) + throw? \in \mathrm{dom} \, slide$

  $\wedge \, position \; currentPlayer \in \mathrm{dom} \, whichSquare$

  $\wedge \, player \neq \langle \, \rangle$

  $\wedge \, \mathrm{ran}(player' \,^\frown place') = \mathrm{ran}(player \,^\frown place)$

  $\wedge \, (player' \neq \langle \, \rangle) \Leftrightarrow (currentPlayer' = head \; player')$

  $\wedge \, \# \, player' + \# place' = numberOfPlayers$

  $\wedge \, \langle \mathrm{ran} \, player', \mathrm{ran} \, place' \rangle \, \mathsf{partition} \, (\mathrm{dom} \, position \cup \{ currentPlayer \})$

Step 5: simplify

We simplify the domain expression further. Using part of the state invariant of *Game* (implicitly included in the precondition schema) together with $player \neq \langle\rangle$ from step 4, we have

$$(player \neq \langle\rangle) \Leftrightarrow (currentPlayer = head\ player) \wedge player \neq \langle\rangle$$
$$\Rightarrow currentPlayer = head\ player$$

□

Using another part of the state invariant of *Game* we can show that

$$\langle ran\ player, ran\ place \rangle\ \mathsf{partition}\ (dom\ position)$$
$$\Rightarrow ran\ player \subseteq dom\ position$$
$$\Rightarrow head\ player \in dom\ position \qquad\qquad [player \neq \langle\rangle]$$
$$\Rightarrow currentPlayer \in dom\ position$$

This means the domain expression simplifies to

$$dom\ position \cup \{currentPlayer\}$$
$$= dom\ position$$

□

We substitute this result into the predicate, and expand the **partition**, to give

$$\exists\ player', place' : \text{iseq}\ PLAYER;\ currentPlayer' : PLAYER \bullet$$
$$whichSquare(position\ currentPlayer) + throw? \in dom\ slide$$
$$\wedge\ position\ currentPlayer \in dom\ whichSquare$$
$$\wedge\ player \neq \langle\rangle$$
$$\wedge\ ran(player' \frown place') = ran(player \frown place)$$
$$\wedge\ (player' \neq \langle\rangle) \Leftrightarrow (currentPlayer' = head\ player')$$
$$\wedge\ \#\ player' + \#place' = numberOfPlayers$$
$$\wedge\ ran\ player' \cup ran\ place' = dom\ position$$
$$\wedge\ ran\ player' \cap ran\ place' = \varnothing$$

Step 6: eliminate *place'*

We substitute the expression for $ran(player' \frown place')$. First, we need to do some manipulation. [Spivey 1992, page 120] gives us that

$$ran\ player' \cup ran\ place' = ran(player' \frown place')$$

So we have ran(*player* ⌢ *place*) = dom *position*, which follows from the state invariant of *Game* and thus does not need to be restated.

[Spivey 1992, page 116] gives us that #(*p* ⌢ *r*) = #*p* + #*r*. We make use of the fact that *player′* and *place′* are injective (from the existential quantification) and that ran *player′* ∩ ran *place′* = ∅, to allow us to say that #(*player′* ⌢ *place′*) = #(ran(*player′* ⌢ *place′*)). We can use the same reasoning on the undashed variables (which are within the state invariant of *Game*) to get a similar undashed identity. We rewrite the expression and reduce it to *numberOfPlayers* = *numberOfPlayers*, as follows.

$$numberOfPlayers$$
$$= \# \, player' + \# place'$$
$$= \#(player' \,^{\frown} place')$$
$$= \#(\mathrm{ran}(player' \,^{\frown} place'))$$
$$= \#(\mathrm{ran}(player \,^{\frown} place))$$
$$= \#(player \,^{\frown} place)$$
$$= numberOfPlayers$$

□

This leaves us with

$$\exists \, player' : \mathrm{iseq} \, PLAYER; \; currentPlayer' : PLAYER \bullet$$
$$whichSquare(position \; currentPlayer) + throw? \in \mathrm{dom} \, slide$$
$$\land \; position \; currentPlayer \in \mathrm{dom} \, whichSquare$$
$$\land \; player \neq \langle \rangle$$
$$\land \; (player' \neq \langle \rangle) \Leftrightarrow (currentPlayer' = head \; player')$$

Step 7: eliminate *player′* and *currentPlayer′*

We satisfy the existential quantification fully. The expression containing *player′* and *currentPlayer′* is satisfiable under any circumstances. Thus, we can eliminate the existential quantification, and are left with

┌─ *preSlideMove* ─────────────────────────────────────
│ *Game*
│ *throw?* : *die*
├──
│ *position currentPlayer* ∈ dom *whichSquare*
│ (*whichSquare*(*position currentPlayer*) + *throw?*) ∈ dom *slide*
│ *player* ≠ ⟨ ⟩
└──

∎

12.2.5   Precondition summary

The other preconditions may be worked out in a similar way. A common approach is then to present a summary of the preconditions in a table.

> ▷ *precondition calculation*
> It is always useful to summarise the preconditions in a table. By looking down the table it is possible, informally, to see whether every possible input has been covered.

Type of move	Precondition
NoMove	*position currentPlayer* $\in$ dom *whichSquare* *whichSquare*(*position currentPlayer*) + *throw*? > *lastSquare* *player* $\neq \langle \rangle$
SlideMove	*position currentPlayer* $\in$ dom *whichSquare* *whichSquare*(*position currentPlayer*) + *throw*? $\in$ dom *slide* *player* $\neq \langle \rangle$
WinMove	*position currentPlayer* $\in$ dom *whichSquare* *whichSquare*(*position currentPlayer*) + *throw*? = *lastSquare* *player* $\neq \langle \rangle$
PlainMove	*position currentPlayer* $\in$ dom *whichSquare* *whichSquare*(*position currentPlayer*) + *throw*? $\qquad \notin$ (dom *slide* $\cup \{$ *lastSquare* $\})$ *player* $\neq \langle \rangle$
StartMove	*position currentPlayer* = *notStarted* *throw*? = *highestScore* *player* $\neq \langle \rangle$
NoStartMove	*position currentPlayer* = *notStarted* *throw*? < *highestScore* *player* $\neq \langle \rangle$

This table presents an informal argument that each possible state of the *Game*, except *player* = $\langle \rangle$, may have some *Move* applied to it. In the next part of the specification, we ensure that when *player* = $\langle \rangle$ no more moves may be taken. By inspection we can see that each precondition that may arise is covered. We can now describe every possible move that a player could make during the main part of the game.

$$
\begin{aligned}
PlayMove \,\widehat{=}\;\; &NoMove \\
\vee\; &SlideMove \\
\vee\; &WinMove \\
\vee\; &PlainMove \\
\vee\; &StartMove \\
\vee\; &NoStartMove
\end{aligned}
$$

12.2.6   Who goes next?

We now consider whose turn it is. There must be at least two players left in the game for turn-taking to apply. There is always a current player, who is the first player in the *player* sequence. Players are moved from the *player* sequence to the *place* sequence if they reach the last square. The turn then passes to the next player.

```
┌─ NextWhenFinished ─────────────────────────────────────────
│ ΔGameMove
├────────────────────────────────────────────────────────────
│ # player ≥ 2
│ whichSquare(position currentPlayer) = lastSquare
│ place' = place ⌢ ⟨currentPlayer⟩
│ player' = tail player
└────────────────────────────────────────────────────────────
```

▷ *sequence operations*
    tail player cuts the first entry off the *player* sequence.

Players are awarded a free turn for throwing the highest score. Otherwise play passes to the next player.

```
┌─ NextWhenNotFinished ──────────────────────────────────────
│ ΔGameMove
├────────────────────────────────────────────────────────────
│ # player ≥ 2
│ whichSquare(position currentPlayer) ≠ lastSquare
│ place' = place
│ player' =
│     if throw? = highestScore
│     then player
│     else tail player ⌢ ⟨head player⟩
└────────────────────────────────────────────────────────────
```

We do not have to say explicitly that $currentPlayer' = head\ player'$, since this follows from the inclusion of $Game'$ in $\Delta GameMove$.

$$NextPlayer \;\hat{=}\; NextWhenFinished \lor NextWhenNotFinished$$

When there is only one player left the game is over. We move the remaining entry in the *player* sequence to the end of the *place* sequence.

```
┌─ GameOver ─────────────────────────────────────────────────
│ ΔGameMove
├────────────────────────────────────────────────────────────
│ # player = 1
│ place' = place ⌢ player
└────────────────────────────────────────────────────────────
```

Note that because of the condition in the state invariant that

⟨ran *player'*, ran *place'*⟩ **partition** dom *position'*

we could deduce that *player'* = ⟨⟩.

To describe the passing of play we need to include *NextPlayer*. A turn is made up of a move and passing the die to the next player. When no more turns can be taken, the only possible outcome is to declare the game over.

$$Move \triangleq (PlayMove \wedge NextPlayer) \vee GameOver$$

12.3   An alternative view

As what one player does makes no difference to the manner in which others play, we could regard the game as a number of players all doing their own thing. Each player proceeds along the board, stopping when the last square is reached. As players make their moves they record how many turns they have taken. When all players have completed the game, the players are ranked according to how many turns they needed to finish.

> ▷ *abstraction*
> This view of snakes and ladders is more abstract. Moreover it ignores one of the stated requirements, that the players should take turns, although note that this model does not *prevent* them from taking turns, it just does not insist that they do.

12.3.1   The player level

The information required about each player is their current position and how many turns they have taken. We do not record a name or other feature to make them distinct; different players are given distinct identities at the game level.

```
┌─ Player ──────────────────────────────────────────
│ position : POSITION
│ turns : ℕ
└───────────────────────────────────────────────────
```

12.3.2   Player operations

The various moves are similar to before, except now we operate at the player level only. Later we use promotion to describe the game level operations.

To start play, the player must throw the highest score. This does not count as a turn; the player earns another go.

```
┌─ StartMoveAlt ──────────────────────────────────────────
│ ΔPlayer
│ throw? : die
├────────────────────────────────────────────────────────
│ position = notStarted
│ throw? = highestScore
│ position' = ready
│ turns' = turns
└────────────────────────────────────────────────────────
```

▷ *promotion*
Promotion imposes some constraints on the way in which we write schemas. Previously, we included *throw?* in the definition of the Δ schema. Now, because we later need a conventional Δ schema to define the promoted operations, we cannot include *throw?* in Δ*Player*. Hence we declare *throw?* each time it is needed.

If a player throws any other number, a turn has still been taken even though no move is possible.

```
┌─ NoStartMoveAlt ────────────────────────────────────────
│ ΔPlayer
│ throw? : die
├────────────────────────────────────────────────────────
│ position = notStarted
│ throw? < highestScore
│ position' = position
│ turns' = turns + 1
└────────────────────────────────────────────────────────
```

As before, we define a schema that describes the main part of a move. We use this to add another turn to the player's count, unless the highest score is thrown. The key part of a main move is that the player has started play. We also need to be assured that the player has not already reached the last square on the board (the reason for this becomes clearer later).

```
┌─ MainMoveAlt ───────────────────────────────────────────
│ ΔPlayer
│ throw? : die
│ newPosn! : ℕ
├────────────────────────────────────────────────────────
│ position ∉ {notStarted, boardPosn lastSquare}
│ newPosn! = whichSquare position + throw?
│ turns' = if (throw? = highestScore) ∧ (newPosn! ≠ lastSquare)
│          then turns else turns + 1
└────────────────────────────────────────────────────────
```

▷ *if then else*
We use the 'if then else' formulation to define *turns'*. If the highest score is thrown then,

provided that the player can move, another throw is allowed as part of the same 'turn'. If the highest score throw allows the player to finish the game or if the highest score is not thrown then the number of turns increases by one.

In the straightforward case, the player advances by the number shown on the die.

```
┌─ PlainMoveAlt ────────────────────────────────
│ MainMoveAlt
│ ──────────────────────────────────────────────
│ newPosn! ∈ square \ (dom slide)
│ position′ = boardPosn newPosn!
└───────────────────────────────────────────────
```

Throws that would take a player beyond the last square are not allowed.

```
┌─ NoMoveAlt ───────────────────────────────────
│ MainMoveAlt
│ ──────────────────────────────────────────────
│ newPosn! > lastSquare
│ position′ = position
└───────────────────────────────────────────────
```

If the player lands on the start of a slide, the resulting position is given by the end of the slide.

```
┌─ SlideMoveAlt ────────────────────────────────
│ MainMoveAlt
│ ──────────────────────────────────────────────
│ newPosn! ∈ dom slide
│ position′ = boardPosn(slide newPosn!)
└───────────────────────────────────────────────
```

We do not identify a finish move. When the player has reached the last square, further moves are prohibited by the inclusion of

$$position \notin \{notStarted, boardPosn\ lastSquare\}$$

in *MainMoveAlt*.

12.3.3   The game level

We need some players and a means of distinguishing them. We do not need a state variable to capture the final placing; it can be calculated after the game is over from the record of the number of turns taken by each player. We use the *PLAYER* given type, from earlier, to label the players.

$$GameAlt \cong [\,player : PLAYER \nrightarrow Player\,]$$

▷ *abstraction*

Previously we used numbers to label the players, by having a sequence; here we use *PLAYER* to label them. Since we do not need any properties peculiar to sequences, we avoid using a sequence declaration.

12.3.4   Game initialisation

At the start of the game, all players are at *notStarted* and none has taken any turns.

┌─ *InitGameAlt* ─────────────────────────────────────
│ *GameAlt'*
├───
│ $\forall\, p : \operatorname{dom} player'\ \bullet$
│ $player'\, p = (\,\mu\, Player \mid position = notStarted \wedge turns = 0\,)$
└───

▷ *definite description*
   The definite description, μ, is useful for constructing an explicit binding.

12.3.5   Promotion

So far we have looked at how the individual players move. As players move their pieces on the board, this has an effect on the whole game. In order to see how the effect of one individual influences the total game, we use the technique of promotion. (Chapter 19 is a tutorial on promotion.)

To promote the player level to game level operations, we define a *framing schema* as follows

┌─ $\Phi\,UpdateGame$ ────────────────────────────────
│ $\Delta\,GameAlt$
│ $\Delta\,Player$
│ *name?* : *PLAYER*
├───
│ $name? \in \operatorname{dom} player$
│ $\theta\,Player = player\ name?$
│ $player' = player \oplus \{name? \mapsto \theta\,Player'\}$
└───

▷ *framing schema*
   The framing schema is used to explain how the individual pieces of local state relate to the overall global state.
▷ *promotion*
   The promoted schemas are stated in terms of the framing schema and the local operations.

The promoted schemas are

$$StartPlayer \;\widehat{=}\; \exists\,\Delta\,Player \bullet \Phi\,UpdateGame \wedge StartMoveAlt$$
$$NoStartPlayer \;\widehat{=}\; \exists\,\Delta\,Player \bullet \Phi\,UpdateGame \wedge NoStartMoveAlt$$
$$NoMovePlayer \;\widehat{=}\; \exists\,\Delta\,Player \bullet \Phi\,UpdateGame \wedge NoMoveAlt$$
$$PlainMovePlayer \;\widehat{=}\; \exists\,\Delta\,Player \bullet \Phi\,UpdateGame \wedge PlainMoveAlt$$
$$SlideMovePlayer \;\widehat{=}\; \exists\,\Delta\,Player \bullet \Phi\,UpdateGame \wedge SlideMoveAlt$$

In total at the game level, the following describes all possible moves.

$$MovePlayer \triangleq StartPlayer$$
$$\lor\ NoStartPlayer$$
$$\lor\ NoMovePlayer$$
$$\lor\ PlainMovePlayer$$
$$\lor\ SlideMovePlayer$$

12.3.6   Finishing the game

When all the players have finished (that is, are at the last square), they are placed into order according to the number of turns taken, as in the following operation.

PlacePlayers

$\Xi GameAlt$

$place! :$ iseq $Player$

$\forall p :$ dom $player \bullet (player\ p).\ position = boardPosn\ lastSquare$

ran $place! =$ ran $player$

$\forall i, j :$ dom $place! \mid i < j \bullet (place!\ i).turns \leq (place!\ j).turns$

▷ *design decision*
We are making a decision here that the first item in the *place* sequence corresponds to the winner. This is the same approach as was taken in the earlier specification of this problem. As we pointed out before, which order is chosen is arbitrary.

▷ *non-determinism*
This operation is non-deterministic, because it does not say exactly what to do with two or more players who take the same number of turns to complete the game.
    The previous formulation does not have this non-determinism at the end of the game; rather it has a non-deterministic allocation of players to the initial *player* sequence.

The complete game is described by

$$PlayGame \triangleq MovePlayer \lor PlacePlayers$$

▷ *non-determinism*
The expression for *PlayGame* shows why we needed to ensure that a precondition of *MainMoveAlt* was that the player had not already completed the game. Otherwise, in *PlayGame* when the player had reached the last square *NoMovePlayer* could apply and the operation to place the players in order might never occur.

12.4   Discussion

Sequences are useful for manipulating the players, both in terms of whose turn it is, and also for devising the final placing. It is often tempting to use a sequence even when order is not important; as in our alternative approach, an unordered set will suffice. Sequences and their associated operations come into play when order really does matter.

Precondition calculation can be time consuming (which is why only one such calculation was presented here), but in an important specification it is essential. One useful outcome from precondition calculation is the ability to present an argument that the operation presents a complete interface. Another is that calculating the precondition is one way to check that the specification of an operation does not contain a contradiction.

Promotion allows us to map operations described at a local level onto those at the global level. It ties a given piece of local state to its position in the global view. The second version of the snakes and ladders is far more simple; the operations are described at a local level and mapped onto their global position. In the first version, we have to worry about whose turn it is and manipulate a sequence of players. These factors lead to a more complicated description of the game. The simplification in the second version is not entirely because of the use of promotion to structure the specification, it is also because we have taken a more abstract view of the system by ignoring the mechanism of turn-taking. Note also that in the first version of the game when there is only one player left that person is automatically placed last. In theory a player might never finish the game. In the second version all players must finish the game to determine the placing.

The lesson here is to notice the consequences of your approach to specification and check to see if they satisfy the true requirements of your customer.

Chapter 13

Refining the Tower of Hanoi

In which the game of the Tower of Hanoi is described in an abstract way, then the state is made more concrete and the operations refined to a popular algorithm for solving the puzzle.

13.1   Problem statement

The Tower of Hanoi is a classic puzzle. It consists of three poles and a set of discs, each of different diameter. Initially all the discs are arranged on one of the poles so that each disc is on top of a larger one (figure 13.1).

   The aim is to move the discs, one at a time, from one pole to another, such that a larger disc is never placed on top of a smaller disc (figures 13.2 and 13.3), until all the discs are arranged on one of the initially empty poles.

   The Tower of Hanoi problem is a classic of computer science. It is based on a game first sold as a toy by the French mathematician Edouard Lucas in 1883 [Gardner 1965]. It in turn is said to be based on the legend of the Benares temple priests in the city of Brahma who have a version with 64 gold discs, and three poles

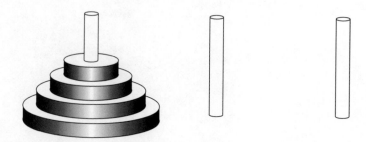

Figure 13.1 The initial state of the Tower of Hanoi.

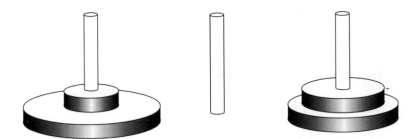

Figure 13.2 A legal state of the Tower of Hanoi.

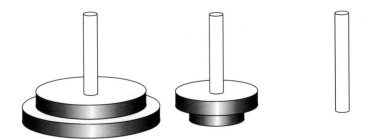

Figure 13.3 An illegal state of the Tower of Hanoi.

made of diamond, each as thick as the body of a bee and a cubit high. When all the moves are complete the world will come to an end in a thunderclap.

Optimal solutions to the n disc puzzle take $2^n - 1$ moves to complete. If the priests move one disc every second it would take them thousands of millions of years to finish the task ... of course, it all depends when they started! [Wells 1987] points out that the 'legend' appeared about a year after the puzzle was introduced.

For an interesting discussion of this problem see [Stewart 1992].

13.2   Top level specification

13.2.1   Description of the state

We need to be able to compare disc sizes, so it makes sense to model them as numbers. Each disc is represented by a number, which represents the diameter of the disc. Each disc must have a non-zero diameter.

$$disc == \mathbb{N}_1$$

▷ *natural numbers*
   Notice that *disc* takes our house style for a 'plain' set. The naturals are not a given type in Z, the integers are.

A pole may be represented by the discs on it. We need to be able to distinguish discs from one another so that we can specify that they are all different. We also need to be able to identify the disc at the top of the pole. Thus, we use sequences to specify poles. A legitimate state of the game is one in which smaller discs are on top of larger discs. We choose to model the bottom of the pole by the beginning of the sequence.

$$pole == sdecr \cap \text{seq } disc$$

▷ *toolkit*
   sdecr is defined in our toolkit extensions (see appendix A.7) and provides a sequence of strictly decreasing numbers. Notice that *sdecr* is injective.
▷ *invariant*
   The constraint that the discs on the pole should be ordered is defined here so that all further use of *pole* must conform to this invariant. Tying the properties of a data type directly to its definition helps to ensure that the data type is never used incorrectly. It also improves modularity.
▷ *accompanying text*
   Whether we model the bottom of the pole as the beginning or the end of the sequence is entirely arbitrary. What does matter is that we record our intention when the model is given. This serves to remind us when specifying the operations what our intentions were, and helps to ensure consistency.

There are three poles in the game, we introduce a constant to describe this.

$$numberOfPoles == 3$$

13.3   First version of the Tower of Hanoi

We use a sequence of poles rather than a set since we need to be able to distinguish the poles other than by the discs upon them (otherwise the starting and the finishing position would be the same and empty poles would merge).

We require that all the poles in the game are distinct. We ensure this by forming a single sequence of the discs and checking that none is repeated. We choose to regard the sequence as starting with the pole which has all the discs on it.

```
┌─ Hanoi1 ─────────────────────────────────────────────
│  poleseq₁ : seq pole
├───────────────────────────────────────────────────────
│  #poleseq₁ = numberOfPoles
│  ⌢/ poleseq₁ ∈ iseq₁ disc
└───────────────────────────────────────────────────────
```

▷ *toolkit*
  iseq₁ is defined as the non-empty injective sequences in our toolkit extensions (see appendix A.5. In this case it ensures that there are some discs in the game.
▷ *sequence, injective*
  Notice that we need to supply a set for iseq₁ to be defined over. The definition of iseq₁ is generic and an appropriate set must be supplied when it is used. This happens easily in declarations but can be overlooked in predicates.
▷ *concatenation, distributed*
  The expression ⌢/ poleseq₁ gathers all the discs into a single sequence.
▷ *sequence, injective*
  Injective sequences have no duplicates. By ensuring that ⌢/ poleseq₁ ∈ iseq₁ disc we check there are no two discs with the same diameter.

13.3.1   Initial and final states

The initial and final states of the game share the property that all the discs are on one pole. We specify this and then use it to determine the initial and the final states.

```
┌─ OneTowerHanoi1 ─────────────────────────────────────
│  Hanoi1
│  p : pole
├───────────────────────────────────────────────────────
│  p = ⌢/ poleseq₁
│  p ∈ ran poleseq₁
└───────────────────────────────────────────────────────
```

▷ *concatenation, distributed*
  ⌢/ poleseq₁ is a single sequence made up of the entries in the sequences in *poleseq₁* and in the same order. So in saying p = ⌢/ poleseq₁ we are saying that the sequence p is the same as all the sequences in *poleseq₁* put together. In other words, p is the only pole with discs on it. In addition we state that p is one of the poles in our collection of poles.

We can pin down the initial pole precisely, we choose it to be the first pole in the sequence.

```
┌─ InitHanoi1 ────────────────────────────────────────
│  OneTowerHanoi1'
│  ────────────────
│  p' = head poleseq₁'
└──────────────────────────────────────────────────────
```

▷ sequence operations
  We use *head* here to identify the first entry in the sequence. We could equally have written *poleseq₁'* 1. We prefer to use toolkit operations where they are available.

The desired state of the game is when all the discs have been transferred to another pole.

```
┌─ EndHanoi1 ─────────────────────────────────────────
│  OneTowerHanoi1
│  ───────────────
│  p ≠ head poleseq₁
└──────────────────────────────────────────────────────
```

▷ discussion
  We have specified *InitHanoi1* as an operation that creates a *OneTowerHanoi1* out of nowhere. In contrast *EndHanoi1* is given as a state that we wish to achieve. We have described the 'final' position as a state because we would like to identify it once reached.

13.3.2 Moving a disc

Moving a disc changes the arrangement of discs on the poles, but not the discs themselves. We state this constraint in the definition of a change of state.

```
┌─ ΔHanoi1 ───────────────────────────────────────────
│  Hanoi1
│  Hanoi1'
│  ──────────────────────────────
│  ran(⌢/ poleseq₁') = ran(⌢/ poleseq₁)
└──────────────────────────────────────────────────────
```

▷ Δ convention
  Notice that we are not using the 'default' definition of the Δ schema. We are including additional information that is true of every change of state of the system. It is convenient to include it here, and thus state it explicitly once only.
▷ concatenation, distributed
  The expression ⌢/ *poleseq₁* creates one sequence of discs containing all the discs that are in the individual sequences in *poleseq₁*.
▷ range
  Taking the range of a sequence gives a set of the entries of the sequence. So ran(⌢/ *poleseq₁*) gives the set of all the discs in the Tower of Hanoi puzzle.

In order to move a disc, the disc at the top of the pole from which are moving must be smaller than the disc at the top of the pole to which we are moving it. This, however, is already imposed by the constraint that the poles at the completion of the move must all be valid poles, and so must be strictly descending sequences. We take the disc from one pole and place it at the top of the other. In order to ensure that the move actually achieves something, we forbid moves that replace the disc in the same position as it started. The poles are labelled by the natural numbers (they are in a sequence), and so we specify the source and target poles by their numbers.

We have a choice of how we specify this operation. We can specify a deterministic move, in which the person making the move chooses the poles to move the disc between. Alternatively, we can specify the operation non-deterministically, where any valid move is allowed to take place, and the actual source and target poles are returned as outputs. We select the non-deterministic approach here, since it leads to a neater specification.

$$
\begin{array}{|l}
\hline
\_\,Move1 \\
\hline
\Delta Hanoi1 \\
from!, to! : \mathbb{N} \\
\hline
\{from!, to!\} \subseteq 1 \mathinner{.\,.} numberOfPoles \\
from! \neq to! \\
poleseq_1\, from! \neq \langle\,\rangle \\
poleseq_1' = poleseq_1 \oplus \{from! \mapsto front\ poleseq_1\ from!, \\
\qquad\qquad\qquad to! \mapsto poleseq_1\ to! \mathbin{\widehat{}} \langle last\ poleseq_1\ from!\rangle\} \\
\hline
\end{array}
$$

▷ *front*
  Notice that we check that $poleseq_1\ from!$ is non-empty in order to ensure that *front* may be applied to it legitimately.

This describes how we move a disc in accordance with the rules of the game. It does not provide us with an algorithm for choosing which disc to move from one pole to another.

13.4   Second version of the Tower of Hanoi

One algorithm for solving the problem is given by Lucas [Lucas 1884]. Imagine the poles arranged in a circle, and make alternate moves. On the odd numbered moves, move the smallest disc one pole clockwise. On the even numbered moves, make the only possible legal move not involving the smallest disc.

In order to specify Lucas' algorithm we need to add a method of determining whether we have an odd or an even move. We define the new state schema. We choose to keep a record of how many moves have been made in order to be able to work out whether a turn is odd or even.

$$
\begin{array}{|l}
\hline
\;\_\_\;Hanoi2 _____ \\
\;\; poleseq_2 : \text{seq } pole \\
\;\; turn : \mathbb{N} \\
\;\; smallestDisc : disc \\
\hline
\;\; \#poleseq_2 = numberOfPoles \\
\;\; \widehat{}/\, poleseq_2 \in \text{iseq}_1\; disc \\
\;\; smallestDisc = min\, (\text{ran}(\widehat{}/\, poleseq_2)) \\
\hline
\end{array}
$$

▷ *minimum*
  The minimum of a set of numbers is given by *min*. So taking the minimum of the set of all the discs identifies the smallest one.

13.4.1   Initial and final states

As before we define the case in which all the discs are on one pole, and hence we can specify initialisation.

$$
\begin{array}{|l}
\hline
\;\_\_\;OneTowerHanoi2 _____ \\
\;\; Hanoi2 \\
\;\; p : pole \\
\hline
\;\; p = \widehat{}/\, poleseq_2 \\
\;\; p \in \text{ran}\; poleseq_2 \\
\hline
\end{array}
$$

$$
\begin{array}{|l}
\hline
\;\_\_\;InitHanoi2 _____ \\
\;\; OneTowerHanoi2' \\
\hline
\;\; turn' = 1 \\
\;\; p' = head\; poleseq_2' \\
\hline
\end{array}
$$

Notice that the initial condition for *Hanoi2* is similar to that for *Hanoi1* except that we have to specify that we strart with turn number one. The end state of *Hanoi2* is also similar to that for *Hanoi1*.

$$
\begin{array}{|l}
\hline
\;\_\_\;EndHanoi2 _____ \\
\;\; OneTowerHanoi2 \\
\hline
\;\; p \neq head\; poleseq_2 \\
\hline
\end{array}
$$

13.4.2   Moving a disc

When a change is made to *Hanoi2* another turn has been taken, but the set of discs in the game are constrained to stay the same.

```
┌─ ΔHanoi2 ──────────────────────────────────────────
│  Hanoi2
│  Hanoi2′
├────────────────────────────────────────────────────
│  turn′ = turn + 1
│  ran(⌢/ poleseq′₂) = ran(⌢/ poleseq₂)
└────────────────────────────────────────────────────
```

Note that because *smallestDisc* is defined as the minimum of all the discs present, and we now constrain the discs present to remain the same, we can deduce that the smallest disc also stays constant. We will need to use this result later.

Each move consists of moving a disc from one pole to another in the prescribed manner. Determining how those poles are chosen is what differentiates the odd and even moves. We describe a general purpose move, which is then adapted by the odd and even moves.

```
┌─ BasicMove2 ───────────────────────────────────────
│  ΔHanoi2
│  from!, to! : ℕ
├────────────────────────────────────────────────────
│  {from!, to!} ⊆ 1 .. numberOfPoles
│  from! ≠ to!
│  poleseq₂ ≠ ⟨⟩
│  poleseq′₂ = poleseq₂ ⊕ {from! ↦ front poleseq₂ from!,
│                 to! ↦ poleseq₂ to! ⌢ ⟨last poleseq₂ from!⟩}
└────────────────────────────────────────────────────
```

For the odd turns, we need to add the pole from which the disc is to be moved. This pole is the one with the smallest disc on top of it. The smallest disc is then moved in a clockwise direction to the top of the next pole.

```
┌─ OddMove ──────────────────────────────────────────
│  BasicMove2
├────────────────────────────────────────────────────
│  turn mod 2 = 1
│  last poleseq₂ from! = smallestDisc
│  to! = (from! mod numberOfPoles) + 1
└────────────────────────────────────────────────────
```

For even turns we must not involve the smallest disc. Of the remaining two poles, provided that either of them have discs on them, the one with the smaller top disc is the pole from which we move and the other is the pole to which we move. We cannot always perform an even move: when all the discs are on the same pole, it is impossible to make a move that does not involve the smallest disc. We begin with an odd move (as given in the initial state) so we need worry only about the end state, when we cannot make an even move. This has the fortunate consequence that, if the end state is reached, the game must terminate.

$$
\begin{array}{|l}
\underline{\;\mathit{EvenMove}\;}\\
\;\;\mathit{BasicMove2}\\
\hline
\;\;\mathit{turn}\;\mathbf{mod}\;2 = 0\\
\;\;\mathit{last\;poleseq_2\;from!} \neq \mathit{smallestDisc}\\
\end{array}
$$

So a complete description of a successful move is given by

$$\mathit{Move2} \,\hat{=}\, \mathit{OddMove} \lor \mathit{EvenMove}$$

13.5   Refinement

This book is principally about specification. However, since the use of refinement is becoming more common, we here give a brief overview of the way in which refinement works. Typically refinement is performed in a number of steps, in which we move gradually towards the concrete design of the system. We concentrate on how to transform the abstract specification into a more concrete one. Methods exist for reaching code from the concrete specification.

An introduction to the notion of refinement is given by [Spivey 1992]. A more detailed description of this process as applied to Z specifications may be found in [Woodcock & Davies 1994]. [Morgan 1990] shows how to calculate the program from the specification, although his approach is not Z specific. [King 1990b] gives the links between Z and Morgan's approach. In this section we show how refinement techniques demonstrate the connection between the two versions of the Tower of Hanoi specification that are given above.

13.5.1   Data refinement

In data refinement the abstract data type in the abstract specification is related to the concrete data type in the concrete specification (the design). This is done by means of a 'retrieve' schema that shows the relationship between the abstract and the concrete state items. This relationship allows us to retrieve the abstract state from the concrete one.

If we have an abstract state called $AState$ and a concrete state called $CState$ then the retrieve schema has the same signature as $AState \land CState$ with additional predicates that shows the relationship between them. $AState$ and $CState$ should not have any common state components.

▷ *readability*
One reason for specifying each version separately and not using schema inclusion (to show how *Hanoi2* builds on *Hanoi1*) is because we are not allowed to have the state schemas sharing components. We have ensured that the presentation of the specification makes this follow automatically, although it is not how it was first written.

The retrieve relation for the Tower of Hanoi

We describe how *Hanoi1* and *Hanoi2* are related. In *Hanoi2* we have the additional state components of *smallestDisc* and *turn*. The smallest disc was not specified in our first version, but it is not hard to see that it is calculated in the same way as for the second version.

$$
\begin{array}{l}
\underline{\mathit{Retrieve\,Two\,One}} \\
\quad \mathit{Hanoi1} \\
\quad \mathit{Hanoi2} \\
\hline
\quad \mathit{poleseq}_2 = \mathit{poleseq}_1 \\
\quad \mathit{smallestDisc} = \mathit{min}(\mathrm{ran}(\widehat{}/\,\mathit{poleseq}_1))
\end{array}
$$

▷ *redundancy*
We effectively repeat the state invariant of *Hanoi2*, in order to make the relationship explicit. This type of redundancy does not give rise to any proof obligations since we are merely repeating what has already been stated.

In this example there is little data refinement. Indeed, the main state variable (*poleseq*) has not changed. The interesting refinement in this case is that of the operations.

13.5.2 Operation refinement

In moving towards a more concrete description of a system, the operations change from describing the 'what' of the operation to the 'how'. We see this in the two versions of the Tower of Hanoi. To begin with, the operation of moving a disc is simply described in terms of moving the top disc from any one pole to any other such that the state invariant is preserved. Then an algorithm is defined in which odd and even moves are separated, and the precise way in which the discs are moved is given. In order to be able to demonstrate the refinement we have to show the following.

Correct initial concrete state Each possible initial concrete state (subscript c) must represent a possible initial abstract state (subscript a). The concrete version should not allow starting points that the abstract specification forbids.

$$
\mathit{Init}_c \vdash \exists \mathit{State}'_a \bullet \mathit{Init}_a \wedge \mathit{Retrieve}'
$$

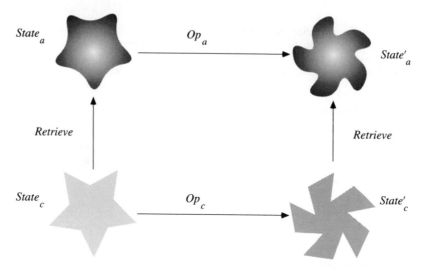

Figure 13.4 Operation refinement. *State*ₐ and *Op*ₐ represent the abstract state and operation, *State*_c and *Op*_c the concrete ones.

Correct operation refinement Whenever the abstract operation terminates so should the concrete operation. In other words, if you are in a state in which the abstract operation is guaranteed to terminate (that is within its precondition) and you apply the retrieve relation, you will be in a state in which the concrete operation is guaranteed to terminate.

$$\text{pre } Op_a \wedge Retrieve \vdash \text{pre } Op_c$$

Correct concrete operation If the abstract operation terminates, then so should the concrete one, and the state in which the concrete operation terminates should represent a possible abstract state in which the abstract operation could terminate. In other words, you can either start in the precondition of the abstract operation, perform the retrieve operation to reach the concrete state and then perform the concrete operation, or you can first perform the abstract operation and then apply the retrieve relation (see figure 13.4).

$$\text{pre } Op_a \wedge Retrieve \wedge Op_c \vdash \exists State'_a \bullet Op_a \wedge Retrieve'$$

Operation input and output variables should have the same names at the various levels of specification in order to support the proof of the operation refinement. If necessary, renaming can be used to achieve this.

13.5.3   Operation refinement for Tower of Hanoi

Here we show that *Move*2 is a refinement of *Move*1. We need to demonstrate that

1. $InitHanoi2 \vdash \exists\, Hanoi1' \bullet InitHanoi1 \wedge RetrieveTwoOne'$
2. pre *Move*1 $\wedge$ *RetrieveTwoOne* $\vdash$ pre *Move*2
3. pre *Move*1 $\wedge$ *RetrieveTwoOne* $\wedge$ *Move*2 $\vdash$
   $\exists\, Hanoi1' \bullet Move1 \wedge RetrieveTwoOne'$

Proving the initial state is correctly refined

We need to show the following

$$InitHanoi2 \vdash \exists\, Hanoi1' \bullet InitHanoi1 \wedge RetrieveTwoOne'$$

Looking at the right hand side, and rewriting using the expression from [Spivey 1992, page 70] that

$$\exists\, D \mid P \bullet Q \Leftrightarrow \exists\, D \bullet P \wedge Q$$

we find that

$\exists\, poleseq_1' : \mathrm{seq}\, pole \bullet$
$\qquad \#poleseq_1' = numberOfPoles$
$\qquad \wedge\; p' \in \mathrm{ran}\, poleseq_1'$
$\qquad \wedge\; \widehat{}/\, poleseq_1' \in \mathrm{iseq}_1\, disc$
$\qquad \wedge\; p' = head\, poleseq_1'$
$\qquad \wedge\; p' = \widehat{}/\, poleseq_1'$
$\qquad \wedge\; poleseq_2' = poleseq_1'$
$\qquad \wedge\; \#poleseq_2' = numberOfPoles$
$\qquad \wedge\; \widehat{}/\, poleseq_2' \in \mathrm{iseq}_1\, disc$
$\qquad \wedge\; smallestDisc' = min\,(\mathrm{ran}(\widehat{}/\, poleseq_2'))$
$\qquad \wedge\; smallestDisc' = min\,(\mathrm{ran}(\widehat{}/\, poleseq_1'))$

Using the one-point rule (see the glossary for a definition) to substitute the expression for $poleseq_1'$ (that is $poleseq_1' = poleseq_2'$) we have

$\#poleseq_2' = numberOfPoles$
$\wedge\; \widehat{}/\, poleseq_2' \in \mathrm{iseq}_1\, disc$
$\wedge\; p' \in \mathrm{ran}\, poleseq_2'$
$\wedge\; p' = head\, poleseq_2'$
$\wedge\; p' = \widehat{}/\, poleseq_2'$
$\wedge\; smallestDisc' = min\,(\mathrm{ran}(\widehat{}/\, poleseq_2'))$

This clearly follows from the expanded form of *InitHanoi2* below

```
┌─ InitHanoi2 ─────────────────────────────────────────
│ poleseq'₂ : seq pole
│ turn' : ℕ
│ smallestDisc' : disc
│ p' : pole
├──────────────────────────────────────────────────────
│ p' = ⌢/ poleseq'₂
│ turn' = 1
│ p' = head poleseq'₂
│ p' ∈ ran poleseq'₂
│ #poleseq'₂ = numberOfPoles
│ ⌢/ poleseq'₂ ∈ iseq₁ disc
│ smallestDisc' = min (ran(⌢/ poleseq'₂))
└──────────────────────────────────────────────────────
```

□

Precondition calculation

We need to calculate the precondition of *Move2*. For a more detailed description of such calculations see section 12.2.4. It is calculated in two parts, using the result that

$$\text{pre } (A \lor B) = \text{pre } A \lor \text{pre } B$$

▷ *precondition calculation*
   Since schema operations are typically built up as a series of disjuncts, it is a useful result that the precondition can be similarly built up.

First we calculate the precondition of an odd move.

$$preOddMove \mathrel{\widehat{=}} \text{pre } OddMove$$

▷ *schema*
   We choose a new name for the result of the precondition calculation because Z does not permit the use of schema operators within schema names.

---
preOddMove

Hanoi2

$\exists\, poleseq'_2 : \text{seq}\, pole;\ turn' : \mathbb{N};\ smallestDisc' : disc;\ from!, to! : \mathbb{N} \bullet$

$\qquad turn' = turn + 1$

$\qquad \wedge\ turn\ \text{mod}\ 2 = 1$

$\qquad \wedge\ \text{ran}(\frown\!/\,poleseq'_2) = \text{ran}(\frown\!/\,poleseq_2)$

$\qquad \wedge\ last\ poleseq_2\ from! = smallestDisc$

$\qquad \wedge\ to! = (from! + 1)\ \text{mod}\ numberOfPoles$

$\qquad \wedge\ \{from!, to!\} \subseteq 1 \mathinner{\ldotp\ldotp} numberOfPoles$

$\qquad \wedge\ from! \neq to!$

$\qquad \wedge\ smallestDisc' = min\,(\text{ran}(\frown\!/\,poleseq'_2))$

$\qquad \wedge\ poleseq'_2 = poleseq_2 \oplus \{from! \mapsto front\ poleseq_2\ from!,$
$\qquad\qquad\qquad to! \mapsto poleseq_2\ to! \frown \langle last\ poleseq_2\ from! \rangle\}$

$\qquad \wedge\ \#poleseq'_2 = numberOfPoles$

$\qquad \wedge\ \frown\!/\,poleseq'_2 \in \text{iseq}_1\ disc$

$\qquad \wedge\ poleseq_2\ from! \neq \langle\,\rangle$

Substituting

$$\text{ran}(\frown\!/\,poleseq'_2) = \text{ran}(\frown\!/\,poleseq_2)$$

into

$$smallestDisc' = min\,(\text{ran}(\frown\!/\,poleseq'_2))$$

we obtain $smallestDisc' = min(\text{ran}(\frown\!/\,poleseq_2))$ which is already within the state invariant of *Hanoi2* and need not be restated.

We also observe that we can always satisfy $turn' = turn + 1$. This leaves us with

---
preOddMove
Hanoi2

$\exists \, poleseq_2' : \text{seq } pole; \; from!, to! : \mathbb{N} \, \bullet$

$\quad \text{ran}(\frown / \, poleseq_2') = \text{ran}(\frown / \, poleseq_2)$

$\quad \wedge \; turn \; \text{mod} \; 2 = 1$

$\quad \wedge \; last \; poleseq_2 \; from! = smallestDisc$

$\quad \wedge \; to! = (from! + 1) \; \text{mod} \; numberOfPoles$

$\quad \wedge \; \{from!, to!\} \subseteq 1 \mathbin{..} numberOfPoles$

$\quad \wedge \; from! \neq to!$

$\quad \wedge \; poleseq_2 \; from! \neq \langle \, \rangle$

$\quad \wedge \; poleseq_2' = poleseq_2 \oplus \{from! \mapsto front \; poleseq_2 \; from!,$
$\qquad\qquad\qquad to! \mapsto poleseq_2 \; to! \frown \langle last \; poleseq_2 \; from!\rangle\}$

$\quad \wedge \; \#poleseq_2' = numberOfPoles$

$\quad \wedge \; \frown / \, poleseq_2' \in \text{iseq}_1 \; disc$

Now we substitute the expression for $polseseq_2'$ into the other parts of the predicate which involve $poleseq_2'$, this gives us

$\#(poleseq_2 \oplus \{from! \mapsto front \; poleseq_2 \; from!,$
$\qquad to! \mapsto poleseq_2 \; to! \frown \langle last \; poleseq_2 \; from!\rangle\}) = numberOfPoles$

$\wedge \;\; \frown /(poleseq_2 \oplus \{from! \mapsto front \; poleseq_2 \; from!,$
$\qquad to! \mapsto poleseq_2 \; to! \frown \langle last \; poleseq_2 \; from!\rangle\}) \in \text{iseq}_1 \; disc$

$\wedge \;\; \text{ran}(\frown /(poleseq_2 \oplus \{from! \mapsto front \; poleseq_2 \; from!,$
$\qquad to! \mapsto poleseq_2 \; to! \frown \langle last \; poleseq_2 \; from!\rangle\})) = \text{ran}(\frown / \, poleseq_2)$

If we can show that these simplify to expressions of the form $a = a$ then $poleseq_2'$ can be eliminated from the existential quantification. For the first part we observe that

$$\text{dom } b \subseteq \text{dom } a \Rightarrow \#(a \oplus b) = \#a$$

Now we know that in this case the domain of the right hand side is $\{from!, to!\}$, and we know from the predicate part

$$\{from!, to!\} \subseteq 1 \mathbin{..} numberOfPoles$$

and hence from the state invariant of *Hanoi2* that $\{from!, to!\}$ is a subset of dom $poleseq_2$. Thus the cardinality of this expression is that of $poleseq_2$ which, from the state invariant of *Hanoi2*, is $numberOfPoles$ as required.

To show the membership of $\text{iseq}_1 \; disc$, we observe that $from!$ and $to!$ are in the domain of $poleseq_2$, if no new discs are added then that is sufficient to ensure that the membership holds, as we know that $^\frown\!/\,poleseq_2 \in \text{iseq}_1\ disc$. Notice that the way in which the operation functions is to remove one disc from *from*! and add it to *to*!, no other discs are moved or introduced. Hence the membership property holds.

It remains to demonstrate that

$$\text{ran}(^\frown\!/(poleseq_2 \oplus \{from! \mapsto front\ poleseq_2\ from!,$$
$$to! \mapsto poleseq_2\ to! ^\frown \langle last\ poleseq_2\ from!\rangle\})) = \text{ran}(^\frown\!/\ poleseq_2)$$

We now make use of the fact that there are three poles, we have named two of them already: *from*! and *to*!. We call the other pole n. Listing the elements of the sequence after the override, we have

$(n, poleseq_2\ n)$
$(from!, front\ poleseq_2\ from!)$
$(to!, poleseq_2\ to! ^\frown \langle last\ poleseq_2\ from!\rangle)$

The distributed concatenation of this is

$$poleseq_2\ n ^\frown front\ poleseq_2\ from! ^\frown poleseq_2\ to! ^\frown \langle last\ poleseq_2\ from!\rangle$$

which simplifies to

$$poleseq_2\ n ^\frown poleseq_2\ from! ^\frown poleseq_2\ to!$$

which can be seen to be $poleseq_2$. Hence the schema simplifies to

```
┌─ preOddMove ──────────────────────────────────────
│ Hanoi2
│ ┌──────────────────────────────────────────────
│ │ ∃ from!, to! : ℕ •
│ │     turn mod 2 = 1
│ │     ∧ last poleseq₂ from! = smallestDisc
│ │     ∧ to! = (from! + 1) mod numberOfPoles
│ │     ∧ {from!, to!} ⊆ 1 .. numberOfPoles
│ │     ∧ from! ≠ to!
│ │     ∧ poleseq₂ from! ≠ ⟨⟩
```

If we can show that $last\ poleseq_2\ from! = smallestDisc$ defines *from*!, we can use the one point rule to eliminate *from*! from the existential quantification.

There is a constraint in *Hanoi2* that says $smallestDisc = min\ (\text{ran}(^\frown\!/\ poleseq_2))$ from which we can deduce that $smallestDisc \in \text{ran}(^\frown\!/\ poleseq_2)$.

That $smallestDisc$ is in the distributed concatenation of the poles implies that it is in at least one of the poles, and the fact that the discs are all different means it is in exactly one pole. *smallestDisc* is the smallest of all the discs, and so is the smallest of those on its pole.

pole is defined to be a descending sequence, and therefore the smallest disc must have the largest index. That is, we have shown that there is exactly one *pole* of $poleseq_2$ whose last element is *smallestDisc*. This clearly defines *from*!.

to! is clearly defined from *from*! and, given that there are three poles, its definition shows it to be distinct from *from*!. Since there are some discs in the game, then it is always possible to pick a non-empty *from*!.

$$preOddMove \triangleq [Hanoi2 \mid turn \bmod 2 = 1]$$

We now look at *EvenMove*. Its precondition is given by

$$preEvenMove \triangleq \mathrm{pre}\ EvenMove$$

    ┌─ *preEvenMove* ─────────────────────────────
    │ *Hanoi2*
    ├──────────────────────────────────
    │ $\exists\, poleseq_2' : \mathrm{seq}\, pole;\ turn', from!, to! : \mathbb{N};\ smallestDisc' : disc\ \bullet$
    │ $turn \bmod 2 = 0$
    │ $\wedge\ \mathrm{ran}(^\frown\!/\, poleseq_2') = \mathrm{ran}(^\frown\!/\, poleseq_2)$
    │ $\wedge\ turn' = turn + 1$
    │ $\wedge\ poleseq_2\, from! \neq \langle\,\rangle$
    │ $\wedge\ \mathrm{last}\ poleseq_2\, from! \neq smallestDisc$
    │ $\wedge\ \{from!, to!\} \subseteq 1 \mathinner{\ldotp\ldotp} numberOfPoles$
    │ $\wedge\ from! \neq to!$
    │ $\wedge\ smallestDisc' = min(\mathrm{ran}(^\frown\!/\, poleseq_2'))$
    │ $\wedge\ poleseq_2' = poleseq_2 \oplus \{from! \mapsto \mathrm{front}\ poleseq_2\, from!,$
    │ $to! \mapsto poleseq_2\, to!\ ^\frown \langle \mathrm{last}\ poleseq_2\, from!\rangle\}$
    │ $\wedge\ \#poleseq_2' = numberOfPoles$
    │ $\wedge\ ^\frown\!/\, poleseq_2' \in \mathrm{iseq}_1\, disc$
    └──────────────────────────────────

Following similar arguments to those in calculating the precondition of *OddMove* this can be simplified to the following schema.

```
┌─ preEvenMove ─────────────────────────────────┐
│ Hanoi2                                         │
├────────────────────────────────────────────── │
│ ∃ from!, to! : ℕ; poleseq'₂ : seq pole •      │
│     turn mod 2 = 0                             │
│   ∧ poleseq₂ from! ≠ ⟨ ⟩                       │
│   ∧ last poleseq₂ from! ≠ smallestDisc         │
│   ∧ {from!, to!} ⊆ 1 .. numberOfPoles          │
│   ∧ from! ≠ to!                                │
└────────────────────────────────────────────────┘
```

We observe that *from!* and *to!* can easily be chosen provided that there are at least two poles with discs on them.

```
┌─ preEvenMove ─────────────────────────────────┐
│ Hanoi2                                         │
├────────────────────────────────────────────── │
│ turn mod 2 = 0                                 │
│ #(ran poleseq₂) = numberOfPoles                │
└────────────────────────────────────────────────┘
```

▷ range
The range of a sequence is the set of entries in it. In the case of *poleseq₂* which is a sequence of sequences, we obtain a set of sequences. Since we know that all the discs within the game are distinct, we will obtain three different elements of its range, unless two of the poles have no discs on them—in which case there would be two elements of the range: the sequence of all the discs and the empty sequence.

So using the result on page 146 the precondition of *Move2* is

$$preMove2 \mathrel{\hat=} \mathrm{pre}\ Move2$$

```
┌─ preMove2 ─────────────────────────────────────┐
│ Hanoi2                                          │
├─────────────────────────────────────────────── │
│ turn mod 2 = 0 ∧ #(ran poleseq₂) = numberOfPoles│
│ ∨                                               │
│ turn mod 2 = 1                                  │
└─────────────────────────────────────────────────┘
```

We also need to calculate the precondition of *Move1*.

$$preMove1 \mathrel{\hat=} \mathrm{pre}\ Move1$$

```
┌─ preMove1 ──────────────────────────────────────────────
│  Hanoi1
├──────────────────────────────────────────────────────────
│  ∃ poleseq₁' : seq pole; from!, to! : ℕ •
│      {from!, to!} ⊆ 1 .. numberOfPoles
│      ∧ ran(⁀/ poleseq₁') = ran(⁀/ poleseq₁)
│      ∧ from! ≠ to!
│      ∧ poleseq₁ from! ≠ ⟨⟩
│      ∧ poleseq₁' = poleseq₁ ⊕ {from! ↦ front poleseq₁ from!,
│                  to! ↦ poleseq₁ to! ⁀ ⟨last poleseq₁ from!⟩}
│      ∧ #poleseq₁' = numberOfPoles
│      ∧ ⁀/ poleseq₁' ∈ iseq₁ disc
└──────────────────────────────────────────────────────────
```

This calculation is similar to that for *OddMove* and so is not given here. The precondition of *Move*1 simplifies to

$$preMoveOne \mathrel{\widehat{=}} [Hanoi1 \mid true]$$

□

Proving the operation is correctly refined

We have to show that

$$\text{pre } Move1 \land RetrieveTwoOne \vdash \text{pre } Move2$$

We first consider the left hand side of the expression, first defining a suitable schema.

$$preMoveOneAndRetrieve \mathrel{\widehat{=}} preMove1 \land RetrieveTwoOne$$

```
┌─ preMoveOneAndRetrieve ─────────────────────────────────
│  Hanoi1
│  Hanoi2
├──────────────────────────────────────────────────────────
│  poleseq₂ = poleseq₁
│  smallestDisc = min (ran(⁀/ poleseq₁))
└──────────────────────────────────────────────────────────
```

The abstract operation will work even in the one tower condition. The concrete operation can be deduced *apart* from this state in which case the concrete operation fails. Thus we cannot show this refinement condition but this is all right for our purposes since the concrete operation 'improves' on the abstract in that if the one tower state is reached the game must terminate.

□

Proving the concrete operation is correct

We need to show that

$$\text{pre } Move1 \land RetrieveTwoOne \land Move2 \vdash$$
$$\exists \, Hanoi1' \bullet Move1 \land RetrieveTwoOne'$$

Looking at the right hand side, we have

$$\exists \, poleseq_1' : \text{seq } pole \bullet$$
$$\#poleseq_1' = numberOfPoles$$
$$\land \, ^\frown\!/ \, poleseq_1' \in \text{iseq}_1 \, disc$$
$$\land \, \{from!, to!\} \subseteq 1 \,.. \, numberOfPoles$$
$$\land \, from! \neq to!$$
$$\land \, poleseq_1 \, from! \neq \langle \, \rangle$$
$$\land \, poleseq_1' = poleseq_1 \oplus \{from! \mapsto front \, poleseq_1 \, from!,$$
$$to! \mapsto poleseq_1 \, to! \, ^\frown \langle last \, poleseq_1 \, from!\rangle\}$$
$$\land \, poleseq_1' = poleseq_2'$$
$$\land \, smallestDisc = min \, (\text{ran}(^\frown\!/ \, poleseq_1'))$$

Using the one-point rule to substitute the expression for $poleseq_1'$ we obtain

$$\#poleseq_2' = numberOfPoles$$
$$\land \, ^\frown\!/ \, poleseq_2' \in \text{iseq}_1 \, disc$$
$$\land \, \{from!, to!\} \subseteq 1 \,.. \, numberOfPoles$$
$$\land \, from! \neq to!$$
$$\land \, poleseq_1 \, from! \neq \langle \, \rangle$$
$$\land \, poleseq_2' = poleseq_1 \oplus \{from! \mapsto front \, poleseq_1 \, from!,$$
$$to! \mapsto poleseq_1 \, to! \, ^\frown \langle last \, poleseq_1 \, from!\rangle\}$$
$$\land \, smallestDisc' = min \, (\text{ran}(^\frown\!/ \, poleseq_2'))$$

Now we look at the left hand side of the expression, we define a schema which describes this, we then expand it.

$$preMove1AndRetrieveAndMove2 \; \hat{=} \; preMove1 \land RetrieveTwoOne \land Move2$$

$\llcorner$ _preMove1AndRetrieveAndMove2_ _____

$\Delta Hanoi2$

$Hanoi1$

$from!, to! : \mathbb{N}$

_____

$\{from!, to!\} \subseteq 1 .. numberOfPoles$

$from! \neq to!$

$poleseq_2 = poleseq_1$

$smallestDisc = min\,(ran(\frown/\,poleseq_1))$

$poleseq_2\,from! \neq \langle\rangle$

$poleseq_2' = poleseq_2 \oplus \{from! \mapsto front\,poleseq_2\,from!,$
$\qquad\qquad\qquad to! \mapsto poleseq_2\,to! \frown \langle last\,poleseq_2\,from!\rangle\}$

$turn' = turn + 1$

$\qquad((turn \bmod 2 = 1$
$\qquad \wedge\, last\,poleseq_2\,from! = smallestDisc$
$\qquad \wedge\, to! = (from! + 1) \bmod numberOfPoles)$

$\vee$

$\qquad(turn \bmod 2 = 0$
$\qquad \wedge\, last\,poleseq_2\,from! \neq smallestDisc))$

We look at the predicate parts of the right hand side in turn, to show that they follow from the above.

1. $\#poleseq_2' = numberOfPoles$ follows from the expression for $poleseq_2'$ above by the same argument that we used in calculating the precondition of _OddMove_.

2. $\frown/\,poleseq_2' \in iseq_1\,disc$ is in the state invariant of $\Delta Hanoi2$.

3. $\{from!, to!\} \subseteq 1 .. numberOfPoles$ and $from! \neq to!$ are both stated directly, above.

4. The expression for $poleseq_2'$ follows from substituting $poleseq_1 = poleseq_2$, as does the condition that $poleseq_2\,from! \neq \langle\rangle$.

5. $smallestDisc' = min\,(ran(\frown/\,poleseq_2'))$ follows from the state invariant of $Hanoi2'$ which is included within $\Delta Hanoi2$ in the declaration.

Thus, we have shown the third theorem of the operation refinement to be correct.

$\square$

Hence, with the exception of the one tower condition in the concrete operation, the concrete version of the specification is a refinement of the abstract version.

■

13.6   Overview of the Tower of Hanoi

Performing the proofs takes time, but is useful in helping to ensure that the specification is correctly formed. A decision must be made as to whether it is worth the effort involved. Clearly for any large problem, there are many such proofs to perform.

As we have said elsewhere, calculation of the preconditions confers benefits in terms of ensuring correct specification of the operation. If you cannot calculate the precondition then something is amiss in your specification of it. Precondition calculation can also demonstrate that the interface to your operation is total. *Move*1 is total; although *Move*2 is not, it turns out that this does not concern us.

Many newcomers to formal methods consider that proof of refinement is the principal focus of using a formal notation. As we have shown elsewhere in this book there is much to be gained from a precise specification of requirements. This is where most practitioners of formal methods concentrate their efforts. Nonetheless there are many benefits to be had from a fully formal development.

The Tower of Hanoi example illustrates a highly important lesson. Systems that you may have to specify do not always have the neat and tidy solutions that the well-chosen, and small, case studies in text books do. Here we have a problem with the concrete operation which fails in one possible state. Provided that we can satisfy ourselves that this is valid then we can permit the 'refinement'.

Our aim in including this chapter is to introduce some of the concepts of refinement and to show how proof is used to demonstrate conformance between two specifications. By attempting such proofs for the two versions of the Tower of Hanoi specifications, we were able to discover an important difference between the way in which the operations worked.

Part III

Style and Tactics

Chapter 14

Be Abstract

In which we illustrate what we mean by abstraction.

14.1   Introduction

There is a temptation to write code, rather than an abstract specification, when writing Z. Resist it. Don't worry though, the temptation *will* come your way again!

By 'code' we mean the description of *how* an algorithm works (for example, by walking along a sequence an element at a time) rather than specifying *what* the outcome should be (for example, identifying a particular element in the sequence). The *how* has lots of irrelevant detail (for example, walking from left to right, or from right to left) that might very well make a different style of implementation impossible or unobvious (for example, processing parts of the sequence in parallel).

In this section, we give a few examples of what we think of as *what*, or non-algorithmic, specifications.

14.2   The blue pencil problem

> **Problem statement.** Define a function *censor* that takes as input a sequence of characters in which there are spaces separating words. The output of the function should be the same as the input except that all four letter words are replaced by four asterisks.

In deciding how to describe this function we must first analyse the types in the system. The requirement is to deal with characters, and we know there are some special instances of characters, namely space and asterisk. As the rest of the characters could be anything we use a given set to model the characters

$$[CHAR]$$

and then identify the special ones.

$$
\begin{array}{|l}
asterisk, space : CHAR \\
\hline
asterisk \neq space
\end{array}
$$

▷ *overspecification*
Notice that we state that *asterisk* and *space* are not the same character; just because we have given them different names does not make them different. However, the different names in the *informal* requirement indicate that they should be different, so it is not overspecification to make them so in the Z.

Now we have to consider how we identify words; unless we can spot words we are not able to apply *censor* to them.

▷ *abstraction*
The usual way to code this problem is to perform some kind of 'look ahead', where we search through the sequence of characters until we spot a space and then we know that we have a word. This approach follows the way that the function might be *implemented* in an imperative programming language, and is rather clumsy to specify. It is far clearer to state in the mathematics what we are told in the English requirement.

The requirement states that 'there are spaces separating words'. Thus we know that whatever else they contain, words do *not* contain spaces. This may be expressed simply by

$$word == \mathrm{seq}_1(CHAR \setminus \{space\})$$

▷ *generic constant*
Notice that we use an expression to instantiate the parameter of the generic sequence.
▷ *sequence, non-empty*
We use a non-empty sequence to ensure that words have at least one character.

It is convenient to identify the four asterisks that are output by the censor function in the event of discovering a four letter word.

$$bleep == uniqseq(4, asterisk)$$

▷ *toolkit*
uniqseq is defined in our extension to the sample toolkit, appendix A.6.

Now we can turn our attention to defining the *censor* function. Recall that what we are asked to do is to take in a sequence of characters and put out a sequence of characters. This provides us with a declaration for the function.

$$censor : \mathrm{seq}\ CHAR \longrightarrow \mathrm{seq}\ CHAR$$

Since *censor* is required to work for any sequence of characters, we require it to be total.

▷ *accompanying text*
  Note that the Z fragment quoted here is part of the explanatory text, not part of the
  formal specification.

How do we define the censor function? Once we have identified a word, we can
check for the length of the word and act accordingly

$\forall\, w : word \bullet$

$\qquad censor\, w = \textbf{if}\ \#w = 4\ \textbf{then}\ bleep\ \textbf{else}\ w$

This gives us a complete description of how *censor* behaves once we have isolated
words. How do we isolate words? All we know about them is that they are
separated by spaces. So if we can identify a space we know that it is not part of a
word. What happens when we censor a space? Why, we leave it as a space.

$\qquad censor\langle space \rangle = \langle space \rangle$

This is the theme that we want, but it still does not tell us what to do with an
arbitrary sequence of characters, within which may be lurking some words. This
expression of the problem lights the way to the solution. Suppose we have an
arbitrary sequence of characters. We feed it into our censor machine, and every
time we find a space we censor it (and output a space). Thus we begin to break
up the sequence around the spaces. Then we can worry about what to do with the
subsequences that are left. It does not matter how we break up the sequence; we
can take a completely non-deterministic approach.

$\forall\, l, r : \text{seq}\ CHAR \bullet$

$\qquad censor(l \frown \langle space \rangle \frown r) = censor\, l \frown \langle space \rangle \frown censor\, r$

▷ *implementation bias*
  Notice that this definition could lead to all manner of implementations, including a parallel
  approach. The more that specifications can be kept free of implementation details the
  better.

If we censor an empty sequence we return an empty sequence. We must add this
to the definition.

▷ *recursive definition*
  When using recursive definitions like this one of *censor* it is necessary to provide an end
  case, otherwise the recursion can never 'bottom out'.

We now put the whole function together and write it, correctly in Z, as an axiomatic
description.

$censor : \text{seq}\ CHAR \longrightarrow \text{seq}\ CHAR$

$censor\langle\rangle = \langle\rangle$

$\forall\, l, r : \text{seq}\ CHAR \bullet$

$\qquad censor(l \frown \langle space \rangle \frown r) = censor\, l \frown \langle space \rangle \frown censor\, r$

$\forall\, w : word \bullet$

$\qquad censor\, w = \textbf{if}\ \#w = 4\ \textbf{then}\ bleep\ \textbf{else}\ w$

Here we are using a recursive definition of *censor* that breaks up the sequence of characters and then censors it in bits. Apart from censoring the non-empty sequences, the only bits we know how to censor are words and spaces. Words do not have spaces in them (by definition) and so they cannot be split up by the predicate. The recursive definition that shows how to break up the sequence around spaces, ensures that we censor whole words, and that words themselves are not broken down.

14.3   Greatest common divisor

> **Problem statement.** Specify the greatest common divisor function. The greatest common divisor (also called the highest common factor) of two numbers is the largest number that exactly divides both.

The coding temptation is to specify something such as Euclid's algorithm (see, for example, [Stewart & Tall 1977, Chapter 8]), which defines a procedure for *calculating* the greatest common divisor. Instead, we give an implicit specification that says what the greatest common divisor *is*, but does not suggest an implementation.

As is often the case, it is easier to specify some auxiliary functions first, then use these to specify the required result more concisely. We take 'number' to mean 'positive integer'. *divisors* is a function that maps a number to the set of all its divisors. This set is never empty because 1 is always a divisor of any number.

$$divisors == (\lambda k : \mathbb{N}_1 \bullet \{ m, n : \mathbb{N}_1 \mid m * n = k \bullet m \})$$

> ▷ *lambda-expression*
> An equivalent form of this definition that does not use a lambda-expression definition is
>
> $$divisors_1 : \mathbb{N}_1 \longrightarrow \mathbb{P}_1\, \mathbb{N}_1$$
> $$\forall k : \mathbb{N}_1 \bullet divisors_1\, k = \{ m, n : \mathbb{N}_1 \mid m * n = k \bullet m \}$$

> ▷ *set comprehension*
> The constructing term in the definition could just as easily be the other number, n.
>
> $$divisors_2 == (\lambda k : \mathbb{N}_1 \bullet \{ m, n : \mathbb{N}_1 \mid m * n = k \bullet n \})$$
>
> Which of these is used makes no difference to the contents of the set. There is no point in trying for a definition that uses both m and n, to save 'wasting' one of them. You should not worry about how you would *construct* such a set.

The greatest common divisor of a pair of numbers is the largest divisor they have in common.

$$gcd == (\lambda i, j : \mathbb{N}_1 \bullet max(divisors\, i \cap divisors\, j))$$

▷ *proof obligation*
    max may be applied only to a non-empty set, so we have to show the set is non-empty in this case.

divisors i and *divisors j* both contain the element 1, hence so does their intersection, so *max* may be safely applied.

▷ *implicit definition*
    This definition closely follows the form of the natural language description. It is implicit because it defines the result merely in terms of its desired properties, not in any constructive manner. It is clear and succinct.

▷ *characteristic tuple*
    The type of the argument that should be supplied to the lambda-expression is given by the characteristic tuple in the declaration, which is a pair of non-zero natural numbers (i, j).

▷ *curried function*
    A definition with the arguments curried, so that they can be applied one at a time ($gcd_1 : \mathbb{N}_1 \longrightarrow \mathbb{N}_1 \longrightarrow \mathbb{N}_1$) rather than as a tuple, is

$$gcd_1 == (\,\lambda\, i : \mathbb{N}_1 \bullet (\,\lambda\, j : \mathbb{N}_1 \bullet max(\,divisors\; i \cap divisors\; j\,)\,)\,)$$

14.4   Maximal common subsequence

Problem statement. Specify the maximal common subsequence function. The maximal common subsequence of two sequences is the longest subsequence that they share.

A sequence is a *subsequence* of another if it contains some of the elements of the latter, in the same order as they occur in the latter, and no other elements. For example, $\langle b, c, f \rangle$ and $\langle a, e \rangle$ are subsequences of $\langle a, b, c, d, e, e, f \rangle$, but $\langle b, d, c \rangle$ and $\langle a, b, g \rangle$ are not. Notice that we do not require that the entries in the subsequence be contiguous in the original sequence.

▷ *accompanying text*
    Giving well chosen examples, and counter-examples, can often aid intuitive understanding of a definition.

So s is a subsequence of t if there is a set of indices that can be extracted from t to give s.

$$
\begin{array}{|l}
\hline
[X]\\
\hline
\_\, subseqOf\, \_ : \mathrm{seq}\, X \leftrightarrow \mathrm{seq}\, X\\
\hline
\forall\, s, t : \mathrm{seq}\, X \bullet s\; subseqOf\; t \Leftrightarrow (\,\exists\, p : \mathbb{P}\,\mathbb{N}_1 \bullet s = p \upharpoonright t\,)\\
\hline
\end{array}
$$

▷ *sequence, extraction*
    $s = p \upharpoonright t$ gives a sequence that consists of the entries of t that appear at the indices given in p, and in the same order.

allSubseq is a function that gives all the subsequences of its argument.

$$
\begin{array}{l}
\boxed{[X]} \\[-2pt]
\hline
allSubseq : \operatorname{seq} X \longrightarrow \mathbb{P}(\operatorname{seq} X) \\
\hline
allSubseq = (\,\lambda\, s : \operatorname{seq} X \bullet \{\, t : \operatorname{seq} X \mid t\ subseqOf\ s \,\}\,)
\end{array}
$$

The common subsequences of two sequences are

$$
\begin{array}{l}
\boxed{[X]} \\[-2pt]
\hline
commonSubseq : \operatorname{seq} X \times \operatorname{seq} X \longrightarrow \mathbb{P}(\operatorname{seq} X) \\
\hline
commonSubseq = (\,\lambda\, s, t : \operatorname{seq} X \bullet allSubseq\ s \cap allSubseq\ t\,)
\end{array}
$$

The maximum common subsequences of two sequences are the longest subsequences they have in common; there may be none, there may be more than one.

$$
\begin{array}{l}
\boxed{[X]} \\[-2pt]
\hline
maxCommonSubseq : \operatorname{seq} X \times \operatorname{seq} X \longrightarrow \mathbb{P}(\operatorname{seq} X) \\
\hline
maxCommonSubseq = (\,\lambda\, s, t : \operatorname{seq} X \bullet \\
\qquad \{\, x : commonSubseq(s, t) \mid \\
\qquad\qquad (\forall\, y : commonSubseq(s, t) \bullet \#x \ge \#y\,)\,\}\,)
\end{array}
$$

$\triangleright$ *implicit definition*
Just like the *gcd* example, this is an implicit definition. Again, it gives no clue as to how to implement it (constructing two sets of all the possible subsequences, forming their intersection, then picking out the longest sequences is unlikely to be acceptable). It is unlikely that any algorithmic specification would be as clear or understandable.

$\triangleright$ *cardinality*
A sequence is a set of pairs, the first element of each pair corresponding to the sequence index, so $\#s$ is the length of the sequence s.

$\triangleright$ *quantifier, scope*
The $\bullet$ in the set comprehension above belongs to the quantifier $\forall\, y$, not to the set comprehension. The scope of quantifier is as far as it can be. In order to reduce possible confusion we have added redundant parentheses.

14.5   Concluding remarks

Abstraction in data and operation specification is different from programming. For specification we are often concerned with specifying what does not change about a state. We use invariants to describe properties and do not concern ourselves with the details of how things change. In many programming languages we are concerned how things change, and we concentrate on making those changes happen.

Abstraction in specifications is a good thing, but there is a balance to be struck. You need to consider the following questions.

What do you really *need* to say? There is often a better, more abstract, specification.

Who is to use the specification? There is no point in being so abstract and
succinct that the specification becomes too difficult to understand. For example, will your readers understand that the expression ran(_ .. _) provides
sets of contiguous numbers?

What are you going to *do* with your specification? It could be hard to carry
out many proofs on the definition of *censor* that we have given; for example,
how would you set about showing that the definition is not loose?

Chapter 15

Sets or Functions?

In which we discuss two different modelling styles.

15.1 Students who do exercises

[Wordsworth 1992, Chapter 2] describes a method for developing and refining Z specifications, using the classic example known as 'Students who do exercises', from [Jones 1980].

> **Problem statement.** Keep track of students enrolled in a class, and which of them have completed the exercises. New students may enrol, unless the class is full. They are assumed not to have done the exercises. Students may leave the class at any time; when they do, those who have completed the exercises receive a certificate.

Wordsworth keeps the model simple, because he wishes to discuss refinement; but is it the best way of *specifying* the problem? In this section, we describe both the way it was specified by Wordsworth (hereinafter referred to as the 'two sets model'), and an alternative model (the 'function model') that could be more resilient to changing requirements.

15.2 The 'two sets model'

The state of the *Class* is modelled as two sets of students, those members who have enrolled, and a subset of them who have done the exercises. The size of the class is constrained to be no greater than *size*.

[*STUDENT*]

$$size : \mathbb{N}$$

─── *Class* ──────────────────────────────
$member, done : \mathbb{F}\,STUDENT$
────────────
$\#member \leq size$
$done \subseteq member$
──

▷ *finite sets*
We have changed $\mathbb{P}\,STUDENT$ in the original to $\mathbb{F}\,STUDENT$ here, to ensure that application of the cardinality operator $\#$ is valid.

The initial state of the *Class* is empty.

$$InitClass \;\hat{=}\; [\,Class' \mid member' = \varnothing\,]$$

We describe three partial operations below, considering only the successful cases.

A new student is enrolled in the class, but not put in the set of students who have done the exercises.

─── *EnrolOK* ──────────────────────────────
$\Delta Class$
$s? : STUDENT$
────────────
$s? \notin member$
$\#member < size$
$member' = member \cup \{s?\}$
$done' = done$
──

An existing student completes the exercises and is moved into the *done* set.

─── *CompleteOK* ──────────────────────────────
$\Delta Class$
$s? : STUDENT$
────────────
$s? \in member \setminus done$
$member' = member$
$done' = done \cup \{s?\}$
──

▷ *set difference*
The expression $s? \in member \setminus done$ is a shorter way of saying

$$s? \in member$$
$$\wedge\; s? \notin done$$

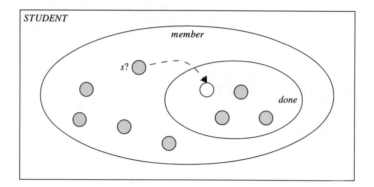

Figure 15.1 The *CompleteOK* operation in the two sets model.

The *CompleteOK* operation in the two sets model may be visualised as in figure 15.1. An existing student who has completed the exercises leaves the class.

$$
\begin{array}{l}
\underline{\quad LeaveCert\ }\underline{\hspace{6cm}} \\
\Delta Class \\
s? : STUDENT \\
\hline
s? \in done \\
member' = member \setminus \{s?\} \\
done' = done \setminus \{s?\} \\
\end{array}
$$

15.3   The 'function model'

Rather than using two sets as above, we instead model the system as a function from *STUDENT* to *STATUS*.

$[STUDENT]$

$STATUS ::= done \mid notDone$

▷ free type, enumerated
The enumerated free type definition of *STATUS* gives us that *done* and *notDone* are its only elements and that they are distinct.

$size : \mathbb{N}$

```
┌─ Class ─────────────────────────────────────────────────────┐
│  member : STUDENT ⇸ STATUS                                   │
│─────────────────────────────────────────────────────────────│
│  #member ≤ size                                              │
└─────────────────────────────────────────────────────────────┘
```

▷ *finite function*
  We use a finite function to ensure that we can validly apply the cardinality operator #.
▷ *cardinality*
  Taking the cardinality of the function *member* gives the number of (student, status) pairs.
  Since *member* is a function, each student appears in only one pair, and so we get the
  number of students, as required. So

$$f : X ⇸ Y ⊢ \#f = \#(\mathrm{dom}\, f)$$

As before, the initial state of the class is empty.

$$InitClass ≙ [\, Class' \mid member' = ∅\,]$$

▷ *function*
  Note that here, *member'* is the empty function, which is an empty set.

The same three operations are specified again below.

```
┌─ EnrolOK ───────────────────────────────────────────────────┐
│  ΔClass                                                      │
│  s? : STUDENT                                                │
│─────────────────────────────────────────────────────────────│
│  s? ∉ dom member                                            │
│  member' = member ∪ {s? ↦ notDone}                          │
└─────────────────────────────────────────────────────────────┘
```

▷ *proof obligation*
  We are following our house style of using ∪ when extending a function's domain (section
  8.4.2). We must demonstrate that it preserves functionality.

Since *s?* is not in the domain of *member*, to unite *member* with a singleton function
that involves *s?* as its domain element does not affect functionality.

```
┌─ CompleteOK ────────────────────────────────────────────────┐
│  ΔClass                                                      │
│  s? : STUDENT                                                │
│─────────────────────────────────────────────────────────────│
│  s? ∈ dom member                                            │
│  member s? = notDone                                        │
│  member' = member ⊕ {s? ↦ done}                            │
└─────────────────────────────────────────────────────────────┘
```

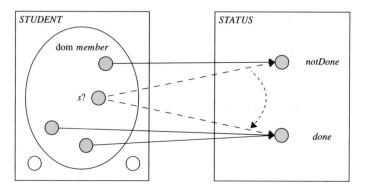

Figure 15.2 The *CompleteOK* operation in the function model.

    LeaveCert _____

    $\Delta\,Class$

    $s? : STUDENT$

    ————————————————————————

    $s? \in \mathrm{dom}\ member$

    $member\ s? = done$

    $member' = \{s?\} \lhd member$

▷ *anti-restriction, domain*

    The expression $member' = \{s?\} \lhd member$ means that $member'$ is the same as $member$
except that any pair involving $s?$ as the first entry has been removed.

The *CompleteOK* operation in the function model may be visualised as in figure 15.2.

15.4   Changing the specification

The specification using the two sets model looks simpler, since there are no overrides or domain anti-restrictions, for example. So what is the advantage of the function model?

Consider having to modify the original specification to include other possible statuses, for example, *exempt* and *failed*, with new schemas for adding students who have been exempted from the exercises, or who have done the exercises but got them wrong.

The function model is easier to modify, since just the free type *STATUS* needs to be extended, and new schemas for the extra operations written. The existing schemas do not have to be changed (except possibly their names, *EnrolOK* to *EnrolNonExemptOK*, for example). But the two sets model would need new (unchanging) sets added to each of the existing schemas.

For this simple example the two sets model is fine, and the function model is overkill. Provided there are just a few sets a 'few sets model' is appropriate, but the possibility that the specification might have to be extended should be borne in mind. If it does the function model would be more appropriate.

Chapter 16

Sets, Quantifiers, or Toolkit?

In which the differences between using explicit set comprehensions, or quantifiers, or sample toolkit operators are examined.

16.1 First n primes

Problem statement. Specify a sequence containing the first n prime numbers, in order.

A prime number is a number that is not composite. So to specify prime numbers, we first specify composite numbers, those that have two or more non-trivial factors (factors not equal to 1 or to the number itself). Note that the number 1 is considered to be neither prime nor composite, so we consider the integers from 2 onwards.

$$\mathbb{N}_2 == \mathbb{N} \setminus \{0, 1\}$$

16.1.1 Using set comprehension

$$composite == \{ i, j : \mathbb{N}_2 \bullet i * j \}$$
$$prime == \mathbb{N}_2 \setminus composite$$

▷ *set comprehension*
Note how we use the constructing term in the set comprehension to build an explicitly composite number.
▷ *abstraction*
The definition of *prime* given here is an example of an abstract specification. It says nothing about how to calculate a prime (if you tested every number to see if it fell into this set it would be hopelessly inefficient). However, it says exactly what is meant by a prime number in a simple way that is easy to understand.

We want an increasing sequence of primes, and we want to ensure that we have consecutive primes.

> $consecutivePrimes ==$
>> $\{\, s : sincr \mid \text{ran } s \subseteq prime \wedge (\forall p : prime \mid p \leq last\ s \bullet p \in \text{ran } s\,)\,\}$

> ▷ *toolkit*
> *sincr* is the set of all strictly increasing sequences of positive numbers, defined in our extension to the sample toolkit, appendix A.7.

By the declaration of p and by the predicate part ran $p \subseteq prime$ we have that p is a strictly increasing sequence of primes. The quantified predicate ensures that we do indeed have an initial sequence of primes.

The required sequence of the first n primes is given by that element of the set of *consecutivePrimes* that has length n.

> $firstnPrimes : \mathbb{N} \longrightarrow consecutivePrimes$
> ---
> $\forall n : \mathbb{N};\ p : consecutivePrimes \mid \#p = n \bullet$
> $firstnPrimes\ n = p$

> ▷ *abstraction*
> We favour this style of solution where we state only what the requirements of the problem are. We have not thought about an algorithm for solving it. Such an algorithm might involve working out how to spot the next prime from any given number. The function *nextPrime* takes an integer and returns the smallest prime number bigger than that integer.

> $nextPrime : \mathbb{Z} \longrightarrow prime$
> ---
> $\forall n : \mathbb{Z};\ p : prime \mid p > n \wedge n+1 \mathinner{\ldotp\ldotp} p - 1 \subseteq composite \bullet$
> $nextPrime\ n = p$

Then *nextPrime* could be used in an alternative definition of *consecutivePrimes*.

> $consecutivePrimes_1 ==$
>> $\{\, s : \text{seq}\ prime \mid head\ s = 2$
>> $\wedge\ (\forall i : 1 \mathinner{\ldotp\ldotp} (\#s - 1) \bullet s(i+1) = nextPrime(s\ i)\,)\,\}$

We find the more abstract specification more readable and more understandable.

16.1.2   Using quantifiers

An alternative definition of prime numbers using a universal quantifier instead of a set comprehension is

> $prime_1 : \mathbb{P}\,\mathbb{N}$
> ---
> $\forall p : \mathbb{N} \bullet p \in prime_1 \Leftrightarrow (\forall x, y : 2 \mathinner{\ldotp\ldotp} (p - 1) \bullet x * y \neq p\,)$

This 'negative style' expression is not as straightforward to read as the set version.

16.1.3   Using the toolkit

Another way to specify composite numbers, but without introducing intermediate variables, is [Gravell 1991]

$$composite_1 == (\_ * \_)(\!(\mathbb{N}_2 \times \mathbb{N}_2)\!)$$

▷ *relation, infix*
Where a relation is declared to be infix, the underscores indicate where parameters are substituted. These underscores become part of the name of the relation and must be given when the relation is referred to by name, as here.
▷ *relational image*
The relational image $\_(\!(\_)\!)$ here takes the multiplication operator, which takes a pair of numbers and gives their product, and returns an operator that takes a *set* of pairs and gives the set of their products. We apply this extended operator to the set of all pairs of numbers greater than 1, and hence get a set of composite numbers.

16.2   Finding the root

Problem statement. Specify the natural number square root. For any natural number this is the integer part (or 'floor') of the corresponding positive real number square root. For example, every number in $9 .. 15$ maps to 3.

In order to work out an appropriate specification of natural number square root, we first need a little informal discussion, using the syntax of 'ordinary' mathematics rather than Z.

The definition of floor r, written $\lfloor r \rfloor$, where r is a real number, is (see Chapter 25)

$$r - 1 < \lfloor r \rfloor \leq r$$

If we put $r = \sqrt{x}$ and $y = \lfloor \sqrt{x} \rfloor$, where $\sqrt{x}$ is the positive real number square root of x (so y is the natural number square root of x), we get

$$\sqrt{x} - 1 < y \leq \sqrt{x}$$

Consider just the right hand inequality, and square (which maintains the inequality, since we are dealing with positive numbers), to get

$$y^2 \leq x$$

Now, consider just the left hand inequality, add one and square, to get

$$x < (y + 1)^2$$

Hence

$$y^2 \leq x < (y + 1)^2$$

16.2.1   Using set comprehension

We convert the above expression into Z to get the definition of natural number square root in terms of a set comprehension:

$$
\begin{array}{|l}
\hline
root : \mathbb{N} \longrightarrow \mathbb{N} \\
\hline
root = \{\, x, y : \mathbb{N} \mid y * y \leq x < (y + 1) * (y + 1) \,\} \\
\end{array}
$$

▷ *accompanying text*
Notice how the accompanying text uses 'plain' mathematics to justify the Z specification of *root*. Its use has an additional advantage; it is clear from the construction that the resulting set comprehension does indeed describe a total function, a fact that would not be obvious if the answer had been stated in isolation.

▷ *transitive relation*
The expression

$$ y * y \leq x < (y + 1) * (y + 1) $$

is an abbreviation for

$$ y * y \leq x \wedge x < (y + 1) * (y + 1) $$

The chain of relations may be used as an abbreviation here because $\leq$ and $<$ are transitive. This can be done with relations that are not transitive, for instance $x \neq y \neq z$ is an abbreviation for $x \neq y \wedge y \neq z$ but it may lead to confusion since it does not give that $x \neq z$.

▷ *set comprehension*
Note that no constructing term, to define the 'shape' of the elements of the set, is necessary in the above set comprehension for *root*. In this case the elements are the same as the default tuple of the declaration. The abbreviated form is equivalent to

$$ root = \{\, x, y : \mathbb{N} \mid y * y \leq x < (y + 1) * (y + 1) \bullet (x, y) \,\} $$

▷ *set comprehension*
A set comprehension can use a schema in the declaration part. Unless the schema has only one variable, the constructing term in the set comprehension may need to be given. If the term is omitted, we get the schema binding, which may not be what is required. If we have a schema that provides the variables x and y, for example

$$ NumberInput \,\widehat{=}\, [\, x, y : \mathbb{N} \,] $$

then it could be used to define root, thus

$$
\begin{array}{|l}
\hline
root_1 : \mathbb{N} \longrightarrow \mathbb{N} \\
\hline
root_1 = \{\, NumberInput \mid y * y \leq x < (y + 1) * (y + 1) \bullet x \mapsto y \,\} \\
\end{array}
$$

Here we must provide the term, otherwise the set would be composed of schema bindings, and hence would not be the same type as the declaration.

16.2.2   Using quantifiers

We can also describe *root* using quantification.

$$
\begin{array}{|l}
\hline
root_2 : \mathbb{N} \longrightarrow \mathbb{N} \\
\hline
\forall x, y : \mathbb{N} \bullet root_2\, x = y \Leftrightarrow y * y \leq x < (y + 1) * (y + 1) \\
\end{array}
$$

16.3   Safe and secure

Problem statement. Describe the state of a secure file system in which each user and each file has a security classification. Read access to files is allowed for users whose security classification is at least as high as the file in question.

We need to compare levels of security, so it makes sense to model these using natural numbers. $\mathbb{N}$ also provides us with a strictly ordered set, which is useful when we wish to distinguish levels of security.

$$class == \mathbb{N}$$

In order to describe the secure file system state we need to introduce given sets for users and files.

$$[USER, FILE]$$

16.3.1   Using set comprehension

The state description is

$\begin{array}{l} \underline{\quad SecureState \underline{}} \\ userClass : USER \nrightarrow class \\ fileClass : FILE \nrightarrow class \\ mayRead : USER \leftrightarrow FILE \\ \underline{} \\ mayRead = \{\, u : \operatorname{dom} userClass\,;\, f : \operatorname{dom} fileClass \mid \\ \qquad\qquad userClass\, u \ge fileClass\, f \,\} \\ \underline{} \end{array}$

16.3.2   Using quantifiers

An alternative form of the predicate, using quantifiers, is

$$\forall u : USER;\, f : FILE \bullet u \mapsto f \in mayRead \Leftrightarrow$$
$$u \in \operatorname{dom} userClass \wedge f \in \operatorname{dom} fileClass \wedge userClass\, u \ge fileClass\, f$$

▷ quantifier, universal
Note that the following are incorrect

$$\forall u : USER;\, f : FILE \mid u \in \operatorname{dom} userClass \wedge f \in \operatorname{dom} fileClass \bullet$$
$$u \mapsto f \in mayRead_X \Leftrightarrow userClass\, u \ge fileClass\, f$$

$$\forall u : \operatorname{dom} userClass\,;\, f : \operatorname{dom} fileClass \bullet$$
$$u \mapsto f \in mayRead_X \Leftrightarrow userClass\, u \ge fileClass\, f$$

because they do not stop a (u, f) pair being in $mayRead$ if the components are not in the domains of $userClass$ or $fileClass$ (recall that $\forall D \mid P \bullet T$ is equivalent to $\forall D \bullet P \Rightarrow T$).

16.3.3   Using the toolkit

A form of the predicate that uses sample toolkit operators is

$$mayRead = userClass \mathbin{\raise.5ex\hbox{$\scriptstyle\circ$}}(\_ \geq \_) \mathbin{\raise.5ex\hbox{$\scriptstyle\circ$}} fileClass^{\sim}$$

This rather compact form may require a little explanation. Consider the first part of the composition (given a name that anticipates the following explanation)

$$mayAccessClass = userClass \mathbin{\raise.5ex\hbox{$\scriptstyle\circ$}}(\_ \geq \_)$$

Substituting the definition of relational composition $\mathbin{\raise.5ex\hbox{$\scriptstyle\circ$}}$ from [Spivey 1992, page 97], and changing those names to something more meaningful, gives

$$mayAccessClass =$$
$$\{\, u : USER;\ c : class;\ z : \mathbb{Z} \mid u\ \underline{userClass}\ c \wedge c \geq z \bullet u \mapsto z \,\}$$

▷ *relation, infix*
  userClass has been underlined here to show its use as an infix relation in this expression.

Hence *mayAccessClass* is a relation between users and all the classes less than or equal to their own class.
  Now compose this with *fileClass*$^{\sim}$, and substitute the definition of $\mathbin{\raise.5ex\hbox{$\scriptstyle\circ$}}$ again

$$mayAccessClass \mathbin{\raise.5ex\hbox{$\scriptstyle\circ$}} fileClass^{\sim}$$
$$= \{\, u : USER;\ c : class;\ f : FILE \mid$$
$$\qquad u\ \underline{mayAccessClass}\ c \wedge c \mapsto f \in fileClass^{\sim} \bullet u \mapsto f \,\}$$
$$= \{\, u : USER;\ c : class;\ f : FILE \mid$$
$$\qquad u\ \underline{mayAccessClass}\ c \wedge f\ \underline{fileClass}\ c \bullet u \mapsto f \,\}$$

Hence this is a relation between users and all the files with a class less than or equal to that of the user, or, in other words, a relation between users and the files they *mayRead*.

16.4   Concluding remarks

We have given various examples using set comprehension, quantifiers, and sample toolkit operators, to define various sets and functions.
  Quantified expressions tend to be a 'translation' of an algorithmic way of thinking, as some sort of *test* for set membership: 'every x in the set has such-and-such a property'. They tend to lead to a clumsy definition that is difficult to read, and difficult to manipulate further.
  Definitions using set comprehensions tend to be more direct, a specification of the set as a whole: 'the set of xs is …'. These definitions tend to be straightforward to read and understand, but may be difficult to manipulate (although not as difficult as quantified expressions).

Using sample toolkit operators can provide compact definitions. These are easier to manipulate since they are direct and various laws are provided, but they can be hard to read and understand.

We recommend using the set comprehension style for most specification work; the toolkit style is appropriate where parts of the specification need to be manipulated (for example, to perform proofs), or where the audience is mathematically sophisticated.

Chapter 17

Sequences are Functions are Relations are Sets

In which we investigate the use and power of operations on sets, relations, functions, and sequences.

17.1 Introduction

A *function*, as defined as part of the sample toolkit, is a *relation* with some additional, constraining predicates to ensure that each element in the domain is related to at most one element in the range. This means that a function is 'really' a relation, and all manipulations that we can do on relations we can also do on functions. We can switch between regarding a function as a function, as a relation or as a set.

The same is true of relations and sets: relations are sets of pairs, and so set operations may be applied to relations. Sequences are special functions (they are finite, and have as their domain an initial portion of the natural numbers), and so function operations, and indeed relation and set operations, can all be applied to sequences.

Such 'distortion' of the meaning of structures can be confusing if not explained, but used correctly, it can lead to clear specifications. Care must be taken when regarding the more general structures as more specific. For example, the set union of two functions need not satisfy the constraints of being a function itself. If it is to be used as a function, a proof obligation may need to be discharged.

This chapter explores the following

- a *mail system*, which shows the benefits of sequences being functions being relations being sets

- a *video encyclopaedia*, which explores the power of relations

179

- *a telephone directory*, which examines the various kinds of functions and illustrates their use
- *the different kinds of function*, which shows how the various functions are related to one another.

17.2   A mail system with aliases

Consider the specification of an electronic mail system, in which mail is sent to a *name*, and each name is associated with a full e-mail *address*. We are not, initially, concerned with the structure of the names or addresses, so we introduce them as given sets.

$$[NAME, ADDRESS]$$

Some names are understood by the system, and have associated addresses. We therefore need a partial function mapping *NAME*s to *ADDRESS*es. It is a function, *address* : $NAME \nrightarrow ADDRESS$, because each name has only one address. We cannot be more specific, such as requiring the function to be injective, because we don't yet know whether we may want multiple names for the same address. We see below that we do need just this.

17.2.1   A simple mail system

We want to allow users to define *aliases*, so that users may address a person or set of persons by a chosen symbolic name. The users use the same kind of names as the system, and so these aliases can be described as a relation on the set *NAME*: an alias is related to all those names (set of persons) for which it acts as an alias. We do not permit an alias to overwrite user names.

We would like to be able to alter the addresses related to each name, and the aliases, so we define a schema describing the current state of the system.

Mail1
$address : NAME \nrightarrow ADDRESS$
$alias : NAME \leftrightarrow NAME$

disjoint $\langle$dom *address*, dom *alias*$\rangle$
ran *alias* $\subseteq$ dom *address*

The disjointness condition ensures that no user names are used also as aliases. The other condition, that ran *alias* $\subseteq$ dom *address*, ensures that the only aliases are those with valid user names. These relations are summarised by example in figure 17.1.

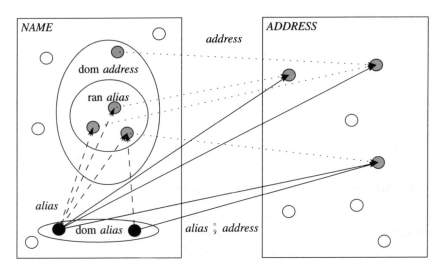

Figure 17.1 An example *Mail* system. The dashed lines represent the *alias* relation; the dotted lines represent the *address* function; the solid lines represent *alias* ⨾ *address*.

From the user-defined aliases and the system-defined mapping between names and addresses, we can generate a relation between names and their ultimate addresses. Informally, we first map a name to the name of which it is an alias (if it has one), and then map this name to its address. To do this, we must regard the partial function *address* : *NAME* ⇸ *ADDRESS* as a *relation*, so that relational composition can be used to combine it with the relation *alias* above.

With the composition *alias* ⨾ *address* we obtain a relation from only alias names to addresses; the direct mapping of names to addresses is excluded. To include this as part of the combined relation we now treat both the composed relation above and the partial function *address* as sets, and form their set union (*alias* ⨾ *address*) ∪ *address*.

This resulting set can, of course, be regarded as a relation, as it is a set of pairs. It could be added as a (derived) component of the mail system

---
Mail2
  Mail1

  aliasedAddress : *NAME* ⟷ *ADDRESS*
  ---
  aliasedAddress = (*alias* ⨾ *address*) ∪ *address*

Although *aliasedAddress* is in general a relation, if we know that it relates exactly one address to a certain name (which it does not in figure 17.1), we can apply it as a function to this name. That is, *aliasedAddress name* is well-defined as function application in precisely those cases where we can prove there is a unique address related to each *name*, that is, if we can prove

$$Mail2 \vdash (\forall n : NAME;\; a_1, a_2 : ADDRESS \mid$$
$$\{n \mapsto a_1, n \mapsto a_2\} \subseteq aliasedAddress \bullet a_1 = a_2)$$

Using the definition of the partial functions, this condition for functionality can be written more concisely.

$$Mail2 \vdash aliasedAddress \in (NAME \nrightarrow ADDRESS)$$

17.2.2   Adding ordering to the mail system

Consider now a mail system with such a notion of aliasing, in which names are to be arranged in some order, maybe alphabetical. An existing aliasing structure is to be used. How would we go about describing the design?

One possibility, which we investigate here, is to use a number as an alias for each name, and to choose the number to represent the position of the name in the ordering.

This requires numbers to be part of names, so we must give some structure to our given set. Names are either positive integers (aliases) or textual ('true' names)

$$[TEXT]$$
$$NAME ::= number \langle\!\langle \mathbb{N}_1 \rangle\!\rangle \mid text \langle\!\langle TEXT \rangle\!\rangle$$

▷ *definition*
  We are 'redefining' *NAME* here. This is not allowed in Z; we are doing this for pedagogical
  reasons.

Next, we must ensure that every 'real' name (that is, in the domain of *address*) is aliased uniquely by a number, and each number aliases no more than one name, (see figure 17.2 for an example). We also want the numbers used to be those running sequentially from 1. These can be added as constraints in the system state schema, which we do below.

Mail3

Mail1

$\forall n : \mathbb{N}_1 \mid number\, n \in \mathrm{dom}\, alias \bullet$
  $\exists_1 t : TEXT \bullet (number\, n)\ \underline{alias}\ (text\, t)$
$\forall t : TEXT \mid text\, t \in \mathrm{ran}\, alias \bullet$
  $\exists_1 n : \mathbb{N}_1 \bullet (number\, n)\ \underline{alias}\ (text\, t)$
$\#(\mathrm{dom}(number \,\mathbin{\fatsemi}\, alias)) = max(\mathrm{dom}(number \,\mathbin{\fatsemi}\, alias))$

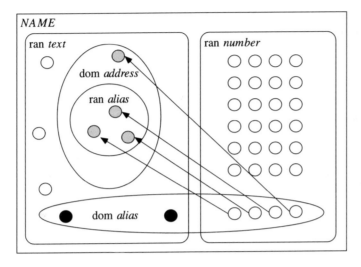

Figure 17.2 An example *Mail3* system.

▷ *relation, infix*
Underlining *alias* allows it to be used in an infix manner. If it had been declared infix, then whenever it is used as an object in its own right, which is most of the time, it would have to be written as (_ *alias* _).

▷ *relational composition*
The expression *number* ⨾ *alias* forms the composition of these two relations to form a new relation in which the integers in the domain of *number* are related to the *NAME*s in the range of *alias*.

alias is still a general relation, in that any name may be aliased to any number of other names. But if we restrict our attention to applying *alias* only to numbers, it becomes a function—imposing functionhood is exactly the restriction we have applied in the complicated predicate above. Indeed, it is an injection. Therefore, whenever $n \in$ dom *number*, we can be sure that *alias*(*number n*) is a well-defined function application, and yields a *NAME*.

Thus the relational composition of *number* and *alias* turns out to be an injective function. We can add this as a derived component to the Mail schema and call it *nameOrder*.

_____ *Mail4* _____
| *Mail3*
| *nameOrder* : $\mathbb{N} \rightarrowtail NAME$
|_____
| *nameOrder* = *number* ⨾ *alias*
|_____

Looking in more detail, *nameOrder* is an injection from a subset of the natural numbers to *NAME*. Recall that this subset of the natural numbers is an interval from 1 to some number. Such a function thus satisfies the requirements for being an *injective sequence*. So we can restate *Mail4* as

$$
\begin{array}{|l}
\_\_Mail4_____ \\
\quad Mail3 \\
\quad nameOrder : \text{iseq } NAME \\
\quad \overline{\qquad\qquad\qquad\qquad\qquad\qquad\qquad} \\
\quad nameOrder = number \,\mathbin{\raise1pt\hbox{$\scriptstyle;$}} alias
\end{array}
$$

nameOrder is therefore a sequence of names, where each name occurs only once. By imposing certain constraints upon *nameOrder* we can force it to be the ordering we wanted.

17.3   A video encyclopaedia

In this section we continue looking at the video specification begun in Chapter 11, in order to illustrate the use of relations.

We extend the definition of a video to include interesting information about it, and we define an encyclopaedia of all those films that have been released on video. The encyclopaedia contains lots of interesting facts extracted from the details about individual videos, and also facts relating different videos.

17.3.1   Information for film buffs

The way that *Video* is defined does not allow us to distinguish between remakes of the same story. For example, *1984* was originally filmed in black and white in 1955, and then remade in 1984 itself with John Hurt as Winston Smith.

Similarly we cannot separate films with different plots but the same title. For example, as well as Hitchcock's *Spellbound* about an amnesiac posing as Dr. Edwards the new head of a mental institution, there is an earlier film directed by John Harlow. In this film a woman who has died is raised from the dead by a medium, which has a detrimental effect on her fiancé.

Film buffs may want to have access to this kind of information. They are likely to wish for details such as director, leading players, year of production and synopsis, academy award nominations and prizes, film company, producer, and interesting facts about the films.

Interesting facts include anecdotes such as when Clark Gable was found not to be wearing an undervest in *It Happened One Night* such garments went out of fashion almost instantly, and the men's underwear industry went into considerable decline. Another interesting fact is that the producers of *The Wizard of Oz* wanted to cut the song *Over the Rainbow* on the grounds that it was too sentimental. They were persuaded to let it stay, and the song received an Oscar [Norman 1980].

We introduce given sets to describe all this extra information

[*COMPANY*, *DIRECTOR*, *FACT*, *PLAYER*, *PRODUCER*, *SYNOPSIS*]

$ACADEMY ::= bestPicture \mid originalStory \mid bestDirector \mid \ldots$

▷ *free type*
In a free type (and indeed in any other definition) items must be supplied, the use of the ellipsis is not legal Z. We have allowed ourselves a little licence in this example.

We extend the definition of *Video* to hold the extra information:

```
┌─ InfoVideo ──────────────────────────────
│ Video
│ award, nomination : 𝔽 ACADEMY
│ cast : 𝔽 PLAYER
│ company : COMPANY
│ director : DIRECTOR
│ facts : 𝔽 FACT
│ producer : PRODUCER
│ released : DATE
│ synopsis : SYNOPSIS
└──────────────────────────────────────────
```

Not every film has a fact of interest, not even to film buffs. Hence we have a *set* of *FACT*s, and allow it to be empty. This also allows for very interesting films, about which there may be several anecdotes. For example, in *Casablanca* the original actor chosen to play Rick was Ronald Reagan; the dramatic tension of the film was partly because the actors didn't know the ending themselves and were given their scripts on a daily basis.

The encyclopaedia consists of a set of the released videos; the interesting facts are represented as subsets of these videos, and relationships between videos.

17.3.2 Many awards

One interesting subset of released videos identifies those films that have scooped many academy awards.

```
┌─ Encyclopaedia ──────────────────────────
│ release : ℙ InfoVideo
│ manyAwards : ℙ InfoVideo
│ ...
├──────────────────────────────────────────
│ manyAwards = { v : release | #v.award > 1 }
│ ...
└──────────────────────────────────────────
```

▷ *definition*
The dots are being used to indicate that the full encyclopaedia has more interesting sets of videos defined.
▷ *schema in set comprehension*
We are declaring v as a schema type in this set comprehension.

The film *It Happened One Night* is a member of *manyAwards*, indeed it was the first film to gather the five most important Oscars [Shipman 1982]. This would also be an interesting fact for the film along with the information that Clark Gable appeared in the film because he was sent to the director, Frank Capra, as a punishment by MGM as he had turned down a rôle opposite his erstwhile lover Joan Crawford. He then won his only Oscar from it [Norman 1980].

17.3.3   Remakes

An item of interest as far as films are concerned is remakes. We can set up a relation to describe which films have been made into other films. We also set up a relation to describe films that are based on other stories.

These relations are included in the encyclopaedia (where *before* is a suitably defined relation on *DATE*).

Encyclopaedia
release : $\mathbb{P}$ *InfoVideo*

$\dots$

remadeAs, basedOn : *InfoVideo* $\longleftrightarrow$ *InfoVideo*

$\dots$

$\forall\, v_1, v_2 : release\ |$
$\qquad v_1 \mapsto v_2 \in remadeAs \lor v_2 \mapsto v_1 \in basedOn \bullet$
$\qquad v_1.released\ \underline{before}\ v_2.released$

The Philadelphia Story was subsequently remade as the musical *High Society*. Whereas the first version was reviewed in the *Hollywood Reporter* as '*There are just not enough superlatives sufficiently to appreciate this show*', the second, which included songs such as *Who wants to be a millionaire*, fell rather flat. Nonetheless, together they provide an element of *remadeAs*. Cary Grant donated his salary from *The Philadelphia Story* to war relief, providing an interesting fact for the film [Halliwell 1985].

It Happened One Night was remade as *You Can't Run Away From It*, thus the encyclopaedia could include it in the set

   dom *remadeAs* $\cap$ *manyAwards*

17.3.4   Films with the same title

The encyclopaedia identifies films with the same title.

```
┌─ Encyclopaedia ─────────────────────────────────────
│  release : ℙ InfoVideo
│
│  . . .
│
│  sameTitle : InfoVideo ⟷ InfoVideo
├─────────────────────────────────────────────────────
│  . . .
│
│  sameTitle = { v₁, v₂ : release | v₁.title = v₂.title ∧ v₁ ≠ v₂ }
```

▷ *relation, binary*
   sameTitle is defined as a set of pairs, a binary relation is nothing more than that.
▷ *identity relation*
   sameTitle could also be defined by

$$sameTitle = \{\ v_1, v_2 : release \mid v_1.title = v_2.title\ \} \setminus \text{id } InfoVideo$$

Subtracting the identity relation has the same effect as insisting that $v_1 \neq v_2$ in the original definition.

Forbidden is a title given to three films, all with different stories. In 1931 the heroine marries someone else to protect the DA she really loves; in 1949 a husband tries to poison his wife because he loves someone else; in 1953 a detective falls for the woman a mobster has hired him to kill.

Films that have the same title but are different stories may be described by the relation *differentStory*:

```
┌─ Encyclopaedia ─────────────────────────────────────
│  release : ℙ InfoVideo
│
│  . . .
│
│  differentStory : InfoVideo ⟷ InfoVideo
├─────────────────────────────────────────────────────
│  . . .
│
│  differentStory = sameTitle \ remadeAs
```

Forbidden would be in the set

$$\text{dom}(differentStory^2 \setminus \text{id } InfoVideo)$$

▷ *relational iteration*
   the iteration *differentStory²* has the same meaning as applying the relation *differentStory* twice: *differentStory ⨾ differentStory*.
▷ *identity relation*
   The identity relation is subtracted here in order to exclude pairs in which films are related to themselves, which could happen when we iterate *differentStory*.

Films such as *The Maltese Falcon*, which has a well regarded original made in 1931 and a highly acclaimed remake made in 1941, would be in the relation

$$remadeAs \cap sameTitle$$

Incidentally, [Halliwell 1985] says of the latter film '...*shows the difference between excellence and brilliance; here every nuance is subtly stressed, and the cast is perfection*'—a review that we should all aim to receive for our Z specifications!

Cyrano de Bergerac has an American version made by Stanley Kramer and a French version starring Gerard Depardieu. And then there is *Roxanne*, a more modern and jokesome tale also starring a man who is nasally challenged, but at least in this version they all live happily ever after.

Since it has been remade and there is at least one film, *Roxanne*, that is based on it, *Cyrano de Bergerac* would be in the set *goodBasis*.

Encyclopaedia

$release : \mathbb{P}\ Info\,Video$

. . .

$goodBasis : \mathbb{P}\ Info\,Video$

. . .

$goodBasis = \text{dom}\ remadeAs \cap \text{ran}\ basedOn$

There are two films called *Heaven Can Wait*. The first is about an elderly playboy sent upstairs by Satan. The second is about a football player taken to heaven by accident, and is a remake of *Here Comes Mr. Jordan*. In that film the eponymous hero is a prizefighter and the film won the academy award for original story. There are many imitations of Mr. Jordan's exploits including *The Horn Blows at Midnight*, *Down to Earth* and *That's the Spirit*.

Heaven Can Wait would be in the set *popularTitleAndStory*.

Encyclopaedia

$release : \mathbb{P}\ Info\,Video$

. . .

$popularTitleAndStory : \mathbb{P}\ Info\,Video$

. . .

$popularTitleAndStory = \text{ran}\ differentStory \cap \text{ran}\ remadeAs$

▷ *range*
In general, $\text{ran}(A \cap B) \subseteq \text{ran}\ A \cap \text{ran}\ B$. So *PopularTitleAndStory* is a superset of $\text{ran}(differentStory \cap remadeAs)$. In this case, the latter set happens to be empty, as can be seen from the definition of *differentStory*, which explicitly subtracts the remakes. Informally it corresponds to the set of all those films that share the same title but are different stories, and are also remakes.

Since there are so many films loosely based on the story of Mr. Jordan, the film would be in the set *veryGoodBasis*.

```
┌─ Encyclopaedia ──────────────────────────────────────────────
│  release : ℙ Info Video
│
│  . . .
│  veryGoodBasis : ℙ Info Video
│  ────────────────────────────
│  . . .
│  veryGoodBasis = { v : goodBasis | #(basedOn ▷ {v}) > 1 }
└──────────────────────────────────────────────────────────────
```

▷ *restriction, range*
   The expression $(basedOn ▷ \{v\})$ gives us those elements of *basedOn* for which the second
   entry is v. So we are looking for films with more than one other film based on them.

More precisely, it would be in the set

$$\{\, v : veryGoodBasis \mid originalStory \in v.award \,\}$$

17.3.5   Different versions of the same story

Many films are based on older stories, rather than other films. We define a relation,
diffVersions, to describe this.

```
┌─ Encyclopaedia ──────────────────────────────────────────────
│  release : ℙ Info Video
│
│  . . .
│  diffVersions : Info Video ⟷ Info Video
│  ──────────────────────────────────────
│  . . .
│  disjoint ⟨diffVersions, id release⟩
└──────────────────────────────────────────────────────────────
```

There are three film versions of *Romeo and Juliet* and there is its modern translation as *West Side Story*. It could appear in the encyclopaedia in the set

$$\mathrm{dom}(diffVersions^2 \setminus \mathrm{id}\ Info Video) \cap \mathrm{ran}\ basedOn$$

17.4   A telephone directory

We describe a simple telephone directory system, based on the Storage Manager
from [Woodcock & Loomes 1988]. It maintains a record of users and their telephone
numbers. There is a fixed number of telephones available and the system has the
following requirements

1. a user may have more than one telephone number
2. a telephone number may be used by more than one person
3. some users might not have a telephone number
4. some telephone numbers may not be allocated.

At the abstract level we are not interested in the details of the users, thus we provide a given set.

$[USER]$

We use natural numbers to model telephone number. Note that only some are available in our system. To express the property that telephone numbers are drawn from a range of numbers we say

$\mid minNo, maxNo : \mathbb{N}$

$$telephone == minNo .. maxNo$$

▷ number range
The expression $minNo .. maxNo$ provides a set of numbers including all those that are at least $minNo$ and all those that are at most $maxNo$.

▷ thinking ahead
Using numbers to specify the telephones is, at this stage, overspecification. There is no requirement to use any numerical operator. Nonetheless it is reasonable to suppose that the client could require that only four digit numbers are allocated, or that desks in an office close to one another have similar numbers.

▷ axiomatic description
If we want to say nothing about telephone numbers other than that they are modelled as numbers, and there are finitely many of them, we would say

$\mid telephone : \mathbb{F}\,\mathbb{N}$

▷ abstraction
To express that all the telephone numbers are four digits then we would choose $minNo = 1000, maxNo = 9999$. This sort of detail would not normally be included in a top-level abstract specification.

Requirements 1, 2 and 3 tell us that there is a relationship between users and their telephone numbers and that this is potentially many–many (see figure 17.3). In Z this is written

$$directory : telephone \leftrightarrow USER$$

Some of the telephones might not be allocated (requirement 4). We describe the set of telephones not allocated by

$$free : \mathbb{P}\, telephone$$

▷ discussion
Why have we used $\mathbb{P}$ to declare $free$ when it is a subset of $telephone$ which is itself finite? We are sticking to our philosophy of declaring items as generally as possible, although here it makes no difference which particular power set is used since we have forced $telephone$ to be finite in order to take its cardinality.

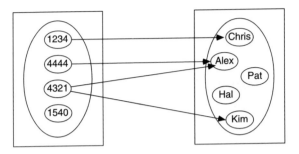

Figure 17.3 General relation between telephones and users.

The schema that describes the state of the telephone system is given by

$$
\begin{array}{l}
\underline{\hspace{0.3cm}\textit{TelephoneSystem}\hspace{5cm}} \\
\textit{directory} : \textit{telephone} \leftrightarrow \textit{USER} \\
\textit{free} : \mathbb{P}\,\textit{telephone} \\
\overline{\hspace{3.5cm}} \\
\textit{free} = \textit{telephone} \setminus (\mathrm{dom}\ \textit{directory})
\end{array}
$$

▷ *schema invariant*
The predicate here is common sense as the telephones that are free are those that have not been allocated. This is the invariant of *TelephoneSystem* and only those combinations of *free* and *directory* that obey this rule provide possible examples of *TelephoneSystem*.

17.4.1   Adding constraints

If we additionally impose a constraint on our telephone system that no-one shares telephones (see figure 17.4) then we could declare the system as

$$
\begin{array}{l}
\underline{\hspace{0.3cm}\textit{NoSharingTS}\hspace{5cm}} \\
\textit{TelephoneSystem} \\
\overline{\hspace{3.5cm}} \\
\textit{directory} \in \textit{telephone} \nrightarrow \textit{USER}
\end{array}
$$

▷ *partial function*
By the predicate *directory* $\in$ *telephone* $\nrightarrow$ *USER* we are ensuring that *directory* is a function; consequently each allocated *telephone* is used by exactly one person.
▷ *readability*
The definition of *NoSharingTS* could equally well be

$$
\begin{array}{l}
\underline{\hspace{0.3cm}\textit{NoSharingTS}_1\hspace{4.5cm}} \\
\textit{directory} : \textit{telephone} \nrightarrow \textit{USER} \\
\textit{free} : \mathbb{P}\,\textit{telephone} \\
\overline{\hspace{3.5cm}} \\
\textit{free} = \textit{telephone} \setminus \mathrm{dom}\ \textit{directory}
\end{array}
$$

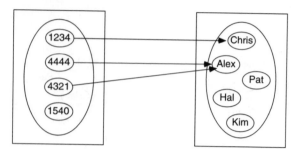

Figure 17.4 No sharing of telephones (partial function).

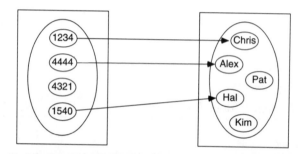

Figure 17.5 No sharing of telephones and one only (injection).

There is always a decision to be made as to whether to include information in the declaration or in the predicate. In each of the examples in this section, we are adding information to the original declaration so it makes sense to draw attention to it by putting it in the predicate. If, on the other hand, the intention had always been to describe a telephone system with no sharing then it would be better to include this information in the declaration.

If, in addition to no sharing, we state that each person with a telephone has access to exactly one (see figure 17.5) then we could write

───── *NoSharingOnlyOneTS* ──────────────────────────────
TelephoneSystem
─────────────
directory ∈ *telephone* ⤖ *USER*
───

▷ *injection*
The use of the injection (⤖) ensures that users cannot have more than one telephone each.

If we insist that every telephone is allocated (see figure 17.6) then we could define the following

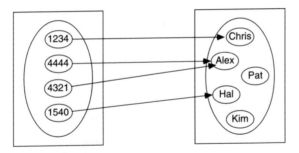

Figure 17.6 All telephones allocated (total function).

```
┌─ FullAllocNoSharingTS ─────────────────────────────
│ TelephoneSystem
│ ───────────────────────────────────────────────────
│ directory ∈ telephone ⟶ USER
└─────────────────────────────────────────────────────
```

▷ *total function*
  The use of the total function (⟶) means that the domain is all of *telephone*. Observe that in this case *free* would always be ∅ so we could reduce this definition to

```
┌─ FullAllocNoSharingTS₁ ────────────────────────────
│ directory : telephone ⟶ USER
└─────────────────────────────────────────────────────
```

If we insist that every user has at least one telephone (see figure 17.7) then we would define the following

```
┌─ AllUsersNoSharingTS ──────────────────────────────
│ TelephoneSystem
│ ───────────────────────────────────────────────────
│ directory ∈ telephone ⟶⟶ USER
└─────────────────────────────────────────────────────
```

▷ *surjection*
  The surjection (⟶⟶) means that *directory* is 'onto'; its range is all of *USER*.

If we insist that every user has one telephone, and every telephone is allocated to one user (see figure 17.8), then we would define the following

```
┌─ AllTS ─────────────────────────────────────────────
│ TelephoneSystem
│ ───────────────────────────────────────────────────
│ directory ∈ telephone ↣⟶ USER
└─────────────────────────────────────────────────────
```

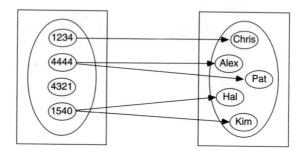

Figure 17.7 Every user has a telephone (surjection).

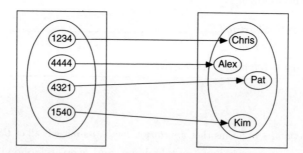

Figure 17.8 Every user has one telephone and every telephone is allocated to one user (bijection).

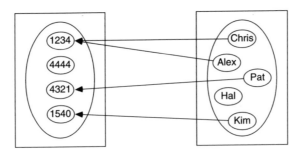

Figure 17.9 No user has more than one telephone (functional inverse).

▷ *bijection*
  The bijection (>—») means that *directory* is total (all telephones allocated), 'onto' (all users assigned a telephone), and one-to-one (no sharing, and no more than one phone each). Bijections are used to provide a 'labelling' of the elements of one set by elements of another, so there is no 'partial bijection'; bijective functions exist only between two sets of the same size.

If we ensure that no user has more than one telephone (see figure 17.9), but sharing is allowed, then we look at the inverse of the relation and insist that it is a function.

$$\begin{array}{|l} \hline \underline{\quad\textit{AtMostOne\,TS}\quad}\qquad\qquad\qquad\qquad\qquad\qquad\qquad \\ \quad \textit{TelephoneSystem} \\ \hline \quad \textit{directory}\sim\; \in\; \textit{USER} \twoheadrightarrow \textit{telephone} \\ \hline \end{array}$$

▷ *readability*
  The example of *AtMostOneTS* would be neater if we had declared the function the other way around in the first instance. Thus

$$\begin{array}{|l} \hline \underline{\quad\textit{AtMostOne\,TS}_1\quad}\qquad\qquad\qquad\qquad\qquad\qquad \\ \quad \textit{directory} : \textit{USER} \twoheadrightarrow \textit{telephone} \\ \quad \textit{free} : \mathbb{P}\,\textit{telephone} \\ \hline \quad \textit{free} = \textit{telephone} \setminus (\mathrm{ran}\;\textit{directory}) \\ \hline \end{array}$$

Note too, that we now take the range of the function in the predicate part.
  It is important to consider carefully which way round to place the sets when declaring relations, and, in particular, functions. Although the domain and range are treated symmetrically, a neater result may be obtained by a little looking ahead.

17.5   The different kinds of function

The telephone example looks at how the various kinds of function may be used, in this section we look at how they are related to one another.

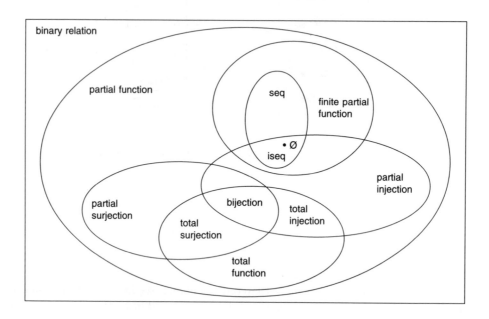

Figure 17.10 Functions from infinite X (in this case, $\mathbb{Z}$) to infinite Y.

The details of the relationships between the different kinds of functions depends in part on the two sets being related. Let's consider the functions from X to Y. If X is a finite set, for example, then the set of all finite functions, $X \nrightarrow Y$, is the same as the set of all partial functions, $X \nrightarrow Y$. But, if X is infinite, the finite functions form a proper subset of the partial functions.

The easiest way to show the connections between the different kinds of functions is to use a Venn diagram. Such a diagram uses ellipses to denote sets, which overlap to show intersections.

The following diagrams show the possible overlappings of different kinds of functions. The empty function $\varnothing$ is also shown since it is an injection (the empty injection) and a sequence (the empty sequence) but never a total function (if X is not empty) nor a surjection (if Y is not empty).

17.5.1 X and Y are both infinite

This is the most general case. Let's assume that X is $\mathbb{Z}$, so that sequences can be included on the diagram. See figure 17.10.

Since X is infinite, there is no overlap between total functions and finite functions. Also, because Y is infinite, no surjection can be finite. Note that if Y is $\mathbb{N}$

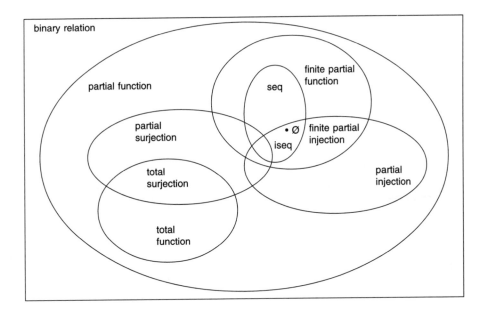

Figure 17.11 Functions from infinite X (in this case, $\mathbb{Z}$) to finite Y.

then we could show bags, but this does not alter the diagram significantly.

17.5.2   *X* infinite and *Y* finite

Again, assume that X is $\mathbb{Z}$, so that sequences can be included on the diagram. See figure 17.11.

Because X is infinite, there are no total finite functions and hence no total finite injections and consequently no bijections.

17.5.3   *X* finite and *Y* infinite

Because X is finite, the sets of finite and partial functions are identical. See figure 17.12.

If X is a subset of $\mathbb{Z}$ that includes an initial segment of $\mathbb{N}_1$ ($\exists\, n : \mathbb{N} \bullet 1 .. n \subseteq X$) then some of the functions from X to Y are sequences. Note that not all possible sequences are included (it is always possible to think of a sequence longer than the number of elements in X), so none of them is drawn in the diagram.

Because X is finite and Y is infinite, there are no surjections and hence no bijections.

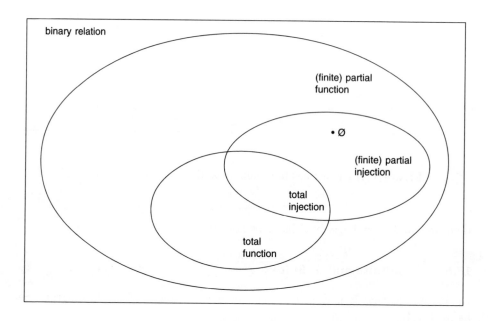

Figure 17.12 Functions from finite X to infinite Y.

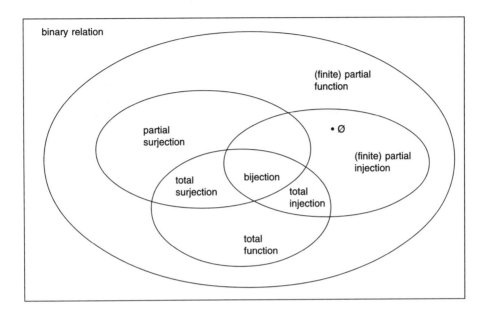

Figure 17.13 Functions from finite X to finite Y.

17.5.4 X and Y are both finite

Because X is finite, the sets of finite and partial functions are identical. Again, no sequences are shown. See figure 17.13.

The diagram is drawn assuming X and Y have the same cardinality, that $\#X = \#Y$, and so bijections exist.

17.6   Concluding remarks

The video encyclopaedia example shows how expressive the notation for relations is. Being able to iterate the relations, take their domains and ranges, and combine them using the set operations means that we can make powerful statements, and that we can make those statements simply.

This power of relations can be used, carefully, with functions and sequences too. Injective sequences are sequences, which are functions, which are relations, which are sets. But going the other way around, before we can treat a set as a relation, we must ensure that it satisfies certain constraints, namely, that the set is a subset of a cross product of two other sets. Relations can be viewed as functions only if they map elements many-to-one or one-to-one, but not many-to-many or one-to-many. Functions can be viewed as sequences only if they have an initial interval of the natural numbers as their domain. Sequences are only injective sequences if entries occur in the sequence once only.

Functions, other than the most elementary partial function, are often shunned. Used judiciously, however, as in the telephone directory example, they can make powerful, concise specification statements. If you wish to draw special attention to the particular kind of function, you can place it in the predicate part of a definition.

Chapter 18

Error Handling Styles

In which we illustrate two different styles for handling error operations.

18.1 Introduction

Handling error cases can be specified neatly in Z through schema disjunction. The usual way to do this, described in the Established Strategy (Chapter 3), uses 'error reports', which have no memory of any previous errors. Sometimes it is necessary to leave a system in a special error state until some explicit recovery takes place. This means the state has to remember that an error has occurred. In this chapter we look at two different approaches to errors.

> **Problem statement.** Specify a bounded stack, which can both underflow and overflow.

18.2 Errors with no memory

$$\vert\ bound : \mathbb{N}$$

bound is the maximum number of elements allowed in the stack.

$$BoundedStack[X] \mathrel{\widehat{=}} [\ stack : \operatorname{seq} X \mid \#stack \le bound\ ]$$

We model a *BoundedStack* as a sequence of elements where the length of the sequence is restricted by the value of *bound*.

> ▷ *generic schema*
> We make *BoundedStack* generic. To use it to store elements of any particular type, we instantiate with that type at the point of use.

18.2.1   Normal operations

Initialising the stack means setting it to the empty sequence.

$$InitOK[X] \mathrel{\widehat{=}} [\, \Delta BoundedStack[X] \mid stack' = \langle\rangle \,]$$

Pushing an element on the stack can be done only if the stack is not full. It adds the input value to the front of the stack.

```
┌─ PushOK[X] ─────────────────────────────────
│  ΔBoundedStack[X]
│  x? : X
│ ───────────────────────────────────────────
│  #stack < bound
│  stack' = ⟨x?⟩ ⌢ stack
└─────────────────────────────────────────────
```

Popping the stack can happen only if the stack is not empty.

```
┌─ PopOK[X] ──────────────────────────────────
│  ΔBoundedStack[X]
│ ───────────────────────────────────────────
│  #stack > 0
│  stack' = tail stack
└─────────────────────────────────────────────
```

Finding the top element of the stack works only if the stack is not empty. It outputs the value of the first element of the stack and leaves the stack unchanged.

```
┌─ TopOK[X] ──────────────────────────────────
│  ΞBoundedStack[X]
│  x! : X
│ ───────────────────────────────────────────
│  #stack > 0
│  x! = head stack
└─────────────────────────────────────────────
```

▷ sequence operations
The operation *head* finds the first entry in the sequence, which is what we want in looking for the top of the stack. Notice that had we specified the stack 'the other way up', by pushing elements onto the end rather than the beginning of the sequence, we would need to use *last* to find the end (top) of the stack.

18.2.2   Error cases

The schemas above specify the *OK* operations on the bounded stack. If an error occurs, the state of the stack is explicitly preserved, and a message reported.

$$REPORT ::= success \mid full \mid empty$$

▷ *free type, enumerated*
 The declaration of *REPORT* is a typical use of enumerated free types in which all the possible messages are listed.

If no error occurs, the *success* message is output.

$$OpOK \triangleq [\, r! : REPORT \mid r! = success \,]$$
$$Init[X] \triangleq InitOK[X] \wedge OpOK$$

Overflow errors occur when the stack is full.

```
┌─ Overflow[X] ──────────────────────────────────
│ ΞBoundedStack[X]
│ r! : REPORT
├────────────────────────────────────────────────
│ #stack = bound
│ r! = full
└────────────────────────────────────────────────
```

An attempt to push an element onto a full stack results in an overflow error. So the full *Push* operation is either a successful operation or an overflow error.

$$Push[X] \triangleq (PushOK[X] \wedge OpOK) \vee Overflow[X]$$

Underflow errors occur when the stack is empty.

```
┌─ Underflow[X] ─────────────────────────────────
│ ΞBoundedStack[X]
│ r! : REPORT
├────────────────────────────────────────────────
│ #stack = 0
│ r! = empty
└────────────────────────────────────────────────
```

An attempt to pop an empty stack results in an underflow error. So the full *Pop* operation is either a successful operation or an underflow error. Similarly for *Top*.

$$Pop[X] \triangleq (PopOK[X] \wedge OpOK) \vee Underflow[X]$$
$$Top[X] \triangleq (TopOK[X] \wedge OpOK) \vee Underflow[X]$$

Notice that this style of specification does not restrict subsequent operations after an error. For example, it is possible to do a successful *Top* immediately after trying to *Push* a value onto a full stack. The unsuccessful *Push* merely reports an error; the stack is left unchanged. The result of the *Top* is to output the top element of the stack as it was before the *Push*.

18.3   Errors with memory

It might be a requirement that, if an error occurs, no further operations are to be allowed until explicit recovery has been done. So if an error occurs the state of the stack is explicitly undefined, and the error 'remembered', allowing no subsequent operations except (re-)initialisation.

$$STATUS ::= ok \mid underflow \mid overflow$$

The *STATUS* is included as part of the state of the bounded stack.

```
┌─ BoundedStackMem[X] ────────────────
│ stack : seq X
│ status : STATUS
├───────────────────────────────
│ #stack ≤ bound
└───────────────────────────────
```

18.3.1   Normal operations

The stack can always be initialised, irrespective of its initial status. This is the only way provided to recover from an error.

```
┌─ InitMem[X] ────────────────────────
│ ΔBoundedStackMem[X]
├───────────────────────────────
│ stack' = ⟨⟩
│ status' = ok
└───────────────────────────────
```

An *OK* operation can occur only if the status of the before stack is *ok*, and it leaves the status unchanged.

```
┌─ ΔBoundedStackMemOK[X] ─────────────
│ ΔBoundedStackMem[X]
├───────────────────────────────
│ status = status' = ok
└───────────────────────────────
```

```
┌─ ΞBoundedStackMemOK[X] ─────────────
│ ΞBoundedStackMem[X]
├───────────────────────────────
│ ΔBoundedStackMemOK[X]
└───────────────────────────────
```

▷ transitive relation
  The expression $status = status' = ok$ provides the desired meaning because $=$ is transitive.

▷ *schema as predicate*

The use of $\Delta BoundedStackMemOK$ as a predicate means that its predicate part is used, its declaration being ignored. And variables used in the predicate must be in scope; this is provided by the declarations in $\Xi BoundedStackMem$.

The definitions of the successful operations proceed as before.

PushMemOK[X]
$\Delta BoundedStackMemOK[X]$
$x? : X$

$\#stack < bound$
$stack' = \langle x? \rangle \frown stack$

PopMemOK[X]
$\Delta BoundedStackMemOK[X]$

$\#stack > 0$
$stack' = tail\ stack$

TopMemOK[X]
$\Xi BoundedStackMemOK[X]$
$x! : X$

$\#stack > 0$
$x! = head\ stack$

18.3.2   Error cases

This time the error report has an extra component—to report that an operation has been attempted on a stack that is in an error state.

$$REPORT ::= success \mid full \mid empty \mid undefined$$

If the stack is in an error state, it stays in that error state. The contents of the stack after the operation are undefined.

Error[X]
$\Delta BoundedStackMem[X]$
$r! : REPORT$

$status \neq ok$
$status' = status$
$r! = undefined$

An overflow error sets the status to *overflow*.

```
┌─ OverflowMem[X] ────────────────────────────
│ ΔBoundedStackMem[X]
│ r! : REPORT
├─────────────────────────────────────────────
│ #stack = bound
│ status = ok
│ status' = overflow
│ r! = full
└─────────────────────────────────────────────
```

Notice that *OverflowMem* only occurs for an *ok* stack. *Error* copes with a stack that has already experienced an error.

So the full *Push* operation is either a successful push (where *OpOK* is defined as before), or an overflow (the stack was full, but with *ok* status), or an error (the stack was already in one of the error states, either *overflow* or *underflow*).

$$PushMem[X] \mathrel{\widehat{=}} (PushMemOK[X] \wedge OpOK) \vee OverflowMem[X] \vee Error[X]$$

An underflow error sets the status to *underflow*.

```
┌─ UnderflowMem[X] ───────────────────────────
│ ΔBoundedStackMem[X]
│ r! : REPORT
├─────────────────────────────────────────────
│ #stack = 0
│ status = ok
│ status' = underflow
│ r! = empty
└─────────────────────────────────────────────
```

The full *PopMem* operation is either a successful pop, or an underflow (the stack was empty, but with *ok* status), or an error (the stack was already in one of the error states). Similarly for *TopMem*.

$$PopMem[X] \mathrel{\widehat{=}} (PopMemOK[X] \wedge OpOK) \vee UnderflowMem[X] \vee Error[X]$$
$$TopMem[X] \mathrel{\widehat{=}} (TopMemOK[X] \wedge OpOK) \vee UnderflowMem[X] \vee Error[X]$$

With this style, it is not possible to do a successful *Top* immediately after trying to *Push* a value onto a full stack. The unsuccessful *Push* changes the *status* of the stack to *overflow*; the subsequent attempt at *Top* reports *undefined*.

18.4   Discussion

It would be possible to specify yet a third error behaviour that combines these two styles: one that does not allow subsequent operations until some sort of error recovery has been performed, yet preserves the values in the stack. Different requirements result in different sorts of behaviour.

Chapter 19

Promotion

In which the secrets of promotion are revealed.

19.1 Introduction

Promotion is a common technique used for structuring specifications. It is used when you have defined a piece of local state with operations on it, then want to collect together multiple instances of this local state into some global state, without having to redefine all the operations. The technique 'promotes' the operations specified on the local state to the relevant operations on instances of the local state within the global state.

19.2 Simple example: a counter

Consider a piece of local state that defines a counter. This stores a number, the current value of the counter

$$Counter \cong [\, c : \mathbb{N} \,]$$

A counter has two operations. It can be incremented

$$Increment \cong [\, \Delta Counter \mid c' = 1 + c \,]$$

and it can be reset to zero

$$Reset \cong [\, \Delta Counter \mid c' = 0 \,]$$

Now consider a system containing a collection of counters. These are distinguished from each other by being named.

$$[NAME]$$

$$CounterCollection \cong [\, collection : NAME \nrightarrow Counter \,]$$

▷ *function*

We ensure the uniqueness of names by setting up a function between the names of the counters and the counters themselves. We could instead have the name of the counter as one of the components of the *Counter* schema, in which case we would need a device to ensure that no two instances of the schemas had the same name.

We define a general schema to update a particular counter without actually specifying what the update does.

$$
\begin{array}{|l}
\hline
\;\Phi\,UpdateCollection \underline{\hspace{8cm}} \\
\;\Delta\,CounterCollection \\
\;\Delta\,Counter \\
\;n? : NAME \\
\hline
\;n? \in \mathrm{dom}\; collection \\
\;\theta\,Counter = collection\; n? \\
\;collection' = collection \oplus \{n? \mapsto \theta\,Counter'\} \\
\hline
\end{array}
$$

▷ *schema binding*

The expression $\theta\,Counter = collection\; n?$ says that the values of the variables of *Counter* are exactly those to which *collection* maps $n?$. (If you feel uncomfortable with θ see section 24.5 for a tutorial.)

▷ *naming convention*

The Φ in this schema name is simply a character; it is not a schema operator. Using a Φ to indicate promotion schemas is a naming convention that not all authors adopt. The letter Φ is used because such schemas are often called 'framing schemas'.

This schema contains the before and after global state, the before and after of some part of the local state, and the name of a part of local state. The predicate ensures that:

- the input name is the name of a counter in the collection
- the before piece of local state has the same value as the named counter's state
- the named counter's new state is the (as yet unspecified) after value of the piece of local state, and all the other counters are unchanged

All that remains in specifying a particular operation is to specify the relation between the before and after pieces of local state. This is exactly what the local operation specifications do. This local state is then hidden in the final definition.

Incrementing one particular counter in the collection is illustrated in figure 19.1 and may be written as

$$
IncrementCollection \;\widehat{=}\; \exists\,\Delta\,Counter \bullet \Phi\,UpdateCollection \wedge Increment
$$

▷ *schema quantification*

In stating what happens when we promote an operation, we are saying that there is a change in a counter state that matches the changes made at the collection level when one of the counters is incremented.

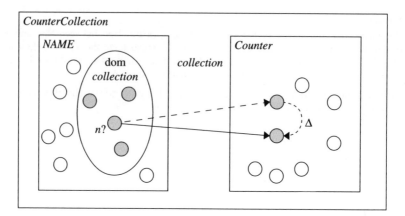

Figure 19.1 A promoted operation. The dashed arrow shows a particular name related to its before *Counter* state, $\theta\, Counter$. The curved arrow labelled Δ shows the result of the local operation *Increment* on this piece of local state. The solid arrow shows the name related to the corresponding after *Counter* state, $\theta\, Counter'$. This defines the effect of the promoted operation *IncrementCollection* on this one element of the promoted state *CounterCollection*.

In order to understand how this works, we expand out the definition here.

$$
\begin{array}{|l}
\quad IncrementCollection1 \\\hline
\Delta\, CounterCollection \\
n? : NAME \\\hline
\exists \Delta\, Counter \bullet \\
\quad n? \in \mathrm{dom}\ collection \\
\quad \wedge\ \theta\, Counter = collection\ n? \\
\quad \wedge\ collection' = collection \oplus \{n? \mapsto \theta\, Counter'\} \\
\quad \wedge\ c' = 1 + c
\end{array}
$$

By appropriate substitution to eliminate the quantified variables, this simplifies to

$$
\begin{array}{|l}
\quad IncrementCollection2 \\\hline
\Delta\, CounterCollection \\
n? : NAME \\\hline
n? \in \mathrm{dom}\ collection \\
collection' = collection \oplus \{n? \mapsto \\
\qquad\qquad (\mu\, Counter_1 \mid c_1 = 1 + (collection\ n?).c\,)\}
\end{array}
$$

▷ *definite description*
The expression ($\mu\ Counter_1 \mid \ldots$) makes a counter with the desired values of its components. (If you feel uncomfortable with μ, see section 24.6 for a tutorial.)

The promoted version of *Reset* is defined similarly.

$$ResetCollection \cong \exists \Delta Counter \bullet \Phi UpdateCollection \land Reset$$

So the global operation on the system of counters has been factored into a local operation on a single counter, and an operation that updates a single counter.

For such a simple example as the counter, with very little state, this technique looks a little contrived. After all, why not just make the system something like *collection* : *NAME* $\nrightarrow \mathbb{N}$? In the next section we look at a more complicated state.

19.3   More complicated local state: an adder

For a local state that has more state components and more complex operations, promotion becomes a powerful structuring mechanism. Consider an *Adder*, which is like a counter, but can be increased by a given input value, and remembers how often it has been reset and increased.

$$Adder \cong [\,count, reset, increase : \mathbb{N}\,]$$

___
IncreaseAdder
$\Delta Adder$
$value? : \mathbb{N}$
___
$count' = value? + count$
$reset' = reset$
$increase' = 1 + increase$
___

___
ResetAdder
$\Delta Adder$
___
$count' = 0$
$reset' = 1 + reset$
$increase' = increase$
___

We now turn our attention to the global state.

$$AdderCollection \cong [\,collection : NAME \nrightarrow Adder\,]$$

The *Update* schema for this collection mirrors the previous definition.

$$
\begin{array}{|l}
\Phi\,UpdateAdder \\
\hline
\Delta AdderCollection \\
\Delta Adder \\
n? : NAME \\
\hline
n? \in \mathrm{dom}\ collection \\
\theta Adder = collection\ n? \\
collection' = collection \oplus \{n? \mapsto \theta Adder'\}
\end{array}
$$

The promoted operations are defined as before.

$$IncreaseAdderCollection \mathrel{\hat=} \exists \Delta Adder \bullet \Phi\,UpdateAdder \wedge IncreaseAdder$$
$$ResetAdderCollection \mathrel{\hat=} \exists \Delta Adder \bullet \Phi\,UpdateAdder \wedge ResetAdder$$

The advantage of the structuring can be seen when one of these definitions is expanded, as a more complicated-looking expansion results.

$$
\begin{array}{|l}
IncreaseAdderCollection1 \\
\hline
\Delta AdderCollection \\
value? : \mathbb{N} \\
n? : NAME \\
\hline
n? \in \mathrm{dom}\ collection \\
collection' = collection \oplus \{n? \mapsto (\mu\, Adder_1\ | \\
\quad\quad count_1 = value? + (collection\ n?).count \\
\quad\quad \wedge\ reset_1 = (collection\ n?).reset \\
\quad\quad \wedge\ increase_1 = 1 + (collection\ n?).increase\,)\}
\end{array}
$$

This can be written more compactly by using the definition of *IncreaseAdder*.

$$
\begin{array}{|l}
IncreaseAdderCollection2 \\
\hline
\Delta AdderCollection \\
value? : \mathbb{N} \\
n? : NAME \\
\hline
n? \in \mathrm{dom}\ collection \\
collection' = collection \oplus \{n? \mapsto (\mu\, IncreaseAdder_1\ | \\
\quad\quad \theta Adder_1 = collection\ n? \\
\quad\quad \wedge\ value?_1 = value? \\
\quad \bullet\ \theta Adder'_1\,)\}
\end{array}
$$

This formulation of promotion, avoiding the use of a framing schema, is used by [Hall 1990], and is described in section 24.6.4.

19.4 Constrained global state: an increasing sequence

The global system state can be more structured than a simple collection of local states. Consider an example where the local states are counters, as before, but now the global state is a sequence of these counters, with the added constraint that the values of the counters must not be decreasing along this sequence.

CounterSequence
_____
line : seq *Counter*
_____
$\forall i, j : \text{dom } line \mid i < j \bullet (line\ i).c \leq (line\ j).c$

▷ *function application*
As sequences are a special instance of functions, they may be applied to elements of their domain.

Updating a counter in the sequence involves selecting a particular index.

Φ *UpdateSequence*
_____
Δ *CounterSequence*
Δ *Counter*
$i? : \mathbb{N}$
_____
$i? \in \text{dom } line$
$\theta\,Counter = line\ i?$
$line' = line \oplus \{i? \mapsto \theta\,Counter'\}$

The promoted operations are defined as before.

$$IncrementSequence \;\widehat{=}\; \exists \Delta\,Counter \bullet \Phi\,UpdateSequence \wedge Increment$$
$$ResetSequence \;\widehat{=}\; \exists \Delta\,Counter \bullet \Phi\,UpdateSequence \wedge Reset$$

If we expand *IncrementSequence* as before, it superficially looks similar to *IncrementCollection2*. We get the expression for what *Counter'* must be to satisfy the operation: the relevant counter's value must be incremented.

IncrementSequence1
_____
Δ *CounterSequence*
$i? : \mathbb{N}$
_____
$i? \in \text{dom } line$
$line' = line \oplus \{i? \mapsto (\mu\,Counter_1 \mid c_1 = 1 + (line\ i?).c)\}$

In this case we also have a global state invariant from $\Delta\,CounterSequence$, requiring *line'* to be a non-decreasing sequence. The *IncrementSequence* operation is undefined if incrementing the chosen counter would not preserve this invariant; there is no $Counter_1$ that satisfies both conditions.

We could change our definition, allowing the counter sequence to be reordered to preserve the invariant. Defining such reordering explicitly is hard. But by making use of the sequence relation *anagram* (see section 21.3) we can give an implicit definition

$$line' \; \underline{anagram} \; (line \oplus \{i? \mapsto \theta\,Counter'\})$$

This allows any reordering of the *line* sequence necessary to preserve the invariant.

19.5   Larger example: a file system

The following specification of a Unix-like file system follows that in [Morgan & Sufrin 1993]. This specification originally appeared in 1984, and was one of the first examples of promotion to appear in the literature. Since Z itself was so new at the time, the paper concentrates on explaining the use of schemas, and so the structuring technique of promotion is not made explicit.

The treatment in this section extends the previous sections, which specified just state changes, by also specifying initial and final states.

> **Problem statement.** Describe a simple file system. There are four operations: read, write, set length and delete. Their informal descriptions are as follows.
>
> **Read a file** Two input parameters are needed: an offset, and a length. The first byte of the file has an offset of zero. A sequence of bytes is output; if the offset is after the end of the file, an empty sequence is returned. The file is unchanged by the operation.
>
> **Write to a file** Two input parameters are needed: an offset, and a sequence of bytes to be written. The file is overwritten by the input bytes from the offset; if the offset is after the end of the file, the gap is padded out with *null* bytes.
>
> **Set the length of a file** If the new length is less than the original length, the file is truncated; if it is more, the file is padded with *null*s.
>
> **Delete a file** The file must be empty before it can be deleted.

19.5.1   Local state

A file is composed of bytes. We do not need to say what bytes are, except that we need a named byte: the *null* mentioned above.

[BYTE]

$$| \; null : BYTE$$

The local state is a file, which is simply a sequence of bytes.

$$File \mathrel{\widehat{=}} [\, file : \mathrm{seq}\, BYTE \,]$$

Initially, a file is empty.

$$InitFile \mathrel{\widehat{=}} [\, File' \mid file' = \langle\, \rangle \,]$$

We now look at the four operations that are possible on a file. First, reading a file. We simply extract the indexes we want; if these are beyond the end of the file, the empty sequence results, as required.

```
ReadFile
ΞFile
offset? : N
length? : N
data! : seq BYTE
─────────────────────
data! = ((offset? + 1) .. (offset? + length?)) ↾ file
```

Note that this definition works for *offset?* = 0, which gives 1 .. *length?*, since we are told that an offset of 0 corresponds to the first byte in the file.

Life is a little more difficult when writing data to a file beyond its end. We do not want a 'gap' in the sequence. So we make the file long enough, by padding it with *null* bytes. We define a function *pad* that pads out a sequence to a given length. For example

$$pad(\langle a, b\rangle, 4, x) = \langle a, b, x, x\rangle$$
$$pad(\langle a, b\rangle, 1, x) = \langle a, b\rangle$$

The definition of *pad* is

```
[X]
pad : seq X × N × X ⟶ seq X
─────────────────────────
∀ s : seq X; n : N; x : X • pad(s, n, x) = uniqseq(n, x) ⊕ s
```

▷ *toolkit*
  uniqseq is defined in our extension to the sample toolkit, appendix A.6. *uniqseq*(n, x) is a sequence of n xs.

We can see from its definition that the length of a padded sequence is

$$s : \mathrm{seq}\, X; n : \mathbb{N}; x : X \vdash \#(pad(s, n, x)) = max\{\#s, n\}$$

▷ *theorem*

We need to use the length of a *pad*ded sequence when arguing the correctness of the *WriteFile* operation, so we document a useful theorem here.

We also need a function, *shift*, that shifts a sequence of bytes rightwards by a given amount. For example

$$shift(\langle a, b, c \rangle, 1) = \{2 \mapsto a, 3 \mapsto b, 4 \mapsto c\}$$

The definition of *shift* is

$$shift == (\lambda\, s : \text{seq}\, BYTE;\ n : \mathbb{N} \bullet \{\, i : \text{dom}\, s \bullet (n + i) \mapsto s\, i\,\})$$

Writing a file from an offset consists of padding the file with *null*s to that offset (in case it is beyond the end of the file), and overwriting this with the input data shifted right by the offset.

```
┌─ WriteFile ─────────────────────────────────────────────────
│ ΔFile
│ offset? : ℕ
│ data? : seq BYTE
├──────────────────────────────────────────────────────────────
│ file′ = pad(file, offset?, null) ⊕ shift(data?, offset?)
└──────────────────────────────────────────────────────────────
```

▷ *proof obligation*

We need to show that *file′* is a sequence, that shifting and overriding has not introduced gaps in the indexes.

The length of the padded file is $max\{\#file, offset?\}$. From the construction of $shift(s, i)$, we can see that its domain is the contiguous set of numbers $(1 + \#s)\,..\,(n + \#s)$. Since the domain of the shifted *data?* starts at $1 + offset?$, there are no gaps introduced by overriding the padded *file* with the shifted *data?*. Hence *file′* is a sequence.

Setting the length of a file involves padding it to the required length, and restricting it to be that length.

```
┌─ SetFile ───────────────────────────────────────────────────
│ ΔFile
│ length? : ℕ
├──────────────────────────────────────────────────────────────
│ file′ = (1 .. length?) ◁ pad(file, length?, null)
└──────────────────────────────────────────────────────────────
```

A file can be deleted, but only if it is empty.

$$CanDeleteFile \;\hat{=}\; [\,File \mid file = \langle\rangle\,]$$

Notice that *CanDeleteFile* does not actually delete a file, it simply tests whether the deletion is possible. The process of removing the file from the system comes later.

19.5.2   Global state

A file system is a mapping from file identifiers to files.

$[FID]$
$FileSystem \cong [\, fs : FID \rightarrowtail File \,]$

Initially, a file system contains no files.

$InitFileSystem \cong [\, FileSystem' \mid fs' = \varnothing \,]$

19.5.3   Promotion schemas

There are three framing schemas. To add a new file to the system it is necessary to input a new identifier for it and test that this is genuinely new. The new file is then assigned to that identifier.

$$
\begin{array}{|l}
\Phi NewFile \underline{\hspace{7cm}} \\
\Delta FileSystem \\
File' \\
fid? : FID \\
\hline
fid? \notin \mathrm{dom}\, fs \\
fs' = fs \cup \{fid? \mapsto \theta File'\} \\
\end{array}
$$

▷ *house style*
 Note that we are following our house style of using $\cup$ rather than $\oplus$ to form fs', in order
 to emphasise that we are extending the domain of fs, not overriding an existing element.

Similarly, updating one of the files in the system is described by

$$
\begin{array}{|l}
\Phi UpdateFile \underline{\hspace{6.5cm}} \\
\Delta FileSystem \\
\Delta File \\
fid? : FID \\
\hline
fid? \in \mathrm{dom}\, fs \\
\theta File = fs\, fid? \\
fs' = fs \oplus \{fid? \mapsto \theta File'\} \\
\end{array}
$$

To delete a file we need to remove its identifier from the records.

```
┌─ ΦRemoveFile ────────────────────────────────────────────
│ ΔFileSystem
│ File
│ fid? : FID
├──────────────────────────────────────────────────────────
│ fid? ∈ dom fs
│ θFile = fs fid?
│ fs' = {fid?} ⩤ fs
└──────────────────────────────────────────────────────────
```

▷ anti-restriction, domain
  The expression $fs' = \{fid?\} \lhd fs$ removes all pairs from fs that have $fid?$ as their first component. In this case there is exactly one such pair, since fs is a function and $fid?$ is in its domain.

19.5.4   Promoted operations

The file operations promoted to the file system are

$$New \mathrel{\widehat{=}} \exists\, File' \bullet \Phi NewFile \wedge InitFile$$

$$Read \mathrel{\widehat{=}} \exists\, \Delta File \bullet \Phi UpdateFile \wedge ReadFile$$

$$Write \mathrel{\widehat{=}} \exists\, \Delta File \bullet \Phi UpdateFile \wedge WriteFile$$

$$Set \mathrel{\widehat{=}} \exists\, \Delta File \bullet \Phi UpdateFile \wedge SetFile$$

$$Remove \mathrel{\widehat{=}} \exists\, File \bullet \Phi RemoveFile \wedge CanDeleteFile$$

Note that we have now performed the removal of the file from the system as promised earlier. We combine the condition in *CanDeleteFile*, which operates at the file level, with the system level *RemoveFile* to describe the complete operation of *Remove*.

So all the work has gone into specifying the individual operations at the lowest level, on a single file, where there is little extra structure to clutter the specification. Then all the operations promote automatically to the higher level, with hardly any work.

19.6   Summary of promotion

Promotion is useful in cases where local items may be operated upon individually and are collected into a global system. We describe a general specification involving promotion, below. We have a global state consisting of several labelled copies of some local state *Local*, possibly constrained in some way

```
┌─ Global ─────────────────────────────────────────────────
│ global : ID ⇸ Local
├──────────────────────────────────────────────────────────
│ optional constraints
└──────────────────────────────────────────────────────────
```

There are three sorts of framing, or promotion, schemas that link the local and global states.

$\Phi NewLocal$ is used to add a new piece of local state to the global state.

┌─ $\Phi NewLocal$ ──────────────────────
│ $\Delta Global$
│ $Local'$
│ $id? : ID$
├──────────────────────────────
│ $id? \notin \mathrm{dom}\ global$
│ $global' = global \cup \{id? \mapsto \theta Local'\}$
└──────────────────────────────

$\Phi UpdateLocal$ is used to change one piece of local state, leaving the other pieces unchanged.

┌─ $\Phi UpdateLocal$ ──────────────────────
│ $\Delta Global$
│ $\Delta Local$
│ $id? : ID$
├──────────────────────────────
│ $id? \in \mathrm{dom}\ global$
│ $\theta Local = global\ id?$
│ $global' = global \oplus \{id? \mapsto \theta Local'\}$
└──────────────────────────────

$\Phi RemoveLocal$ is used to delete a piece of local state from the global state.

┌─ $\Phi RemoveLocal$ ──────────────────────
│ $\Delta Global$
│ $Local$
│ $id? : ID$
├──────────────────────────────
│ $id? \in \mathrm{dom}\ global$
│ $\theta Local = global\ id?$
│ $global' = \{id?\} \lhd global$
└──────────────────────────────

The promoted global operations corresponding to local ones are

$$New \mathrel{\widehat{=}} \exists Local' \bullet \Phi NewLocal \wedge InitLocal$$
$$GlobalOp_n \mathrel{\widehat{=}} \exists \Delta Local \bullet \Phi UpdateLocal \wedge LocalOp_n$$
$$Remove \mathrel{\widehat{=}} \exists Local \bullet \Phi RemoveLocal \wedge CanDeleteLocal$$

There are also rules that allow data refinements to be promoted correctly. Describing these is beyond the scope of this book; the interested reader is referred to [Lupton 1991].

Section 24.6.4 describes another way of looking at promotion, which shows its connection with an object based specification style.

Part IV

Z Notation Details

Chapter 20

Using Free Types

In which free type definitions are explored and explained.

20.1 Introduction

The notation for free type definitions does not add anything new to the Z language (as we illustrate in this chapter). However, it provides a convenient tool for describing enumerated types, disjoint unions and recursive structures. We look at each of these uses in turn.

20.2 Enumerated free type

One common error made when trying to specify a new type that has a few distinct elements is to write an abbreviation definition something like

$$ SUIT_X == \{\clubsuit, \diamondsuit, \heartsuit, \spadesuit\} $$

What such a specifier usually wants this to mean is that $SUIT_X$ is a new type with the four elements listed. Unfortunately, it says no such thing. What it actually does is introduce a new global constant, $SUIT_X$, as an abbreviation for the set display on the right hand side. The type of $SUIT_X$ is the same as the type of the set display, but

- the elements need to have been defined previously for their types to be known
- unless stated explicitly, there is no guarantee that the four elements are distinct (it might be that case that $\diamondsuit$ and $\heartsuit$ are merely different names for the same element in this set)
- there is no guarantee that the four elements exhaust the type; there could be other elements not listed in the set display.

To achieve the desired effect, what is needed is a free type definition.

$$SUIT ::= \clubsuit \mid \diamondsuit \mid \heartsuit \mid \spadesuit$$

Such a definition is syntactically equivalent to

$$[SUIT]$$

$$
\begin{array}{|l}
\clubsuit, \diamondsuit, \heartsuit, \spadesuit : SUIT \\
\hline
\langle\{\clubsuit\}, \{\diamondsuit\}, \{\heartsuit\}, \{\spadesuit\}\rangle \text{ partition } SUIT
\end{array}
$$

and so it is exactly what we want. It introduces the given set $SUIT$, says that the four elements are of this type, that they are distinct, and that they exhaust the type, so there are no more elements of this type hiding somewhere.

20.3   Money and the arithmetic operations

Problem statement. Specify the coins in circulation in Britain that are legal tender (so disallowing the odd peseta left over from holiday and forced into a vending machine). Disregard commemorative issues such as crowns, £2, £5 and £10.

A first approach might be to say

$$COIN_0 == \{1, 2, 5, 10, 20, 50, 100\}$$

This does not have the problem of the card suit example above; the values in the set are (distinct) numbers and so elements of $COIN_0$ have the type $\mathbb{Z}$. But too much type information is lost as coins are indistinguishable from 'ordinary' numbers, whereas they should have a type of their own.

So, following the card suit example, we might say

$$
\begin{aligned}
COIN_1 ::= \ &onePenny \\
\mid \ &twoPence \\
\mid \ &fivePence \\
\mid \ &tenPence \\
\mid \ &twentyPence \\
\mid \ &fiftyPence \\
\mid \ &onePound
\end{aligned}
$$

Now each member of $COIN_1$ has a name, and is of type $COIN_1$. That is all they are. In particular, there are no operations defined on $COIN_1$s, but we probably want to be able to add (and subtract!) their values.

We could define a total function from coins to their values

$$
\begin{array}{|l}
coin\,Value : COIN_1 \longrightarrow \mathbb{N} \\
\hline
coin\,Value = \{onePenny \mapsto 1, \ldots, onePound \mapsto 100\}
\end{array}
$$

but there is a neater way. Instead, define

$$value == \{1, 2, 5, 10, 20, 50, 100\}$$
$$COIN ::= coin\langle\!\langle value \rangle\!\rangle$$

The definition of $COIN$ is syntactically equivalent to

$$[COIN]$$

$$
\begin{array}{|l}
coin : value \rightarrowtail COIN
\end{array}
$$

The members of this $COIN$ cannot be confused with 'ordinary' integers, but all the operations that apply to integers are available to members of $COIN$. So the value of coins may be added together or subtracted from one another, for example

$$\forall\, n : \mathbb{N};\ c_1, c_2 : COIN \mid n = (coin^\sim c_1 + coin^\sim c_2) \bullet \ldots$$

They may be multiplied by integers and even divided by integers if those operations are required.

20.4   A pack of cards

We now complete the specification of a pack of cards begun in section 20.2. We have the four suits, now we want the card face values. To specify the order of these cards, it would be convenient to use the arithmetic operator $+$. So we define

$$FACE ::= pips\langle\!\langle 2 \mathinner{\ldotp\ldotp} 10 \rangle\!\rangle \mid jack \mid queen \mid king \mid ace$$

The definition of $FACE$ is syntactically equivalent to

$$[FACE]$$

$$
\begin{array}{|l}
pips : 2 \mathinner{\ldotp\ldotp} 10 \rightarrowtail FACE \\
jack, queen, king, ace : FACE \\
\hline
\langle \operatorname{ran} pips, \{jack\}, \{queen\}, \{king\}, \{ace\} \rangle \text{ partition } FACE
\end{array}
$$

It is also convenient to give a name to the inverse of the injection

$$face\,Value == pips^\sim$$

▷ *free type, disjoint union*

The inverses of the injections tend to be used as much as, if not more than, the injections themselves. [Macdonald 1991] recommends giving the inverse of each injection a name that indicates the meaning of the type of its range (the domain of the original function), because the inverse function applied to an element of the free type returns one of these things. In other words, the function *faceValue* applied to a *FACE* returns its value, an element of the set $2 \mathrel{..} 10$. This style saves cluttering up the specification with explicit inverses.

Then we can define the order of cards (taking ace high, so it has no next card) as

$$
\begin{array}{|l}
\hline
nextFace : FACE \nrightarrow FACE \\
\hline
\mathrm{dom}\, nextFace = FACE \setminus \{ace\} \\
\forall\, c : (\mathrm{ran}\, pips) \setminus \{pips\, 10\} \bullet nextFace\, c = pips(1 + faceValue\, c) \\
nextFace(pips\, 10) = jack \\
nextFace\, jack = queen \\
nextFace\, queen = king \\
nextFace\, king = ace \\
\end{array}
$$

If we had defined the cards as an enumerated type, the definition of *nextFace* would have been much longer. The relation *higherFace* can be defined simply as the transitive closure of *nextFace*

$$ higherFace == nextFace^{+} $$

▷ *transitive closure*

$nextFace^{+}$ is the transitive closure of the relation *nextFace*. In general, using the transitive closure operation is a concise way to build the 'is descendent of' relation from the appropriate 'is child of' relation.

Now a card is

$$ Card \mathrel{\hat=} [\, face : FACE;\; suit : SUIT\,] $$

▷ *schema versus Cartesian product*

Card could have been defined as a Cartesian product instead

$$ Card_1 == FACE \times SUIT $$

Later on, however, we want to extract the *suit* and *face* components of a *Card*. As a schema, this becomes *c.face* and *c.suit*; as a Cartesian product, it would be the less informative *first c* and *second c*. Using a schema does have a drawback, however. If we had used a Cartesian product, we could write down the values of particular cards, for example $(A, \heartsuit)$ and $(10, \diamondsuit)$. There is no analogous notation for writing down the value of a schema binding explicitly.

▷ *schema binding*

[Spivey 1992] uses the meta-notation $\langle x_1 \Rrightarrow v_1, \ldots, x_n \Rrightarrow v_n \rangle$ to write down an explicit binding for the schema $[\, x_1 : X_1, \ldots, x_n : X_n\,]$, but does not include it as part of the Z language. The Z Standard includes notation for explicit bindings. (See also the discussion of θ and bindings in section 24.5.)

20.5   Disjoint union free type

Problem statement. The Stodgy Engineering Corporation has recently merged with the Pushy Systems House. The payrolls are to be merged and the salaries of the former employees of the Stodgy Engineering Corporation to be raised by ten per cent while the former employees of the Pushy Systems House, who are grossly overpaid, are to take a pay cut of £500.

In the past both companies used numbers for their staff payroll numbers. We cannot just merge the payrolls, since some numbers may have been used in both the old payrolls. We need to keep the old pay numbers distinct. So we use a free type definition

$$PAYNUMBER ::= stodgy\langle\!\langle \mathbb{N} \rangle\!\rangle \mid pushy\langle\!\langle \mathbb{N} \rangle\!\rangle$$

In order to make the salary adjustments we need the original salaries. An obvious way to do this is by using a function from *PAYNUMBER* to pay, which in this case we model as $\mathbb{N}$ to describe the number of pounds paid. All members of the Pushy Systems House are currently paid more than the £500 cut they are soon to receive.

$$
\begin{array}{|l}
oldSalary : PAYNUMBER \nrightarrow \mathbb{N} \\
\hline
\forall p : \text{ran } pushy \bullet oldSalary \, p > 500
\end{array}
$$

This is not a total function; there are an infinite number of *PAYNUMBER*s, but rather fewer employees.

▷ *abstraction*
It is appropriate to use numbers to model the salaries as we need to perform arithmetical operations on them.

To make the salary changes we must first establish from which company an individual came and then apply the appropriate formula. Recall that the definition of *PAYNUMBER* includes the definition of two injections, $stodgy : \mathbb{N} \rightarrowtail PAYNUMBER$ and $pushy : \mathbb{N} \rightarrowtail PAYNUMBER$, with disjoint ranges. Thus we can determine the original employer of a given employee by examining the range of the injections.

$$
\begin{array}{|l}
newSalary : PAYNUMBER \nrightarrow \mathbb{N} \\
\hline
\forall p : \text{dom } oldSalary \bullet \\
\quad (p \in \text{ran } stodgy \Rightarrow newSalary \, p = oldSalary \, p * 11 \text{ div } 10) \\
\quad \wedge (p \in \text{ran } pushy \Rightarrow newSalary \, p = oldSalary \, p - 500)
\end{array}
$$

Because of the declaration of *newSalary*, the expression *oldSalary p* − 500 in the second branch must not be negative. This is so, from the condition on *oldSalary*.

There is a further proof obligation, arising from this use of implication. If both antecedents happen to be true, then both consequents must be true, which would imply

$$oldSalary\ p * 11\ \mathsf{div}\ 10 = oldSalary\ p - 500$$

meaning that the employee concerned was paying the employer about £5000 for the privilege of working. This situation is impossible under our model of non-negative salaries (as well as being highly unlikely in practice!).

So we need to show that both antecedents cannot be true simultaneously. We also want to show that at least one is always true when p is in the domain of *oldSalary*, otherwise that employee's new salary is not defined.

This obligation may be discharged quite simply by observing that the ranges of *stodgy* and *pushy* partition *PAYNUMBER*.

> ▷ *proof obligation*
> In this specification we have demonstrated that everything works out as expected when implication is used. If we were deliberately leaving the specification loose such arguments would be unnecessary.

20.6   A file system: barking up the wrong tree

The use of tree structures is ubiquitous in both the specification and implementation of computer systems. An obvious way of specifying a tree is to employ a 'recursive' free type definition, yet this may not always be the most useful. In the following sections we explore and compare the use of a free type definition and of an alternative approach to model a file system and specify an operation on it.

> **Problem statement.** A file system consists of a named *root directory*, which may be empty or may contain file system objects, called *nodes*. A node is either a named directory, which may contain further nodes, or a named file, which contains data. No two nodes immediately contained within any directory may share the same name.
>
> We require the *Move* operation to be specified; the operation corresponds roughly to (the successful part of) a mv in Unix. Given the path name (a sequence of names that identifies a node by navigating the file system from the root directory to the node itself) of an existing node and a new path name that does not currently identify a node, the operation transfers the existing node (and its contents, if any) to the location identified by the new path name.

20.6.1   Using a free type definition

We first show how to model the file system using a recursive free type definition.

The state of the file system

We introduce given sets for the names of nodes and for the data held by files.

$$[\mathit{NAME}, \mathit{DATA}]$$

Each node in a file system is either a file or a directory.

$$\mathit{NODE} ::= \mathit{file}\langle\!\langle \mathit{NAME} \times \mathit{DATA} \rangle\!\rangle$$
$$\qquad\quad | \quad \mathit{directory}\langle\!\langle \mathit{NAME} \times \mathbb{F}\,\mathit{NODE} \rangle\!\rangle$$

▷ *free type, recursive*
Notice that we use $\mathbb{F}\,\mathit{NODE}$ in the recursive part of the definition of NODE and not the larger $\mathbb{P}\,\mathit{NODE}$. This finiteness condition is sufficient to ensure that NODE is well-defined. (See also the discussion on page 245.)

Now we define some useful functions. The function $\mathit{nodesOf}$ maps a directory to the set of nodes immediately within it. The function $\mathit{subDirsOf}$ maps a directory to the set of subdirectories immediately within it (that is, all nodes excluding ordinary files). The function parent maps a directory to its parent directory (if it has one).

$$
\begin{array}{|l}
\mathit{nodesOf} : \mathrm{ran}\,\mathit{directory} \longrightarrow \mathbb{F}\,\mathit{NODE} \\
\mathit{subDirsOf} : \mathrm{ran}\,\mathit{directory} \longrightarrow \mathbb{F}\,\mathit{NODE} \\
\mathit{parent} : \mathit{NODE} \nrightarrow \mathit{NODE} \\
\hline
\mathit{nodesOf} = \mathit{directory}^{\sim}\, \fatsemi\, \mathit{second} \\
\forall\, d : \mathrm{ran}\,\mathit{directory} \bullet \mathit{subDirsOf}\ d = \mathit{nodesOf}\ d \setminus \mathrm{ran}\,\mathit{file} \\
\mathit{parent} = \{\, d : \mathrm{ran}\,\mathit{directory};\ n : \mathit{NODE} \mid n \in \mathit{nodesOf}\ d \bullet n \mapsto d \,\}
\end{array}
$$

▷ *projection function*
$\mathit{nodesOf}$ takes the inverse of $\mathit{directory}$ (which is functional since $\mathit{directory}$ is an injection) and composes it with second, to give the second item in the pair, a set of NODEs. This is a useful device for situations where you have a function from a single item to a pair of items, but want a function that maps to only one of them.

The relation isIn relates a node to any other node that ultimately contains it.

$$
\begin{array}{|l}
\_\,\mathit{isIn}\,\_ : \mathit{NODE} \leftrightarrow \mathit{NODE} \\
\hline
(\_\,\mathit{isIn}\,\_) = \{\, n : \mathit{NODE};\ d : \mathrm{ran}\,\mathit{directory} \mid n \in \mathit{nodesOf}\ d \,\}^{+}
\end{array}
$$

▷ *relation, infix*
The underscores in the declaration indicate that isIn is intended as an infix relation. Notice that the underscores are part of the name, as shown in the predicate.
▷ *transitive closure*
We build the 'isImmediatelyIn' relation as an explicit set comprehension, then extend it to the general 'isIn' relation by forming the transitive closure.

The function *name* returns the name of a node.

$$
\begin{array}{|l}
name : NODE \longrightarrow NAME \\
\hline
name = (\,\lambda\, d : \operatorname{ran} file \bullet first(file^{\sim}\, d)\,) \\
\qquad\quad \cup\,(\,\lambda\, d : \operatorname{ran} directory \bullet first(directory^{\sim}\, d)\,)
\end{array}
$$

▷ *free type*
This style of definition 'by cases', one case for each branch of the free type, is a useful cliché.

▷ *proof obligation*
We define *name* as the union of two functions, and so are obliged to show that this union preserves functionality.

Since the domains of the two functions, ran *file* and ran *directory*, are disjoint, by construction of the free type, their union is also a function.

We're nearly there! We now define a file system to be a directory in which no two nodes immediately contained within it, or in the same subdirectory of the file system, share the same name.

$$
\begin{aligned}
fileSys == \{\,root, d : \operatorname{ran} directory \mid (d\ isIn\ root \lor d = root) \\
\land\,(\,\forall\, m, n : nodesOf\ d \mid m \neq n \bullet name\ m \neq name\ n\,) \bullet root\,\}
\end{aligned}
$$

Finally, the state of the file system is specified by the (rather uninteresting) schema *fileSystem*.

$$
FileSystem \,\widehat{=}\, [\,fileSystem : fileSys\,]
$$

The move operation

We must first specify what is meant by the *path name* of a node. The path name of a node n that is in a file system d is given by a sequence of names, beginning with the name of d and ending with the name of n. The intermediate members of the path name are the names (in order) of the enclosing directories, moving successively from d to n. The relation *pathName* relates a node and the path names of all nodes (subdirectories and files) contained in it.

$$
\begin{array}{|l}
pathName : NODE \longleftrightarrow \operatorname{seq} NAME \\
\hline
pathName = \{\,n : NODE \bullet n \mapsto \langle name\ n\rangle\,\} \\
\qquad\quad \cup\, \{\,d : \operatorname{ran} directory;\ p : \operatorname{seq} NAME \mid \\
\qquad\qquad\quad p \in pathName(\!|nodesOf\ d|\!) \bullet d \mapsto \langle name\ d\rangle \,\widehat{\ }\, p\,\}
\end{array}
$$

▷ *relational image*
nodesOf d gives the set of nodes in directory d. Applying the relational image of *pathName* to this set gives the set of all path names within d. Concatenating the name of d to the beginning of each member of this set gives the set of all path names from d.

▷ *relational image*
When d contains no nodes, the relational image gives an empty set, and so there is no such p, and the set comprehension is empty. The case is covered by the first term of the union, which gives the path name $\langle name\ d\rangle$.

▷ *recursion*

It is not immediately obvious that this recursive definition is well-formed. Note that for finite directory structures the set *nodesOf d* will eventually be either empty, or all files not in the range of *directory*, and so the recursion terminates.

A proper path name is a sequence of names of length at least two

$$path == \{\, p : \text{seq } NAME \mid \#p \geq 2 \,\}$$

We now require the following functions

- *subNode* returns the node corresponding to the given file system and path name
- *remove* returns a file system with the node identified by the given path name removed
- *add* returns a file system with the given node added to the place in the given file system identified by the given path name.

It is tedious to specify these functions, as a value drawn from the set *fileSys* is just the *root* of the file system. Every manipulation of the file system requires us to enter the system at the root directory and navigate ourselves to the node of interest. We provide a full specification here only for the function *remove*, which is enough to give the general idea.

$$
\begin{array}{|l}
\hline
subNode : fileSys \times path \rightarrow\!\!\!\rightarrow NODE \\
remove : fileSys \times path \rightarrow\!\!\!\rightarrow fileSys \\
add : NODE \times path \times fileSys \rightarrow\!\!\!\rightarrow fileSys \\
\hline
remove = \\
\quad (\, \lambda\, fs : fileSys;\ p : path \mid \#p = 2 \land fs \mapsto p \in pathName \bullet \\
\qquad\quad directory(name\ fs, \{\, n : nodesOf\ fs \mid name\ n \neq p\,2 \,\})\,) \\
\\
\quad \cup \\
\\
\quad \{\, fs, n : fileSys;\ p : path \mid \#p > 2 \land fs \mapsto p \in pathName \\
\qquad\quad \land n \in nodesOf\ fs \land name\ n = p\,2 \bullet \\
\qquad\quad (fs, p) \mapsto remove(n, tail\ p) \,\} \\
\hline
\end{array}
$$

A *Move* operation takes the input path names *from?* (identifying the node to be moved) and *to?* (identifying the location in the file system where the node is to be moved to). The following preconditions are required

- the node must exist
- the front of *to?* must identify an existing directory node
- there must not already be an existing node identified by *to?* (that is, no overwriting of nodes).

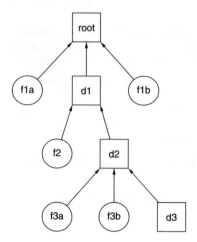

Figure 20.1 An example element of *fileSys*, shown as a tree.

```
┌─ Move ─────────────────────────────────────────────────────────────
│ ΔFileSystem
│ from?, to? : path
├──────────────────────────────────────────────────────────────────
│ fileSystem ↦ from? ∈ pathName
│ fileSystem ↦ front to? ∈ pathName
│ subNode(fileSystem, front to?) ∈ ran directory
│ fileSystem ↦ to? ∉ pathName
│ fileSystem′ =
│       add(subNode(fileSystem, from?), to?, remove(fileSystem, from?))
└──────────────────────────────────────────────────────────────────
```

▷ *sequence operations*
The expression *front to?* identifies that part of the destination path name which must be an existing path (that is, all but the last part of the name).

20.6.2   Discussion

We have seen that the specification of the file system in terms of a recursive free type definition is quite difficult. This difficulty lies in the fact that the nodes in the file system are not equally available to us; we have immediate access only to the *root* of the tree. For example, the file system shown abstractly as a tree in figure 20.1 is represented using the free type structure as

$$
\begin{aligned}
&directory(root, \{\\
&\quad file(f_{1a}, data),\\
&\quad directory(d_1, \{\\
&\qquad file(f_2, data),\\
&\qquad directory(d_2, \{\\
&\qquad\quad file(f_{3a}, data),\\
&\qquad\quad file(f_{3b}, data),\\
&\qquad\quad directory(d_3, \varnothing)\\
&\qquad \})\\
&\quad \}),\\
&\quad file(f_{1b}, data),\\
&\})
\end{aligned}
$$

In order to access components deep in the structure, the whole structure has to be explicitly traversed.

This inequality of access has two important consequences for specification:

- it is difficult to specify state invariants and operations that involve relationships between different tree nodes
- it is hard to define operations that change the structure of a tree

The following section introduces a different way of specifying a tree that does not suffer from these drawbacks.

20.6.3   Avoiding the free type definition

In this section we try again, respecifying the problem using a different model. Our new approach involves the separation of the *structure* of a tree from the *contents* of its nodes. It relies heavily on the treatment of trees in [Brown *et al.* 1986].

Application oriented theory

It is convenient to define a set of trees, for use later. This could be done as one definition, but we prefer to split it into four stages, to make clear which properties are being added at each stage. First we define *digraph X*, the set of directed graphs over X.

$$ digraph\ X == \{\, n : \mathbb{P}\,X;\ e : X \leftrightarrow X \mid (\mathrm{dom}\ e \cup \mathrm{ran}\ e) \subseteq n \,\} $$

A directed graph is a set of nodes and a homogeneous relation describing the directed edges connecting some of these nodes. See figure 20.2. Notice that we have to include a set of nodes in addition to the edge relation between them, in order to be able to have a digraph containing unconnected nodes.

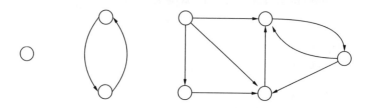

Figure 20.2 A directed graph.

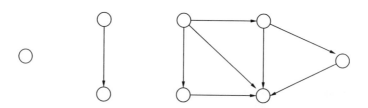

Figure 20.3 A directed acyclic graph.

Next we define *dag X*, the set of directed acyclic graphs over X.

$$dag\ X == \{\, n : \mathbb{P}\,X;\ e : X \leftrightarrow X \mid (n, e) \in digraph\ X \wedge \mathsf{disjoint}\ \langle e^+, \mathrm{id}\ X\rangle \,\}$$

A directed acyclic graph is a digraph that contains no cycles, see figure 20.3.

▷ *transitive closure*
e^+ is the transitive closure of the directed edge relation, so it relates all nodes that can be reached by one or more steps along the edges.

▷ *disjoint*
disjoint $\langle e^+, \mathrm{id}\ X\rangle$ says that no node can be reached in one or more steps from itself. So there are no cycles in the graph.

Next we define *condag X*, the set of connected directed acyclic graphs.

$$condag\ X == \{\, n : \mathbb{P}\,X;\ e : X \leftrightarrow X \mid (n, e) \in dag\ X \wedge (e \cup e^\sim)^* = n \times n \,\}$$

A connected dag is a dag that does not have separate pieces. See figure 20.4.

▷ *relational inverse*
$e^\sim$ is the relational inverse of the directed edge relation: it describes the case where the nodes are joined by edges in the other direction. So $e \cup e^\sim$ describes an edge relation where the nodes are joined by edges in both directions, or, equivalently, by undirected edges.

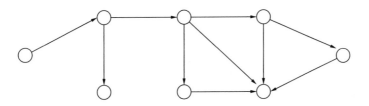

Figure 20.4 A connected directed acyclic graph.

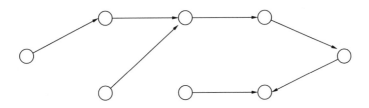

Figure 20.5 A tree.

▷ *reflexive transitive closure*
e^* is the reflexive transitive closure of the edge relation, so it relates all nodes that can be reached by zero or more steps along directed edges. Thus $(e \cup e^\sim)^*$ describes the relation between nodes that can be reached, in one direction or the other, by zero or more steps.

▷ *Cartesian product*
$n \times n$ is the Cartesian product of n with itself: the set of all pairs of nodes. The condition therefore states that all nodes can be reached from all others in zero or more steps, hence, the graph is connected.

Finally we define *tree X*, the set of trees.

$$tree\, X == \{\, n : \mathbb{P}\, X;\ e : X \leftrightarrow X \mid (n, e) \in condag\, X \wedge e \in X \twoheadrightarrow X \,\}$$

A trees is a connected dag where each node is related to at most one other—often called its *parent*. See figure 20.5.

These definitions are reusable if we ever want to have another tree structure. So the definitions have been folded up into a reusable toolkit *tree* (see appendix A.3).

Generic trees

We first define a non-empty tree that is generic in its node type N. This consists of a *tree* as defined above, along with some auxiliary definitions that are useful later.

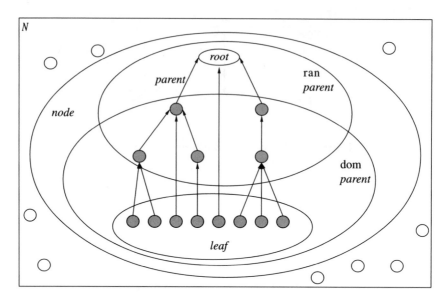

Figure 20.6 The sets *leaf* and *node*, and the function *parent*.

$$\begin{array}{l}
\underline{\hspace{1em}Tree[N]\hspace{8em}} \\
t : tree\ N \\
parent : N \nrightarrow N \\
node, leaf : \mathbb{P}_1\ N \\
child : N \leftrightarrow N \\
root : N \\
\overline{\hspace{1em}} \\
(node, parent) = t \\
leaf = node \setminus \text{ran}\ parent \\
\{root\} = node \setminus \text{dom}\ parent \\
child = parent^\sim
\end{array}$$

The tree t consists of a non-empty set of *node*s and a directed edge function called *parent*. The set of *leaf* nodes are those that are not in the range of *parent*, those that have no descendents. The *root* node is the single node that has no parent. It is convenient to name the inverse of the parent function; it is called *child*. See figure 20.6.

▷ *generic schema*
   This generic schema definition of a tree is applicable for any node type N. The desired type of the node is supplied when the schema is used.

The state of the file system

We declare given sets for the names of nodes, the data held by files, and for nodes themselves.

$$[DATA, NAME, NODE]$$

Note that we are defining *NODE* as a given set in this version rather than the free type definition that we had before. The free type definition is a given set with some additional structure.

We model the file system as a tree. The structure is provided by the schema *Tree* and the contents of the nodes are provided by functions from the nodes to appropriate values. The following state invariants are required

- all nodes are named
- a file (a node that contains data) must be a leaf node
- no two nodes immediately contained within a directory share the same name

```
┌─ FileSystem0 ────────────────────────────────────────────
│ Tree[NODE]
│ name : NODE ⤖ NAME
│ data : NODE ⤖ DATA
├──────────────────────────────────────────────────────────
│ dom name = node
│ root ∉ dom data ⊆ leaf
│ ∀ n : node • (∀ c, d : child(|{n}|) | c ≠ d • name c ≠ name d )
└──────────────────────────────────────────────────────────
```

▷ *generic schema*
  Whenever we use the generic schema *Tree[N]* we must supply an actual parameter for the generic parameter *N*. Here we are creating a tree of *NODEs*.
▷ *relation, infix*
  The expression

$$root \notin dom\ data \subseteq leaf$$

  is shorthand for

$$root \notin dom\ data$$
$$dom\ data \subseteq leaf$$

For convenience we add to the state schema a derived function *namedNode*, which returns the node in the tree corresponding to a given non-empty sequence of names.

```
 ___ FileSystem1 _____
| FileSystem0
| namedNode : seq₁ NAME ⤖ NODE
|_____
| namedNode =
|       { path : seq₁ NODE | head path = root
|                  ∧ ( ∀ i, j : dom path | j = i + 1
|                          • path i ↦ path j ∈ child )
|               • path ⨟ name ↦ last path }
|_____
```

▷ *sequence operations*
The expression *head path = root* checks that the first entry in the path name is the root of the file system.
▷ *sequence operations*
The expression *last path* gives the last entry in the path name, which is the name of the file.
▷ *relational composition*
We use *path ⨟ name* to build a sequence of names from a sequences of nodes and a function from nodes to names.

The move operation

A path name is a sequence of names of length at least two (as in the first attempt at the specification).

$$path == \{\, p : \text{seq } NAME \mid \#p \geq 2 \,\}$$

The specification of the *Move*1 operation is now trivial, because all nodes are equally accessible to us. We require the same preconditions as in the previous version of *Move*.

```
 ___ Move1 _____
| ΔFileSystem1
| from?, to? : path
|_____
| from? ∈ dom namedNode
| front to? ∈ dom namedNode
| namedNode(front to?) ∉ dom data
| to? ∉ dom namedNode
| root' = root
| parent' = parent ⊕{namedNode from? ↦ namedNode(front to?)}
|_____
```

20.7   Free types in detail

20.7.1   Structural induction

Recursive free type definitions can be powerful, and they have their own proof technique, *structural induction*. The classic example of a recursive free type definition is a binary tree. Here we use a slightly different formulation from the file system example; now the nodes, not the leaves, hold the data.

[*DATA*]

$$BINTREE ::= leaf$$
$$\quad\quad\quad | \ node \langle\!\langle DATA \times BINTREE \times BINTREE \rangle\!\rangle$$

As in all recursive definitions, (at least) one branch is not recursive; the single element *leaf* gives the base case. The other branch is recursive, with *BINTREE* defined as the composition of a *DATA* element and two other (smaller) *BINTREE*s. If we want to prove some property for all *BINTREE*s

$$t : BINTREE \vdash \mathcal{P}\,t$$

then we use the technique of proof by structural induction, so called because it uses the structure of the definition, together with the technique of mathematical induction.

▷ *prefix relation*
   $\mathcal{P}\,x$ is shorthand for $x \in (\mathcal{P}\_)$, where $\mathcal{P}\_ : \mathbb{P}\,X$

Such a proof requires one proof for each branch of the definition

$$\vdash \mathcal{P}\,leaf$$
$$d : DATA;\ s, t : BINTREE \mid \mathcal{P}\,s;\ \mathcal{P}\,t \vdash \mathcal{P}\,(node(d, s, t))$$

For example, assume we have defined a function that reverses a tree by swapping its recursively reversed subtrees

$$revtree : BINTREE \longrightarrow BINTREE$$
$$revtree\ leaf = leaf$$
$$\forall\,d : DATA;\ s, t : BINTREE \bullet$$
$$\quad\quad revtree(node(d, s, t)) = node(d, revtree\ t, revtree\ s)$$

Now suppose we want to prove that reversing a tree twice leaves it unchanged, that is

$$t : BINTREE \vdash (revtree \circ revtree)t = t$$

Then we have to prove two things. The *leaf* branch of the proof is

$(revtree \circ revtree)leaf$
$= revtree\ leaf$ [from definition]
$= leaf$ [from definition]

□

The *node* branch of the proof is

$(revtree \circ revtree)s = s$ [hypothesis 1]
$(revtree \circ revtree)t = t$ [hypothesis 2]

$(revtree \circ revtree)(node(d, s, t))$
$= revtree(node(d, revtree\ t, revtree\ s))$ [from definition]
$= node(d, (revtree \circ revtree)s, (revtree \circ revtree)t)$ [from definition]
$= node(d, s, t)$ [from hypotheses 1 and 2]

□

Notice how the proof was assisted by the form of the definition of *revtree*. As a general rule, let the form of functions over recursive free types follow the structure of the free type definition itself. This makes the function easier to define, and any induction proofs easier to do.

20.7.2   Schemas in the domain

[King *et al.* 1988] use free types to define an abstract syntax for Z itself. Their definition of predicates (their section 5.5) uses schemas as the domains of their injections

$Param \triangleq [\, op_1, op_2 : PRED\,]$

$PRED ::= negate\langle\!\langle PRED \rangle\!\rangle$
$\quad\quad | \quad conjoin\langle\!\langle Param \rangle\!\rangle$
$\quad\quad | \quad \ldots$

It might appear that the definition above is ill-formed, since *Param* is used in the definition of *PRED* before it itself has been declared. Remember that the 'declaration before use' condition requires only that it be possible to reorder a specification so that everything is declared before use, not that it is presented in that order. It is possible to reorder the above definition by rewriting it as

$[PRED]$
$Param \triangleq [\, op_1, op_2 : PRED\,]$

$$negate : PRED \rightarrowtail PRED$$
$$conjoin : Param \rightarrowtail PRED$$
$$\ldots$$
$$\langle \operatorname{ran} negate, \operatorname{ran} conjoin, \ldots \rangle \text{ partition } PRED$$

▷ *tool support*
Z tools tend to enforce a declaration before use order, because this makes it possible to perform various checks in a single pass. If your Z tool does enforce this order, but permits repeated declarations, you can use schemas in free type definitions by writing something like

$$[PRED]$$
$$Param \mathrel{\widehat{=}} [\, op_1, op_2 : PRED \,]$$
$$PRED ::= \ldots$$

This use of schemas is particularly useful when the domain of an injection is quite complicated. For example, a ternary tree (just to go one better than the usual binary example) could be defined as

$$TreeNode \mathrel{\widehat{=}} [\, data : DATA;\ left, mid, right : TERNTREE \,]$$

$$TERNTREE ::= tleaf$$
$$\mid branch \langle\!\langle TreeNode \rangle\!\rangle$$

20.7.3   The structure of free types

This section explains the structure of free types in some detail. A free type definition is a bit of syntactic sugar for introducing a new type with some associated structure. For example, the free type declaration

$$IDCHAR ::= a \langle\!\langle ALPHA \rangle\!\rangle$$
$$\mid d \langle\!\langle DIGIT \rangle\!\rangle$$
$$\mid underscore$$

is equivalent to (assuming that the types *ALPHA* and *DIGIT* have already been defined)

$$[IDCHAR]$$

$$a : ALPHA \rightarrowtail IDCHAR$$
$$d : DIGIT \rightarrowtail IDCHAR$$
$$underscore : IDCHAR$$
$$\langle \operatorname{ran} a, \operatorname{ran} d, \{underscore\} \rangle \text{ partition } IDCHAR$$

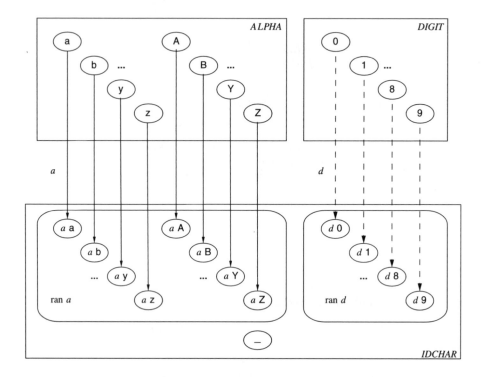

Figure 20.7 The elements of the *IDCHAR* free type.

Pictorially, this can be shown as the three types, *IDCHAR*, *ALPHA* and *DIGIT*, and the two injections (one-to-one functions) *a* and *d* between them; see figure 20.7. Notice that the elements of the free type do not all have names of their own, some are built up from the names of the injection and its argument.

The mapping functions are total injections, so there is one element in *IDCHAR* for every element in *ALPHA*, and one for every element in *DIGIT*. The ranges of the all the functions, and the singleton set, partition *IDCHAR*, so there is no overlap between the ranges, and there are no other 'spare' elements in *IDCHAR*.

With a recursive free type definition, the type itself occurs as component of the domain of at least one injection. This can be thought of as defining how to build complex elements of the type from simpler elements. Such a definition always yields an infinite type, because complex elements themselves can always be used to build yet more complex elements, and so on. For example, consider the simplest recursive definition, *NAT*

$$NAT ::= zero \mid next \langle\!\langle NAT \rangle\!\rangle$$

The elements of *NAT* are

    zero
    next(*zero*)
    next(*next*(*zero*))
    next(*next*(*next*(*zero*)))
    . . .

▷ *induction*
This shows the connection between structural induction and classical mathematical induction. Assume we want to prove some property for all *NAT*s

$$n : NAT \vdash \mathcal{P}\, n$$

This requires one proof for each branch of the definition (see also the discussion in section 20.7.1).

$$\vdash \mathcal{P}\, zero$$
$$n : NAT \mid \mathcal{P}\, n \vdash \mathcal{P}\, (next\, n)$$

which is the classic requirement for proof by induction. Similar forms of proof can also be used for non-recursive free types, one proof for each branch, although there is no need for the inductive 'assumption' step.

More complicated expressions can be used in the domains of a free type's injections. For example, consider the free type definition of well-formed formulae (taken from [Diller 1990, Chapter 9])

$$
\begin{aligned}
WFF ::=\ &atom \langle\!\langle ID \rangle\!\rangle \\
\mid\ &negation \langle\!\langle WFF \rangle\!\rangle \\
\mid\ &conjunction \langle\!\langle WFF \times WFF \rangle\!\rangle \\
\mid\ &disjunction \langle\!\langle WFF \times WFF \rangle\!\rangle \\
\mid\ &implication \langle\!\langle WFF \times WFF \rangle\!\rangle \\
\mid\ &equivalence \langle\!\langle WFF \times WFF \rangle\!\rangle
\end{aligned}
$$

This includes terms like *WFF* × *WFF*. A picture of a few of the elements of this type, and how they are related by the various injections, is shown in figure 20.8. That the ranges of the injections are disjoint means that there is only ever one arrow *to* an element as each element is built up from primitive components in a unique way (this is sometimes called the 'no confusion' property). That the ranges partition the type means that all the elements are built up from the primitive components only, so there are no extra spurious elements (this is sometimes called the 'no junk' property).

Care has to be taken when building recursive free types as some definitions are impossible to satisfy. The following, for example, is an inconsistent free type definition

$$IMPOS ::= tooBig \langle\!\langle \mathbb{P}\, IMPOS \rangle\!\rangle$$

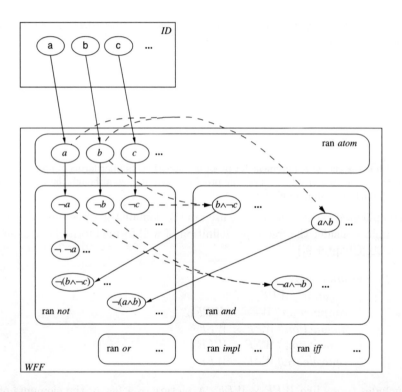

Figure 20.8 Some elements of the *WFF* free type. (The names of the injections have been abbreviated, for clarity.)

It is impossible to have a *total* injection from a set's power set to that set; the power set is just 'too big', there are not enough elements in the target set for a one-to-one mapping. It is a standard mathematical result that the cardinality of a power set $\mathbb{P}\,X$ is strictly greater than the cardinality of the set X, even if the set is infinite (see, for example, [Stewart & Tall 1977, Chapter 12, proposition 5]).

Since relations are just power sets, $X \leftrightarrow Y == \mathbb{P}(X \times Y)$, they are also too big to use in a domain. Functions, although a subset of relations, can also turn out to be too big.

Sets of all finite subsets, and the finite functions (which include sequences), however, are not too big, and can be used in recursive definitions. For example

$$OK ::= finSet\langle\!\langle \mathbb{F}\,OK \rangle\!\rangle$$
$$\;\;\;\;\; |\;\; finFun\langle\!\langle OK \twoheadrightarrow OK \rangle\!\rangle$$
$$\;\;\;\;\; |\;\; finSeq\langle\!\langle \mathrm{seq}\,OK \rangle\!\rangle$$

▷ *finiteness*
 This is one of the few times it is necessary to specify explicitly that various sets are finite. [Spivey 1992, 3.10.2] discusses this in more detail, and gives a sufficient condition for a free type definition to be consistent.

It is possible to write a pointless definition such as

$$EMPTY ::= nothing\langle\!\langle EMPTY \rangle\!\rangle$$

With this sort of definition, there is no base case to the recursion, nothing for the construction of complex elements to start from. The 'no junk' property ensures that the construction cannot start from some other primitive element in the type as there is none. So *nothing* is the empty injection.

At first sight, it might look as if

$$OKF ::= finiteSet\langle\!\langle \mathbb{F}\,OKF \rangle\!\rangle$$
$$OKS ::= sequence\langle\!\langle \mathrm{seq}\,OKS \rangle\!\rangle$$

are also a problem. But these do have a base point for starting to build elements of the type: the empty set and the empty sequence. Nonetheless there is a problem with using $\mathbb{F}_1$ or seq_1.

20.8   Concluding remarks

Free types are useful for defining a new type in terms of other, disjoint types, and for capturing recursive structures.

Recursive free type definitions are useful when any definitions or proofs make use of *structural induction* over the structure of the free type. For example, see the proof of *revtree* in section 20.7.1, and the specification of a four function calculator in section 22.2.

The use of a free type springs immediately to mind to specify recursive structures such as trees. As the file system example in section 20.6 shows, such an approach is not necessarily appropriate. Using a free type to model the file system permits access to the tree from the root only and results in awkward definitions of the operations. The operations do not follow a structural induction style, and so a free type definition is inappropriate in this case.

A good guide to the suitability of a model is the simplicity with which the relevant operations may be defined. If they are difficult to describe then there may well be a better way of describing the system state.

Chapter 21

Using Bags

In which bags are described and shown to be more useful than generally supposed.

21.1 The ins and outs of bags

Bags are rarely addressed on Z courses or in introductory tutorials. We attempt to rectify that omission in this chapter.

A bag is a collection of elements in which an element may occur more than once. It is sometimes known as a *multiset*. The order of elements is unimportant. A bag thus has more structure than a set (where number of occurrences is not considered) but less than a sequence (where the order of elements is important).

In Z we define a bag over a type X to be a function from the type onto the number of times the given item occurs in the bag; we do not record elements that do not occur in the bag.

$$\text{bag } X == X \nrightarrow \mathbb{N}_1$$

▷ *abbreviation definition, generic*
This definition is generic on type X. So we can now have a bag of any type. Operations that are defined generically on bags may be used on bags of any type.

Bags have a special 'bag bracket' notation to display the entries in the bag. The notation

$$\llbracket \underbrace{a_1, \ldots, a_1}_{k_1 \text{ times}}, \ldots, \underbrace{a_n, \ldots, a_n}_{k_n \text{ times}} \rrbracket$$

is used to represent the bag

$$\{a_1 \mapsto k_1, \ldots, a_n \mapsto k_n\}$$

For example, the bag

$$[\![f, l, o, c, c, i, n, a, u, c, i, n, i, h, i, l, i, p, i, l, i, f, i, c, a, t, i, o, n]\!]$$

is equivalent to

$$\{f \mapsto 2, l \mapsto 3, o \mapsto 2, c \mapsto 4, i \mapsto 9, n \mapsto 3,$$
$$a \mapsto 2, u \mapsto 1, h \mapsto 1, p \mapsto 1, t \mapsto 1\}$$

Since the order of the items in the bag display is irrelevant, the following all represent the same bag

$$[\![a, s, c, e, r, t, a, i, n]\!]$$
$$[\![c, a, r, t, e, s, i, a, n]\!]$$
$$[\![s, e, c, t, a, r, i, a, n]\!]$$
$$[\![a, a, c, e, i, n, r, s, t]\!]$$
$$\{a \mapsto 2, c \mapsto 1, e \mapsto 1, i \mapsto 1, n \mapsto 1, r \mapsto 1, s \mapsto 1, t \mapsto 1\}$$

[Hayes 1990] uses a different definition of bags and offers more toolkit operations for bags than [Spivey 1992]. For example, he allows negative occurrences of bag entries.

21.2   What's in a bag?

We can determine whether or not an item is in a bag using the infix bag membership relation $(\_ \mathrel{\mathsf{E}} \_)$. This is the bag version of $\in$ for sets. We can also discover how many times an item appears in the bag using the toolkit function *count*. This extends a bag into a total function that returns zero if the item is not in the bag. The definition of *count* has some interesting features.

$$
\begin{array}{l}
=[X] \\
\hline
count : \mathrm{bag}\, X \twoheadrightarrow X \to \mathbb{N} \\
\hline
\forall b : \mathrm{bag}\, X \bullet count\, b = (\lambda x : X \bullet 0) \oplus b \\
\hline
\end{array}
$$

▷ *bijection*
  count is a bijection. Hence it is
  – *total*: any bag can be counted
  – *onto*: all functions $f : X \to \mathbb{N}$ are in the range of *count*; given an f, the corresponding bag can be formed by removing zero from f's range
  – *one-to-one*: each bag is a different function, and so each 'extended bag' formed by *count* is also a different function.

Because of the existence of this bijection, there is no theoretical difference between defining bags as partial functions excluding zero from their range, and total functions including zero. Which representation is chosen is a matter of convenience. The partial function approach makes the definition of bag membership slightly more convenient ($x \in b \Leftrightarrow x \in \text{dom}\, b$, rather than $x \in b \Leftrightarrow count\, b\, x > 0$), but is harder to extend to negative occurrences of elements. This ability to make a partial function total with a bijection depends on there being an element not in the range of the partial function (zero in this case).

▷ *curried function*
Function arrows associate to the right, so

$$\text{bag}\, X \rightarrowtail\mkern-14mu\rightarrow X \longrightarrow \mathbb{N} \ \text{ and }\ \text{bag}\, X \rightarrowtail\mkern-14mu\rightarrow (X \longrightarrow \mathbb{N})$$

are equivalent. Hence *count b* is a function from elements to their number of occurrences in bag *b*, and *count b x* gives the number of *x*s in *b*.

▷ *bag operations*
The toolkit operator ♯ is an infix, and hence uncurried, variant of *count*. Although it is possible to use *count* with a single argument, there is no equivalent expression using ♯; it must be given both arguments.

▷ *overriding*
In the definition of *count* the function that maps every item to zero is overridden by the function that is the bag. This means that for entries in the bag, *count* reports the number of times that that each appears in the bag. Otherwise *count* gives zero.

▷ *lambda-expression*
Compare the definition of

$$count\, b = (\lambda x : X \bullet 0) \oplus b$$

with the equivalent

$$count\, b\, x = \textbf{if } x \in b \textbf{ then } b\, x \textbf{ else } 0$$

21.3   Throwing things into a bag

The toolkit function *items* converts a sequence into a bag. If *s* is a sequence, *items s* is the bag in which each element maps to the number of times it appears in *s*. One way to think about *items* is by analogy to a game of Scrabble[1]; at the end of the game the sequence of tiles on the board are gathered up into a (physical) bag of tiles. The tiles in the bag are the same as those that were on the board, but the information about their order has been lost.

We can use *items* to define anagrams. We define an *anagram* of a sequence to be any other sequence containing exactly the same elements, with each element occurring the same number of times in each sequence. In other words, the respective bags are the same.

$$\begin{array}{l}
\underline{[X]}\\
\quad anagram : \text{seq}\, X \leftrightarrow \text{seq}\, X\\
\hline
\quad anagram = \{\, s, t : \text{seq}\, X \mid items\, s = items\, t \,\}
\end{array}$$

---

[1]Scrabble[TM] is a registered trademark of Spear's Games.

A true anagram is one in which the two sequences are not the same, so we remove identity pairs from the anagram relation.

$$
\boxed{\begin{array}{l}
=[X]=\\[2pt]
\quad trueAnagram : \operatorname{seq} X \longleftrightarrow \operatorname{seq} X \\[6pt]
\hline
\quad trueAnagram = anagram \setminus \operatorname{id}(\operatorname{seq} X)
\end{array}}
$$

▷ *identity relation*
This definition of *trueAnagram* says that the true anagrams are the ones that are anagrams, but not the ones where there has been no 'real' reordering of the elements.

▷ *discussion*
We give a direct description of all the anagram and true anagram pairs. Another way to have defined these concepts would have been

$$
\boxed{\begin{array}{l}
=[X]=\\[2pt]
\quad anagram, trueAnagram : \operatorname{seq} X \longleftrightarrow \operatorname{seq} X \\[6pt]
\hline
\quad \forall\, s, t : \operatorname{seq} X \bullet \\
\qquad (s \mapsto t \in anagram \Leftrightarrow items\ s = items\ t) \\
\qquad \wedge\, (s \mapsto t \in trueAnagram \Leftrightarrow s \mapsto t \in anagram \wedge s \neq t)
\end{array}}
$$

This version says 'for any two sequences that satisfy these criteria, it follows that they are anagrams of each other'. The version with the set comprehension is more direct, it says 'all the anagrams are defined like this'.

21.4   Joining bags together and taking them apart

Two bags may be combined using the toolkit operator *bag union*. This creates a new bag in which the number of times each item appears is equal to the sum of the number of times in which it appeared in the original two bags. (A better name would be *bag sum*.) Bag union is used extensively in the following example.

Bag difference can be used to remove the contents of one bag from another. Note that if c has more xs than does b, then the bag $b \uplus c$ has no xs. If bags were allowed to have negative occurrences, a more natural definition of bag difference would in such a case have a negative number of xs.

21.5   A game of Scrabble

In a game of Scrabble each player has some tiles with letters inscribed on them. These tiles have to be arranged into words and placed on the board in the manner of a crossword. Usually players have seven tiles; when they place a word on the board they draw more tiles to replace those used up. These tiles are kept in a cloth bag to ensure that the players cannot see those remaining. Below we refer to this cloth bag and its contents as the 'pool' of tiles. When there are no more tiles in the pool, players continue to form words until an individual player has no tiles remaining, or no player can form and place a word. We introduce a given set for tiles

$$[\mathit{TILE}]$$

▷ *thinking ahead*
In a Scrabble set, different tiles have different scores associated with them. It is better to model the player's hand as a bag of tiles, rather than a bag of the characters on the tiles, because later it may be necessary to modify the specification to include scoring. If tiles are used, the given set *TILE* can be replaced by a schema type such as

$$Tile \; \widehat{=} \; [\, char : CHAR; \; score : \mathbb{N} \,]$$

There is a standard number of tiles that a player should have (if there are sufficient tiles available).

$$\mid \; noOfTiles : \mathbb{N}$$

Players are modelled by the bag of tiles currently in their hand. They are assigned identifiers when promoted to the game level of the specification. It is there that we distinguish between two players who may have the same set of *TILE*s.

$$
\begin{array}{l}
\_\,Player \underline{\hspace{7cm}} \\
\quad hand : \mathrm{bag} \; TILE \\
\rule{7cm}{0.4pt} \\
\quad sizebag \; hand \leq noOfTiles \\
\rule{8.5cm}{0.4pt}
\end{array}
$$

▷ *toolkit*
The function *sizebag* is defined in our extension to the standard toolkit, appendix A.9.

21.5.1   Levels of the specification

We specify Scrabble at two different levels: the player level and the game level. The player details will be promoted to the game level later on.

At the player level, tiles are used by placing them on the board or returning them to the pool, and new tiles are acquired from the pool. At the game level, the pool of tiles is diminished as tiles are drawn from it or increased (temporarily) by tiles returned to it. Players should maintain a certain number of tiles (usually seven) but if there are insufficient remaining in the pool they cannot do so.

21.5.2   Player level operations

Forming some tiles into a word and putting those tiles down on the board is described by

```
┌─ PlayWord ─────────────────────────────────────────────
│ ΔPlayer
│ word : seq TILE
├─────────────────────────────────────────────────────────
│ hand' ⊎ items word = hand
└─────────────────────────────────────────────────────────
```

▷ *implicit definition*
We do not give an explicit definition for the value of *hand'*, instead we show how it relates to *hand*. This is perfectly in order in Z and is an illustration of why it is important **not** to think of '=' as assignment.

▷ *bag operations*
Writing

$$hand' = hand \uplus items\ word$$

would not achieve the same effect, since ⊎ removes members of the bag only if they were there in the first place. Thus such an expression would permit a word to be put down made with tiles other than those currently in the player's hand.

▷ *bag operations*
We could avoid this problem by including an extra constraint using the sub-bag relation

$$items\ word \sqsubseteq hand$$

If a player is unable to go, some of the tiles may be returned to the pool.

```
┌─ ReturnTiles ──────────────────────────────────────────
│ ΔPlayer
│ return : bag TILE
├─────────────────────────────────────────────────────────
│ hand' ⊎ return = hand
└─────────────────────────────────────────────────────────
```

Notice that the predicate prevents tiles not currently in the player's hand from being in *return*.

After using up some tiles either by returning them or by placing a word on the board, a player may draw some more.

```
┌─ ReplenishHand ────────────────────────────────────────
│ ΔPlayer
│ take : bag TILE
├─────────────────────────────────────────────────────────
│ hand' = hand ⊎ take
└─────────────────────────────────────────────────────────
```

If the 'word' that a player puts down is successfully challenged (for example by not being in the dictionary used, or being a proper noun) the tiles must be taken back by that player, and play passes to the next player. Taking back the tiles is described by

```
┌─ TakeBackWord ────────────────────────────────────┐
│ ΔPlayer                                            │
│ word : seq TILE                                    │
├────────────────────────────────────────────────── │
│ hand' = hand ⊎ items word                          │
└────────────────────────────────────────────────────┘
```

A turn of placing a word that must then be withdrawn is given by

$$ChallengedWord \; \widehat{=} \; PlayWord \; ; \; TakeBackWord$$

▷ *schema composition*
   The schema composition matches the resulting *hand'* from *PlayWord* with the initial *hand* in *TakeBackWord*.

This should leave the player's hand unchanged, and so it should be possible to prove the following theorem

$$ChallengedWord \vdash \Xi Player$$

In other words, given the hypothesis *ChallengedWord* (which introduces declarations and constraints), then the property of $\Xi Player$ holds.

We prove this theorem in section 23.3.2.

▷ *proof obligation*
   It is good practice to demonstrate that where an operation is meant to 'undo' another, that it really does. In general, it should be possible to show that $\Xi State$ may be deduced from the combined result of the two operations. (There are likely to be 'extra' variables resulting from the composition of the operations so the result is not necessarily equivalent to $\Xi State$).

21.5.3   Game level operations

The state of a game consists of a number of players, a player whose turn it currently is, and the pool of tiles still available. The players are arranged into a sequence, and play progresses along the sequence. When the end of the sequence is reached play starts again from the beginning. (According to the rules, at the beginning of the game each player draws a tile. The player with the earliest letter in the alphabet starts, and play passes to the left.) Scrabble is a game for between two and four players

$$least == 2$$
$$most == 4$$

The complete game has a sequence of players, one of whom is currently playing, a bag of letters remaining (the *pool*), some letters placed on the board, and a record of all the letters in the game (on Scrabble boards there is usually a list of how many of each letter there are).

```
┌─ Game ────────────────────────────────────────────────
│ currentPlayer : ℕ
│ players : seq Player
│ pool, allTiles, onBoard : bag TILE
│ inHands : bag TILE
├───────────────────────────────────────────────────────
│ currentPlayer ∈ dom players
│ #players ∈ least .. most
│ inHands = ⨄{ i : dom players • i ↦ (players i).hand }
│ onBoard ⊎ pool ⊎ inHands = allTiles
└───────────────────────────────────────────────────────
```

▷ *redundancy*
The variable *inHands* is a derived function, introduced for convenience. It makes the subsequent expression of *allTiles* easier to read.

▷ *toolkit*
⨄, distributed bag union, is a toolkit operator defined in appendix A.10.

We give the players an identity here by placing them in a sequence. Their identity is given by their place (index) in the sequence. They never change this position. Notice that the sequence cannot be injective since two players may have the same *TILE*s.

During a game, the number of players involved does not change, nor does the record of the tiles that exist, so we include these constraints in $\Delta Game$.

```
┌─ ΔGame ───────────────────────────────────────────────
│ Game
│ Game'
├───────────────────────────────────────────────────────
│ #players' = #players
│ allTiles' = allTiles
└───────────────────────────────────────────────────────
```

▷ *discussion*
Directly saying that the length of the *players* sequence does not change achieves the same effect as we achieved in the specification of Snakes and Ladders (Chapter 12) by saying that

$$\#players + \#place = numberOfPlayers$$

The approach chosen here is probably neater as it says what we want directly, and does not require a separate variable to represent the number of players; it merely asserts that the number does not change.

Note that we will have to ensure that the order in which the players take their turns remains the same. We cannot say that the sequence does not change since each *Player* is defined by the tiles held.

For our purposes, we assume that at the start of the game the first player has already been chosen (who we shall make the first in the sequence) and that each player has already drawn the requisite number of tiles.

```
┌─ InitGame ──────────────────────────────────────────
│ Game'
├──────────────────────────────────────────
│ currentPlayer' = 1
│ onBoard' = [[ ]]
│ ∀ p : ran players' • sizebag p.hand = noOfTiles
└──────────────────────────────────────────
```

Notice that the success of this initialisation requires a minimum number of tiles to be available.

Drawing tiles from the pool also changes the overall state of the game, and the details of a player who is drawing tiles. The mechanics of a player drawing tiles is given by *ReplenishHand*, so we include this. If there are sufficient tiles available then players can make up their quota, if not, all the remaining tiles are taken from the pool.

```
┌─ DrawFromPool ──────────────────────────────────
│ ΔGame
│ ReplenishHand
├──────────────────────────────────────────
│ pool' ⊎ take = pool
│ sizebag take = min{noOfTiles − sizebag hand, sizebag pool}
└──────────────────────────────────────────
```

▷ *minimum*
  The predicate part here says that the number of tiles taken should either be as many as required, or if that is more than the number available then all remaining in the pool.

The return of tiles to the pool does not involve an explicit player, merely the collection of tiles to be returned.

```
┌─ Return ─────────────────────────────────────────
│ ΔGame
│ return : bag TILE
├──────────────────────────────────────────
│ pool' = pool ⊎ return
└──────────────────────────────────────────
```

Both *DrawFromPool* and *Return* are partial descriptions of operations. They do not say what happens to *players* or to *currentPlayer*. These schemas are combined with others to give the full description of the operations. As we shall see, the returned tiles could come directly from a player's hand, or, in the case of a good player, they are tiles put to one side while new tiles are taken (in order to ensure the new tiles do not include any of the unwanted returned ones). They do not say what happens to the tiles on the board, either, because this can be deduced from the tiles in the pool and the tiles in the players' hands by using the invariant.

21.5.4   Combining player level and game level operations

We now promote the player level operations to the game level by way of a framing schema.

$$
\begin{array}{|l}
\underline{\Phi\,UpdateGame}\\
\Delta\,Game\\
\Delta\,Player\\
\hline
\theta\,Player = players\ currentPlayer\\
players' = players \oplus \{\,currentPlayer \mapsto \theta\,Player'\,\}
\end{array}
$$

$\triangleright$ *discussion*

Usually a framing schema has an input variable to identify explicitly the piece of local state to be manipulated. In this case, we know that the player (the local state) to be manipulated is the current player. So this framing schema ensures that the player we are dealing with is the current player.

When a player returns tiles, they are lost from that player's hand, but not necessarily returned to the pool immediately. Note that players are not allowed to discard more tiles than are available in the pool of tiles.

$$Discard \;\widehat{=}\; \exists\,\Delta\,Player \bullet [\,\Phi\,UpdateGame;\ ReturnTiles \mid$$
$$sizebag\ return \le sizebag\ pool\,]$$

The process of drawing new tiles at the game level is

$$Draw \;\widehat{=}\; \exists\,\Delta\,Player \bullet \Phi\,UpdateGame \wedge DrawFromPool$$

A normal turn involves playing a word and then drawing some tiles to replace those put down.

$$PlainGo \;\widehat{=}\; PlayWord \,\fatsemi\, DrawFromPool$$

We use this description in the complete specification of a normal turn.

$$NormalTurn \;\widehat{=}\; \exists\,\Delta\,Player \bullet [\,\Phi\,UpdateGame;\ PlainGo\,]$$

If the word is challenged then the player must take that word back. At the game level this is

$$UndoTurn \;\widehat{=}\; \exists\,\Delta\,Player \bullet \Phi\,UpdateGame \wedge ChallengedWord$$

If a player wishes to discard some tiles and draw some new ones, there are two ways of doing this. A good player places the rejected tiles on one side, and returns them to the pool *after* drawing new tiles.

Good players swap their tiles thus

$$GoodSwap \;\widehat{=}\; Discard \,\fatsemi\, Draw \,\fatsemi\, Return$$

whereas a poorer player swaps tiles thus

$PoorSwap \triangleq Discard \,\vdots\, Return \,\vdots\, Draw$

A player may also 'pass'. This can happen only if the player cannot go and there are no tiles left in the pool for a swap. (This is our interpretation of the summary of the rules that we have seen).

$Pass \triangleq [\Xi Game; \Xi Player \mid pool = [\![\,]\!]\,]$

A turn can be described by the disjunction of all the possible turns.

$Turn \triangleq NormalTurn$
$\qquad\quad \vee\ GoodSwap$
$\qquad\quad \vee\ PoorSwap$
$\qquad\quad \vee\ Pass$
$\qquad\quad \vee\ UndoTurn$

Passing the play from one player to the next is another game level operation, and is described thus

---
NextPlayer
$\Delta Game$

$currentPlayer' =$
$\quad$ **if** $currentPlayer = \#players$ **then** 1 **else** $currentPlayer + 1$

▷ *if then else*
The use of the 'if . . . then . . . else' construction here neatly captures what we wish to express. If we are at the end of the sequence of players, we start again at the beginning, otherwise we move along one.

The complete description of a turn is given by having a turn and then passing the play to the next player.

$CompleteTurn \triangleq Turn \,\vdots\, NextPlayer$

▷ *discussion*
In Snakes and Ladders (Chapter 12) the current player is always the first in the sequence and we manipulate the entries in the sequence to maintain this. Here, we walk along the sequence. In Snakes and Ladders the current player is modelled as a player (that is a range element in the sequence) whereas here the current player is modelled as an index (that is a domain element of the sequence). The domain element is often a more convenient way to manipulate the sequence as there is no need to index into the sequence. In the case of Snakes and Ladders we move entries from the *players* sequence to the *place* sequence since in this case it is easier to deal with the range elements of the sequence directly.

The game finishes when a player has no tiles remaining, and no tiles are left in the pool. This player is not necessarily the winner; we have not modelled scoring in this specification.

21.6   Poker hands

We now use the definition of playing cards from section 20.4 to define some poker hands [Phillips 1960]. A poker hand consists of five (different!) cards. *hand* is the set of all possible poker hands.

$$hand == \{\, c : \mathbb{P}\ Card \mid \#c = 5 \,\}$$

▷ *cardinality*
The cardinality, or size of set, operator $\#$ may be applied only to finite sets. There is a proof obligation to show that it is not being applied to an infinite subset of *Card*.
    Card is a schema with two components, each of which is an element of a finite set. Hence the bindings of *Card* also form a finite set, hence $\#$ is being applied correctly.

One way of looking at a hand is to consider just its suits: 'I've got all clubs', 'I've got three hearts and two diamonds'. The function *suit* takes a hand and returns a bag of its suits.

$$
\begin{array}{|l}
suit : hand \longrightarrow \text{bag } SUIT \\
\hline
\forall\, h : hand\ \bullet \\
\quad \exists\, c : \text{iseq } Card;\ s : \text{seq } SUIT \mid \\
\qquad \text{ran } c = h \wedge \#s = 5 \\
\qquad \wedge\ (\forall\, i : \text{dom } s \bullet s\, i = (c\, i).suit\,) \bullet \\
\quad suit\ h = items\ s
\end{array}
$$

c is a sequence of cards formed from the hand, s is the corresponding sequence of suits, and *suit* gives the bag formed from this sequence. Most of the complexity arises from trying to extract the suit component of the card schema; life would have been no easier if *Card* had been defined as a Cartesian product.

▷ *sequence, injective*
An injective sequence iseq (every element different) was used for c, to stop such sequences as $c = \langle \spadesuit K, \spadesuit A, \heartsuit A, \diamondsuit A, \clubsuit A, \clubsuit A, \clubsuit A \rangle$, which satisfies the predicate ran $c = h$, but would tend to cause trouble during a game of poker! Alternatively, c could have been defined as an ordinary sequence of length 5.

$$c : \text{seq } Card \mid \ldots \#c = 5 \ldots$$

Another way of looking at a hand is to consider just its faces: 'I've got four kings', 'I've got three tens and two aces'. The function *face* takes a hand and returns a bag of its faces.

$$
\begin{array}{|l}
face : hand \longrightarrow \text{bag } FACE \\
\hline
\forall\, h : hand\ \bullet \\
\quad \exists\, c : \text{iseq } Card;\ s : \text{seq } FACE \mid \\
\qquad \text{ran } c = h \wedge \#s = 5 \\
\qquad \wedge\ (\forall\, i : \text{dom } s \bullet s\, i = (c\, i).face\,) \bullet \\
\quad face\ h = items\ s
\end{array}
$$

▷ *discussion*

This function is similar to *suit*. Unfortunately a general form cannot be given using schemas or Cartesian products, since there is no way to pass the function the desired schema component or position in the Cartesian product, and even if there were, there would be no way to specify the type of the result. If all the components were of the same type, they could be formed into a sequence, and the relevant index passed to the function.

Some hands are distinguished by having all the cards of the same suit. In this case, the bag of suits would have only one component.

$$sameSuit == \{\, h : hand \mid \#(suit\ h) = 1\,\}$$

Some hands are distinguished by having a consecutive sequence of face values. For such hands the bag of faces would have five elements (one for each face value), and they could be formed into a sequence of faces in which each element was the *nextFace* of the previous.

$$consecutive == \{\, h : hand;\ s : \text{seq}\ FACE;\ b : \text{bag}\ FACE \mid$$
$$b = face\ h \wedge \#b = 5 \wedge items\ s = b$$
$$\wedge\ (\forall\,i : 1 .. 4 \bullet s(i+1) = nextFace(s\ i)\,)$$
$$\bullet\ h\,\}$$

We now have enough machinery to define the various special hands that are significant in the game of poker.

A *royalStraightFlush* is a hand where all the cards have the same suit, have consecutive values and the highest card is an ace. For example, $\heartsuit A\,K\,Q\,J\,10$.

$$royalStraightFlush == \{\, h : hand \mid h \in consecutive \cap sameSuit$$
$$\wedge\ (\exists\,c : h \bullet c.face = ace\,)\,\}$$

▷ *conjunction*

$h \in consecutive \cap sameSuit$ is a shorter form of $h \in consecutive \wedge h \in sameSuit$. This shows the connection between conjunction and intersection.

A *straightFlush* is a hand where all the cards have the same suit and have consecutive values, but is not a *royalStraightFlush*. For example, $\clubsuit J\,10\,9\,8\,7$.

$$straightFlush == (consecutive \cap sameSuit) \setminus royalStraightFlush$$

A *flush* is a hand where all the cards have the same suit but do not have consecutive values. For example, $\clubsuit A\,J\,9\,3\,2$.

$$flush == sameSuit \setminus consecutive$$

A *straight* is a hand where the cards have consecutive values but are not all the same suit. For example, $\heartsuit 10\,7, \Diamond 9, \spadesuit 8, \clubsuit 6$.

$$straight == consecutive \setminus sameSuit$$

Various hands are distinguished by having cards of the same face value. These can be defined in terms of the bag of faces. For example, if a hand has four cards of one face value and one of another, its bag of faces b looks like $[\![f_1, f_1, f_1, f_1, f_2]\!]$, or $\{f_1 \mapsto 4, f_2 \mapsto 1\}$. So $\#b = 2$ and $\exists f : FACE \bullet b \,\sharp\! f = 4$. Similar arguments hold for other combinations.

The hands called *fours* have four cards with the same face value. For example, $\heartsuit\,9\,2, \diamondsuit\,9, \spadesuit\,9, \clubsuit\,9$. So *fours* has two groups of values, one with four elements (the four of the same face), the other with one (the odd one out).

$$fours == \{\, h : hand; f : FACE; b : \text{bag } FACE \mid$$
$$b = face\ h \wedge \#b = 2 \wedge b \,\sharp\! f = 4 \bullet h \,\}$$

A *fullHouse* has two cards of one value and three of another. For example, $\heartsuit\,9\,4, \diamondsuit\,9, \clubsuit\,4, \spadesuit\,4$.

$$fullHouse == \{\, h : hand; f : FACE; b : \text{bag } FACE \mid$$
$$b = face\ h \wedge \#b = 2 \wedge b \,\sharp\! f = 3 \bullet h \,\}$$

The hands called *threes* have three cards with the same face value, and the other two different (from the three the same, and also from each other). For example, $\heartsuit\,A\,10, \clubsuit\,J\,10, \spadesuit\,10$. So *threes* has three groups of values, one with three elements (the three of the same face), the others with one (the two odd ones out).

$$threes == \{\, h : hand; f : FACE; b : \text{bag } FACE \mid$$
$$b = face\ h \wedge \#b = 3 \wedge b \,\sharp\! f = 3 \bullet h \,\}$$

The hands called *twoPairs* are those that have two pairs (but are not *fours*). For example, $\heartsuit\,9\,4\,2, \diamondsuit\,9, \clubsuit\,4$. So *twoPairs* has three groups of values, two with two elements, the other with one.

$$twoPairs == \{\, h : hand; f : FACE; b : \text{bag } FACE \mid$$
$$b = face\ h \wedge \#b = 3 \wedge b \,\sharp\! f = 2 \bullet h \,\}$$

Finally, a *pair* has two cards with the same face value, and no others the same. For example, $\heartsuit\,A\,10, \diamondsuit\,10, \spadesuit\,3, \clubsuit\,J$. So a *pair* has four groups of values, one with two elements, the others with one.

$$pair == \{\, h : hand; f : FACE; b : \text{bag } FACE \mid$$
$$b = face\ h \wedge \#b = 4 \wedge b \,\sharp\! f = 2 \bullet h \,\}$$

21.7   Concluding remarks

Bags can be a useful device in a specification. They are often used together with sequences, using *items* to connect a sequence with its associated bag. Be aware that sometimes you may define a function as $X \nrightarrow \mathbb{N}$ without at first realising that it is a bag (as happened to us in our space flight database example). It can be useful to define a bag explicitly, to make the specification clearer, and to make it obvious (especially to yourself) that the bag operators are available.

Chapter 22

A Four Function Calculator

In which a four function calculator is specified in an axiomatic style, is compared with a solution involving schemas, and loose specification is investigated.

22.1 Introduction

This example looks at two ways of specifying what is often called a 'four function' calculator with memories. A fairly concrete specification is given using schemas, along with a more abstract specification using axiomatic descriptions, with a discussion of why the more abstract version forces the use of axiomatic descriptions rather than schemas.

> **Problem statement.** Specify a calculator that provides the four arithmetical functions (addition, subtraction, multiplication and division), a change sign operation, can store results of calculations in its memories, can retrieve values from a memory, and can reset (clear) all its memories and zero the display.

In order to keep things simple, only integer values are allowed (once upon a time even expensive calculators used to be like this) and errors like overflow are not considered.

22.1.1 Input abstraction

We must select the level of abstraction to use for this specification. The critical decision is in terms of the inputs to the calculator; what do we model as being the input for which we expect an output? At one extreme, the most concrete, the inputs to the calculator correspond exactly to keystrokes. So there is an operation to press the '1' key, and another to press the '+' key. It works at the level of keystrokes. At the other extreme all forms of input are ignored except the request for the calculator to execute a certain expression and store it in a certain place. It works at the level of expressions. At a middle level we input the arithmetic operations, so we can input an integer, or the request to 'add' or 'subtract', etc.

The choice of abstraction has some consequences. The most abstract specification allows us to ignore completely the details of input/output. The interface is not specified, and so we can concentrate purely on the results to be achieved by the calculator. The least abstract specification is the easist to implement. It forces the specifier to address detailed issues of the interface, which is good if that is the area the specifier want to focus on, but bad if the overall behaviour has not yet been investigated.

We present here two choices: the most abstract (expressions) and a medium level of abstraction (arithmetic operations). It turns out that the most abstract does not lend itself to specification using schemas, but is better expressed using axiomatic descriptions. We see why later. The medium abstraction requires some design decisions to made; specifically either adding additional operations for nesting arithmetic operations or disallowing nested operations entirely. It is naturally expressed using schemas.

22.2   A solution using axiomatic descriptions

22.2.1   Store

We introduce a given set for labelling the memories.

> $[MEMORY]$

> ▷ *abstraction*
> On a real calculator, memory locations might be numbered (for example, 0 to 15) or named (for example, A to Z). But such detail is not needed in the specification, so we leave it out.

The store of the calculator is given by the mapping from its memories to the values stored there

> $store == MEMORY \longrightarrow \mathbb{Z}$

> ▷ *function*
> A total function is used here because whether we have explicitly stored a value in memory or not, every memory location has some value in it. If we intended the calculator to distinguish between those memory locations containing defined values and those not (by some form of tagging of the memory), we could use a partial function.

The initial store (when the calculator is switched on) has a zero in all the memories.

$$
\begin{array}{|l}
\hline
initStore : store \\
\hline
\forall\, m : MEMORY \bullet initStore\ m = 0 \\
\hline
\end{array}
$$

We have introduced a named constant, *initStore*, that represents the all-zero memory. Its name suggests that this is the store when the calculator is initialised, but this has not been captured in the Z.

22.2.2   Syntax

As we have chosen to consider entire expressions as the inputs to the calculator, we need a type definition of these. To treat all inputs in a consistent way, we introduce the idea of a calculator session, which consists of all the expressions (arithmetic manipulation for calculating values) and commands (modifications to memory) in a sequence.

The various kinds of expression can be specified using a free type definition.

$$
\begin{aligned}
EXPR ::= \ &number \langle\!\langle \mathbb{Z} \rangle\!\rangle \\
         \mid\ &memory \langle\!\langle MEMORY \rangle\!\rangle \\
         \mid\ &changeSign \langle\!\langle EXPR \rangle\!\rangle \\
         \mid\ &add \langle\!\langle EXPR \times EXPR \rangle\!\rangle \\
         \mid\ &subtract \langle\!\langle EXPR \times EXPR \rangle\!\rangle \\
         \mid\ &multiply \langle\!\langle EXPR \times EXPR \rangle\!\rangle \\
         \mid\ &divide \langle\!\langle EXPR \times EXPR \rangle\!\rangle
\end{aligned}
$$

▷ *free type, recursive*
This is a typical recursive definition. There are primitive branches, where the recursion can bottom out: *number* provides an integer value, and *memory* provides the value stored in a memory. And there are the recursive branches, building bigger expressions from smaller ones: *changeSign* changes the sign of the value of an expression, and the rest provide the four arithmetic operations, each combining two expressions.

▷ *abstraction*
Notice that this syntax is defined abstractly; it gives no indiction of the format that might be used to enter the expressions into the calculator. This is deliberate. The same abstract syntax can be used for a variety of different concrete syntaxes. For example, the abstract form

$$multiply(add(number\ 2, memory\ A), number\ 4)$$

could be written in 'algebraic notation' as
```
( 2 + A ) * 4
```
or in 'reverse Polish notation' as
```
2 A + 4 *
```

The descriptions of what the expressions do are completely informal at this point; the next section changes this.

▷ *discussion*
  There is the extra step of parsing the chosen concrete notation, but that is not covered here.
  In fact, some practitioners argue that it is a waste of time and effort to use Z to specify
  'well-understood' topics like parsing, for which there are existing formalisms (for example,
  BNF) and tools (for example, lex and yacc); the argument being that specification effort
  is better spent on the less well-understood areas of the application.

The various kinds of commands can be specified similarly

$$CMD ::= save\langle\!\langle EXPR \times MEMORY \rangle\!\rangle$$
$$\mid \; clear$$
$$\mid \; sequence\langle\!\langle \text{seq } CMD \rangle\!\rangle$$

There are commands to save the value of an expression in a memory, and to clear
all the memories. Commands can be sequenced (done one after the other).
    A session (from switching on the calculator) is simply a command (notice that
a command can be composed of a sequence of commands)

$$SESSION ::= session\langle\!\langle CMD \rangle\!\rangle$$

22.2.3 Semantics

Although the meaning of the various expressions and commands are explained
informally along with the syntax specifications above, they too need to be specified properly. The specification provides the semantics of the various constructs,
by defining various 'meaning functions', which map each piece of syntax to the
mathematical function it denotes.
    Expressions do not change the store (this is done by the *save* operation), but
they do need the store (well, the *memory* one does). So the meaning of an expression is a mapping from the expression to a number (the value of the expression) in
the context of a store.
    The first argument of the meaning function is a piece of syntax, and the func-
tion is mapping it to a mathematical value, or meaning. It is a convention in
denotational semantics to use 'fat square brackets', $[\![\,]\!]$, to enclose the syntax, to
distinguish it from the mathematical meaning. However, this is not allowed in Z,
since those brackets are used for bag displays, so here we use ordinary parenthesis
to enclose the syntactic argument.

- The value of a *number* expression is simply the number.
- A *memory* expression yields the value stored in the memory.
- A *changeSign* expression negates the value of its argument.
- An *add* expression adds the values of its two arguments.
- The other arithmetical expressions are defined similarly, using the Z mathe-
  matical toolkit definitions.

The complete meaning function is defined using the structure of the free type definition, one definition for each component of the free type.

$$\mathcal{M}_E : EXPR \longrightarrow store \nrightarrow \mathbb{Z}$$
$$\forall\, e, f : EXPR;\; n : \mathbb{Z};\; m : MEMORY;\; s : store \bullet$$
$$\mathcal{M}_E(number\ n)s = n$$
$$\wedge\ \mathcal{M}_E(memory\ m)s = s\ m$$
$$\wedge\ \mathcal{M}_E(changeSign\ e)s = -(\mathcal{M}_E(e)s)$$
$$\wedge\ \mathcal{M}_E(add(e,f))s = \mathcal{M}_E(e)s + \mathcal{M}_E(f)s$$
$$\wedge\ \mathcal{M}_E(subtract(e,f))s = \mathcal{M}_E(e)s - \mathcal{M}_E(f)s$$
$$\wedge\ \mathcal{M}_E(multiply(e,f))s = \mathcal{M}_E(e)s * \mathcal{M}_E(f)s$$
$$\wedge\ \mathcal{M}_E(divide(e,f))s = \mathcal{M}_E(e)s\ \mathsf{div}\ \mathcal{M}_E(f)s$$

▷ *curried function*
The meaning function $\mathcal{M}_E$ is declared to be a curried function. Hence the arguments can be supplied one at a time.

Note that the resulting function is not total because division by zero is not defined. Division by zero, although syntactically correct, does not mean anything. A fuller specification of the calculator would need to make this function total, possibly by including an error state for division by zero, or by choosing an arbitrary result.

▷ *implementation bias*
Note that neither of these choices is disallowed by the current specification since what is not defined can be implemented in any way you like.
▷ *axiomatic description*
The behaviour of evaluating an expression is much more easily expressed using a function than it would be using predicates on state variables. Consider, for example, the following model of the calculator with *store* as before, together with a display to show the user the result of evaluating an expression.

$$\begin{array}{|l}
\hline
Calc \\
\hline
store : MEMORY \longrightarrow \mathbb{Z} \\
display : \mathbb{Z} \\
\hline
\end{array}$$

How, then, would we express the operation to evaluate an input expression? The free type definition of *EXPR* forces any operations on *EXPR* to be defined recursively. There is no way of recursively 'applying' operations defined in schemas, and so we are forced to write

$$\begin{array}{|l}
\hline
Evaluate \\
\Delta Calc \\
exp? : EXPR \\
\hline
store' = store \\
display' = \mathcal{M}_E(exp?)store \\
\hline
\end{array}$$

and then define $\mathcal{M}_E$ separately in an axiomatic description. The *Evaluate* schema is left as unnecessary clutter, with all the real specification residing in $\mathcal{M}_E$.

Now that we have the semantics defined, we can calculate the value denoted by the example expression written in algebraic notation as $(2 + A) * 4$ (in this case, let's assume the value stored in memory A is 3, so that $s\,A = 3$)

$$\mathcal{M}_E(multiply(add(number\,2, memory\,A), number\,4))s$$
$$= \mathcal{M}_E(add(number\,2, memory\,A))s * \mathcal{M}_E(number\,4)s$$
$$= (\mathcal{M}_E(number\,2)s + \mathcal{M}_E(memory\,A)s) * 4$$
$$= (2 + s\,A) * 4$$
$$= (2 + 3) * 4$$
$$= 20$$

□

The effect of a command is to change the store.

- The *clear* command gives an initial store.
- The *save* command finds the value of its expression in the current store, and returns a new store with that value stored in the appropriate memory, and the other memories unchanged.
- An empty sequence of commands has no effect on the store.
- For a non-empty sequence of commands, the commands in the tail are evaluated in the store as modified by the first command.

Again, the meaning function definition is based around the structure of the *CMD* free type definition.

$$\mathcal{M}_C : CMD \longrightarrow store \nrightarrow store$$

$\forall s : store \bullet$
$\quad \mathcal{M}_C(clear)s = initStore$
$\forall e : EXPR; \, m : MEMORY; \, s : store \bullet$
$\quad \mathcal{M}_C(save(e, m))s = s \oplus \{m \mapsto \mathcal{M}_E(e)s\}$
$\forall s : store \bullet$
$\quad \mathcal{M}_C(sequence\langle\rangle)s = s$
$\forall c : CMD; \, cc : seq\,CMD; \, s : store \bullet$
$\quad \mathcal{M}_C(sequence(\langle c\rangle \frown cc))s = \mathcal{M}_C(sequence\,cc)(\mathcal{M}_C(c)s)$

Again, this results in a partial function since if an expression in a *store* command includes division by zero, the effect of the command is undefined.

A session starts out with an initially clear store, then performs the command specified.

$$\mathcal{M}_S : SESSION \nrightarrow store$$

$\forall c : CMD \bullet$
$\quad \mathcal{M}_S(session\,c) = \mathcal{M}_C(c)initStore$

▷ *axiomatic description*

This time a schema would be a little more effective. We have been encouraged through the use of axiomatic descriptions to model sequences of commands, which is unusual in Z. If we ignore sequencing, and use the state model introduced earlier, we can define the *Clear* and *Update* commands as

```
┌─ Clear ─────────────────────────────────────────
│  ΔCalc
├──────────────────────────────────────────────────
│  store' = initStore
│  display' = 0
└──────────────────────────────────────────────────
```

```
┌─ Update ────────────────────────────────────────
│  ΔCalc
│  memory? : MEMORY
├──────────────────────────────────────────────────
│  store' = store ⊕ {memory? ↦ display}
│  display' = display
└──────────────────────────────────────────────────
```

The decision has been made to clear the display on *Clear* as well as clearing the store.

22.3   A solution using schemas

Now we take a middle level of abstraction, not as abstract as the axiomatic specification given above (because it considers as inputs individual arithmetic operations rather than entire expressions) but not as concrete as a specification at the level of individual keystrokes.

22.3.1   The state

We must make some decisions about the model of the calculator state in addition to those made in the more abstract specification. As we choose to model individual arithmetic operations, we need a system model that is capable of holding the arguments to the operation before we invoke it. As before, the calculator has a memory. It has a display, which conventionally displays either the last value calculated or the last value entered. Because all operations are either unary or binary, we need have no more than two arguments available, one of which is the display. The other is modelled as an additional state variable.

```
┌─ Calculator ────────────────────────────────────
│  store : MEMORY → ℤ
│  display : ℤ
│  arg2 : ℤ
└──────────────────────────────────────────────────
```

22.3.2   Operations

We need to model the process of constructing the arguments for an operation. In a real calculator this action may be recognised in more than one way, for example after pressing a number of digits, pressing the '+' key signals both the end of argument construction and the choice of next operation. The end of the next argument construction is signalled by pressing the '=' key, which also serves to request the execution of the add operation. For our purposes, these distinctions may be ignored, and the operation defined in isolation.

$$
\begin{array}{|l}
\hline
\ Enter \underline{\hspace{7cm}} \\
\Delta\,Calculator \\
value? : \mathbb{Z} \\
\hline
store' = store \\
display' = value? \\
arg2' = display \\
\hline
\end{array}
$$

Whatever value was being displayed is routed into an internal holding place ($arg2$) to act as a secondary argument to a binary operation, if one is needed.

The arithmetic operations act on the display and the second argument, leaving the result in the display. For example, add can be specified as follows

$$
\begin{array}{|l}
\hline
\ Add \underline{\hspace{8cm}} \\
\Delta\,Calculator \\
\hline
store' = store \\
display' = display + arg2 \\
\hline
\end{array}
$$

▷ *loose specification*
  Notice that we do not record the fate of $arg2$. We leave this to subsequent operations (for example, the next enter) to define.

The other operations are similar.

Storing a value in memory or extracting a value from memory requires knowing which memory location to access. How this value is entered need not concern us. We assume it is the value in the display that is stored in memory.

$$
\begin{array}{|l}
\hline
\ UpdateStore \underline{\hspace{6cm}} \\
\Delta\,Calculator \\
memory? : MEMORY \\
\hline
store' = store \oplus \{memory? \mapsto display\} \\
display' = display \\
arg2' = arg2 \\
\hline
\end{array}
$$

Recalling a value from memory is similar, with the recalled value being placed in the display. The old value of the display is moved into the secondary argument.

```
┌─ Recall ────────────────────────────────────────────
│ ΔCalculator
│ memory? : MEMORY
│ ─────────────────────────────────────────────────
│ store' = store
│ display' = store memory?
│ arg2' = display
└─────────────────────────────────────────────────────
```

Clearing the memory of the calculator can be defined. In this case, we must also make a choice of what value to leave in the display and in the secondary argument. Zero seems the most suitable choice in all cases.

```
┌─ ClearDisplay ──────────────────────────────────────
│ ΔCalculator
│ ─────────────────────────────────────────────────
│ store' = initStore
│ display' = 0
│ arg2' = 0
└─────────────────────────────────────────────────────
```

▷ *readability*

Here, we have used the special value *initStore* defined in the abstract specification to shorten the specification, but have explicitly written out the zero values for *display* and *arg2*. As the system model is richer here, we may do better to define a state of the whole calculator representing an initial state, and define *ClearDisplay* as the operation that results in this state. Thus

```
┌─ ZeroCalculator ────────────────────────────────
│ Calculator
│ ───────────────────────────────────────────────
│ ∀ m : MEMORY • store m = 0
│ display = 0
│ arg2 = 0
└─────────────────────────────────────────────────
```

```
┌─ ClearDisplay0 ─────────────────────────────────
│ ΔCalculator
│ ───────────────────────────────────────────────
│ θCalculator' = θZeroCalculator
└─────────────────────────────────────────────────
```

Here, *ZeroCalculator* is a state, whereas *ClearDisplay0* is an operation that yields the state as specified in *ZeroCalculator*.

▷ *schema binding*

The expression $\theta Calculator' = \theta ZeroCalculator$ says that the values of the variables after the operation to clear the display are those of that calculator in which all values are zero.

22.4   Comparison of the two approaches

Although the most popular form of system specification uses schemas to describe the state and schemas to describe operations as relationships between before and after states, axiomatic descriptions can also be used, as has been shown by this example. The secure properties method described in Chapter 4 uses axiomatic descriptions heavily.

We can draw some general conclusions on the relative use of the two approaches.

- We do not have to use schemas to specify systems.

- Axiomatic descriptions are appropriate when the outcome, rather than how you got there, or any side effects, is of importance.

- The specification of a system using only axiomatic descriptions results in a collection of *constraints*, not a state that varies.

- If free types are used to construct a complex data type, it is likely that axiomatic descriptions will be needed to capture a significant amount of system behaviour (this is because schema definitions cannot be couched in the recursive manner needed with free types).

22.5   Different ways of under-specifying

As we have seen, it is not necessary to specify every last little detail in order to capture the desired functionality. There are three kinds of under-specification: loose, non-deterministic, and undefined. In this section we explore the differences in more detail.

Consider a simple example of an incrementer, which has an operation that increases the value in the state by one unit, up to a maximum of 250. First, consider a 'fully defined' specification.

$$
\begin{array}{|l}
\hline
\_\textit{IncrementDefinite} _____ \\
\textit{value}, \textit{value}' : \mathbb{N} \\
\hline
(\textit{value} + 1 \le 250 \wedge \textit{value}' = \textit{value} + 1) \\
\vee \\
(\textit{value} + 1 > 250 \wedge \textit{value}' = \textit{value}) \\
\hline
\end{array}
$$

We now look at how this specification may be modified to remove some of its definition.

22.5.1   Loose specification

If the specification states that a variable takes on a single value under certain circumstances, but does not specify what this value is, the specification is *loose*.

The incrementer can be made loose by extracting the definitions of the amount of the increment (1) and the limiting value (250) into axiomatic descriptions, and then leaving the actual values unspecified.

$$\begin{array}{|l}
inc, limit : \mathbb{N} \\
\hline
limit > 100
\end{array}$$

$$\begin{array}{|l}
\underline{\ IncrementLoose\ } \\
value, value' : \mathbb{N} \\
\hline
value + inc \leq limit \wedge value' = value + inc \\
\vee \\
value + inc > limit \wedge value' = value
\end{array}$$

The incrementer now always increments by the same, fixed amount, but we do not know what it is. Similarly, there is always a maximum figure, but we know only that it exceeds 100.

22.5.2   Non-deterministic specification

If the specification allows a number of values to be suitable, and does not constrain the one chosen to always be the same, the specification is *non-deterministic*. The incrementer can be made non-deterministic by allowing it to increase the value of the state, but by an unspecified amount each time.

$$\begin{array}{|l}
\underline{\ IncrementNonDet\ } \\
value, value' : \mathbb{N} \\
\hline
value' > value \wedge value' \leq limit \\
\vee \\
value' = value
\end{array}$$

This can equally well be expressed as the presence, at any one time, of a positive amount of increase. This amount of increase can be different each time the operation is invoked.

$$\begin{array}{|l}
\underline{\ IncrementNonDet0\ } \\
value, value' : \mathbb{N} \\
\hline
\exists\, n : \mathbb{N} \bullet \\
\quad value + n \leq limit \wedge value' = value + n \\
\quad \vee \\
\quad value + n > limit \wedge value' = value
\end{array}$$

22.5.3   Undefined specification

The specification may be undefined in some cases, in other words there are no values to meet the specification. In these cases, an implementation may do anything. The previous examples of the incrementer defined a behaviour under all circumstances. The specification can be relaxed

$$
\begin{array}{|l}
\hline
\text{\_\_\_} \textit{IncrementUndefined} \text{_____} \\
\quad \textit{value}, \textit{value}' : \mathbb{N} \\
\hline
\quad \textit{value} + 1 \leq 250 \\
\quad \textit{value}' = \textit{value} + 1 \\
\hline
\end{array}
$$

and now it is undefined in the case where the *value* cannot be incremented and stay within bounds.

22.5.4   Abstracted detail

All specifications have flexibility in the way in which they can be interpreted in the real world. None of the specifications of the incrementer explain how *value* is represented in the real world; it may be a binary representation in a computer memory, or a dial in a mechanical counter, or fingers on a person's hand.

Chapter 23

Making Schemas Work for You

In which the power and potential of that special Z feature, the schema, is demonstrated.

23.1 Introduction

Schemas are a powerful tool, providing the ability to help structure specifications, as we show in the case studies. In this chapter we look at

- schemas as types
- schema composition, and hiding schema variables
- what schema negation really means
- schemas as predicates, and how this allows negation to be used safely
- schema quantification.

23.2 Schemas as types

There are four different ways to define a new type in a specification

- declaring a given set
- constructing a power set from an existing type
- constructing a Cartesian product from existing types, to give tuples of ordered elements
- constructing a schema type from existing types, to give schema bindings of named but unordered elements.

For examples of schemas used as types see Chapter 11 in which the schema *Video* is used extensively as a type; the alternative view of Snakes and Ladders (section 12.3) where *Player* is used as a type; or Chapter 10 where the schema *Flight* is used as a type.

A schema can be used to model part of a state, which can then also be used as a type. Operations on the state can be defined using state transition functions (see Chapter 4), which treat the state as a whole, or by using operation schemas (see Chapter 3), which include the components of the before and after states in the operation.

23.3   Schema composition and hiding

23.3.1   Schema composition explained

If we have two schemas each specifying an operation, then schema composition may be thought of as applying one operation after the other. As with relational composition it must be possible to pass from the initial state through both operations in order to achieve a final state.

> ▷ *non-determinism*
> Consider $A \,\S\, B$. If A non-deterministically defines more than one final state only some of which satisfy the precondition of B, then those states are the only ones considered when forming $A \,\S\, B$. This is known as *angelic non-determinism*.
>
> A programming language composition $A; B$ does not necessarily behave angelically. It may well choose one of the final states of A that lets it become 'stuck'. A backtracking language like Prolog can implement angelic non-determinism by retreating and trying a different final state if it does become stuck.
>
> Notice the difference between the fat semi-colon used to describe specification composition ($\S$) and the 'ordinary' one used in programming (;). This difference in notation helps to draw attention to the difference in behaviour.

The composition of schemas S and T is written $S \,\S\, T$. The meaning is as follows. All matching variables that are primed in S (for example, x') and unprimed in T (hence, x) are renamed to a common name (for example, to x_0), giving $S[x_0/x']$ and $T[x_0/x]$ in this case. The two renamed schemas are conjoined and the renamed variables hidden to give $(S[x_0/x'] \land T[x_0/x]) \setminus (x_0)$. Conjunction requires the renamed variables, and any other common variables, to have the same type. The resulting schema has all the unmatched variables of the two schemas including all inputs and outputs.

23.3.2   Schema composition example

We want to prove the theorem from section 21.5.2, that

$$PlayWord \,\S\, TakeBackWord \vdash \Xi Player$$

This says that if a player first plays a word then takes it back, the effect is to leave the state unchanged as if the player had done nothing.

Below we work through the schema composition, showing how it is formed and thus demonstrating that $\Xi Player$ may be deduced from it.

The composition *Play Word $\,_{9}^{\circ}\,$ TakeBackWord* is equivalent to

$$(\, Play Word[hand_0/hand'] \wedge$$
$$\qquad TakeBackWord[hand_0/hand] \,) \setminus (hand_0)$$

▷ *schema hiding*
  We should check that the variables being hidden are components of the schema. $hand_0$ is a component of the conjunction since $hand'$ is in *Play Word* and we rename it to be $hand_0$.

Step 1: expand the schemas as necessary

We take the definitions of *Play Word* (page 252) and *TakeBackWord* (page 253) and expand them enough to reveal the shared variables.

Play Word
$hand, hand'$: bag *TILE*
$word$: seq *TILE*

$sizebag\ hand \leq noOfTiles$
$sizebag\ hand' \leq noOfTiles$
$hand' \uplus items\ word = hand$

TakeBackWord
$hand, hand'$: bag *TILE*
$word$: seq *TILE*

$sizebag\ hand \leq noOfTiles$
$sizebag\ hand' \leq noOfTiles$
$hand' = hand \uplus items\ word$

Step 2: rename the intermediate variables

We rename any variables with the same underlying names that are primed in the first schema and unprimed in the second. We use a subscript 0 for this renaming.

$$Play WordI \;\widehat{=}\; Play Word[hand_0/hand']$$
$$TakeBackWordI \;\widehat{=}\; TakeBackWord[hand_0/hand]$$

The expansion of *Play WordI* is

```
┌─ PlayWordI ─────────────────────────────────────────
│ hand, hand₀ : bag TILE
│ word : seq TILE
├─────────────────────────────────────────────────────
│ sizebag hand ≤ noOfTiles
│ sizebag hand₀ ≤ noOfTiles
│ hand₀ ⊎ items word = hand
└─────────────────────────────────────────────────────
```

Step 3: conjoin the intermediate schemas

PlayWordI and *TakeBackWordI* are conjoined. We call this *Intermediate*.

$$Intermediate \mathrel{\widehat{=}} PlayWordI \wedge TakeBackWordI$$

The expanded form of *Intermediate* is

```
┌─ Intermediate ──────────────────────────────────────
│ hand, hand₀, hand' : bag TILE
│ word : seq TILE
├─────────────────────────────────────────────────────
│ sizebag hand ≤ noOfTiles
│ sizebag hand₀ ≤ noOfTiles
│ sizebag hand' ≤ noOfTiles
│ hand₀ ⊎ items word = hand
│ hand' = hand₀ ⊎ items word
└─────────────────────────────────────────────────────
```

Step 4: hide the intermediate variable $hand_0$

The effect of hiding a variable is to remove it from the declaration part of the schema and existentially quantify over it in the predicate part. We call this *IntermediateH*

$$IntermediateH \mathrel{\widehat{=}} Intermediate \setminus (hand_0)$$

Expanded in full it is

```
┌─ IntermediateH ─────────────────────────────────────
│ hand, hand' : bag TILE
│ word : seq TILE
├─────────────────────────────────────────────────────
│ ∃ hand₀ : bag TILE •
│     sizebag hand ≤ noOfTiles
│     ∧ sizebag hand₀ ≤ noOfTiles
│     ∧ sizebag hand' ≤ noOfTiles
│     ∧ hand₀ ⊎ items word = hand
│     ∧ hand' = hand₀ ⊎ items word
└─────────────────────────────────────────────────────
```

Step 5: simplify the schema

We would like to be able to remove the existential quantification and hence remove all references to the intermediate variables. For this we need to use the *one point rule* (see the glossary).

We determine the required expression for $hand_0$ as follows

$$hand_0 \uplus items\ word = hand$$

$$\Rightarrow (hand_0 \uplus items\ word) \uplus items\ word = hand \uplus items\ word$$

$$\Rightarrow hand_0 = hand \uplus items\ word \qquad\qquad \text{[Spivey 1992, page 126]}$$

We now substitute the expression for $hand_0$ into $hand'$. Any expressions that do not involve a quantified variable may be pulled out of the quantification. We simplify

$$hand' = hand_0 \uplus items\ word$$

$$= (hand \uplus items\ word) \uplus items\ word$$

$$= hand$$

This leaves us with

$$
\begin{array}{l}
\hline
\ IntermediateH \underline{\hspace{8cm}} \\
\ hand, hand' : \text{bag } TILE \\
\ word : \text{seq } TILE \\
\hline
\ sizebag\ hand \leq noOfTiles \\
\ sizebag\ hand' \leq noOfTiles \\
\ hand' = hand \\
\ \exists\, hand_0 : \text{bag } TILE \bullet \\
\qquad sizebag(hand \uplus items\ word) \leq noOfTiles \\
\hline
\end{array}
$$

Step 6: simplify further

We have (see appendix A.9)

$$sizebag(hand \uplus items\ word) \leq sizebag\ hand$$

$$\Rightarrow sizebag(hand \uplus items\ word) \leq noOfTiles$$

$\Box$

▷ *discussion*
 We do not specify *hand'* simply to be *hand ⊎ items word*, because that would not constrain the value of *word* sufficiently. Even so the above manipulation shows that, because the specification as written constrains *word* to be a sub-bag of *hand*, *hand'* (here renamed to $hand_0$) does in fact equal this value.

Since we have an expression for $hand_0$ that satisfies the quantifier it can be deleted from the predicate. This leaves

```
┌─ IntermediateH ────────────────────────────────
│  hand, hand' : bag TILE
│  word : seq TILE
├─────────────────────────────────────────────────
│  sizebag hand ≤ noOfTiles
│  sizebag hand' ≤ noOfTiles
│  hand' = hand
└─────────────────────────────────────────────────
```

Step 7. simplify into the final form of the composition

We can now simplify the schema, back into a version that uses schema inclusion

```
┌─ Final ────────────────────────────────────────
│  ΞPlayer
│  word : seq TILE
└─────────────────────────────────────────────────
```

From this it is clear that the predicate of $\Xi Player$ follows, and the theorem is proved.

∎

23.4   Schema normalisation

A declaration introduces a new variable, and says what its type is. It may also include more information, an implicit predicate, that restricts the variable's value to be drawn from a subset of the complete type. For example, declaring x to be a sequence of X says it is a set of pairs of numbers and Xs, but only a set that also has the property of being a sequence.

A declaration that includes no such implicit predicate, that is just a pure type, is known as a *signature*. The predicate part of a schema conjoined with all the implicit predicates from the declarations is known as the *property* of the schema. A schema written as a signature and property (rather than declaration and predicate) is said to be *normalised*. Some schema operators are defined in terms of normalised schemas.

Normalising a schema is straightforward. For example, if we write σS for the signature of a schema S, then the normalised form of

$$
\begin{array}{|l}
\hline
S \\
\hline
x : \operatorname{seq} X \\
T \\
r : R \\
\hline
p \\
\hline
\end{array}
$$

is

$$
\begin{array}{|l}
\hline
S \\
\hline
x : \mathbb{P}(\mathbb{Z} \times X) \\
\sigma T \\
r : \sigma R \\
\hline
x \in \operatorname{seq} X \\
T \\
r \in R \\
p \\
\hline
\end{array}
$$

Here the T in the predicate part means the property of T, and $r \in R$ means r is a binding that satisfies the property of R. (See section 23.6 for more discussion on the use of schemas as predicates.)

23.5   Schema negation

In this section we discuss schema negation and show why it is defined in terms of signature and property rather than declaration and predicate.

23.5.1   A simple telephone directory

This example builds on the telephone directory introduced in section 17.4, in which a telephone directory system was defined as

$$
\begin{array}{|l}
\hline
\textit{TelephoneSystem} \\
\hline
directory : telephone \leftrightarrow USER \\
free : \mathbb{P}\, telephone \\
\hline
free = telephone \setminus (\operatorname{dom} directory) \\
\hline
\end{array}
$$

23.5.2   The initial state of the telephone system

The initial state, in which no telephones have been allocated, is given by

$$\begin{array}{l}
\underline{\quad InitTelephoneSystem \underline{}} \\
\quad TelephoneSystem' \\
\hline
\quad free' = telephone \\
\quad directory' = \varnothing \\
\hline
\end{array}$$

▷ *initial state*
It is good practice to give the initial state of the system. This demonstrates that at least one instantiation of the system exists. The initial state is a good choice for this existence proof because starting from the initial state the operations transform the system from one legal state to another.

▷ *redundancy*
Strictly we do not need both lines of the predicate since one can be deduced given the state invariant.

23.5.3   When it is not the initial state

It would be tempting to write ¬ *InitTelephoneSystem* for states of the telephone system that are not the initial one, but it results in something rather different as we see below.

Before negating a schema we must normalise it.

▷ *normalisation*
In the case of the telephone system we have the information about what *telephone* really is and the included schema *TelephoneSystem'* within the declaration. The property information is removed from the declaration to leave the underlying types. The property parts are put into their proper place, below the line in the schema box.

Substituting for *TelephoneSystem'* we get

$$\begin{array}{l}
\underline{\quad InitTelephoneSystem \underline{}} \\
\quad directory' : telephone \leftrightarrow USER \\
\quad free' : \mathbb{P}\, telephone \\
\hline
\quad free' = telephone \setminus (\mathrm{dom}\ directory') \\
\quad free' = telephone \\
\quad directory' = \varnothing \\
\hline
\end{array}$$

We move the implicit property information from the declaration into the predicate.

```
┌─ InitTelephoneSystem ──────────────────────────
│ directory′ : ℕ ↔ USER
│ free′ : ℙ ℕ
├─────────────────────────────────────────────────
│ free′ = telephone \ (dom directory′)
│ free′ = telephone
│ directory′ = ∅
│ directory′ ∈ telephone ↔ USER
│ free′ ∈ ℙ telephone
└─────────────────────────────────────────────────
```

▷ *normalisation*
You might think that the expression $\mathbb{Z} \leftrightarrow USER$ should be normalised to $\mathbb{P}(\mathbb{Z} \times USER)$. However, since $X \leftrightarrow Y$ is an abbreviation for $\mathbb{P}(X \times Y)$ [Spivey 1992, page 95] the use of the relation arrow adds no property information, and thus the expression is already normalised.

Simplifying leaves the normalised initial state schema

```
┌─ InitTelephoneSystem ──────────────────────────
│ directory′ : ℤ ↔ USER
│ free′ : ℙ ℤ
├─────────────────────────────────────────────────
│ free′ = telephone
│ directory′ = ∅
└─────────────────────────────────────────────────
```

When the predicate is negated we obtain the following

```
┌─ ¬ InitTelephoneSystem ─────────────────────────
│ directory′ : ℤ ↔ USER
│ free′ : ℙ ℤ
├─────────────────────────────────────────────────
│ ¬ (free′ = telephone
│      ∧ directory′ = ∅)
└─────────────────────────────────────────────────
```

Using the De Morgan's law that states

$$\neg\,(p \wedge q) \Leftrightarrow (\neg\,p \vee \neg\,q)$$

[Morgan & Sanders 1989, page 5, law 16] we have

```
┌─ ¬ InitTelephoneSystem ─────────────────────────
│ directory′ : ℤ ↔ USER
│ free′ : ℙ ℤ
├─────────────────────────────────────────────────
│ free′ ≠ telephone
│ ∨ directory′ ≠ ∅
└─────────────────────────────────────────────────
```

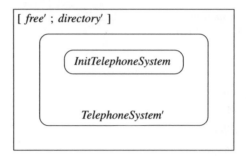

Figure 23.1 The states involved in *TelephoneSystem'*.

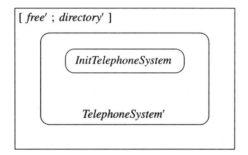

Figure 23.2 Negating *InitTelephoneSystem*.

This allows values of the variables that would not form legitimate members of *TelephoneSystem*. You can see why this happens if you consider what the definition of *InitTelephoneSystem* is really saying. It is a special case of *TelephoneSystem'* (figure 23.1), the one in which

$$free' = telephone \wedge directory' = \varnothing$$

When we negate *InitTelephoneSystem* we take any other possible values for *free'* and *directory'* except the ones in *InitTelephoneSystem*, even ones not in *Telephone-System'* (figure 23.2).

The situation we actually wish to describe is states of the telephone system that are not the initial one (figure 23.3). In order to ensure that we keep within *TelephoneSystem'*, we need to conjoin its state invariant back in. So the description of the telephone system states that are not the initial state is given by

$$NotInitTelephoneSystem \mathrel{\widehat{=}} \neg\, InitTelephoneSystem \wedge TelephoneSystem'$$

▷ *schema negation*
   This use of schema negation with conjunction may be thought of as 'not this but that'; 'not the initial state of the telephone directory, but a legitimate state of *TelephoneSystem'*'.

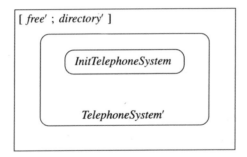

Figure 23.3 *TelephoneSystem'* excluding *InitTelephoneSystem*.

Application of various laws of the logical calculus demonstrates that this definition has the effect of reintroducing the state invariant and leaving the predicate we would expect. We now work this through.

The simplified normalised version of *TelephoneSystem'* is

TelephoneSystem' _____
$directory' : \mathbb{Z} \longleftrightarrow USER$
$free' : \mathbb{P}\,\mathbb{Z}$

$free' = telephone \setminus (\mathrm{dom}\ directory')$
$directory' \in telephone \longleftrightarrow USER$

We conjoin it with ¬ *InitTelephoneSystem* to give

NotInitTelephoneSystem _____
$directory' : \mathbb{Z} \longleftrightarrow USER$
$free' : \mathbb{P}\,\mathbb{Z}$

$(free' \neq telephone$
$\lor directory' \neq \varnothing)$
$free' = telephone \setminus (\mathrm{dom}\ directory')$
$directory' \in telephone \longleftrightarrow USER$

Recall the distributive law [Morgan & Sanders 1989, page 4, law 7]

$$(p \lor q) \land r \Leftrightarrow (p \land r) \lor (q \land r)$$

Applying this result to the predicate gives us

$(free' \neq telephone$
$\land\ free' = telephone \setminus (\mathrm{dom}\ directory')$
$\land\ directory' \in telephone \longleftrightarrow USER)$
$\lor$

$$(directory' \neq \emptyset$$
$$\wedge\ free' = telephone \setminus (dom\ directory')$$
$$\wedge\ directory' \in telephone \longleftrightarrow USER)$$

Using de Morgan's law again we factor out the common parts

$$(free' \neq telephone \vee directory' \neq \emptyset)$$
$$\wedge\ free' = telephone \setminus (dom\ directory')$$
$$\wedge\ directory' \in telephone \longleftrightarrow USER$$

Combining the predicate part

$$directory' \in telephone \longleftrightarrow USER$$

back into the declaration of the schema and using

$$free' = telephone \setminus (dom\ directory')$$

to allow us to write that $free' : \mathbb{F}\ telephone$, we have

$$
\begin{array}{|l}
\hline
\_NotInitTelephoneSystem\rule{5cm}{0pt}\\
\quad directory' : telephone \longleftrightarrow USER\\
\quad free' : \mathbb{F}\ telephone\\
\hline
\quad (free' \neq telephone \vee directory' \neq \emptyset)\\
\quad free' = telephone \setminus (dom\ directory')\\
\hline
\end{array}
$$

Using schema inclusion, this reduces to

$$
\begin{array}{|l}
\hline
\_NotInitTelephoneSystem\rule{5cm}{0pt}\\
\quad TelephoneSystem'\\
\hline
\quad free' \neq telephone\\
\quad \vee\\
\quad directory' \neq \emptyset\\
\hline
\end{array}
$$

■

We could use a schema as predicate to write this schema

$$
\begin{array}{|l}
\hline
\_NotInitTelephoneSystem\rule{5cm}{0pt}\\
\quad TelephoneSystem'\\
\hline
\quad \neg\ InitTelephoneSystem\\
\hline
\end{array}
$$

as explained below in section 23.6. When using schemas as predicate parts, all the variables must already be in scope; the property parts of their declarations cannot be negated. The moral of this tale is that it is better to be safe with a negated schema as a predicate than sorry with a negated schema as a declaration.

Readers may be interested in an alternative semantics for schema negation, which is expounded in [Hayes 1991]. There the author proposes different interpretations of schema operators that would allow them to behave in a more 'natural' manner.

23.6   Schemas as predicates

As well as the more familiar use for specifying types, states and operations, schemas can also be used to specify predicates. This is illustrated below. Although for such a simple example it might be argued that the explicit form is actually often shorter than the form using predicates, the latter often expresses the specifier's intention more clearly. For more complicated predicates this style also leads to simpler, more modular, specifications.

23.6.1   A list with a current position

Consider the specification of a variable length list of *ITEM*s with an 'index': a position in the list that is remembered. (This example is adapted from the description of lists in [Meyer 1988, appendix A.2].) The list is modelled as a sequence of elements of type *ITEM*, and the index position as a natural number. We allow the index to be just off the beginning of the list or just off the end, as well as pointing at an element in the list.

$$
\begin{array}{|l}
\hline
\_\,MemList\,_____ \\
\quad list : \mathrm{seq}\ ITEM \\
\quad index : \mathbb{N} \\
\hline
\quad index \in 0\,..\,(1 + \#list) \\
\hline
\end{array}
$$

▷ *cardinality*
  Recall that a sequence is really a set of pairs in which the first item represents the position of the second item in the sequence. Taking the cardinality of the sequence thus gives us the length of the sequence.

We define some operations on this list such as moving the index. This leads to much checking whether the list is empty, whether the index is off one end or the other, and whether the required position is valid. So first we define some schemas to help us.

An empty list is a zero length list. Notice that in such a list a valid index position could be 0 or 1.

$$EmptyList \;\hat{=}\; [\,MemList \mid \#list = 0\,]$$

23.6.2   Simple use as a predicate

The index is off the start of a non-empty list if it is at position zero. For an empty list, the index is always considered to be off the start, even if its position is 1.

$$IndexOffStart \cong [\, MemList \mid EmptyList \lor index = 0\,]$$

Here the schema *EmptyList* appears in the predicate part of *IndexOffStart*. What is the effect of this? The variables in its declaration become bound to any variables of the same name and type that are in scope. These are the ones in *IndexOffStart*'s declaration from the included *MemList*, which in this case are exactly those in *EmptyList*'s declaration. Then a schema as predicate is just the property part of the schema (that is, of the predicate of the *normalised* schema), with this binding of its declared variables.

▷ *normalisation*
It necessary to normalise the schema in order to identify all of its predicate (often called the property of the schema).

▷ *declarations, combining*
All the components of the schema used as a predicate must be in scope and have the same type for this sort of expression to be allowed.

Working through this in steps we first expand *IndexOffStart*

```
┌─ IndexOffStart ──────────────────────────────
│  list : seq ITEM
│  index : ℕ
├──────────────────────────────────────────────
│    index ∈ 0 .. (1 + #list)
│    #list = 0
│    ∨
│    index = 0
└──────────────────────────────────────────────
```

In this case we can see that *IndexOffStart* is just

```
┌─ IndexOffStart ──────────────────────────────
│  MemList
├──────────────────────────────────────────────
│    #list = 0 ∨ index = 0
└──────────────────────────────────────────────
```

and could also have been written, with a slightly different emphasis, as

$$IndexOffStart \cong EmptyList \lor [\, MemList \mid index = 0\,]$$

▷ *schema, unnamed*
Normally schemas are given a name since only the name has global scope. In some contexts such as with

$$[\, MemList \mid index = 0\,]$$

it is convenient to use a schema 'in-line', without giving it a name.

The index's being off the end of the list is expressed similarly

$$IndexOffEnd \cong [\, MemList \mid EmptyList \lor index = 1 + \#list\,]$$

23.6.3   Negating a predicate

Similar definitions can be made for the index pointing at the first or last element of the list. In these cases we need the list not to be empty.

$$IndexAtFirst \;\widehat{=}\; [\,MemList \mid \neg\; EmptyList \land index = 1\,]$$
$$IndexAtLast \;\widehat{=}\; [\,MemList \mid \neg\; EmptyList \land index = \#list\,]$$

Now we have the negation of a schema as predicate. There are often problems in negating a schema; it does not always do what is wanted because any implicit predicates in the declaration are also negated (see the discussion in section 23.5). However, it does work here. Expanding *IndexAtFirst* shows this. First, we substitute the definition of *MemList* in the declaration

```
┌─ IndexAtFirst ─────────────────────────────
│ list : seq ITEM
│ index : ℕ
├─────────────────────────────────────────────
│ index ∈ 0 .. (1 + #list)
│ ¬ EmptyList
│ index = 1
└─────────────────────────────────────────────
```

Next we normalise by turning the declaration into a signature making the implicit predicates explicit.

```
┌─ IndexAtFirst ─────────────────────────────
│ list : ℙ(ℤ × ITEM)
│ index : ℤ
├─────────────────────────────────────────────
│ list ∈ seq ITEM
│ index ≥ 0
│ index ∈ 0 .. (1 + #list)
│ ¬ EmptyList
│ index = 1
└─────────────────────────────────────────────
```

▷ signature
  The signature of *list* : seq *ITEM* is *list* : $\mathbb{P}(\mathbb{Z} \times ITEM)$, the fact that *list* is a sequence is part of the property of the schema.

Now we normalise the *EmptyList* schema and negate it.

```
┌─ NotEmptyList ──────────────────────────────────
│ list : ℙ(ℤ × ITEM)
│ index : ℤ
├──────────────────────────────────────────────
│ ¬ (list ∈ seq ITEM
│     ∧ index ≥ 0
│     ∧ index ∈ 0 . . 1 + #list
│     ∧ #list = 0)
└──────────────────────────────────────────────
```

We substitute the predicate of this schema into the expanded *IndexAtFirst*, and now find that the variables are properly bound (the ¬ has also been pulled inside the brackets)

```
┌─ IndexAtFirst ──────────────────────────────────
│ list : ℙ(ℤ × ITEM)
│ index : ℤ
├──────────────────────────────────────────────
│ list ∈ seq ITEM
│
│ index ≥ 0
│
│ index ∈ 0 . . 1 + #list
│
│ (list ∉ seq ITEM
│     ∨ index < 0
│     ∨ index ∉ 0 . . (1 + #list)
│     ∨ #list ≠ 0)
│
│ index = 1
└──────────────────────────────────────────────
```

The only part of the predicate inside the brackets that can be true is the last part, since the negation of all the other parts also occurs outside the brackets (because $p \land (\neg p \lor q) \Leftrightarrow p \land q$). The predicate simplifies to the following.

```
┌─ IndexAtFirst ──────────────────────────────────
│ list : ℙ(ℤ × ITEM)
│ index : ℤ
├──────────────────────────────────────────────
│ list ∈ seq ITEM
│
│ index ≥ 0
│
│ index ∈ 0 . . (1 + #list)
│
│ #list ≠ 0
│
│ index = 1
└──────────────────────────────────────────────
```

Substituting *MemList* (page 285) back in gives

```
┌─ IndexAtFirst ─────────────────────────────────
│ MemList
├────────────────────────────
│ #list ≠ 0
│ index = 1
└─────────────────────────────────────────────────
```

which is exactly what we wanted.

∎

▷ *schema negation*
Note that something like

$$S1 \mathrel{\widehat{=}} [\, MemList \mid \neg \; EmptyList \lor pred \,]$$

is *not* the same as

$$S2 \mathrel{\widehat{=}} \neg \; EmptyList \lor [\, MemList \mid pred \,]$$

The predicate $\neg \; EmptyList$ has its intuitive meaning of 'being a *MemList*, but not an empty one', whereas the schema $\neg \; EmptyList$ means 'being anything (of the right signature) that is not an empty *MemList*'.

Negating schemas as predicates does do what is wanted, provided the declarations (signature plus implicit predicates) being matched are the same in the two schemas. The implicit predicates in the outer schema stop the unwanted effects of negating them in the included schema.

23.6.4   Some operations

Just one more definition is needed before we start defining operations on the list. Some operations have a list index as input, which has to be checked.

$$ValidIndex \mathrel{\widehat{=}} [\, MemList;\; i? : \mathbb{N} \mid \neg \; EmptyList \land i? \in \mathrm{dom}\; list \,]$$

▷ *redundancy*
Notice that $i? \in \mathrm{dom}\; list$ prevents *MemList* from being empty. Nonetheless we include $\neg \; EmptyList$ as part of the predicate to make this explicit. Note too that $i? \in \mathrm{dom}\; list$ does not follow from the list being non-empty since we cannot be sure it is that particular $i?$ that is in the list.

Operations either query the state leaving it unchanged, or change it. In the operations below, either the list or the index is changed, but not both. So the following are useful

$$\Delta MemListContents \mathrel{\widehat{=}} [\, \Delta MemList \mid index' = index \,]$$
$$\Delta MemListIndex \mathrel{\widehat{=}} [\, \Delta MemList \mid list' = list \,]$$

Two obvious operations are querying and changing the value of the ith element in the list, provided that $i?$ is actually in the domain of the list.

```
┌─ AtIth ──────────────────────────────
│ ΞMemList
│ i? : ℕ
│ v! : ITEM
├──────────────────────────────────────
│ ValidIndex
│ v! = list i?
└──────────────────────────────────────
```

```
┌─ PutIth ─────────────────────────────
│ ΔMemListContents
│ i? : ℕ
│ v? : ITEM
├──────────────────────────────────────
│ ValidIndex
│ list' = list ⊕ {i? ↦ v?}
└──────────────────────────────────────
```

Here the declarations of the including and included schemas are not identical since there are more variables in the declaration of *PutIth* than in the declaration of *ValidIndex*. The variables declared in *ValidIndex* bind to the before state variables of $\Delta MemList$ and to the input variable $i?$.

▷ *schema hiding*
These definitions can easily be adapted to the queries and changes at the index position, by requiring $i?$ to be the index position, and hiding it from view

$$AtThis \mathrel{\widehat{=}} [\,AtIth \mid i? = index\,] \setminus (i?)$$
$$PutThis \mathrel{\widehat{=}} [\,PutIth \mid i? = index\,] \setminus (i?)$$

Note that these are partial operations. If the current position is off an end, then *ValidIndex* is *false*.

23.6.5   Decorating a predicate

Other operations are ones that change the index's position. For example, it could be moved to the first element of a non-empty list

$$GotoFirst \mathrel{\widehat{=}} [\,\Delta MemListIndex \mid \neg\ EmptyList \wedge IndexAtFirst'\,]$$

▷ *schema decoration*
Often schemas are decorated as part of the declaration of another schema, but it is perfectly possible to decorate a schema when it is being used as a predicate as with *IndexAtFirst'*. The declared variables bind to the after state variables in the delta list (in the declaration), so the expansion becomes

$$
\begin{array}{|l|}
\hline
\_GotoFirst\_\rule{0pt}{0pt}\hspace{3cm}\\
\Delta MemListIndex\\
\hline
\#list \neq 0\\
index' = 1\\
\hline
\end{array}
$$

Similarly, moving to the last element can be written as

$$GotoLast \mathrel{\widehat{=}} [\,\Delta MemListIndex \mid \neg\; EmptyList \wedge IndexAtLast'\,]$$

23.6.6   Schemas in theorems

Schemas can be used in the consequent part of theorems. For example, the theorem

$$EmptyList \vdash IndexOffStart$$

states that if the empty list is assumed, then it is true that the index is off the start of the list.

▷ *theorem*
$EmptyList \vdash IndexOffStart$ may be read as 'given *EmptyList* it can be shown that the property of *IndexOffStart* holds'. The use of *EmptyList* on the left hand side of this expression declares the local variables in the expression.

23.6.7   Quadrilaterals specification

This section uses a slightly more complicated example to illustrate the advantages of using schemas as predicates.

The specification below consists of defining a general *Quadrilateral*, then defining more restrictions on it in order to define a *Rectangle* and a *Rhombus* from a *Parallelogram*, and a *Square* from a *Rectangle* and a *Rhombus*.

Vectors

Two-dimensional vectors are used to specify the quadrilaterals. Their components, length and so on, are real numbers $\mathbb{R}$ (see the real number toolkit of Chapter 25).

$$VECTOR == \mathbb{R} \times \mathbb{R}$$

▷ *house style*
$\mathbb{R}$ is a type if we use the extended toolkit. $\mathbb{R} \times \mathbb{R}$ is also a type, so we choose a name written in upper case, *VECTOR*, to indicate that it is a name for a type.

The zero vector, and the vector operations modulus (length), vector addition, and vector dot product are used. They have their conventional definitions (but not their conventional symbols, since this would require overloading various operators, not usual practice in Z).

$$
\begin{array}{|l}
\mathbf{0} : VECTOR \\
length : VECTOR \longrightarrow \mathbb{R} \\
\_ \maltese \_ : VECTOR \times VECTOR \longrightarrow VECTOR \\
\_ \bullet \_ : VECTOR \times VECTOR \longrightarrow \mathbb{R} \\
\hline
\mathbf{0} = (0, 0) \\
\forall\, v : VECTOR;\ x, y : \mathbb{R} \mid v = (x, y) \bullet \\
\qquad length\ v * length\ v = x * x + y * y \\
\qquad \wedge\ length\ v \geq 0 \\
\forall\, v_1, v_2 : VECTOR;\ x_1, x_2, y_1, y_2 : \mathbb{R} \mid v_1 = (x_1, y_1) \wedge v_2 = (x_2, y_2) \bullet \\
\qquad v_1 \maltese v_2 = (x_1 + x_2,\ y_1 + y_2) \\
\qquad \wedge\ v_1 \bullet v_2 = x_1 * x_2 + y_1 * y_2
\end{array}
$$

An abstract quadrilateral

A *Quadrilateral* is a four sided closed figure. The edges of a closed figure sum to zero. We use vectors to represent the sides, not the corners, of the quadrilateral; the quadrilaterals have no location given. Notice this definition allows edges to cross or be zero.

> ▷ *abstraction*
> This definition is loose, but at the right level of abstraction for our purposes. There is no point in constraining a definition unless it is necessary.

$$
\begin{array}{|l}
\_\, Quadrilateral \underline{\hspace{4cm}} \\
v1, v2, v3, v4 : VECTOR \\
\hline
v1 \maltese v2 \maltese v3 \maltese v4 = \mathbf{0}
\end{array}
$$

A *Parallelogram* is a *Quadrilateral* with opposite edges equal in length and opposite in direction.

$$Parallelogram \cong [\, Quadrilateral \mid v1 \maltese v3 = \mathbf{0} \,]$$

> ▷ *schema as predicate*
> This could have been written using *Quadrilateral* as a predicate, thus

$$
\begin{array}{|l}
\_\, Parallelogram \underline{\hspace{4cm}} \\
v1, v2, v3, v4 : VECTOR \\
\hline
Quadrilateral \\
v1 \maltese v3 = \mathbf{0}
\end{array}
$$

A *Rhombus* is a *Parallelogram* that also has adjacent sides of the same length.

$$Rhombus \cong [\, Parallelogram \mid length\ v1 = length\ v2 \,]$$

A *Rectangle* is a *Parallelogram* that also has perpendicular adjacent sides.

$$Rectangle \mathrel{\widehat{=}} [\, Parallelogram \mid v1 \boldsymbol{.} v2 = 0\,]$$

A *Square* is both a *Rhombus* and a *Rectangle*.

$$Square \mathrel{\widehat{=}} [\, Rhombus;\ Rectangle\,]$$

A quadrilateral in place

Consider a system that needs to specify a variety of closed figures. These are specified by a set of edges, a position, and a tag noting their type. This tag might be needed to distinguish between, say, a *Square* and a *Rectangle* that just happened to have all its sides the same length. Such a *Rectangle* could possibly be stretched parallel to one edge, whereas a *Square* could not.

$$TAG ::= aQuad \mid aRect \mid aParallelogram \mid aRhombus \mid aSquare$$

QuadFigure
Quadrilateral
$position : VECTOR$
$t : TAG$

$t = aQuad$
$\lor\ (t = aParallelogram \land Parallelogram)$
$\lor\ (t = aRhombus \land Rhombus)$
$\lor\ (t = aRect \land Rectangle)$
$\lor\ (t = aSquare \land Square)$

The predicate ensures that the edges and type of the quadrilateral are consistent. A *QuadFigure* that has a tag saying it is a *Rectangle* must satisfy the predicate *Rectangle*. It is not constrained from satisfying a stronger condition.

Expanding out the schemas as predicates in the above gives

QuadFigure
Quadrilateral
$position : VECTOR$
$t : TAG$

$t = aQuad$
$\lor\ (t = aParallelogram \land v1 \maltese v3 = \mathbf{0})$
$\lor\ (t = aRhombus \land v1 \maltese v3 = \mathbf{0} \land length\ v1 = length\ v2)$
$\lor\ (t = aRect \land v1 \maltese v3 = \mathbf{0} \land v1 \boldsymbol{.} v2 = 0)$
$\lor\ (t = aSquare \land v1 \maltese v3 = \mathbf{0} \land length\ v1 = length\ v2 \land v1 \boldsymbol{.} v2 = 0)$

Now the advantages of factoring out the complicated conditions as named predicates become apparent. There is much repetition of the same conditions, and it is not obvious just what the significance of the conditions is. As is always the case with repeated expressions there is more potential for error. For example, changing the representation from explicitly numbered edges to a sequence of edges (allowing the specification of triangles and pentagons too) would require a lot of changes in the expanded version, but none at all in the version using predicates; only the schemas defining the predicates would have to be changed.

23.6.8   Summary

Using a schema as a predicate is a way of giving a *name* to a predicate. This allows it to be used in different places, and can make the specifier's intention clearer. It also increases modularity, confining changes to a single place. Such predicates can be decorated making it possible to specify required final states more clearly. They can also be negated, with a more intuitive meaning when used as predicates than when used as schemas.

23.7   Quantifying schemas—for the best result

Requirements are often expressed in terms of some known constraints on an acceptable state, together with an overall requirement that a chosen state is the 'best' available at the time. For example, a program to calculate the shortest route between two points can be specified first by defining what constitutes a 'route', and then demanding the shortest of these. Such specifications need to refer to all possible states that satisfy some schema, and this is most naturally expressed as universal or existential quantification.

23.7.1   Order lists

Consider elements of a sequence that can be put into order according to a *partial ordering*. A partial ordering does not specify the relative order of some of the elements, which are considered equivalent for ordering purposes. Elements of a sequence can be put into order according to a partial ordering relation in more than one way. The specification of an 'insert new element' operation may require that the new sequence is correctly ordered, and that the sequence chosen is as close to the previous sequence as possible. That is, the new sequence is correctly ordered, and as little reordering as possible has been done when the new element was introduced. Take as an example the partial ordering shown in figure 23.4.

Given the elements to be sorted as

$$a, c_1, c_2, c_3, d$$

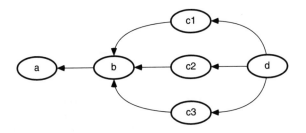

Figure 23.4 A partial ordering: $a < b < \{c_1, c_2, c_3\} < d$

these can be ordered correctly in any of the following six ways

a, c_1, c_2, c_3, d
a, c_2, c_1, c_3, d
a, c_1, c_3, c_2, d
a, c_2, c_3, c_1, d
a, c_3, c_1, c_2, d
a, c_3, c_2, c_1, d

If the first ordering is chosen, then b is added to the sequence, we would expect to produce

a, b, c_1, c_2, c_3, d

rather than, say,

a, b, c_3, c_2, c_1, d

Both are valid according to our ordering, but the first seems a 'better' choice, because it involves less reordering.

There is a temptation to make the design decision involved in choosing the best state. A more abstract approach is to capture the intuitive notion of 'best' directly, and then *derive* the design step.

In this example, we must first model the partial ordering. A partial ordering $\prec$ is transitive and anti-symmetric. The relation $\preccurlyeq$ is extended to be reflexive.

$[ITEM]$

$$
\begin{array}{|l}
\_\prec\_ : ITEM \leftrightarrow ITEM \\
\_\preccurlyeq\_ : ITEM \leftrightarrow ITEM \\
\hline
(\_\prec\_) = (\_\prec\_)^{+} \\
(\_\prec\_) \cap (\_\prec\_)^{\sim} = \varnothing \\
(\_\preccurlyeq\_) = (\_\prec\_)^{*}
\end{array}
$$

▷ *transitive closure*
  The expression $(\_ \prec \_) = (\_ \prec \_)^+$ says that the relation is equal to its transitive closure, which is the same as saying that it is transitive.
▷ *reflexive transitive closure*
  The expression $(\_ \preccurlyeq \_) = (\_ \prec \_)^*$ says that $\preccurlyeq$ is $\prec$ with the addition of all the reflexive pairs.
▷ *relation, infix*
  These relations have been defined as infix, using underscores to mark the position of the arguments. Another approach would be not to define them as infix, and underline them in order to use them as infix. But this would create confusing symbols such as $\underline{\prec}$ and $\underline{\preccurlyeq}$
▷ *loose specification*
  This definition does not say what the partial order is, it simply defines just enough properties to ensure that it is a partial order. Hence we cannot make the definition generic; it is not uniquely defined.

We wish to consider only ordered sequences of the elements.

```
┌─ Ordered ─────────────────────────────────────────────
│ list : seq ITEM
│ ──────────────────────────────────────────────────────
│ ∀ i, j : dom list | i ≤ j • ¬ (list j ≺ list i)
└───────────────────────────────────────────────────────
```

A simple insertion of a new element into the list preserves the invariant (the partial ordering) and preserves the elements in the list, but does not necessarily preserve the detailed ordering.

```
┌─ SimpleInsert ────────────────────────────────────────
│ Δ Ordered
│ i? : ITEM
│ ──────────────────────────────────────────────────────
│ items list' = items list ⊎ ⟦ i? ⟧
└───────────────────────────────────────────────────────
```

▷ *bag operations*
  The predicate considers the list as a bag, which preserves the number of elements in the list, but ignores their relative positions. It requires only that the new list has the same elements as the old list plus one extra. ⊎ forms a new bag in which *items list'* adds *i*? into *items list*.

We now want to impose the extra constraint that the new list is somehow 'as close as possible' to the old list. Staying at a requirements level, and shunning early design decisions, we must capture the intuitive notion of 'close'.

It is not critical to this example to understand the following construction of a function to define 'close', and you may freely skip it if you feel mathematically queasy. It is sufficient to know that it results in a function *distance* that gives a numerical value that represents how much reordering has been performed from one sequence to another. The smaller this value, the 'closer' the two sequences.

23.7.2   Deriving the 'best fit' function

There is a well-known theorem (to people who spend their lives playing with permutations!) that says that every permutation can be expressed as the sequential composition of 'transpositions', where each transposition swaps two adjacent elements. For example, the permutation

$$abc \longrightarrow cba$$

can be expressed as

$$abc \longrightarrow bac \longrightarrow bca \longrightarrow cba$$

We define a generic constant *swap*

$$\boxed{\begin{array}{l} \hline [X] \\ \hline swap : \operatorname{seq} X \longleftrightarrow \operatorname{seq} X \\ \hline swap = \{\, s, t : \operatorname{seq} X; \, x, y : X \bullet (s \frown \langle x, y \rangle \frown t) \mapsto (s \frown \langle y, x \rangle \frown t) \,\} \end{array}}$$

  ▷ *set comprehension*
  Note that the constructing term in a set comprehension can be quite complicated. Here it
  is doing all the 'work'.

The minimum number of transpositions needed to perform the permutation is known as the *length* of the permutation.

$$\boxed{\begin{array}{l} \hline [X] \\ \hline length : \operatorname{seq} X \times \operatorname{seq} X \nrightarrow \mathbb{N} \\ \hline \operatorname{dom} length = \{\, s, t : \operatorname{seq} X \mid items\ s = items\ t \,\} \\ \forall\, s, t : \operatorname{seq} X \mid items\ s = items\ t \bullet \\ \qquad length(s, t) = min\{\, n : \mathbb{N} \mid s \mapsto t \in swap^n \,\} \end{array}}$$

  ▷ *relational iteration*
  $s \mapsto t \in swap^n$ means that s is related to t if some number of swaps can transform s to t.

This nearly gives us a notion of closeness, if we say that two sequences are close if the length of the permutation necessary to move from one to the other is small. In our case the two sequences do not have identical elements—one has an extra element.

   We therefore define the distance between two sequences that differ by one element as the distance after that element is removed from the longer sequence. The definition needs to be able to handle cases such as $s = ab$ and $t = bab$, the permutation distance depends on which b is removed from t, we choose the minimum.

$$
\begin{array}{l}
\underline{[X]}\\
distance : \mathrm{seq}\, X \times \mathrm{seq}\, X \nrightarrow \mathbb{N}\\
\overline{}\\
\mathrm{dom}\; distance = \{\, s, t : \mathrm{seq}\, X;\; x : X \mid\\
\qquad\qquad\qquad items\, t = items\, s \uplus [\![x]\!] \bullet (s,t) \,\}\\
\forall\, s, t : \mathrm{seq}\, X \mid (s,t) \in \mathrm{dom}\; distance \bullet\\
\qquad distance(s,t) = min\{\, x : X;\; beg, end : \mathrm{seq}\, X \mid\\
\qquad\qquad items\, s = items\,(beg \frown end)\\
\qquad\qquad \wedge\; t = beg \frown \langle x \rangle \frown end \bullet\\
\qquad\qquad\qquad length(s, beg \frown end) \,\}
\end{array}
$$

We are now in a position to use this function to define an insert operation that reorders elements as little as possible.

$$
\begin{array}{l}
\underline{BestInsert}\\
SimpleInsert\\
\overline{}\\
\forall\, SimpleInsert_0 \mid i?_0 = i? \wedge \theta\, Ordered_0 = \theta\, Ordered \bullet\\
\qquad distance(list_0, list'_0) \geq distance(list, list')
\end{array}
$$

▷ *schema decoration*
  The subscript 0 acts as a decoration.

BestInsert is a *SimpleInsert* operation with the additional constraint that it is not possible to find another *SimpleInsert* operation that starts with the same list, inserts the same element into it, but ends with a list that is strictly closer to the original list than this operation achieved.

This approach can be used whenever an operation is needed that is the 'best' of a collection of potential operations.

In this particular case, the 'best' operation can be just as easily described directly. It is the operation that splits the existing list in two and inserts the new element in between the two parts in such a way that the new element is inserted in a correct position in its order. That is,

$$
\begin{array}{l}
\underline{DirectInsert}\\
SimpleInsert\\
\overline{}\\
\exists\, beg, end : \mathrm{seq}\, ITEM \bullet\\
\qquad beg \frown end = list\\
\qquad \wedge\; beg \frown \langle i? \rangle \frown end = list'
\end{array}
$$

The data invariant implicit in *SimpleInsert* ensures that the lists are correctly partially ordered. Sometimes there is no such straightforward definition of 'best' as illustrated in the next section.

23.7.3   Reversed lists

Consider a more complicated case where the lists are allowed to be ordered in either ascending or descending order, and we are required to specify an operation to reverse the ordering on a list. That is, if a list is ordered ascending, reorder it descending, but with a minimum amount of reshuffling, and vice versa. This would require, for example, the list

$$a, b, c_1, c_2, c_3, d$$

to be reversed to

$$d, c_1, c_2, c_3, b, a$$

and not to

$$d, c_3, c_2, c_1, b, a$$

Following the same approach as for the simply ordered list, we can define what it means for a list to be ordered in ascending order and what it means to be ordered in descending order. The lists under consideration are then the union of these two sets of lists.

__*Ascending*_____
$list : \text{seq } ITEM$
_____
$\forall\, i, j : \text{dom } list \mid i \leq j \bullet \neg\, (list\; j \prec list\; i)$
_____

__*Descending*_____
$list : \text{seq } ITEM$
_____
$\forall\, i, j : \text{dom } list \mid i \geq j \bullet \neg\, (list\; j \prec list\; i)$
_____

$$EitherOrdered \;\hat{=}\; Ascending \lor Descending$$

To reverse the ordering in such a list the elements in the resulting list must be the same as the elements in the given list. The before and after lists must each satisfy opposite ordering conditions; that is, either the before list is ascending and the after list is descending, or the before list is descending and the after list is ascending.

__*SimpleReverse*_____
$\Delta\, EitherOrdered$
_____
$items\; list' = items\; list$
$(Ascending \land Descending') \lor (Descending \land Ascending')$
_____

As before this schema describes an operation that does what we want to do, in that after the operation the list is reversed, but it lacks the condition to ensure that a minimum of reshuffling has taken place. We can add this minimality condition exactly as we did before. We can use the length of the permutation from one list to the other directly as the measure of closeness, because the two lists are the same size.

$$
\begin{array}{|l}
\hline \text{\_\_} \textit{BestReverse} \text{_____} \\
\quad \textit{SimpleReverse} \\
\hline
\quad \forall\, SimpleReverse_0 \mid \theta\, EitherOrdered_0 = \theta\, EitherOrdered \bullet \\
\qquad length(list_0, list_0') \geq length(list, list') \\
\hline
\end{array}
$$

In this case defining the reverse operation directly would be difficult, and inappropriate for requirements specification, although the step would have to be made at some time during design.

23.8   Concluding remarks

Schemas can be used in far more ways than just in the 'ordinary' devices of inclusion, conjunction and disjunction. We can hide those components that may not be needed for a particular purpose without needing to define a new schema. Schemas that define operations may be composed to form new operations, in which one always follows the other taking the final state of the previous operation as its initial state.

You can negate a schema, but this operation is applied to the normalised version of the schema, and may have unexpected results. It needs to be used with care. Schemas may be used as predicates, and it is here that schema negation behaves well. We recommend using it principally in such contexts. It is also possible to quantify over schemas, and this allows you to make powerful statements about the behaviour of the system being specified.

The schema is a highly useful device; it makes an extremely useful contribution to producing well-structured, succinct specifications. It makes Z what it is!

Chapter 24

Exploiting the Power of the Language

In which advice is given on some of the more advanced features of Z.

24.1   Introduction

Z has many powerful features. Often the concepts involved are simple but it can be hard to find examples that explain their use. In this chapter we illustrate the following language features using small examples

- domain and range restriction, revealing the symmetry between them
- generic definitions
- disjoint sets and partitions
- schema binding formation, θ
- definite description notation, μ

24.2   Red tape and (domain and range) restriction

Problem statement. Specify a *bureaucracy* which consists of *bureaucrats* and *committees*. Every bureaucrat serves on at least three different committees and every committee is served on by at least three different bureaucrats. Given two distinct committees exactly one bureaucrat serves on both. Given two distinct bureaucrats there is exactly one committee on which they both serve [Stewart & Tall 1977].

24.2.1   The state

We have a fairly simple state, with the bureaucrats and the committees as the state items. We represent these by given sets, and use a relation between them to record which bureaucrat serves on which committee.

$$[BUREAUCRAT, COMMITTEE]$$

servesOn relates the bureaucrats and the committees on which they serve. The domain and range of this relation give the sets of actual bureaucrats and committees (the given sets record all possible bureaucrats and committees, not just those serving or being served on).

$$
\begin{array}{|l}
servesOn : BUREAUCRAT \leftrightarrow COMMITTEE \\
bcrat : \mathbb{P}\, BUREAUCRAT \\
com : \mathbb{P}\, COMMITTEE \\
\hline
bcrat = \mathrm{dom}\, servesOn \\
com = \mathrm{ran}\, servesOn
\end{array}
$$

This gives a simple, abstract definition of the system.

24.2.2   The constraints on the state

First, we express the condition that every bureaucrat serves on at least three committees. This falls out simply by using domain restriction

$$\forall\, b : bcrat \bullet \#(\{b\} \lhd servesOn) \geq 3$$

 ▷ *axiomatic description*
  Normally we would advise against the later addition of predicates to previously declared global variables, but here we are building up the constraints in steps and so this presentation is appropriate. When all the constraints have been explained, we gather them together and present them as one declaration.

At this point we observe that we need to take the cardinality of the relation (albeit a restriction of it). We cannot do this unless we know that the relation is finite. So we must add this into our predicates.

$$servesOn \in BUREAUCRAT \leftrightarrow\!\!\!\!+\!\!\!\!\rightarrow COMMITTEE$$

 ▷ *toolkit*
  The set of finite relations, ↔↔, is defined in our extension to the standard toolkit, appendix A.4.

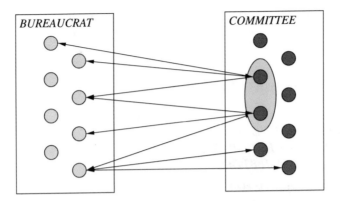

Figure 24.1 *BUREAUCRAT*s and their *COMMITTEE*s. The shaded area shows the two distinct committees, each of which we wish to be part of a pair, in order to give us at least two pairs in the restricted relation. If there is a unique domain element then we have exactly two pairs.

The requirement that each committee is served on by at least three bureaucrats is described using range restriction.

$$\forall\, c : com \bullet \#(servesOn \rhd \{c\}) \geq 3$$

Now we look at the requirement that given two distinct committees there is exactly one bureaucrat who serves on them both. This can be described using restrictions

$$\forall\, c_1, c_2 : com \mid c_1 \neq c_2 \bullet \exists_1 b : bcrat \bullet \#(\{b\} \lhd servesOn \rhd \{c_1, c_2\}) = 2$$

▷ *quantifier, unique existential*
  $\exists_1 b$ means that there is a unique b that satisfies the expression $\#(\{b\} \lhd servesOn \rhd \{c_1, c_2\}) = 2$.
▷ *restriction, domain*
  This example demonstrates the symmetry between domain and range restriction. We could have directly constructed the pairs in which we are interested. Instead, we restrict the relation to the two committees in question, then restrict that to a single bureaucrat. Finally, we require there to be two pairs in the remaining relation, and that there be a unique solution as to who that bureaucrat can be. Figure 24.1 may help to illustrate this point.
    This approach is more abstract since we do not have to name the pairs in question. Thus this definition is more readily extensible. If we wished to have two bureaucrats common to each committee, we would need to name four pairs, $(b_1, c_1), (b_1, c_2), (b_2, c_1), (b_2, c_2)$, and it becomes more complex and less readable as the number who should be in common grows. In the definition that uses the restrictions, much less work needs to be done to extend the requirement.

Likewise, we can describe the fact that two bureaucrats have only one committee in common.

$$\forall b_1, b_2 : bcrat \mid b_1 \neq b_2 \bullet \exists_1 c : com \bullet \#(\{b_1, b_2\} \lhd servesOn \rhd \{c\}) = 2$$

Combining the predicates that we have described, the complete description of *servesOn* is

> $servesOn : BUREAUCRAT \leftrightarrow COMMITTEE$
> $bcrat : \mathbb{P}\, BUREAUCRAT$
> $com : \mathbb{P}\, COMMITTEE$
> ---
> $bcrat = \mathrm{dom}\, servesOn$
>
> $com = \mathrm{ran}\, servesOn$
>
> $\forall b : bcrat \bullet \#(\{b\} \lhd servesOn) \geq 3$
>
> $\forall c : com \bullet \#(servesOn \rhd \{c\}) \geq 3$
>
> $\forall c_1, c_2 : com \mid c_1 \neq c_2 \bullet$
> $\quad \exists_1 b : bcrat \bullet \#(\{b\} \lhd servesOn \rhd \{c_1, c_2\}) = 2$
>
> $\forall b_1, b_2 : bcrat \mid b_1 \neq b_2 \bullet$
> $\quad \exists_1 c : com \bullet \#(\{b_1, b_2\} \lhd servesOn \rhd \{c\}) = 2$

> ▷ *readability*
> There is always a decision to be made as to how much information about the properties of the variables should be given in the declaration and how much stated explicitly in the predicates. There is no ready answer to this, as much depends on the reader, but one rule of thumb is to describe what we *really* want to say in the predicate, and put incidental detail into the declaration. The finiteness of *servesOn* is needed only so that we may apply cardinality. Thus, this has been merged into the declaration.

24.3   Genericity

24.3.1   Generic constants

A *generic constant* definition is used to introduce new constants defined in terms of generic parameters. Typically one is used to define an operator that depends only on the shape of its operands rather than their types. The format of a generic constant is

> [formal generic parameters]
> declaration in terms of the generic parameters
> ---
> predicate in terms of the generic parameters

Generic constants are used to define the mathematical toolkit operators. For example, taking the union of two sets (which can be performed on any type of sets provided only that the two sets are of the same type) is defined using a generic constant.

Although generic constant definitions may superficially resemble schema boxes, they should not be confused with them. They are never used directly, for example by schema inclusion, and the generic operations that they define have global scope within the specification. Consequently the name of the operator being defined must be new, and must not be used for anything else subsequently. The formal parameters are local to the definition.

If there are general notions that you wish to use often in your specifications, it is worthwhile to define an appropriate generic constant. For example, when working out how many elements there are in a bag, *sizebag* reports the number of items in the bag.

$$
\begin{array}{l}
[X] \\
\hline
sizebag : \mathrm{bag}\ X \longrightarrow \mathbb{N} \\
\hline
sizebag\ [\![\,]\!] = 0 \\
\forall\, b : \mathrm{bag}\ X;\ x : X \bullet sizebag(b \uplus [\![x]\!]) = 1 + sizebag\ b
\end{array}
$$

▷ *cardinality*
The cardinality of a bag gives the number of *distinct* items in the bag, not the total number. For the bag

$$ B = [\![a_1, \ldots, a_1, \ldots, a_n, \ldots, a_n]\!] = \{a_1 \mapsto k_1, \ldots, a_n \mapsto k_n\} $$

the cardinality is $\#B = n$, the number of pairs in the set B, not the number of items in it.

From now on we can use the operation *sizebag* on bags of any type, and it gives the number of elements in the bag. The formal generic parameters are replaced by the actual parameters at the point of use.

These generic constructions define *constants*. The definition must uniquely determine the value of the constant for *every* possible value of the formal generic parameters. So care should be taken to ensure that there is no non-determinism in the definition. A common pitfall is that the definition depends on there being sufficient members of the type. For example

$$
\begin{array}{l}
[X] \\
\hline
threeDifferent : \mathbb{P}\, X \\
\hline
\# threeDifferent = 3
\end{array}
$$

is not permissible as a generic constant definition; when X has more than three members it does not determine the value of *threeDifferent* uniquely, and when X has fewer than three members it is impossible to determine the value of *threeDifferent*.

Another common pitfall in defining generic constants is leaving the domain of a generic partial function unspecified. The error here is that the specification is loose, which is not permitted for generic constants.

When the constant being defined is a function (as in the case of *sizebag*) then it is easy to discharge this proof obligation. It is a question of ensuring that the predicate defines a unique value for each element of the function's domain. We discharge this by inspection in the case of *sizebag*.

The 'name' defined in the generic constant can be a symbol, for example, anti-filter on sequences. This operator takes a sequence and a set and returns a sequence that contains only those items not in the set provided. We define it in terms of filter, $\upharpoonright$, which takes a sequence and a set and returns a sequence that contains only those items in the set provided. (This definition has been added to our extended toolkit in appendix A.8.)

$$
\begin{array}{|l}
\hline
[X] \\
\hline
\_ \downharpoonright \_ : \operatorname{seq} X \times \mathbb{P} X \longrightarrow \operatorname{seq} X \\
\hline
\forall T : \mathbb{P} X;\ s : \operatorname{seq} X \bullet \\
\quad s \downharpoonright T = s \upharpoonright (X \setminus T) \\
\hline
\end{array}
$$

The use of the formal generic parameter X ensures that everything 'matches': the set and the sequence must be composed of elements of the same type.

The same rules apply to the introduction of new symbols as to the introduction of new names.

24.3.2   Generic abbreviation definitions

The generic constant described above is a generalisation of the abbreviation definition. Abbreviation definitions can also take generic parameters.

As we saw earlier, we can define a *finite relation*. We require that both the domain and the range of the relation are finite, useful in the cases when we wish to take the cardinality of a relation. For a function it is sufficient to have a finite domain, the number of elements in the function must then be finite. For a relation, we must ensure that both 'ends' are finite. More precisely we are interested in ensuring only that we have a finite number of pairs. As we may want to use this concept often, it makes sense to define a new symbol for it.

$$ X \leftrightarrowtail Y == \mathbb{F}(X \times Y) $$

As with the generalised version, the symbol or name defined must be new and must not be used subsequently to mean anything else. The formal generic parameters (X and Y) are local to the definition and are replaced by the actual parameters at the point of use.

The generic item defined can be a name as well as a symbol.

24.4   Disjoint and partition

The sample toolkit relation disjoint [Spivey 1992, page 122] is useful for specifying that the sets in some collection have no elements in common; that, when taken in pairs, they have an empty intersection.

$$
\begin{array}{l}
\underline{\hspace{0.3em}}[X, L] \rule{11cm}{0.4pt}\\
\text{disjoint } \_ : \mathbb{P}(L \twoheadrightarrow \mathbb{P}\,X)\\
\rule{11cm}{0.4pt}\\
\forall D : L \twoheadrightarrow \mathbb{P}\,X \bullet\\
\quad \text{disjoint } D \Leftrightarrow (\forall\, i, j : \operatorname{dom} D \mid i \neq j \bullet D\,i \cap D\,j = \varnothing)\\
\rule{11cm}{0.4pt}
\end{array}
$$

▷ *prefix relation*
  disjoint is defined as a prefix relation, so disjoint x is shorthand for $x \in$ disjoint $\_$. disjoint is the set of all functions $L \twoheadrightarrow \mathbb{P}\,X$ that enjoy the disjoint property.
▷ *set*
  In this definition of disjoint, the sets have to be labelled, in order to distinguish otherwise identical sets. This is why the type of disjoint is $\mathbb{P}(L \twoheadrightarrow \mathbb{P}\,X)$, and not $\mathbb{P}\,\mathbb{P}\,X$, as you might originally have thought. L is the set from which the labels are drawn.

In practice, the labels are often numbers, obtained by taking a sequence of sets. For example

$$\text{disjoint } \langle \{1\}, \{2, 3\}, \{4, 5\} \rangle$$

The labels could be something else, for example, consider a collection of named users who have each been allocated a set of resources. The condition that users cannot share resources can be written using disjoint

$$
\begin{array}{l}
\underline{\hspace{0.3em}} \textit{NoSharing} \rule{9cm}{0.4pt}\\
\textit{allocate} : \textit{NAME} \twoheadrightarrow \mathbb{P}\,\textit{RESOURCE}\\
\rule{9cm}{0.4pt}\\
\text{disjoint } \textit{allocate}\\
\rule{9cm}{0.4pt}
\end{array}
$$

Here the set *NAME* provides the labels, and the predicate states that

$$\forall\, n, m : \operatorname{dom} \textit{allocate} \mid n \neq m \bullet \textit{allocate}\; n \cap \textit{allocate}\; m = \varnothing$$

The relation partition is a relation between a collection of labelled sets and another set, W. These sets partition W if they are disjoint, and if they comprise the whole of W.

$$
\begin{array}{l}
\underline{\hspace{0.3em}}[X, L] \rule{11cm}{0.4pt}\\
\_ \text{ partition } \_ : (L \twoheadrightarrow \mathbb{P}\,X) \leftrightarrow \mathbb{P}\,X\\
\rule{11cm}{0.4pt}\\
\forall D : L \twoheadrightarrow \mathbb{P}\,X; \; W : \mathbb{P}\,X \bullet\\
\quad D \text{ partition } W \Leftrightarrow\\
\qquad \text{disjoint } D\\
\qquad \wedge \bigcup \{\, i : \operatorname{dom} D \bullet D\,i \,\} = W\\
\rule{11cm}{0.4pt}
\end{array}
$$

▷ *generalised union*
The use of $\bigcup$ here allows us to find the union across all the sets in the set of labelled sets.

Again the labels are usually numbers, if we are using a sequence of sets; but they could be any labels. For example, to say that the resources are not shared, and also all allocated, we could write

```
┌─ AllAllocated ───────────────────────────────────────────
│  allocate : NAME ⤀ ℙ RESOURCE
│ ─────────────────────────────────────────────────────────
│  allocate partition RESOURCE
└───────────────────────────────────────────────────────────
```

▷ *discussion*
This technique of defining a function over general labelled sets, $L \nrightarrow X$, rather than over sets labelled with a number, $\operatorname{seq} X$, is useful in other areas, too. For example, we define distributed bag sum, $\biguplus : (L \nrightarrow \operatorname{bag} X) \longrightarrow \operatorname{bag} X$, this way (see appendix A.10), and use it in the definition of *Venus* (section 10.3.4) to sum over a set of bags labelled by passenger id, $PID \nrightarrow \operatorname{bag} CLASS$.

24.5   Bindings and theta

Some Z users have difficulty with θ. This is unsurprising: Z has no notation for writing down explicitly what θS denotes, and so definitions and explanations have to resort to circumlocutions. In this section we try to demystify theta.

$\mathbb{N}$ represents a set, the set of natural numbers. Similarly a schema S represents a set, the set of all its *bindings*. A binding is an assignment of values to a schema's components such that they obey its predicate. If a variable is declared with a schema type, $s : S$, then the variable's value is one of these bindings. This is exactly the same as saying if a variable is declared as $x : \mathbb{N}$, then x has the value of one of the members of $\mathbb{N}$.

▷ *schema binding*
We can write particular values of $\mathbb{N}$, for example $3 \in \mathbb{N}$, but there is no equivalent notation for particular schema bindings, $?? \in S$; hence the circumlocutions. [Spivey 1992] uses meta-notation like $\langle x \Rrightarrow 3; y \Rrightarrow 42 \rangle$ to write down a binding, but this notation is not part of the Z language itself.
With the current language, a mu-expression gives one of the more compact ways of specifying a particular binding (see section 24.6.3).

Schemas can also be used by inclusion. If a schema S is included in another, we may still want to talk about the associated value of its components, say before and after an operation. We can do this with the schema binding θS (or $\theta S'$ for the after state binding).

This is how the expression

$\theta Counter = collection\ n?$

used in Chapter 19 on promotion works. It just says that the binding (associated values) of the piece of local state *Counter* is the same as that of the piece of state pointed to by $n?$. Similarly, all that

$$collection' = collection \oplus \{n? \mapsto \theta\, Counter'\}$$

says is that in the after state of *collection*, $n?$ now points to a piece of state that has the same binding as the after piece of local state, *Counter'*.

This is also how the ΞS convention works. The definition

$$\Xi S \cong [\, S; S' \mid \theta S = \theta S'\,]$$

says that the values associated with the components of S are the same as the values associated with the components of S'. In other words, the state doesn't change.

The same convention can be used for just *part* of the state. For example, say you had a schema defined by including two others

$$A \cong [\, S; T \mid \text{a predicate}\,]$$

and you wanted to define an operation that changed the value of S's components, but not those of T's. You could use the Δ and Ξ conventions to write

$$OpA \cong [\, \Delta S; \Xi T \mid \text{op definition}\,]$$

▷ *schema binding*

A word of warning: there is a subtlety in the use of θ. It picks up the properties and values of its components from the current environment, not from the schema definition. This can have unexpected results. If θS is used in the predicate part of a schema that includes S in its declaration, it picks up S's declaration, and everything behaves as expected. But if θS is used in a schema that does not include S, or if it is used outside a schema, then it picks up any available local and global variable definitions with the same names and types. If there are no such variables, θS is undefined (this will be detected by a type checker, if you are using one). If there are variables with the same name and type, the resultant binding is probably not what is wanted.

24.6 Definite description, mu-expression

The definite description (or mu-expression) has the form

$$\mu\, \text{SchemaText} \bullet \text{Expression}$$

The expression $\mu\, S \bullet E$ takes the variables introduced by S and then gives them values that make the property of S true; the value of the mu-expression is then the value of E (if E is omitted, the value of the characteristic tuple is used).

The mu-expression is defined only if there is a *unique* way of giving values to the variables to make the property of S true. The mu-expression is a choice operator, but there must be a unique element to choose. For example

$$\mu\, n : \mathbb{N} \mid n > 3 \bullet n + 2$$

is not defined; there are many choices of the value of n that satisfy the property. Neither is

$$\mu\, n : \mathbb{N} \mid n < 0 \bullet n + 2$$

defined; there are no choices of the value of n that satisfy the property. However

$$\mu\, n : \mathbb{N} \mid 1 < n < 3 \bullet n + 2$$

is defined; there is a unique choice of the value of n that satisfies the property: $n = 2$. So this mu-expression has the value 4.

> ▷ *quantifier, unique existential*
> People often ask what the difference is between using a unique existential quantifier and a mu-expression. The quantifier is used as part of a predicate that may or may not be true; the mu-expression says *choose* the unique value that satisfies this expression.
> ▷ *proof obligation*
> Use of a mu-expression often results in a proof obligation that a choice of values is possible, and is unique.
> ▷ *definite description*
> Some authors use a more relaxed uniqueness requirement, and let the mu-expression be defined exactly when there is a unique value for the expression. Using this definition
>
> $$\mu\, n : \mathbb{Z} \mid n = -2 \lor n = 2 \bullet n * n$$
>
> would be defined, since, whether n is chosen to be -2 or 2, the expression is uniquely determined as 4.

24.6.1   A definition of *squash* using mu

[Spivey 1992, page 118] defines a *squash* operation, which takes a function with the domain drawn from $\mathbb{N}_1$ and turns it into a sequence. His definition for this is

$$
\begin{array}{l}
\underline{\quad[X]\quad} \\
\hline
squash : (\mathbb{N}_1 \nrightarrow X) \longrightarrow \mathrm{seq}\, X \\
\hline
\forall f : \mathbb{N}_1 \nrightarrow X \bullet \\
\quad squash\, f = f \circ (\mu\, p : 1\, ..\, \#f \rightarrowtail\!\!\!\rightarrow \mathrm{dom}\, f \mid p \circ succ \circ p^{\sim} \subseteq (\_ < \_)) \\
\end{array}
$$

> ▷ *finite function*
> Only finite functions can be squashed to sequences because sequences are defined to be finite in the sample mathematical toolkit.
> ▷ *bijection*
> The bijection $\rightarrowtail\!\!\!\rightarrow$ ensures that we end up with a 'relabelled' copy of the domain of f.

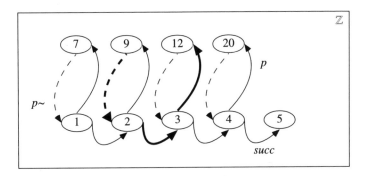

Figure 24.2 *squash*: an example of $p \circ succ \circ p^{\sim}$.

▷ *successor function*
  The use of *succ* allows us to progress to the next item in the domain of p.
▷ *backward relational composition*
  The expression $p \circ succ \circ p^{\sim}$ creates a set of pairs that are the composition of the three
  functions mentioned in which the composition starts from the right hand side.

Understanding this definition takes a little thought. What it does is find a bijection
that compacts the domain of the function to be squashed, and composes this with
the function to create the desired sequence. The domain of p is an initial sequence
of the naturals because we are using it to create a sequence. It is also chosen to
be the correct size.

  The purpose of the composition $p \circ succ \circ p^{\sim}$ is to check that p really does impose
an order on the elements of dom f. Looking at the parts of this in turn:

1. Examining the composition part, we calculate it 'backwards'. First we take
    the inverse of p (so we move from the domain of f to an initial sequence of
    $\mathbb{N}_1$).

2. Then we move to the next one along in the domain of p by composing with
    succ.

3. Then we map back to the domain of f by composing with p. The resulting
    set of pairs must be a subset of the less-than relation (because then we have
    imposed an order on dom f).

4. There must be a unique p that satisfies these constraints, so we pick it and
    compose it with f. This compacts the domain of f into a sequence, as re-
    quired.

For example, take f with $\{7, 9, 12, 20\}$ as its domain. Then p must be

$$p = \{1 \mapsto 7, 2 \mapsto 9, 3 \mapsto 12, 4 \mapsto 20\}$$

Figure 24.2 shows the composition imposing an order on the elements of $\operatorname{dom} f$. The outcome of the composition is

$$p \circ succ \circ p^{\sim} = \{7 \mapsto 9, 9 \mapsto 12, 12 \mapsto 20\}$$

$$f \circ p$$
$$= \{7 \mapsto a, 9 \mapsto b, 12 \mapsto c, 20 \mapsto d\} \circ \{1 \mapsto 7, 2 \mapsto 9, 3 \mapsto 12, 4 \mapsto 20\}$$
$$= \{1 \mapsto a, 2 \mapsto b, 3 \mapsto c, 4 \mapsto d\}$$

□

▷ *backward relational composition*
There are some places where the composition 'drops out', for example, 20 is in the original 'source' set, but does not become an element of the domain of the composition. This has no effect on the composition. Relational composition is angelic: it is formed only of those pairs for which a complete path from beginning to end may be found. Parts that 'drop out' are ignored by the final composition.

▷ *proof obligation*
There is a proof obligation to demonstrate that the mu-expression is defined (that is, that p may be chosen uniquely). This may be awkward to discharge.

24.6.2   An alternative definition of *squash*

The above shows a use of μ, although the expression for *squash* is awkward to read because it contains many different pieces of notation. We prefer the following definition of *squash*.

$$
\begin{array}{l}
\boxed{\begin{array}{l}
\underline{[X]} \\
squash : (\mathbb{N}_1 \nrightarrow X) \longrightarrow \operatorname{seq} X \\[4pt]
\hline
squash \, \varnothing = \langle\,\rangle \\
\forall f : \mathbb{N}_1 \nrightarrow X; \; i : \mathbb{N}_1; \; x : X \mid i < min(\operatorname{dom} f) \bullet \\
\quad squash(f \cup \{i \mapsto x\}) = \langle x \rangle \frown squash \, f
\end{array}}
\end{array}
$$

▷ *maximum*
We could equally well define *squash* using the maximum of a set by replacing the last part with

$$\forall f : \mathbb{N}_1 \nrightarrow X; \; i : \mathbb{N}_1; \; x : X \mid i > max(\operatorname{dom} f) \bullet$$
$$squash(f \cup \{i \mapsto x\}) = squash \, f \frown \langle x \rangle$$

▷ *implementation bias*
We could also define *squash* without assuming either a left–right or right–left implementation. Such a definition, which could be implemented on a parallel machine, would be

$$\begin{array}{l} =[X]\!=\!\!=\!\!=\!\!=\!\!=\!\!=\!\!=\!\!=\!\!=\!\!=\!\!=\!\!=\!\!=\!\!= \\[2pt] squash : (\mathbb{N}_1 \nrightarrow X) \longrightarrow seq\,X \\[4pt] \hline squash\varnothing = \langle\,\rangle \\[2pt] \forall\,i : \mathbb{N}_1;\, x : X \bullet squash\,\{i \mapsto x\} = \langle x\rangle \\[2pt] \forall\,f, g : \mathbb{N}_1 \nrightarrow X \mid max(\mathrm{dom}\,f) < min(\mathrm{dom}\,g) \bullet \\[2pt] \qquad squash(f \cup g) = squash\,f \,^\frown squash\,g \end{array}$$

▷ *readability*

We prefer this 'constructive' style of recursive definition, where a compound expression $(f \cup g)$ is expressed in terms of its components, rather than the more common 'subtractive' style, where a single expression is split into two parts, as illustrated below.

$$\begin{array}{l} =[X]\!=\!\!=\!\!=\!\!=\!\!=\!\!=\!\!=\!\!=\!\!=\!\!=\!\!=\!\!=\!\!=\!\!= \\[2pt] squash : (\mathbb{N}_1 \nrightarrow X) \longrightarrow seq\,X \\[4pt] \hline squash\varnothing = \langle\,\rangle \\[2pt] \forall\,f : \mathbb{N}_1 \nrightarrow X;\, i : \mathbb{N}_1 \bullet \\[2pt] \qquad squash\,f = squash((1 .. (i-1)) \lhd f) \,^\frown \langle f\,i\rangle \\[2pt] \qquad\quad ^\frown squash(((i+1) .. (max(\mathrm{dom}\,f))) \lhd f) \end{array}$$

Whether you find a recursive definition, either 'constructive' or 'subtractive', more readable than the direct definition given by Spivey is a question of how familiar you are with the recursive style, and with the toolkit. You should be guided by your audience: it is for your readers that the specification is being created.

24.6.3   Defining a schema binding

Although there is no direct way of writing down a particular schema binding, μ can be used to construct one relatively compactly. Given

$$S \triangleq [\,x : X;\, y : Y;\, \ldots\,]$$

we can define a specific binding with explicit values x_0, y_0, ... for the components:

$$b = (\,\mu\,S \mid x = x_0 \wedge y = y_0 \wedge \ldots\,)$$

This can be read as 'make an S where x is x_0, y is y_0, ...'. This is uniquely defined, by construction, provided that the supplied values satisfy the property of S.

24.6.4   Quadrilateral drawing system

As a further example of the use of μ, we present here part of a specification of a quadrilateral drawing system. We concentrate on defining the state and operations on a quadrilateral. The style followed is that of [Hall 1990] and the specification is based on that given in [Stepney *et al.* 1992].

This example builds on the quadrilateral drawing system introduced in section 23.6.7. The difference in style between this presentation and that given previously are because here we follow a more object oriented style. We use the definitions of *VECTOR*, **0**, ✠ and *Quadrilateral* from section 23.6.7.

A quadrilateral is defined by its identity (using a given set of identifiers), by its four sides, and by its *position* (which we introduce to give the displacement of the quadrilateral from the origin of the drawing system).

[*QUAD*]

┌─ *Quad* ─────────────────────────────────
│ *self* : *QUAD*
│ *edges* : *Quadrilateral*
│ *position* : *VECTOR*
└──

The whole drawing system may be described in terms of a set of quadrilateral identifiers and a function that relates the identifier to the instance of a quadrilateral. This function ensures the individuality of the quadrilaterals.

┌─ *DrawingSystem* ─────────────────────────
│ *quads* : $\mathbb{F}$ *Quad*
│ *idQuad* : *QUAD* $\rightarrowtail$ *Quad*
├──
│ *idQuad* = { *q* : *quads* • *q.self* $\mapsto$ *q* }
└──

The drawing system is thus described in terms of the objects it contains.

Operations on Quadrilaterals

We define operations in terms of single objects, then calculate their effect on the whole system. We define a general operation on a quadrilateral that simply says that no matter what else changes, the quadrilateral's identity does not.

$$\Delta Quad \;\widehat{=}\; [\, Quad;\; Quad' \mid self' = self \,]$$

Translation of a quadrilateral is given by

┌─ *TranslateQuad* ─────────────────────────
│ $\Delta Quad$
│ *move?* : *VECTOR*
├──
│ *position'* = *position* ✠ *move?*
│ *edges'* = *edges*
└──

This operation describes only single objects. In order to describe the effect of the translation of one quadrilateral upon the whole drawing system the following approach is adopted

$$
\begin{array}{|l}
\hline
\;\; ChangePositionSystem \underline{\hspace{6cm}} \\
\;\; \Delta DrawingSystem \\
\;\; q? : QUAD \\
\;\; move? : VECTOR \\
\hline
\;\; idQuad' = idQuad \oplus \{\, q? \mapsto (\, \mu \; TranslateQuad_1 \mid \\
\qquad\qquad \theta Quad_1 = idQuad \; q? \\
\qquad\qquad \wedge \; move?_1 = move? \; \bullet \\
\qquad \theta Quad'_1 \,)\} \\
\hline
\end{array}
$$

▷ *readability*

In order to avoid name clashes, the schema *TranslateQuad* has been decorated with a subscript 1. Another approach is to choose the names in the outer operation with care. For example, *translation?* could be used instead of *move?* (so as to avoid a clash with the inner operation described in the included schema). We prefer using decoration, as we believe it makes the schema more readable.

▷ *abstraction*

Note that as a result of this change in *idQuad* the *quads* set is altered too, but this is not stated explicitly.

The way in which the operation works is that we update our record of the quadrilaterals (*idQuad*) by the new details of *q?* given by the definition of the translation on *q?*. We choose the only possible instantiation of *TranslateQuad* that moves the given quadrilateral by the given amount (*move?*).

▷ *promotion*

What we are describing here is a more specific version of promotion. *idQuad* has been set up to give an exact identification of quadrilaterals. Each quadrilateral knows its own identifier and *idQuad* maps that identifier to the quadrilateral with that name. Thus we do not need to match up the quadrilateral with the right set of values; we can find it directly.

24.6.5 Whether to use a mu-expression

Mu-expressions can be useful, but they should be used sparingly as many readers find them awkward to comprehend. Using a mu-expression also gives rise to a proof obligation to demonstrate that the mu-expression is defined and unique. A mu-expression does provide a compact way of defining a schema binding.

Chapter 25

A Real Number Toolkit

In which an alternative toolkit is presented and used.

25.1   Defining the alternative toolkit

The sample toolkit [Spivey 1992, Chapter 4] has no support for real numbers, only integers. But real numbers can be useful in some specifications—we do not always wish to build mathematical models of just discrete data structures. Some authors simply use real numbers without further comment, for example, [Hayes 1990], [Mahoney & Hayes 1991], [Woodcock 1991].

In this section we describe what a 'real number toolkit' might look like. There is a tension between putting in too many rarely used operators and leaving out ones that are used a lot. We have tried to err on the minimalist side. A more thorough treatment is given by [Valentine 1993].

25.1.1   Real numbers

Spivey parachutes in the integers and leaves the arithmetic operators undefined, saying that it is possible to define them using *succ* [Spivey 1992, section 4.4]. He discusses this in more detail in [Spivey 1988, section 5.2]. The Z Standard does define the operators.

It is possible to construct the reals from the natural numbers, but easier just to take their existence as an axiom [Stewart & Tall 1977, Chapter 9]. So, following Spivey, a real number toolkit can just parachute in the well-known reals, and leave the well-known arithmetic operators undefined. (We are assuming that the sample toolkit is unchanged up to this point, so we will say nothing more about sets, relations and functions as defined in [Spivey 1992, sections 4.1 to 4.3].) So we now have

$$\mathbb{N} \subset \mathbb{Z} \subset \mathbb{R}$$

25.1.2   Real operators

Operators for real numbers can be broken down into three categories

Unchanged existing operators those defined in the sample toolkit that can be incorporated unchanged.

Modified existing operators those defined in the sample toolkit that can be incorporated with a modification to their range and domain.

New operators no appropriate operator is defined in the sample toolkit, so new ones need to be defined.

Unchanged existing operators

The following carry over to the real number toolkit unchanged

- relational iteration, R^k
- integer number range, $n \mathinner{\ldotp\ldotp} m$
- size of a finite set, $\#S$
- sequences, and their operators

Modified existing operators

Some operators need to be extended to have a real range and domain. These are the arithmetic operators, and (possibly) bags. Following the presentation given in [Spivey 1992, sections 4.4 and 4.6]

$$[\mathbb{R}]$$

$\mathbb{Z}, \mathbb{N} : \mathbb{P}\,\mathbb{R}$
$\_ + \_ , \_ - \_ , \_ * \_ : \mathbb{R} \times \mathbb{R} \longrightarrow \mathbb{R}$
$- : \mathbb{R} \longrightarrow \mathbb{R}$
$\_ < \_ , \_ \leq \_ , \_ > \_ , \_ \geq \_ : \mathbb{R} \leftrightarrow \mathbb{R}$
(definitions omitted)

---

div and mod need more careful definition, especially for negative arguments. Spivey merely says they use truncation towards minus infinity, and that they obey certain laws. A definition consistent with these statements is

$$\begin{array}{|l}
\_\,\mathsf{div}\,\_ : \mathbb{R} \times (\mathbb{R} \setminus \{0\}) \longrightarrow \mathbb{Z} \\
\_\,\mathsf{mod}\,\_ : \mathbb{R} \times (\mathbb{R} \setminus \{0\}) \longrightarrow \mathbb{R} \\
\hline
\forall\, a, b : \mathbb{R} \mid b \neq 0 \bullet \\
\quad a\ \mathsf{div}\ b = \lfloor a \,/\, b \rfloor \\
\quad \wedge\ a\ \mathsf{mod}\ b = a - (a\ \mathsf{div}\ b) * b
\end{array}$$

where real division, x/y, and floor, $\lfloor x \rfloor$, are new real toolkit operators defined in the next section.

If Hayes's suggested bag extension [Hayes 1990] is taken up, it might be worthwhile in a real toolkit to provide bags that can have non-integral occurrences

$$\mathsf{bag}\ X == X \longrightarrow \mathbb{R}$$

New operators

Real versions of unchanged operators
Some of the operators exist in distinct real and integral forms. Real number division (compare div), intervals (compare number range $n \mathrel{..} m$), and upper and lower bounds (compare *min* and *max*) are needed.

Division is the well-known real arithmetic operator

$$\begin{array}{|l}
\_\,/\,\_ : \mathbb{R} \times (\mathbb{R} \setminus \{0\}) \longrightarrow \mathbb{R} \\
\hline
\text{(definitions omitted)}
\end{array}$$

The standard mathematical notation for an open interval, one that does not include the end points, is (l, u); for a closed interval, one that does include the end points, is $[l, u]$; and for mixed intervals, open one end and closed the other, is $[l, u)$ and $(l, u]$. However, we suggest a slightly different notation, to reduce confusion of open intervals with tuples. This notation echoes the discrete integer interval notation.

$$\begin{array}{|l}
(\_ \ldots \_) : \mathbb{R} \times \mathbb{R} \longrightarrow \mathbb{P}\,\mathbb{R} \\
[\_ \ldots \_] : \mathbb{R} \times \mathbb{R} \longrightarrow \mathbb{P}\,\mathbb{R} \\
(\_ \ldots \_] : \mathbb{R} \times \mathbb{R} \longrightarrow \mathbb{P}\,\mathbb{R} \\
[\_ \ldots \_) : \mathbb{R} \times \mathbb{R} \longrightarrow \mathbb{P}\,\mathbb{R} \\
\hline
\forall\, l, u : \mathbb{R} \bullet \\
\quad (l \ldots u) = \{r : \mathbb{R} \mid l < r < u\} \\
\quad \wedge\ [l \ldots u] = \{r : \mathbb{R} \mid l \leq r \leq u\} \\
\quad \wedge\ (l \ldots u] = \{r : \mathbb{R} \mid l < r \leq u\} \\
\quad \wedge\ [l \ldots u) = \{r : \mathbb{R} \mid l \leq r < u\}
\end{array}$$

Notice that $(l \mathrel{..} u) = \{k : \mathbb{Z} \mid l \leq k \leq u\}$ is a parenthesised expression denoting a discrete set of integers, which may contain either endpoint if they too are integers. Contrast this with $(l \ldots u) = \{k : \mathbb{R} \mid l < k < u\}$, where the parentheses are part of the expression, which denotes a connected set of real numbers that does *not* contain the endpoint values. Designing new notation that keeps close to standard mathematical notation, but does not conflict with standard Z notation, is challenging; the results are not always totally satisfactory.

Minimum and maximum elements of a set are less easy to define when reals abound. What is usually done is to define the *least upper bound* and the *greatest lower bound*, which are not necessarily members of the sets.

$$lub : \mathbb{P}_1 \mathbb{R} \nrightarrow \mathbb{R}$$
$$glb : \mathbb{P}_1 \mathbb{R} \nrightarrow \mathbb{R}$$
(definitions omitted)

Rounding to integers
The operators that round reals down (floor) and up (ceiling) to the nearest integer are

$$\lfloor \_ \rfloor : \mathbb{R} \rightarrow \mathbb{Z}$$
$$\lceil \_ \rceil : \mathbb{R} \rightarrow \mathbb{Z}$$
$$\forall\, r : \mathbb{R} \bullet$$
$$\quad r - 1 < \lfloor r \rfloor \leq r$$
$$\quad \wedge\, r \leq \lceil r \rceil < r + 1$$

Functions
New classes of functions can be defined, for example, continuous functions, and functions with a countable domain.

Powers
Raising numbers to powers can be defined as follows

$$\_ \uparrow \_ : \mathbb{R} \times \mathbb{R} \nrightarrow \mathbb{R}$$
$$\forall\, r : \mathbb{R}; \ n : \mathbb{N} \bullet$$
$$\quad r \uparrow 0 = 1$$
$$\quad \wedge\, r \uparrow (n + 1) = r * (r \uparrow n)$$
$$\forall\, r : \mathbb{R} \setminus \{0\}; \ n : \mathbb{N} \bullet$$
$$\quad r \uparrow (-n) = 1 / (r \uparrow n)$$
(further definitions for real exponents omitted)

The more conventional notation of r^n is not used, to avoid confusion with the notation for relational iteration.

▷ *recursive definition*
  We have used a recursive definition, each positive power is defined in terms of the next lower one; a base case is provided for raising to the power of zero.

Other functions

Trigonometric functions, exponentials, and logarithms should probably be included in a real toolkit. The inverses of the trigonometric functions should have their domains and ranges defined explicitly, since this is often a source of confusion and ambiguity, but otherwise well-known mathematical definitions can be omitted.

For example

$$\begin{array}{|l}
\sin : \mathbb{R} \longrightarrow \mathbb{R} \\
\arcsin : \mathbb{R} \nrightarrow \mathbb{R} \\
\hline
\forall \phi : \mathbb{R}; \; n : \mathbb{Z} \bullet \sin \phi = \sin(\phi + 2 * n * \pi) \\
(\text{definitions omitted}) \\
\mathrm{dom}\,\arcsin = [(-1) \ldots 1] \\
\mathrm{ran}\,\arcsin = [0 \ldots 2 * \pi) \\
\forall \phi : \mathbb{R} \bullet \exists n : \mathbb{Z} \bullet \arcsin(\sin \phi) = \phi + 2 * n * \pi
\end{array}$$

This defines arcsin to be a function, and a kind of inverse for sin, leaving $\sin^{-1}$ to refer to the inverse *relation* in the usual Z way.

25.1.3   Syntax for real numbers

The syntax for integers is built into the base Z language, because there is no mechanism in Z for extending the syntax of identifiers (the 'meaning' of a digit string in Z is: 'this is the name of a member of the set $\mathbb{Z}$').

To keep the real number toolkit as a proper addition to Z, rather than redefining the base language to include syntax for real numbers such as 3.14159 and 0.$\dot{1}$4285$\dot{7}$, concrete real numbers have to be written as the division of integers, for example, $31415/10000 < \pi < 31416/10000$.

Exponentiation can be used for large or small numbers. For example $c = 3 * 10 \uparrow 8$, $m = 9 * 10 \uparrow -31$.

Various 'well-known' constants should be made available, for example

$$\begin{array}{|l}
\pi, e : \mathbb{R} \\
\hline
(\text{definitions omitted})
\end{array}$$

25.1.4   Complex numbers

Complex numbers, if required, can be constructed from the reals [Stewart & Tall 1977, Chapter 11] via

$$\mathbb{C} == \mathbb{R} \times \mathbb{R}$$

and various complex operators could be defined, for example

$$
\begin{array}{|l}
i : \mathbb{C} \\
\underline{\ } +_c \underline{\ } , \underline{\ } *_c \underline{\ } : \mathbb{C} \times \mathbb{C} \to \mathbb{C} \\
\hline
i = (0, 1) \\
\forall\, x_1, y_1, x_2, y_2 : \mathbb{R} \bullet \\
\quad (x_1, y_1) +_c (x_2, y_2) = (x_1 + x_2, y_1 + y_2) \\
\quad \wedge\ (x_1, y_1) *_c (x_2, y_2) = (x_1 * x_2 - y_1 * y_2, x_1 * y_2 + x_2 * y_1)
\end{array}
$$

Alternatively, complex numbers could be parachuted in as the most fundamental numerical type, and then we would have

$$\mathbb{N} \subset \mathbb{Z} \subset \mathbb{R} \subset \mathbb{C}$$

25.1.5   Multiple toolkits

Such a real number toolkit could replace the sample toolkit. Apart from the given set of numbers changing from $\mathbb{Z}$ to $\mathbb{R}$, few changes would be needed to existing specifications with the real toolkit suggested above.

Alternatively, users could say which toolkit they wanted to use. In this case a mechanism for such a statement would be needed. This more general approach would allow complex numbers to be parachuted in if required, and allow any other application-specific toolkits to be slotted in sensibly.

25.2   Fixed point arithmetic

Fixed point numbers are a subset of real numbers. For example, money could be modelled as reals correct to 2 decimal places

$$sterling == \{\, m : \mathbb{R} \mid \lfloor 100 * m \rfloor = 100 * m \,\}$$

When the halfpence piece still existed, requiring 3 decimal places, with the third place being either 0 or 5, it could have be accommodated with the same mechanism

$$oldSterling == \{\, m : \mathbb{R} \mid \lfloor 200 * m \rfloor = 200 * m \,\}$$

Real addition and subtraction can be used for fixed point numbers. But a special multiplication operation needs to be defined (for example, for calculating 13.9% interest on a loan or 17.5% tax on a purchase). Obvious choices are rounding up, or down, or to the nearest penny. A less obvious choice, used in some tax calculations, rounds down to the nearest 10 pence. Alternatively, it might be desired to keep a more accurate (more decimal places) internal representation, and round to the

nearest penny only when billing. For example, petrol prices are calculated in units
of tenths of a penny per litre, and rounded only when the final bill is presented.

It is not difficult to specify any of these choices. The important thing is that
some choice can be explicitly and unambiguously documented.

25.3   Physical units

The physical world is classically modelled as a continuum. This needs real numbers,
not discrete integers.

As we want to be able to add lengths together, to say one time occurs before
another and so on, we define the units thus

$TIME == \mathbb{R}$
$LENGTH == \mathbb{R}$

▷ *given set*
  When modelling physical quantities, do not use something like

  $[TIME, LENGTH]$

  As given sets, these are structureless and have no operations available.
▷ *abbreviation definition*
  This device of assigning an existing type to the name of a set in the specification is very
  useful. It helps to remind the reader and the writer of the specification of the intended
  usage of the new sets (*TIME* and *LENGTH* in our case) and thus can help to avoid (some)
  silly errors.

This approach is adequate for simple problems without lots of different physical
quantities that need to be combined. Notice, however, that even though variables
can be declared to be of type *TIME* or *LENGTH*, there is no error in a definition
like

> $now : TIME$
> $height : LENGTH$
> $weird : \mathbb{R}$
> ___
> $weird = now + height$

The problem is that the 'semantics' rests solely in the meaning ascribed to the
names by the reader, not in the mathematics. We want to be able to specify that
metres can be divided by seconds, but not added to them. The point to recognise
here is that a physical quantity like a length has two components: its magnitude
and its physical dimension. Dimensional analysis in physics is based on the fact
that any dimension can be reduced to powers of length, mass, and time (sometimes
augmented with temperature and electric charge). Hence we can write

$UNIT ::= \mathcal{L} \mid \mathcal{M} \mid \mathcal{T} \mid \Theta \mid \mathcal{Q}$
$dimension == UNIT \rightarrow \mathbb{Z}$
$physical == \mathbb{R} \times dimension$

Physical quantities can be dimensionless (in fact, particular values of physical quantities are significant only when they are dimensionless, since only then do they remain unchanged by a change in units).

$$\begin{array}{|l}
zeroD : dimension \\
\hline
zeroD = (\lambda\, u : UNIT \bullet 0)
\end{array}$$

Then acceleration due to gravity, and the speed of light, for example, could be represented as

$$\begin{array}{|l}
g : physical \\
c : physical \\
\hline
g = (98\,/\,10,\ zeroD \oplus \{\mathcal{L} \mapsto 1, \mathcal{T} \mapsto -2\}) \\
c = (3 * 10 \uparrow 8,\ zeroD \oplus \{\mathcal{L} \mapsto 1, \mathcal{T} \mapsto -1\})
\end{array}$$

▷ *overriding*
  We set all values to the zero dimension and then override with the dimensions we actually want. This follows the same method as is used to define bag count.

It would be wonderful to be able to describe an abbreviated form of these quantities, to be able to write, using conventional SI units, expressions like $g = 9.8\,\mathrm{m\,s}^{-2}$ and $c = 3.0 * 10^8\,\mathrm{m\,s}^{-1}$. Unfortunately, this is not possible with Z as it stands. Explicit abbreviations can be made, however, like

$$\begin{aligned}
\mathsf{ms}^{-1} &== zeroD \oplus \{\mathcal{L} \mapsto 1, \mathcal{T} \mapsto -1\} \\
\mathsf{ms}^{-2} &== zeroD \oplus \{\mathcal{L} \mapsto 1, \mathcal{T} \mapsto -2\} \\
speed &== \{\, p : physical \mid second\ p = \mathsf{ms}^{-1} \,\} \\
acceleration &== \{\, p : physical \mid second\ p = \mathsf{ms}^{-2} \,\}
\end{aligned}$$

Notice that here, 'ms^{-2}' is a single name, written using some 'strange' font, and should not be confused with relational iteration.

▷ *projection function*
  We use the projection function *second*, which takes the second entry of an ordered pair.

This enables us to write things like

$$\begin{array}{|l}
g : acceleration \\
c : speed \\
\hline
g = (98\,/\,10,\ \mathsf{ms}^{-2}) \\
c = (3 * 10 \uparrow 8,\ \mathsf{ms}^{-1})
\end{array}$$

Addition and subtraction of physical quantities is defined only for units with the same dimensions

$$\begin{array}{|l}
\_ +_u \_ : physical \times physical \nrightarrow physical \\
\_ -_u \_ : physical \times physical \nrightarrow physical \\
\hline
(\_ +_u \_) = \{ r_1, r_2 : \mathbb{R}; \ d_1, d_2 : dimension \mid d_1 = d_2 \bullet \\
\qquad ((r_1, d_1), (r_2, d_2)) \mapsto (r_1 + r_2, d_1)\} \\
(\_ -_u \_) = \{ r_1, r_2 : \mathbb{R}; \ d_1, d_2 : dimension \mid d_1 = d_2 \bullet \\
\qquad ((r_1, d_1), (r_2, d_2)) \mapsto (r_1 - r_2, d_1)\}
\end{array}$$

Physical quantities with different dimensions can be multiplied and divided. Each component in their dimensions is added or subtracted, respectively

$$\begin{array}{|l}
\_ \boxplus \_ : dimension \times dimension \longrightarrow dimension \\
\_ \boxminus \_ : dimension \times dimension \longrightarrow dimension \\
\hline
\forall d_1, d_2 : dimension; \ u : UNIT \bullet \\
\quad (d_1 \boxplus d_2)u = d_1\ u + d_2\ u \\
\quad \wedge\ (d_1 \boxminus d_2)u = d_1\ u - d_2\ u
\end{array}$$

$$\begin{array}{|l}
\_ *_u \_ : physical \times physical \longrightarrow physical \\
\_ /_u \_ : physical \times (physical \setminus \{d : dimension \bullet (0, d)\}) \nrightarrow physical \\
\hline
\forall r_1, r_2 : \mathbb{R}; \ d_1, d_2 : dimension \bullet \\
\quad (r_1, d_1) *_u (r_2, d_2) = (r_1 * r_2, d_1 \boxplus d_2) \\
\forall r_1 : \mathbb{R}; \ r_2 : \mathbb{R} \setminus \{0\}; \ d_1, d_2 : dimension \bullet \\
\quad (r_1, d_1)/_u(r_2, d_2) = (r_1\ /\ r_2, d_1 \boxminus d_2)
\end{array}$$

Using this approach, it is possible to ascertain the dimensional consistency of expressions. Consider the following

$$kg == zeroD \oplus \{\mathcal{M} \mapsto 1\}$$
$$N == zeroD \oplus \{\mathcal{L} \mapsto 1, \mathcal{T} \mapsto -2, \mathcal{M} \mapsto 1\}$$
$$J == zeroD \oplus \{\mathcal{L} \mapsto 2, \mathcal{T} \mapsto -2, \mathcal{M} \mapsto 1\}$$
$$mass == \{\, p : physical \mid second\ p = kg\,\}$$
$$force == \{\, p : physical \mid second\ p = N\,\}$$
$$energy == \{\, p : physical \mid second\ p = J\,\}$$

▷ abbreviation definition
Note that we are not following our house style here, which would require the use of (say) n and j for newtons and joules. However, this would conflict with conventional use in physics. We prefer to adopt the pre-existing convention, to minimise confusion.

Then in the definition

$f : force$
$m : mass$
$a : acceleration$
$E : energy$

$f = m *_u a$
$E = m *_u c *_u c$
$E = m *_u a$

the first two expressions are dimensionally consistent

$second(m *_u a)$
$\quad = (zeroD \oplus \{\mathcal{M} \mapsto 1\}) \boxplus (zeroD \oplus \{\mathcal{L} \mapsto 1, \mathcal{T} \mapsto -2\})$
$\quad = zeroD \oplus \{\mathcal{L} \mapsto 1, \mathcal{T} \mapsto -2, \mathcal{M} \mapsto 1\}$
$\quad = \mathsf{N}$
$\quad = second\ f$

$\square$

$second(m *_u c *_u c)$
$\quad = (zeroD \oplus \{\mathcal{M} \mapsto 1\}) \boxplus (zeroD \oplus \{\mathcal{L} \mapsto 1, \mathcal{T} \mapsto -1\})$
$\quad\quad \boxplus (zeroD \oplus \{\mathcal{L} \mapsto 1, \mathcal{T} \mapsto -1\})$
$\quad = zeroD \oplus \{\mathcal{L} \mapsto 2, \mathcal{T} \mapsto -2, \mathcal{M} \mapsto 1\}$
$\quad = \mathsf{J}$
$\quad = second\ E$

$\square$

but the third is not

$second(m *_u a)$
$\quad = (zeroD \oplus \{\mathcal{M} \mapsto 1\}) \boxplus (zeroD \oplus \{\mathcal{L} \mapsto 1, \mathcal{T} \mapsto -2\})$
$\quad = zeroD \oplus \{\mathcal{L} \mapsto 1, \mathcal{T} \mapsto -2, \mathcal{M} \mapsto 1\}$
$\quad = \mathsf{N}$
$\quad \neq second\ E$

$\square$

25.3.1   Discussion

Multiplication or division of a physical quantity by a real number can be achieved by considering the number to be dimensionless (having the dimension component equal to *zeroD*).

[Hayes 1990] notes that the definition of *dimension* is similar to that for bags, except that the function is total, and that negative values are allowed. He proposes an extension to bags that would allow them to be used for dimensions. The function ⊞ would then become simply bag addition, where the number of times an item appears in the resulting bag is the sum of the times it appears in the original bags (confusingly called 'bag union' in the standard toolkit), see section 21.4. Analogously, the function ⊟ would become bag subtraction, where the number of times an item appears in the resulting bag is the difference between the times it appears in the original bags, hence the requirement for negative occurrences.

Chapter 26

And Finally ...

In which the book is summarised and the future considered.

Writing Z specifications is not an easy task. This is not because Z is inherently difficult, rather it is because you are forced to think what the system you are describing is really about. The abstraction required can be hard to learn but, with practice, Z users become 'better and better' as the saying has it.

Where a team of people is working on a specification a house style is needed. Such a style extends beyond the typographical conventions, such as in Chapter 8, towards a common approach. A suitable approach can be adapted from the many published examples.

Using Z helps you to understand your system more clearly and produce a more complete and succinct specification. Such specifications help you to build your system more quickly and with fewer errors. None of these effects is guaranteed, but Z assists by encouraging you to think more abstractly about your problem.

We have examined specification and the issue of abstraction in some detail. We have looked briefly at proof at the specification level, and proofs of refinement. If you need to develop your system more formally these aspects must be addressed and some further study is appropriate. The interested reader is referred to [Morgan 1990], [Prehn & Toetenel 1991] and [Woodcock & Davies 1994].

The number of tools available for Z is increasing. Such tools ease the problems of using Z since they can assist in presenting the specifications and they can find small errors. As tool support for refinement and proof matures, it will become feasible for more projects to address these areas.

Government standards, in Britain and elsewhere, are already demanding the use of formal methods on certain projects. As the calls for reliable software become louder the use of formal methods such as Z will increase. Z is one of the best documented and best supported formal notations in the UK. We believe that it has a strong future, which we look forward to with interest and optimism.

Part V

Appendices

Appendix A

Extension to the Sample Toolkit

In which we add some useful operations to the Sample Toolkit.

A.1   The sample toolkit

The sample toolkit [Spivey 1992, Chapter 4] describes common structures compactly. It orients its data types towards mathematical simplicity, rather than computer implementation, and hence simplifies reasoning about properties of the systems.

The definitions in the sample toolkit are not the last word. There are many other useful operations possible; indeed we use some in our specifications in this book. These extra definitions are summarised below, in a style similar to the sample toolkit.

A.2   Distributed operators

Many sample toolkit operators have a declaration like $op : Y \times Y \longrightarrow Y$. They take a pair of arguments, and return a value of the same type that is some combination of the argument's values. Examples include set union and intersection, relational composition and overriding, binary arithmetic operators, sequence concatenation, and bag union. It is occasionally useful to have a *distributed* form of these operators, that takes some collection of arguments and combines them all in one go. For example, generalised union and intersection, and distributed concatenation, are defined in the sample toolkit.

Although it is not possible to define a generic Z function that takes an operator and returns the distributed version, it is possible to take a systematic approach to defining individual distributed operators.

Consider some particular infix binary operator $\_ \diamond \_ : Y \times Y \longrightarrow Y$. The name of the distributed form is conventionally written either as a larger version of the same symbol, $\Diamond$, or as the symbol followed by a slash, $\diamond/$. The former looks neater in printed specifications; the latter is easier to distinguish from the non-distributed form in handwritten specifications.

If $\diamond$ is an associative operator like sequence concatenation, where $(x \diamond y) \diamond z = x \diamond (y \diamond z)$, a distributed form of $\diamond$ that takes a *sequence* of arguments of type Y can be defined as follows. Let the result of the distributed operator on the empty sequence be $e : Y$. (The value of e differs according to the actual operator; it is often the empty set, but for set intersection, for example, it is Y.) Then

$$
\begin{array}{|l}
\hline
\llap{=}[Y]\rlap{\rule{2cm}{0.4pt}}\\
\quad \Diamond : \operatorname{seq} Y \longrightarrow Y \\
\hline
\quad \Diamond \langle \rangle = e \\
\quad \forall y : Y \bullet \Diamond \langle y \rangle = y \\
\quad \forall s, t : \operatorname{seq} Y \bullet \Diamond(s \frown t) = (\Diamond s) \diamond (\Diamond t) \\
\hline
\end{array}
$$

Note that this style of definition uses our preferred recursive form of splitting the sequence into two arbitrary subsequences, rather than splitting it into *head* and *tail*, or into *front* and *last* (see also the discussion in section 9.3.6).

Some binary operators are left-associative, for example, some sort of subtraction operator like set difference, arithmetic minus or bag difference, where $x \ominus y \ominus z = (x \ominus y) \ominus z \neq x \ominus (y \ominus z)$. In such a case a *front* and *last* form of specification captures the correct associativity.

$$
\begin{array}{|l}
\hline
\llap{=}[Y]\rlap{\rule{2cm}{0.4pt}}\\
\quad \Diamond : \operatorname{seq} Y \longrightarrow Y \\
\hline
\quad \Diamond \langle \rangle = e \\
\quad \forall y : Y; \ s : \operatorname{seq} Y \bullet \Diamond(s \frown \langle y \rangle) = (\Diamond s) \diamond y \\
\hline
\end{array}
$$

For right-associative operators, a *head* and *tail* form captures the correct associativity.

$$\boxed{\begin{array}{l} [Y] \\ \hline \diamondsuit : \operatorname{seq} Y \longrightarrow Y \\ \hline \diamondsuit\langle\,\rangle = e \\ \forall y : Y;\ s : \operatorname{seq} Y \bullet \diamondsuit(\langle y\rangle \frown s) = y \diamond (\diamondsuit s) \end{array}}$$

If $\diamond$ is an idempotent operator like set union or intersection, where $x \diamond x = x$, then the distributed form can be safely applied to a *set* of arguments, rather than to a sequence. (The use of a sequence stops identical arguments being 'lost' when $\diamond$ is not idempotent.)

$$\boxed{\begin{array}{l} [Y] \\ \hline \diamondsuit : \mathbb{P}\, Y \longrightarrow Y \\ \hline \diamondsuit\varnothing = e \\ \forall y : Y \bullet \diamondsuit\{y\} = y \\ \forall s, t : \mathbb{P}\, Y \bullet \diamondsuit(s \cup t) = (\diamondsuit s) \diamond (\diamondsuit t) \end{array}}$$

If $\diamond$ is commutative as well as associative, where $x \diamond y = y \diamond x$, then the distributed form can be applied to an *unordered* labelled set of arguments, rather than to a sequence (where the labels are numbers, which give an order).

$$\boxed{\begin{array}{l} [L, Y] \\ \hline \diamondsuit : (L \nrightarrow Y) \longrightarrow Y \\ \hline \diamondsuit\varnothing = e \\ \forall l : L;\ y : Y \bullet \diamondsuit\{l \mapsto y\} = y \\ \forall s, t : L \nrightarrow Y \mid \mathsf{disjoint}\ \langle \operatorname{dom} s, \operatorname{dom} t\rangle \bullet \\ \qquad \diamondsuit(s \cup t) = (\diamondsuit s) \diamond (\diamondsuit t) \end{array}}$$

The extra condition, that the domains of s and t are disjoint, is needed to ensure that the recursive step does split the function into two separate parts. In the pure associative case, the sequence concatenation gives us this condition for free; in the idempotent case it is not necessary, since duplicates do not matter. This general labelled form of definition may look a little more clumsy than the sequence style, but sometimes the extra freedom that comes from having a more general label than a number can be useful (see section 24.4). If this form is used, it can also be applied to a sequence of arguments, since a sequence is just a special case of a labelled set. We use this style to define a distributed bag union operator in section A.10.

A.3   Directed acyclic graphs

Name

$digraph$ – directed graphs

$digraph_1$ – non-empty directed graphs

dag – directed acyclic graphs

dag_1 – non-empty directed acyclic graphs

$condag$ – connected directed acyclic graphs

$condag_1$ – non-empty connected directed acyclic graphs

$tree$ – trees

$tree_1$ – non-empty trees

Definition

$$digraph\ X == \{\, v : \mathbb{P}\,X;\ e : X \leftrightarrow X \mid (\operatorname{dom} e \cup \operatorname{ran} e) \subseteq v \,\}$$

$$digraph_1\ X == (digraph X) \setminus \{(\varnothing, \varnothing)\}$$

$$dag\ X == \{\, v : \mathbb{P}\,X;\ e : X \leftrightarrow X \mid (v, e) \in digraph\ X \wedge \mathsf{disjoint}\ \langle e^+, \operatorname{id} X\rangle \,\}$$

$$dag_1\ X == dag\ X \cap digraph_1\ X$$

$$condag\ X == \{\, v : \mathbb{P}\,X;\ e : X \leftrightarrow X \mid (v, e) \in dag\ X \wedge (e \cup e^\sim)^* = v \times v \,\}$$

$$condag_1\ X == condag\ X \cap digraph_1\ X$$

$$tree\ X == \{\, v : \mathbb{P}\,X;\ e : X \leftrightarrow X \mid (v, e) \in condag\ X \wedge e \in X \rightarrowtail X \,\}$$

$$tree_1\ X == tree\ X \cap digraph_1\ X$$

Description

$digraph\ X$ is the set of directed graphs over X. A directed graph is a set of vertices and a homogeneous relation describing the directed edges connecting some of these vertices. See figure 20.2.

$dag\ X$ is the set of directed acyclic graphs over X. These are digraphs that contain no cycles, that is, the transitive closure of the edge relation does not include any vertices that are mapped to themselves. See figure 20.3.

$condag\ X$ is the set of connected directed acyclic graphs: those graphs that do not have separate pieces. So every vertex is joined to every other vertex, in one direction or the other, by zero or more hops. See figure 20.4.

$tree\ X$ is the set of trees: connected dags where each element is related to at most one other—its *parent*. See figure 20.5.

$digraph_1$, dag_1, $condag_1$ and $tree_1$ exclude the empty graph.

A.4 Finite relation

Name

$\longleftrightarrow$ — Finite relations

Definition

$$X \longleftrightarrow Y == \mathbb{F}(X \times Y)$$

Description

If X and Y are sets, then $X \longleftrightarrow Y$ is the set of *finite binary relations* between X and Y. Each such relation is a finite subset of $X \times Y$.

Laws

$$X \longleftrightarrow Y \subseteq X \leftrightarrow Y$$

A.5 Non-empty injective sequences

Name

iseq_1 — non-empty injective sequences

Definition

$$\mathrm{iseq}_1 X == \{\, s : \mathrm{iseq}\, X \mid \#s > 0 \,\}$$

Description

$\mathrm{iseq}_1 X$ is the set of non-empty injective sequences over X. As the elements are injective they have no duplicate entries.

Laws

$$\mathrm{iseq}_1 X = \mathrm{iseq}\, X \setminus \{\langle\rangle\}$$

A.6   Sequences of a single element

Name

$\quad$ *monoSeq* $\;-$ sequences of a single element
$\quad$ *monoSeq₁* $-$ non-empty sequences of a single element
$\quad$ *uniqseq* $\quad-$ monosequences of a given length and element

Definition

$$monoSeq\ X == \{\, s : seq\ X \mid \#(ran\ s) \leq 1 \,\}$$
$$monoSeq_1\ X == \{\, s : monoSeq\ X \mid \#s > 0 \,\}$$

$\underline{\quad[X]\quad}$
$\quad uniqseq : \mathbb{N} \times X \longrightarrow monoSeq\ X$
$\overline{\quad}$
$\quad \forall\, n : \mathbb{N};\ x : X \bullet$
$\qquad uniqseq(n, x) \in monoSeq\{x\}$
$\qquad \wedge\ \#(uniqseq(n, x)) = n$

Description

monoSeq X is the set of sequences that map to a single element. *monoSeq₁ X* excludes the empty sequence.

$\quad$ *uniqseq(n, x)* is a monosequence consisting of n (possibly zero) occurrences of x.

Laws

$$monoSeq_1\ X = monoSeq\ X \setminus \{\langle\rangle\}$$
$$uniqseq(0, x) = \langle\rangle$$

A.7   Ascending and descending sequences

Name

    incr $-$ increasing sequence of numbers
    sincr $-$ strictly increasing sequence of numbers
    decr $-$ decreasing sequence of numbers
    sdecr $-$ strictly decreasing sequence of numbers

Definition

$$incr == \{\, s : \mathrm{seq}\, \mathbb{N}_1 \mid (\forall\, i, j : \mathrm{dom}\, s \mid i < j \bullet s\, i \le s\, j)\,\}$$
$$sincr == \{\, s : \mathrm{seq}\, \mathbb{N}_1 \mid (\forall\, i, j : \mathrm{dom}\, s \mid i < j \bullet s\, i < s\, j)\,\}$$
$$decr == \{\, s : \mathrm{seq}\, \mathbb{N}_1 \mid (\forall\, i, j : \mathrm{dom}\, s \mid i < j \bullet s\, i \ge s\, j)\,\}$$
$$sdecr == \{\, s : \mathrm{seq}\, \mathbb{N}_1 \mid (\forall\, i, j : \mathrm{dom}\, s \mid i < j \bullet s\, i > s\, j)\,\}$$

Description

incr is the set of finite sequences of positive numbers, where the numbers do not decrease along the sequence. *sincr* is the set of finite sequences of positive numbers, where the numbers increase along the sequence. Similarly *decr* does not increase, and *sdecr* decreases.

Laws

    $sincr \subset incr$
    $sdecr \subset decr$
    $rev\, (\!|incr|\!) = decr$
    $rev\, (\!|sincr|\!) = sdecr$

A.8   Anti-extraction and anti-filter

Name

$\downarrow$ — anti-extraction

$\mathord{\downharpoonleft}$ — anti-filtering

Definition

$$
\begin{array}{|l}
\hline
\rule{0pt}{1.2em}[X]\!=\!=\!=\!=\!=\!=\!=\!=\!=\!=\!=\!=\!=\!=\!=\\
\hline
\quad \_\downarrow\_ : \mathbb{P}\,\mathbb{N}_1 \times \operatorname{seq} X \longrightarrow \operatorname{seq} X \\
\quad \_\downharpoonleft\_ : \operatorname{seq} X \times \mathbb{P}\,X \longrightarrow \operatorname{seq} X \\
\hline
\quad \forall\, n : \mathbb{P}\,\mathbb{N}_1;\ s : \operatorname{seq} X \ \bullet \\
\qquad n \downarrow s = squash(n \lhd s) \\
\quad \forall\, s : \operatorname{seq} X;\ x : \mathbb{P}\,X \ \bullet \\
\qquad s \downharpoonleft x = squash(s \rhd x) \\
\hline
\end{array}
$$

Description

$n \downarrow s$ is a sequence that contains only those elements in the sequence s that do not have indices in the set n, in the same order as in s.

$s \downharpoonleft x$ is a sequence that contains only those elements in the sequence s that are not in the set x, in the same order as in s.

Laws

$$n \downarrow s = (\mathbb{N}_1 \setminus n) \upharpoonleft s$$
$$\varnothing \downarrow s = s$$
$$s \downharpoonleft x = s \upharpoonleft (X \setminus x)$$
$$s \downharpoonleft \varnothing = s$$

A.9   Number of items in a bag

Name

    sizebag – number of items in a bag

Definition

$$
\begin{array}{|l}
\hline
[X] \\
\hline
sizebag : \mathrm{bag}\, X \longrightarrow \mathbb{N} \\
\hline
sizebag[\![\,]\!] = 0 \\
\forall x : X \bullet sizebag[\![x]\!] = 1 \\
\forall a, b : \mathrm{bag}\, X \bullet \\
\quad sizebag(a \uplus b) = sizebag\ a + sizebag\ b \\
\hline
\end{array}
$$

Laws

$$sizebag(items\ s) = \#s$$
$$sizebag\ b - sizebag\ c \le sizebag(b \uplus c) \le sizebag\ b$$
$$c \sqsubseteq b \Rightarrow sizebag(b \uplus c) = sizebag\ b - sizebag\ c$$

A.10   Distributed bag union

Name

    $\uplus$ – bag union of a labelled set of bags

Definition

$$
\begin{array}{|l}
\hline
[L, X] \\
\hline
\uplus : (L \nrightarrow \mathrm{bag}\, X) \longrightarrow \mathrm{bag}\, X \\
\hline
\uplus\varnothing = [\![\,]\!] \\
\forall l : L;\ x : \mathrm{bag}\, X \bullet \uplus\{l \mapsto x\} = x \\
\forall s, t : L \nrightarrow \mathrm{bag}\, X \mid \mathsf{disjoint}\ \langle \mathrm{dom}\ s, \mathrm{dom}\ t\rangle \bullet \\
\quad \uplus(s \cup t) = (\uplus s) \uplus (\uplus t) \\
\hline
\end{array}
$$

Appendix B

Glossary and Cross References

Organisation of glossary

Within this glossary we have provided definitions of the terms used in this book.
Alternative names are included in the index and the page references there point at
the principal terms of this glossary. Definitions that use terms defined elsewhere
in the glossary are indicated in *slanted type*.

The structure of glossary entries themselves is explained in the preface on
page xiv.

abbreviation definition

> $Name == Expression$

Name must be new, and becomes global in the specification. It stands for *Expression*
wherever it appears in the specification.

> page 79: Space flights: documenting intended usage
> page 114: Snakes and Ladders: used to define constants
> page 116: Snakes and Ladders: advantage of using
> page 322: Real toolkit (physical units): renaming existing types
> page 324: Real toolkit (physical units): breaking house style

abbreviation definition, generic

An abbreviation definition may have a generic parameter. For example, X is a
generic parameter in

> $\mathbb{P}_1 X == \mathbb{P} X \setminus \{\varnothing\}$

An actual set is substituted for the generic parameter X at the point of use. This
is usually transparent; the substitution is not shown.

See section 24.3.2 for more details.

> page 247: Bags: definition of bag

340

abstraction

An abstract Z specification should convey its meaning clearly. The aim is to specify what the system should do, not how it does it (the mechanics should be left to the programming stage).

See Chapter 14 on abstraction for a number of small examples of abstract specification. See also *implementation bias*.

accompanying text

The informal text and diagrams accompanying a piece of formal Z are there to explain the mathematics, and relate it to the objects in the real world being specified. They may also draw attention to particular consequences of the specification, or redundancy or looseness in the specification.

antecedent

In a logical implication statement $p \Rightarrow q$, the antecedent is p.

See also *consequent*.

anti-restriction, domain

Also known as 'domain subtraction', 'domain co-restriction'.

$s \lhd r$ is a relation comprising the set of just those pairs in r whose first (domain) elements are *not* in s. For example

$$\{1,3\} \lhd \{2 \mapsto b, 3 \mapsto c, 4 \mapsto d\} = \{2 \mapsto b, 4 \mapsto d\}$$

page 170: Sets or functions: use in *LeaveCert*
page 218: Promotion: removing files

anti-restriction, range

Also known as 'range subtraction', 'range co-restriction'.

$r \rhd s$ is a relation comprising the set of just those pairs in r whose second (range) elements are *not* in s. For example

$$\{2 \mapsto b, 3 \mapsto c, 4 \mapsto d\} \rhd \{c, e\} = \{2 \mapsto b, 4 \mapsto d\}$$

page 84: Space flights: use in definition of *alloc*

anti-symmetric relation

A relation r is anti-symmetric if $(a \ r \ b) \wedge (b \ r \ a) \Rightarrow a = b$.

applicative-style specification

The name used in this book for functional-style specification (specification in terms of function application, rather than in terms of state transition schemas). We use this term to to avoid confusion with 'functional specification', used by some as the name for the specification of a system's functionality.

axiomatic description

An axiomatic description takes the form

$$\begin{array}{|l} \text{declaration} \\ \hline \text{predicate} \end{array}$$

The names declared must be new to the specification, and they become global. The predicate does not have to constrain the variables uniquely—the specification may be *loose*. A declaration may be given on its own, thus

$$\begin{array}{|l} \text{declaration} \end{array}$$

which means that there is no constraining predicate.

A predicate constraining variables declared elsewhere may appear on its own. We prefer to avoid separating predicates from their declarations in this way, since a later constraint may come as a surprise to the reader. It may also cause problems where proofs of properties of the specification relied on earlier, weaker, conditions.

backward relational composition

The backward relational composition of two relations r and s, written $s \circ r$, is equivalent to the *relational composition* $r \, \mathbin{\raise0.3ex\hbox{$_9^9$}} \, s$. This form is most often used to compose *functions*, in which case $(f \circ g)(x) = f(g(x))$.

See also *function application, relational composition.*

bag

Also known as 'multiset'.

A bag is a *function* that maps an item to the number of times it occurs in the bag.

$$\text{bag } X == X \nrightarrow \mathbb{N}_1$$

A particular bag may be written using function notation, or as a bag display.

See Chapter 21, on using bags, for further description. See also *bag operations.*

bag membership

Also known as *in*, but generally written as $\in$.

See *bag operations* for an example.

bag operations

The sample toolkit defines a number of operations for bags.

$[\![\ldots]\!]$	bag display	$[\![a, a, b, c, c]\!] = \{a \mapsto 2, b \mapsto 1, c \mapsto 2\}$
$[\![\,]\!]$	empty bag	$[\![\,]\!] = \varnothing$
count	multiplicity	$count[\![a, a, b, d]\!]a = 2$
$\sharp$	multiplicity	$[\![a, a, b, d]\!]\sharp a = 2$
$\otimes$	bag scaling	$[\![a, a, b, d]\!] \otimes 2 = [\![a, a, a, a, b, b, d, d]\!]$
$\sqsubseteq$	bag membership	$b \sqsubseteq [\![a, a, b, d]\!]$
$\sqsubseteq$	sub-bag	$[\![a, d]\!] \sqsubseteq [\![a, a, b, d]\!]$
$\uplus$	bag sum	$[\![a, a, b, d]\!] \uplus [\![a, b, b, c]\!] = [\![a, a, a, b, b, b, c, d]\!]$
$\cup$	bag difference	$[\![a, a, b, d]\!] \cup [\![a, b, b, c]\!] = [\![a, d]\!]$
items	sequence to bag	$items\langle a, b, a, d\rangle = [\![a, a, b, d]\!]$

page 71: Word count: *items*
page 85: Space flights: sub-bag used to constrain *alloc*
page 88: Space flights: bag difference in *SpareOK*
page 92: Space flights: sub-bag used in *ClassFull*
page 249: Bags: infix bag count
page 252: Bags (Scrabble): bag difference
page 252: Bags (Scrabble): sub-bag
page 296: Schemas: bag union

bijection

A bijection, written $\rightarrowtail\!\!\!\twoheadrightarrow$, is a *total function* that is both an *injection* and a *surjection*. An example of a bijection is shown in figure 17.8.

See section 17.5 for a discussion of the different kinds of functions and how they are related.

page 193: Sequences are sets (telephone directory): labelling a set
page 248: Bags: bag count
page 310: Language (mu): definition of *squash*

cardinality

The cardinality of a finite set s, written $\#s$, is the number of elements in the set. For example

$$\#\{a, b, b, c, d, d\} = \#\{a, b, c, d\} = 4$$
$$\#\langle a, b, b, c, d, d\rangle = \#\{1 \mapsto a, 2 \mapsto b, 3 \mapsto b, \ldots, 6 \mapsto d\} = 6$$
$$\#[\![a, b, b, c, d, d]\!] = \#\{a \mapsto 1, b \mapsto 2, \mapsto 1, d \mapsto 2\} = 4$$

page 164: Be abstract (maximal common subsequence): length of a sequence
page 169: Sets or functions: of the function *member*
page 258: Bags (poker): proof that a particular set is finite
page 285: Schemas: length of a sequence
page 305: Language (genericity): unexpected result for a bag

Cartesian product

Also known as 'cross product'.

The Cartesian product $Y_1 \times Y_2 \times \ldots \times Y_n$ is the set of all n-tuples $(n \geq 2)$ of elements $(y_1, y_2, \ldots, y_n)$ where $y_i \in Y_i$. A Cartesian product may be formed from two or more sets. Where the sets involved are types, the Cartesian product itself is a type. Cartesian product is not associative. For example

$$\{a, b\} \times \{1, 2\} \times \{\gamma\} = \{(a, 1, \gamma), (a, 2, \gamma), (b, 1, \gamma), (b, 2, \gamma)\}$$
$$\{a, b\} \times (\{1, 2\} \times \{\gamma\}) = \{(a, (1, \gamma)), (a, (2, \gamma)), (b, (1, \gamma)), (b, (2, \gamma))\}$$

See also *schema versus Cartesian product*.

page 235: Free types (file system tree): use in *condag*

characteristic tuple

- the characteristic tuple of declaration $a : A; \ldots; b : B$ is $(a, \ldots, b)$
- the characteristic tuple of schema S is the *schema binding* θS.

The characteristic tuple of a *schema text* S may be written χS.

In a set comprehension, if S is a schema text, then $\{S\}$ is the set of values taken by the characteristic tuple of its declaration as constrained by its predicate, $\{S \bullet \chi S\}$.

lambda-expressions and *definite descriptions* also use characteristic tuples (see [Spivey 1992, page 58]).

page 163: Be abstract (greatest common divisor): used in a lambda-expression

component selection

If a schema S has been declared as

$$S \triangleq [x : X; y : Y]$$

and a variable s has been declared of schema type S, as $s : S$, then we can access the individual components of s by using component selection: $s.x$, $s.y$

concatenation

sequences can be joined together by concatenation. This forms a new sequence, with the order of the entries preserved. For example

$$\langle h, o, n, e, y \rangle \frown \langle p, o, t \rangle = \langle h, o, n, e, y, p, o, t \rangle$$

page 63: Word count: use to split up a sequence

concatenation, distributed

A sequence of *sequences* may be 'flattened' to a single sequence, using distributed concatenation.

$$\frown / \langle \langle h, o, n, e \rangle, \langle \rangle, \langle y \rangle, \langle p, o, t \rangle \rangle = \langle h, o, n, e, y, p, o, t \rangle$$

conjunction

Also known as 'logical and'.

The conjunction of two *predicates*, written $p \wedge q$, is true exactly when both p and q are true.

consequent

In a logical implication statement $p \Rightarrow q$, the consequent is q.

See also *antecedent*.

contingent

A predicate is contingent if it is true under some possible interpretations (assignment of values to variables).

See also *tautology*.

curried function

A function with multiple arguments, declared such that the arguments may be applied one at a time (named after the mathematician Haskell B. Curry). For example

$$curried : A \longrightarrow B \longrightarrow C$$

is the curried form of

$$uncurried : (A \times B) \longrightarrow C$$

curried may be applied to a single argument $a : A$ to yield a result that is a function of type $B \longrightarrow C$: *curried* $a \in B \longrightarrow C$. This resulting function may then be applied to an argument $b : B$ to yield a result of type C: *curried* $a\, b \in C$.

uncurried must be applied to a pair of arguments, $(a, b) : A \times B$, yielding a result of type C: *uncurried*$(a, b) \in C$.

dashed

Also known as 'primed'.

A name for a variable with a dash *decoration*, for example a'. By convention, a decoration of $'$ is taken to indicate the 'after' variables of an operation.

declaration

A declaration introduces new variables and provides type information about them. This is always in the form: $x : X$. The X from which the x is drawn may contain *property* information. If it does not, then it is a *signature*.

declarations, circular

A circular declaration is one that is defined in terms of itself. This is not permitted in Z. For example, consider

$$
\begin{array}{|l}
\hline
\text{\_\_ } Bad \text{ _____} \\
numbers : \mathbb{P}\,\mathbb{N} \\
name : numbers \longrightarrow NAME \\
\hline
\end{array}
$$

This schema declares *name* in terms of *numbers*, but *numbers* is itself declared in the same declaration, and so is not yet in scope. The declaration of *name* refers to a previous declaration of *numbers*, if any, which is probably not what is intended. The specification should be recast as

$$
\begin{array}{|l}
\hline
\text{\_\_ } Good \text{ _____} \\
numbers : \mathbb{P}\,\mathbb{N} \\
name : \mathbb{N} \longrightarrow NAME \\
\hline
\text{dom } name = numbers \\
\hline
\end{array}
$$

since *numbers* is in scope in the predicate part.

Circular declarations should not be confused with *recursive definitions* which, in general, are allowed in Z.

declarations, combining

The declarations of schemas may be combined using inclusion or the *schema calculus*. Variables with the same name are 'identified' (that is, considered to be the same) provided that their underlying type is the same. If variables with the same name do not have the same type, then the declarations cannot be combined.

page 286: Schemas: schema as predicate

decoration

A decoration is a special character (for example, ? and !) that is added to the usual textual name of an object. It is considered to be part of the name of that object. A variable can have more than one decoration and these are arranged in a *sequence*. a'_0 is different from a_0'.

See also *decoration convention, schema decoration.*

decoration convention

By convention, a decoration of ' is taken to indicate the 'after' variables of an operation, where the 'before' variables are undecorated. ? is taken to indicate input variables, and ! indicates output variables.

definition

There are a number of ways of defining items in Z, depending on the intended use.

See also *abbreviation definition, axiomatic description, generic constant, generic schema, free type, given set, schema definition.*

page 182: Sequences are sets (mail alias): cannot redefine items
page 185: Sequences are sets (videos): use of ellipsis not permitted

definite description

Also known as 'mu-expression'.

The definite description expression

$$(\mu \, \text{SchemaText} \bullet \text{Expr})$$

is defined exactly when there is a unique assignment of values to the variables in the *schema text*'s declaration that makes its property true. This assignment of values is then used to determine the value of the expression, which is the value of the definite description. If the expression is omitted, the value is the *characteristic tuple* of the schema text.

See section 24.6 for more details.

Δ convention

By convention if no other definition of ΔS is given it is taken to be

$$\Delta S \mathrel{\widehat{=}} S \wedge S'$$

The Δ is part of the name of the schema and is used to indicate 'change' of the state. If ΔS is defined explicitly, for example to include other variables and predicates, it overrides the default convention.

See also Ξ *convention*.

design decision

Be aware of design decisions taken in a specification. Make sure to document them and to check with the client or users that they agree with these decisions.

disjoint

A labelled collection of sets (often represented as a sequence, although the labelling does not have to be numerical) is disjoint if every pair of the sets has an empty *set intersection*. For example

$$\mathsf{disjoint}\ \langle \{a, b, d\}, \{c, e\}, \{f\} \rangle$$

See section 24.4 for a detailed description. See also *partition*.

disjunction

Also known as 'logical or'.

The disjunction of two *predicates*, written $p \vee q$, is true when one or other, or both, of p and q are true.

domain

The domain of a binary *relation* r, written dom r, is the set of first elements of the ordered pairs that make up r. For example

$$\text{dom}\{2 \mapsto b, 3 \mapsto c, 4 \mapsto d\} = \{2, 3, 4\}$$

See also *range*.

equivalence relation

A *relation* that is *reflexive*, *symmetric* and *transitive*.

An equivalence relation on a set *partitions* that set into subsets where all the elements of each subset are related to each other, and are not related to any elements of any of the other subsets.

error reporting

An abstract specification does not need to be able to deal with all possible inputs, provided that it is stated explicitly with what inputs it can cope. Nonetheless, it is good practice for the specification to cover all eventualities by reporting erroneous inputs.

See Chapter 18 for a discussion on the treatment of errors.

finite function

A finite function, written $\rightarrowtail\!\!\!\rightarrow$, is a *partial function* that has a finite domain.

See section 17.5 for a discussion of the different kinds of functions and how they are related.

> page 169: Sets or functions: cardinality
> page 310: Language (mu): use in the definition of *squash*

finiteness

The *cardinality* of a set is defined only where the set is finite. Thus it is sometimes important to know that a particular set is finite.

See also *finite function, finite sets, sequence*.

> page 245: Free types (detail): use in free type definition

finite sets

The set of all the finite subsets of a set X is written $\mathbb{F}\,X$. Where X is a finite set, then $\mathbb{F}\,X = \mathbb{P}\,X$. For the set of all non-empty finite subsets, we write $\mathbb{F}_1\,X$. For example

$$\mathbb{F}\{1, 2, 3\} = \{\varnothing, \{1\}, \{2\}, \{3\}, \{1, 2\}, \{1, 3\}, \{2, 3\}, \{1, 2, 3\}\}$$

See also *power set*.

> page 167: Sets or functions: use with cardinality operator

framing schema

A schema specified for use in *promotion*. It describes how the local state relates to the global state.

See Chapter 19 for a discussion of promotion.

> page 131: Snakes and Ladders: relating local to global state

free type

There are three principal ways of using free types: as an enumerated type, as a disjoint union and as a recursive type. These have separate entries below. A free type is made up of one or more branches of any of these types. A free type is declared as follows

$$TYPENAME ::= branch_1 \mid \ldots \mid branch_n$$

The order of the branches is not significant. Free types are explained in detail in section 20.7. Note that in the Z Standard, free types are renamed 'structured sets'.

> page 185: Sequences are sets (videos): items in branches must be specified
> page 230: Free types (file system tree): definition by cases

free type, disjoint union

A disjoint union is one way of using a free type definition, in which there is no recursion.

See Chapter 20 for details.

> page 81: Space flights: advantage over partitioning a type
> page 115: Snakes and Ladders: naming of injections
> page 115: Snakes and Ladders: naming the inverse of the injection
> page 115: Snakes and Ladders: use to have a wide function domain
> page 225: Free types (pack of cards): naming the inverse of the injection

free type, enumerated

An enumerated type is the simplest way of using a free type. It defines a new type by introducing the new values that constitute the elements of that type explicitly. These names are global and must therefore be new. For example

$$SEASON ::= spring \mid summer \mid autumn \mid winter$$

defines a new type *SEASON* with exactly four elements *spring*, *summer*, *autumn*, *winter*, none of which must have been defined before.

> page 102: Video shop: plain numbers cannot be used
> page 168: Sets or functions: definition of *STATUS*
> page 202: Error handling: declaring output messages

free type, recursive

Recursion is permitted in free type definitions.
   See section 20.7 for details of how this is handled.

> page 229: Free types (file system tree): finite occurrences of the type being defined
> page 263: Calculator: need for primitive branches

function

A function, written $\nrightarrow$, is a relation in which, for each domain element, there is a unique range element to which it is related.
   See Chapter 17 for a description of how functions are used. See section 17.5 for a discussion of the different kinds of functions and how they are related. See also *bijection, finite function, injection, partial function, surjection, total function.*

> page 169: Sets or functions: empty function is the empty set
> page 209: Promotion: use in promotion
> page 262: Calculator: total or partial function?

function application

A function may be applied to elements of its domain to produce a 'result'. Where the function is a *sequence* this is equivalent to indexing into a sequence. We recommend avoiding putting parentheses around the argument where possible, to reduce clutter. So we prefer $f\,x$ to $f(x)$.

> page 213: Promotion: indexing into a sequence

generalised intersection

Also known as 'distributed intersection'.

If X is a set of sets then $\bigcap X$ contains all items that are members of every member of X. For example,

$$\bigcap\{\{a, b, c\}, \{b, c, d\}, \{a, b\}, \{b\}\} = \{b\}$$

See also *set intersection*.

generalised union

Also known as 'distributed union'.

If X is a set of sets then $\bigcup X$ contains all elements that are members of some member of X. For example,

$$\bigcup\{\{a, b, c\}, \{b, c, d\}, \{a, b\}, \{b\}\} = \{a, b, c, d\}$$

See also *set union*.

page 307: Language (disjoint and partition): definition of partition

generic constant

A method for adding new operations to a *toolkit*.
See section 24.3.1 for a detailed explanation. See also *toolkit*.

page 72: Word count: definition of generic *uniq*
page 160: Be abstract (blue pencil): expression for the actual parameter

generic schema

Schemas may be defined with generic parameters. The generic parameter is instantiated by supplying an actual parameter at the point of use of the schema. The form is

$$
\begin{array}{|l}
\hline
\mathit{Name}[\text{generic parameters}] \underline{\hspace{5cm}} \\
\text{declaration involving the generic parameters} \\
\hline
\text{predicate involving the generic parameters} \\
\hline
\end{array}
$$

page 201: Error handling: definition of *BoundedStack*[X]
page 236: Free types (file system tree): definition of *Tree*[N]
page 237: Free types (file system tree): instantiation of generic schema

given set

Also known as 'basic set', 'parachuted set'.

   This is a method of introducing new types and is used when the structure of the elements is irrelevant. The names become global in the specification and thus must be new. The form is

$$[TYPEONE, TYPETWO, TYPETHREE]$$

   page 322: Real toolkit (physical units): loss of operations

global variable

A global variable is one that always has a meaning within the specification.

homogeneous

A homogeneous relation is one where the domain and range are of the same type.

house style

As Chapter 8 explains, it is a good idea to define standards for writing Z specifications. Within this book we have adopted such a standard.

   page 84: Space flights: layout of declarations in a schema
   page 87: Space flights: splitting schema operations
   page 217: Promotion: extending a function
   page 291: Schemas: naming *VECTOR*

hypothesis

A hypothesis is a theory which is stated about a specification but has yet to be proved.

identity relation

The relation id X maps every element of the set X to itself. For example

$$\text{id}\{a, b, c\} = \{a \mapsto a, b \mapsto b, c \mapsto c\}$$
$$\text{id}\,\mathbb{N}_1 = \{1 \mapsto 1, 2 \mapsto 2, 3 \mapsto 3, \ldots\}$$

   page 70: Word count: use in definition of *upperseq*
   page 187: Sequences are sets (videos): use to exclude reflexive pairs in *SameTitle*
   page 187: Sequences are sets (videos): use to exclude reflexive pairs in *differentStory*
   page 250: Bags: use to identify true anagrams

if and only if

Also known as 'logical equivalence'.

   $p \Leftrightarrow q$ ('p exactly when q') is true when the *predicates* p and q have the same truth value.

if then else

The expression **if** p **then** $expr_1$ **else** $expr_2$ has the value of $expr_1$ if the *predicate* p is *true*, otherwise it has the value of $expr_2$.

> page 69: Word count: 'negative' condition
> page 129: Snakes and Ladders: use in *MainMoveAlt*
> page 257: Bags (Scrabble): use in *NextPlayer*

implementation bias

A specification exhibits implementation bias if it unnecessarily excludes some implementations. An abstract specification should, so far as is possible, be free of implementation bias.

> page 73: Word count: splitting a sequence
> page 161: Be abstract (blue pencil): parallel implementation possible
> page 265: Calculator: what is not specified does not inhibit implementation
> page 312: Language (mu): removing implementation bias from *squash*

implicit definition

An implicit definition is not 'constructive'; it does not tell you directly how to calculate something. For example, square root may be defined as

$$squareroot\ x * squareroot\ x = x$$

This may be thought of as 'if you knew how to calculate the square root of the number, then when you square it you obtain the number you first thought of'.

See also *recursion*.

> page 69: Word count: explicit definition may be more understandable
> page 163: Be abstract (greatest common divisor): versus constructive definition
> page 164: Be abstract (maximal common subsequence): use for clarity
> page 252: Bags (Scrabble): before state in terms of after state in Scrabble

implies

Also known as 'logical implication'.

$p \Rightarrow q$ is true when the *predicate* p is *false* or when q is *true*. It is equivalent to $\neg\, p \lor q$. Notice that when p is false, then q may take any value. If implication is used in predicates there is a *proof obligation* to show that the specification still behaves sensibly when the antecedent p is false. For this reason, some authors avoid the use of implication.

in

A *relation* between *sequences*: s in t holds if s is a contiguous subsequence of t, that is, if $u \frown s \frown v = t$.

See also *prefix, suffix.*

The name *in* (note the different typographical style) is used by some authors for bag membership, but this use has been overtaken by $\in$.

See *bag operations.*

page 64: Word count: use in *lexicon*

induction

A proof technique applicable to recursive *free types* (which includes natural numbers).

See section 20.7.1.

page 243: Free types (detail): structural and classical induction

initial state

An initial state of the system should always be specified, not least because it demonstrates that at least one state exists. If it is not possible to give an example of a state that satisfies all the constraints then there is an inconsistency in the specifications. The provision of an initial state does not mean that there are no inconsistencies. Initial states are often stated as operations that create the initial state out of 'thin air', and have only an 'after' state.

page 85: Space flights: naive definition

page 118: Snakes and Ladders: initial state of snakes and ladders

page 280: Schemas: initial state of the telephone directory

injection

An injection is a one-one *function*. It may be partial $\rightarrowtail$, total $\rightarrowtail$ or finite $\rightarrowtail\!\!\!\!+$. An example of an injection is shown in figure 17.5.

See section 17.5 for a discussion of the different kinds of functions and how they are related.

page 192: Sequences are sets (telephone directory): no sharing and one each

integers

The set of integers, $\mathbb{Z} = \{\ldots, -2, -1, 0, 1, 2, \ldots\}$, is a given set in the sample toolkit.

invariant

When an object is defined, the predicate constrains the value in the declaration to exhibit a certain property. As the object invariably exhibits this constraining property, the property is sometimes called an 'invariant'.

See also *schema invariant*.

page 136: Tower of Hanoi: definition of *pole*

lambda-expression

λ SchemaText $\bullet$ Expr

A lambda-expression is a way to define a *function* without the need to name it, or to define a named function using an *abbreviation definition*. The function's parameters are given by the *characteristic tuple* of the *schema text*, the domain is constrained by the *property*, and the value is given by the expression.

Let S be a schema text, χS its *characteristic tuple*, and $f\ S$ some function of the variables declared in S. Then a lambda-expression may be considered to be syntactic sugar for the set comprehension:

$$(\lambda S \bullet f\ S) \equiv \{\ S \bullet (\chi S, f\ S)\ \}$$

page 74: Word count: Unix pipe
page 111: Video shop: defining the query *listByCertificate*
page 162: Be abstract (greatest common divisor): equivalent form using a quantifier
page 249: Bags: definition of bag count

let

Also known as 'local definition'.

There are two forms of let constructs

- *let expression*
  A let expression is written

    let $x_1 == e_1;\ \ldots;\ x_n == e_n \bullet expr$

  Its value is that of the *expr* when each of the x_i takes the value given by the corresponding e_i. The x_i have local scope that extends to the *expr*.

- *let predicate*
  A let predicate is written

    let $x_1 == e_1;\ \ldots;\ x_n == e_n \bullet p$

  It is true exactly when the predicate p is true, where each of the x_i takes the value given by the corresponding expression e_i.

The types of the local variables x_i are determined implicitly by the types of the corresponding e_i.

Note that an expression such as, for example, **let** $e == root\,9 \bullet \ldots$ could instead be written as $\exists\, e : \mathbb{N} \mid e = root\,9 \bullet \ldots$

> page 111: Video shop: use in $AddVideoOK_1$

loose specification

A specification is loose if it states that a variable takes on a single value under certain circumstances, but does not specify what that value is.

See section 22.5.1 for a discussion of loose specification. See also *non-determinism*.

> page 80: Space flights: of *localDay*
> page 82: Space flights: tightening a loose specification
> page 103: Video shop: of *ageToday*
> page 268: Calculator: definition of *Add*
> page 296: Schemas: defining a partial order

maplet

The maplet notation $x \mapsto y$ is an alternative form of (x, y). We adopt maplets as our house style for elements of binary *relations* (section 8.4.1).

mathematical type

There are three ways of defining mathematical types in Z: *given sets*, *power sets* and *Cartesian products*. Z also provides *schema types*.

maximum

A sample toolkit function, written *max*, that gives the largest value of a set of numbers. For example

$$max\{5, 8, 42, -4, 0\} = 42$$

See also *minimum*.

> page 312: Language (mu): definition of *squash*

minimum

A sample toolkit function, written *min*, that gives the smallest value of a set of numbers. For example

$$min\{5, 8, 42, -4, 0\} = -4$$

See also *maximum*.

> page 140: Tower of Hanoi: selecting the smallest disc
> page 255: Bags (Scrabble): how many tiles to take

naming convention

By convention, there are a number of special symbols in Z that are taken to have particular meanings. In our house style (section 8.2) we give our rules for naming variables.

See also Δ *convention, decoration convention,* Ξ *convention.*

> page 68: Word count: using underscores
> page 209: Promotion: Φ in promotion schemas

natural numbers

The set of natural numbers, $\mathbb{N} = \{0, 1, 2, \ldots\}$, is defined as a subset of $\mathbb{Z}$ in the sample toolkit.

> page 136: Tower of Hanoi: naturals are not a given type

negation

Also known as 'logical not'.

The negation of a *predicate*, written ¬ p, is true exactly when p is false, and vice versa.

non-determinism

A specification is non-deterministic if it allows a number of values to be suitable, and does not constrain the one chosen to always be the same. There are many opportunities for giving non-deterministic descriptions within Z specifications. For a top level abstract specification this is usually a good thing, since there is no point in forcing a system to make a particular choice unless you have to. During the *refinement* process the non-determinism should be reduced, but it is better to leave this for as long as possible to allow appropriate decisions to be made about requirements and efficiency of implementation.

See section 22.5.2 for a discussion of non-determinism. See also *loose specification.*

> page 24: Established Strategy: documentation
> page 29: Security properties: determinism is important for secure systems
> page 132: Snakes and Ladders: *place* sequence
> page 132: Snakes and Ladders: determinism is sometimes required
> page 274: Schemas: angelic non-determinism

normalisation

Normalisation is the removal of any *property* information from the declaration into the predicate part of a schema, leaving just the *signature,* σS, behind. The result of normalising schema S is $[\sigma S \mid S]$. Normalisation is necessary before some of the *schema calculus* operators can be applied.

number range

The set of numbers $m \mathbin{..} n$ ('m upto n') is the set of all integers from m to n inclusive. For example: $1 \mathbin{..} 3 = \{1, 2, 3\}$; $3 \mathbin{..} 3 = \{3\}$; $3 \mathbin{..} 1 = \varnothing$.

one-point rule

Let s be a *set*, t be a term in which x does not occur free, and p be some *predicate*. Then

$$(\exists x : s \mid x = t \bullet p) \Leftrightarrow (t \in s \wedge p[t/x])$$

In other words, if we have to find a value for x to make p hold, but we have an expression for x that still allows us to deduce p, then we can replace every occurrence of x by term t and remove the existential quantifier (so long as x does not occur free in t). This rule is useful in simplifying expressions.

See, for example, sections 12.2.4, 13.5.3.

overriding

$r \oplus s$ is the binary *relation* r overridden by the binary relation s.

$$r \oplus s = ((\operatorname{dom} s) \mathbin{\lhd\!\!\!-} r) \cup s$$

Where r and s share *domain* elements, then the pairs in s are used in the resulting relation, otherwise it is the pairs in r. For example

$$\{2 \mapsto b, 3 \mapsto c, 4 \mapsto d, 4 \mapsto e\} \oplus \{2 \mapsto f, 2 \mapsto a, 4 \mapsto g\}$$
$$= \{2 \mapsto f, 2 \mapsto a, 3 \mapsto c, 4 \mapsto g\}$$

Overriding is often used to 'update' one element of a *function* by overriding it with a single pair. If this pair 'extends' the function, our house style is to write $f \cup \{n \mapsto a\}$, rather than $f \oplus \{n \mapsto a\}$, to highlight this fact.

overspecification

Overspecification involves supplying more detail than is required about an item
or operation in the system. This may unnecessarily constrain a subsequent implementor. Overspecification should be avoided!

    page 78: Space flights: avoid enumerating a type when the details will not be used
    page 78: Space flights: avoid using numbers where not required
    page 160: Be abstract (blue pencil): distinguishing items unnecessarily

partial function

All functions are partial (written $\nrightarrow$). An example of a partial function is shown
in figure 17.4.

    See section 17.5 for a discussion of the different kinds of functions and how they
are related. See also *function*.

    page 191: Sequences are sets (telephone directory): property of functions

partition

A labelled collection of sets (often represented as a sequence, although the labelling
does not have to be numerical) partitions another set X if the labelled sets are
pairwise *disjoint* and if their union is the whole set X. For example

$$\langle\{a, b, d\}, \{c, e\}, \{f\}\rangle \text{ partition } \{a, b, c, d, e, f\}$$

    See section 24.4 for a more detailed explanation. See also *disjoint*.

    page 105: Video shop: distinguishing *staff* and *members*
    page 117: Snakes and Ladders: in definition of game

power set

The power set of a set X, written $\mathbb{P}\,X$, is the set of all the subsets of X. Where X
is a type, then $\mathbb{P}\,X$ is also a type. For the set of all non-empty subsets, we write
$\mathbb{P}_1\,X$. For example

$$\mathbb{P}\{1, 2, 3\} = \{\varnothing, \{1\}, \{2\}, \{3\}, \{1, 2\}, \{1, 3\}, \{2, 3\}, \{1, 2, 3\}\}$$
$$\mathbb{P}\varnothing = \{\varnothing\}$$

See also *finite sets*.

    page 82: Space flights: constructing the expression for *price*

precondition calculation

Within Z it is possible to calculate the precondition of each schema operation using the special precondition schema notation pre S. 'pre' is a schema operator. Contrast Δ or Ξ, which are merely a part of the schema name with conventional meanings.

See section 3.3.7 for one approach to the use of precondition calculation. See section 12.2.4 for a detailed presentation of a precondition calculation.

> page 122: Snakes and Ladders: use of pre
> page 126: Snakes and Ladders: table of preconditions
> page 146: Tower of Hanoi: disjunction distributes over pre

predicate

A logical statement that is either *true* or *false*.

prefix

A *relation* between *sequences*: s prefix t holds if s is an initial subsequence of t, that is, if $s \frown u = t$.

See also *suffix, in*.

prefix relation

A prefix *relation* is written

$$\mid \quad prerel\_ : \mathbb{P}\,X$$

prerel x is shorthand for $x \in (prerel\_)$.

> page 239: Free types (detail): binary tree
> page 307: Language (disjoint and partition): disjoint

projection function

The Z notation offers two projection functions that take pairs and project onto the first or second elements of the pair. $first(x, y) = x$ and $second(x, y) = y$.

> page 65: Word count: first
> page 229: Free types (file system tree): functions to pairs from single items
> page 323: Real toolkit (physical units): second

promotion

A technique in which an operation on a single item is used to specify global operations on a state.

See Chapter 19 for a detailed explanation.

> page 129: Snakes and Ladders: constraints on schema definitions
> page 131: Snakes and Ladders: framing schema
> page 315: Language (mu): use of mu

proof

The degree of rigour with which a proof is performed depends upon the importance of the specification.

See section 6.2 for a discussion of proof. See also *proof obligation, theorem.*

page 33: Security properties: proof is not 'all or nothing'

proof, existence

One proof that should be carried out is that there is some possible *initial state* of a specification.

proof obligation

Also known as 'proof opportunity'.

There are a number of aspects of specifications that the specifier is 'obliged' to prove, for example, that the specification is non-empty. Proof obligations should always be stated, and are often discharged to some degree of rigour.

page 22: Established Strategy: initial state exists
page 31: Security properties: formal proof needed
page 32: Security properties: uniqueness of mu-expression
page 85: Space flights: existence of initial state
page 110: Video shop: using set union with *catalogue* function
page 111: Video shop: using cardinality with *catalogue* function
page 162: Be abstract (greatest common divisor): use of partial function max
page 169: Sets or functions: preserved functionality of *member* in *EnrolOK*
page 216: Promotion: overriding a sequence with a function
page 228: Free types (merger): using implication
page 230: Free types (file system tree): union of two function
page 253: Bags (Scrabble): demonstration that operations really 'undo'
page 310: Language (mu): of uniqueness
page 312: Language (mu): use of mu

property

A schema can be considered as composed of its *signature* and its property. The property constrains the variables and describes the relationship between them (if any). The property includes the explicit predicate 'below the line', and any implicit predicates concealed within the declaration.

When using a schema as a predicate, the predicate that results is the schema's property (that is, it includes the implicit predicates from the declaration).

Variables declared in other contexts may also have property information stated about them, for example in an *axiomatic description.*

prototyping

Rapid prototyping is a technique used in the development process to explore and test possible design and implementation strategies. Without prototyping it is unlikely that the true requirements will be elicited.

quantifier, existential

The general form is

$$\exists \, d \mid p \bullet q$$

where $d \mid p$ is a *schema text* and q is a predicate. It is true if q is true for some possible value of the variables in the schema text.

It is equivalent to $\exists \, d \bullet p \wedge q$. It makes no difference to the meaning which conditions are put in p, and which in q. It is a matter of style or emphasis. View p as a constraint on the variables, and q as the result in which you are interested. The predicate p may be omitted.

See also *schema quantification*.

quantifier, scope

The scope of a quantifier is to the end of the 'sentence' in which it appears, which may need to be indicated by parentheses. The quantifiers bind less tightly than any of the propositional connectives.

See also *schema quantification*.

page 164: Be abstract (maximal common subsequence): parentheses for clarity

quantifier, unique existential

The general form is

$$\exists_1 \, d \mid p \bullet q$$

where $d \mid p$ is a *schema text* and q is a predicate. It is true if q is true for one, and only one, possible value of the variables in the schema text.

page 303: Language (red tape): use in *servesOn*
page 310: Language (mu): versus mu-expression

quantifier, universal

The general form is

$$\forall \, d \mid p \bullet q$$

where $d \mid p$ is a *schema text* and q is a predicate. It is true if q is true for all the possible values of the variables in the schema text.

It is equivalent to $\forall \, d \bullet p \Rightarrow q$.

page 176: Sets, quantifiers, toolkit (security classes): predicate part or term?

range

The range of a binary *relation* r, written ran r, is the set of second elements of the
ordered pairs that make up r. For example

$$\text{ran}\{2 \mapsto b, 3 \mapsto c, 4 \mapsto d\} = \{b, c, d\}$$

See also *domain*.

> page 72: Word count: range of a sequence is a singleton
> page 138: Tower of Hanoi: set of all discs
> page 151: Tower of Hanoi: poles with no discs
> page 188: Sequences are sets (videos): range does not distribute over intersection

readability

A specification should be readable by someone other than the writer. The writer
should assist the reader as much as possible in understanding the intention. Readability is about far more than just the names of variables. It affects the whole way
in which Z is written.

> See also *redundancy*.

> page 78: Space flights: listing given sets in alphabetical order
> page 90: Space flights: local variables in schemas
> page 102: Video shop: using *uCert*
> page 142: Tower of Hanoi: presentation of a specification differs from development
> page 191: Sequences are sets (telephone directory): declaration or predicate
> page 195: Sequences are sets (telephone directory): declarations
> page 269: Calculator: what to define explicitly and what to package up as a schema
> page 304: Language (red tape): what information to put in the declaration
> page 313: Language (mu): definition of our *squash*
> page 315: Language (mu): renaming versus decoration

recursive definition

Recursion provides a convenient tool for abstract specification. Recursive definitions are defined in terms of themselves, except that there is always a base case
where the definition 'bottoms out'. For example, factorial may be defined by

$$\underline{\quad}! : \mathbb{N} \longrightarrow \mathbb{N}$$
$$0! = 1$$
$$\forall n : \mathbb{N} \bullet (n + 1)! = n! * (n + 1)$$

Although the main part of the definition is defined in terms of itself, the base case
means that a value for factorial can always be found.

> page 73: Word count: definition of *uniq*
> page 161: Be abstract (blue pencil): providing an end case
> page 319: Real toolkit: definition of exponentials

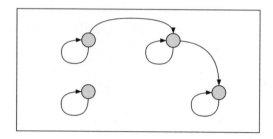

Figure B.1 A reflexive relation.

redundancy

Z specifications often include redundancy in the specifications. That is, a predicate may introduce no new constraints, but merely be a consequence of some other predicates. Such redundant information is usually included in order to make the specification more readable. This introduces a *proof obligation* to show that the redundant predicate is not inconsistent. On the other hand, since a redundant predicate often expresses a desired property of the specification, were it to be omitted there would be a proof obligation to show that it could be deduced.

page 108: Video shop: definition of *HireOK*
page 143: Tower of Hanoi: repetition of predicates already stated
page 254: Bags (Scrabble): introducing variables for convenience
page 280: Schemas: 'unnecessary' predicates
page 289: Schemas: 'unnecessary' predicates

refinement

Also known as 'reification', meaning 'to make more concrete'.

Refinement is a process of turning a more abstract specification into a more concrete one. The usual symbol used to show that one specification refines another is *Spec* ⊑ *Design*: 'specification is refined by design'. (Unfortunately, the sample toolkit uses the same symbol to represent the sub-bag relation.)

See Chapter 13 for an example of refinement. See also *retrieve relation*.

reflexive relation

A binary *relation* in which every element is related to itself. This is illustrated in figure B.1. The *identity relation* is a subset of every reflexive relation.

reflexive transitive closure

Written r^*, it is the smallest binary *relation* containing r that is both *transitive* and *reflexive*. If r is considered as defining the places that can be reached in one 'hop', then r^* defines all the places that can be reached in zero or more hops.

If r^+ is the transitive closure, then $r^* = \text{id}\, X \cup r^+$.

relation

A set of the form $\mathbb{P}(X_1 \times \ldots \times X_n)$. Its elements are tuples of the form $(x_1, \ldots, x_n)$, where each x_i is drawn from the corresponding X_i.

See Chapter 17 for a discussion of how relations underlie functions and sequences.

relation, binary

A *relation* of the form $\mathbb{P}(X \times Y)$, usually written $X \leftrightarrow Y$. A binary relation is a set of pairs.

relation, infix

A binary *relation* may be used in an infix manner by declaring it between underscores.

$$\mid \; \_\, r \,\_ : X \leftrightarrow Y$$

The underscores are part of the name of the relation, so to use it in a non-infix way, we need to write

$$(x, y) \in (\_\, r \,\_)$$

An 'ordinary' relation can be used in an infix manner by underlining it, thus

claudette <u>*likes*</u> *croissants*

When declaring relations it is best to omit the underscores if the relation is mainly to be used in an 'ordinary' way, and resort to underlining for the rare occasions on which it is used as an infix relation. If you anticipate that the relation will mainly be used as an infix one then declare it using underscores.

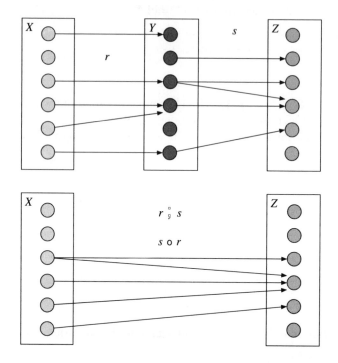

Figure B.2 Relational composition in action.

relational composition

Relational composition is a way of combining two binary *relations*. The composition of $r : X \leftrightarrow Y$ and $s : Y \leftrightarrow Z$, written $r \mathbin{\raise0.5ex\hbox{$\scriptstyle\circ$}\mkern-6mu\lower0.3ex\hbox{$\scriptstyle 9$}} s$, relates a member x of X to a member z of Z provided that there is a member y of Y to which r relates x and which s relates to z. This is illustrated in figure B.2.

See also *backward relational composition*.

page 75: Word count: comparison with backward relational composition
page 183: Sequences are sets (mail alias): use in *Mail3*
page 238: Free types (file system tree): used with a sequence

relational image

The relational image $r(\!(s)\!)$ of a set s through a relation r is the set of all elements y to which r relates some member x of s. The relational image of set s through relation r may be thought of as 'applying' relation r to set s. The result is a set in which each member is related by r to some member of s. Relational image is not an exact analogue of function application; the relational image may be applied to items outside its *domain* without difficulty, whereas if a function is applied to an item outside its domain the result is undefined. For example

$$\{1 \mapsto a, 1 \mapsto b, 2 \mapsto c, 3 \mapsto a\}(\!|\{0, 1, 3\}|\!) = \{a, b\}$$

relational inverse

The inverse of the binary *relation* r, written $r^\sim$, consists of the pairs in r with their order reversed. For example

$$\{1 \mapsto a, 1 \mapsto b, 2 \mapsto c, 3 \mapsto a\}^\sim = \{a \mapsto 1, b \mapsto 1, c \mapsto 2, a \mapsto 3\}$$

If r is *homogeneous*, then $r^\sim = r^{-1}$. If r is non-homogeneous, r^{-1} is not defined, but $r^\sim$ is.

relational iteration

A *homogeneous* relation may be iterated, or applied multiple times. It can be written *iter k r*, but is more usually written r^k. k may be any member of $\mathbb{Z}$. For example

$$r = \{a \mapsto b, b \mapsto c, c \mapsto d, d \mapsto e\} = r^1$$
$$r^2 = \{a \mapsto c, b \mapsto d, c \mapsto e\}$$
$$r^{-1} = \{b \mapsto a, c \mapsto b, d \mapsto c, e \mapsto d\} = r^\sim$$

restriction, domain

A relation may be restricted to a smaller *domain*. $s \lhd r$ is a relation comprising the set of just those pairs in r whose first (domain) elements are also in s. For example

$$\{1, 3\} \lhd \{2 \mapsto b, 3 \mapsto c, 4 \mapsto d\} = \{3 \mapsto c\}$$

restriction, range

A relation may be restricted to a smaller *range*. $r \triangleright s$ is a relation comprising the set of just those pairs in r whose second (range) elements are also in s. For example

$$\{2 \mapsto b, 3 \mapsto c, 4 \mapsto d\} \triangleright \{c, e\} = \{3 \mapsto c\}$$

page 70: Word count: use in definition of *upperseq*
page 189: Sequences are sets (videos): use in *veryGoodBasis*

retrieve relation

The retrieve relation is used in *refinement*. It specifies how the state components of the abstract and concrete states are related. It is stated as part of a retrieve schema.

See section 13.5.1 for further discussion.

reuse

With careful design, some aspects of a Z specification may be reusable in other contexts. This can help to reduce the work of the specifier. It can also assist the reader, because if a concept has already been understood further effort is not required when it reappears. The sample toolkit is reused extensively.

schema

A schema may be used to describe some part of the state or an operation on the state. The name of the schema has global scope; its variables have local scope. A horizontal schema is written

$Name \hat{=} [\,\text{declaration} \mid \text{predicate}\,]$

The same schema written in vertical form is

```
 ┌─ Name ──────────────────────────────
 │  declaration
 ├──────────────────────────────────────
 │  predicate
 └──────────────────────────────────────
```

The two forms are equivalent. Horizontal schema definition should be reserved for those that are short enough to fit onto one line. A schema can also be defined in terms of its *signature* and its *property*.

page 84: Space flights: use horizontal definitions for small ones
page 122: Snakes and Ladders: cannot use schema operators in names
page 146: Tower of Hanoi: cannot use schema operations in schema names

schema as declaration

A schema may be used wherever a declaration is expected, for example, by inclusion, in quantification, and in set comprehensions. The effect is the same as if the declarations and constraints were copied in at the point of use, subject only to the lexical scope rule that if in the schema there is any reference to a name global to that schema, the reference remains to the object recognised at the point of schema definition, irrespective of any alternative offered at the point of schema use.

See also *schema inclusion, schema quantification, schema in set comprehension.*

schema as predicate

Schemas may be used as predicates provided the variables of the schema are already in scope.

See section 23.6 for further explanation.

page 204: Error handling: use of *BoundedStackMemOK*
page 292: Schemas: obtaining a different emphasis

schema as type

Schemas may be used as types in the same way as *mathematical types*.
See section 23.2 for further explanation.

page 103: Video shop: definition of *Video*
page 110: Video shop: adding a new video

schema binding

The binding of the values of the variables in a schema S is indicated by θS.
See section 24.5 for an explanation.

page 30: Security properties: use in state transitions
page 89: Space flights: use to match route numbers and details
page 209: Promotion: use in promotion
page 226: Free types (pack of cards): meta-notation
page 269: Calculator: use in *ClearDisplay0*
page 308: Language (theta): meta-notation
page 309: Language (theta): θ takes values from current environment

schema calculus

Various logical operations may be applied to schemas.

See Chapters 10 and 23, which illustrate various aspects of the schema calculus. See also *schema conjunction, schema disjunction, schema iff, schema implication, schema negation, schema quantification.*

schema composition

$S \, \semi \, T$ is the schema composition of two schema operations, where the 'after' state of S is identified with the 'before' state of T.

See section 23.3 for an example.

page 253: Bags (Scrabble): definition of *ChallengedWord*

schema conjunction

$S \wedge T$ merges the declarations of S and T and conjoins their predicates (which is equivalent to merging their *signatures* and conjoining their *properties*).

$$S \wedge T = [\sigma S; \sigma T \mid S \wedge T]$$

schema cross reference

A schema cross reference is a list of schema names together with the page number in the specification on which their declarations appear. This can be a useful aid to a reader, and indeed the writer, of a specification, since it helps in finding the definitions, and is essential for large specifications. We provide a comprehensive cross reference in our index.

schema decoration

An operation on schemas in which each of the components is systematically decorated with a special mark. If $S \cong [a, b : X]$ then $S' \cong [a', b' : X]$. Note that S and S' have the same type.

See also *decoration convention*.

page 30: Security properties: using subscripts
page 290: Schemas: decorating a predicate
page 298: Schemas: using numerical subscripts

schema disjunction

$S \vee T$ merges the *signatures* of S and T and disjoins their *properties*.

$$S \vee T = [\sigma S; \sigma T \mid S \vee T]$$

In order to expand a schema disjunction, it may be necessary to make provision for components that are mentioned in one declaration and not in the other. Partial *normalisation* may be necessary.

page 88: Space flights: use in operation specification

schema expansion

The process of 'flattening out' any schema calculus expression and schema inclusions, so that the remaining schema has declarations entirely in terms of variables, is sometimes known as schema expansion. This expansion may be done partially, in order to reveal sufficient details of the variables that are interesting in the given context.

See also *normalisation*.

schema hiding

$S \setminus (x_1, \ldots, x_n)$ hides the variables $x_1, \ldots, x_n$ from the schema S. The variables must exist in the schema. This is equivalent to quantifying existentially by those variables in the predicate part of S.

See also *schema projection*.

> page 107: Video shop: definition of Δ *VideoShopHire*
> page 275: Schemas: hidden variables must be schema components
> page 290: Schemas: adapting existing definitions

schema iff

$S \Leftrightarrow T$ is a merged schema in which the *signatures* are combined and the *properties* joined by logical equivalence.

$$S \Leftrightarrow T = [\sigma S; \sigma T \mid S \Leftrightarrow T]$$

schema implication

$S \Rightarrow T$ is a merged schema in which the *signatures* are combined, and the *properties* are joined by logical implication.

$$S \Rightarrow T = [\sigma S; \sigma T \mid S \Rightarrow T]$$

We advise avoiding this construct because $S \Rightarrow T$ is equivalent to $\neg S \vee T$, and *schema negation* may have unintended results. If you do use it note the consequences for merging the declarations; *normalisation* may be required.

schema in set comprehension

Schemas may be used to supply the declaration and predicate for a set comprehension.

See also *schema as declaration*, *schema as predicate*.

> page 89: Space flights: using *Route*
> page 186: Sequences are sets (videos): using *Video* as a type

schema inclusion

Schema names may be included in the declarations of other schemas. The declarations are merged and the predicates conjoined.

See also *schema as declaration*.

> page 84: Space flights: use in specification of a state

schema invariant

The invariant of a state schema is its *property*. There may be many possible assignments of values to the variables in the signature, but only those that obey the property part of the schema give a legitimate occurrence of the state.

> page 191: Sequences are sets (telephone directory): invariant of *TelephoneSystem*

schema negation

$\neg S$ has the same *signature* as the schema S, and the negated *property* part.

$$\neg S = [\sigma S \mid \neg S]$$

Because the predicate part of negated $S \;\widehat{=}\; [d \mid p]$ is $\neg S$ (so implicit predicates in the declaration are negated), rather than $\neg p$ (where implicit predicates in the declaration are not negated), this may have unintended results, and should be used with caution.

If the schemas are used as predicates, then schema negation behaves as expected (section 23.6.3). See also section 23.5 for more details.

> page 282: Schemas: 'not this but that'
> page 289: Schemas: use in *EmptyList*

schema piping

$S \gg T$ is the schema piping of two operations, where the output variables of S, those decorated with !, are identified with the input variables of T, those decorated with ?, and then hidden. The resulting operation has the inputs of the first schema and the outputs of the second.

Schema piping is unlikely to be in the Z Standard and we do not recommend its use.

schema projection

$S \upharpoonright T$ has all the variables of schema S hidden, except for those in schema T. See also *schema hiding*.

> page 30: Security properties: definition of *TransOp*

schema quantification

Schemas can be used to supply the declaration and predicates of quantifications

$$\forall S \bullet \text{SchemaExpression}$$
$$\exists S \bullet \text{SchemaExpression}$$

The effect is as if the declarations and predicates of the schema had been copied out at this point (but see the point about lexical rules in *schema as declaration*).

> page 209: Promotion: use in promotion

schema renaming

The components of a schema may be renamed, provided that the names given do not conflict with others in that schema. Renaming is written

$$S[new_1/old_1, \ldots, new_n/old_n]$$

schema text

A schema text is a declaration and a predicate (the predicate may be omitted if it is a tautology).

schema, unnamed

The name of a schema has global scope, its components have local scope only. Thus it makes sense to give each schema a name, however, within a schema calculus expression it is sometimes convenient to introduce an unnamed schema. Typically this is quite short. More detailed schemas are likely to be referred to elsewhere and thus need to be named.

> page 94: Space flights: use in *AddFlight*
> page 286: Schemas: use in *IndexOffStart*

schema, updating a single component

A compact way of defining an operation schema that updates a single component only, while leaving all the other components unchanged, is to hide that component, dashed and undashed, from the Ξ state schema, and conjoin the operation that updates the variable. Suppose a is the only component of S we wish to change. Then we could write

$$\Delta SOnlyA \mathrel{\widehat{=}} \Xi S \setminus (a, a') \wedge \Delta S$$

> page 107: Video shop: definition of $\Delta\,VideoShopHire$

schema versus Cartesian product

An element of a *schema type* (a *schema binding*) is an unordered, named, collection of elements of various types; an element of a *Cartesian product* (an n-tuple) is an ordered, unnamed, collection of elements of various types.

A single component can be picked out of a schema binding using *component selection*, *s.x*. A special projection function needs to be defined in order to pick a component from an n-tuple. (Projection functions for pairs, *first* and *second*, are defined in the sample toolkit.)

A particular n-tuple value can be written down quite easily, as $(x, y, \ldots, z)$. There is no similar notation for writing down a particular schema binding; a more indirect approach is necessary (see section 24.5).

The Z Standard removes this asymmetry by supplying a notation for Cartesian component selection and for schema bindings.

> page 226: Free types (pack of cards): advantages and disadvantages

scope

Z has scope rules for its variables, depending upon how they are introduced.

See also *abbreviation definition, axiomatic description, given set, schema*.

sequence

$$\operatorname{seq} X == \{ f : \mathbb{N} \nrightarrow X \mid \operatorname{dom} f = 1 \ldots \#f \}$$

A sequence, as defined in the sample toolkit, is finite, and has as its indices an initial subsequence of the non-zero naturals.

sequence, extraction

For a set of numbers n and a sequence s, $n \upharpoonright s$ creates a sequence containing only those elements in s that appear at the indexes given in n, and in the same order. For example

$$\{2, 4, 6\} \upharpoonright \langle a, b, c, d, e \rangle = \langle b, d \rangle$$

> page 163: Be abstract (maximal common subsequence): use in *subseqOf*

sequence, filtering

For a sequence s and a set of values v, $s \upharpoonright v$ creates a new sequence that contains precisely those entries in sequence s that are elements of set v, and in the same order. For example

$$\langle a, b, c, d, e \rangle \upharpoonright \{b, d, f\} = \langle b, d \rangle$$

> page 63: Word count: removing non-space characters

sequence, injective

An injective sequence, written iseq X, has no duplicates. Notice that for an injective sequence $\# \operatorname{ran} s = \# s$.

sequence operations

The sample toolkit defines a number of operations for sequences.

head s	the first element of *s*	$head\langle a, b, c \rangle = a$
last s	the final element of *s*	$last\langle a, b, c \rangle = c$
front s	*s* without its last	$front\langle a, b, c \rangle = \langle a, b \rangle$
tail s	*s* without its head	$tail\langle a, b, c \rangle = \langle b, c \rangle$

See also *concatenation, in, prefix, sequence extraction, sequence filtering, squash, suffix*.

sequence, non-empty

$\operatorname{seq}_1 X$ is the set of non-empty sequences with entries drawn from set X.

set

A set in Z is a collection of elements of the same type.

set comprehension

The full form of a set comprehension is

$$\{ d \mid p \bullet t \}$$

where $d \mid p$ is a *schema text*. Either of the predicate p and the constructing term t may be omitted. The predicate p is used to constrain the allowed values declared in d; if it is omitted it is taken to be *true*. The constructing term is used to define the 'shape' of the elements in the set; if it is omitted then the shape is the *characteristic tuple* of the declaration. For example

$$squareEvens == \{\, x : \mathbb{N} \mid x \bmod 2 = 0 \bullet x * x \,\}$$
$$squares == \{\, x : \mathbb{N} \bullet x * x \,\}$$
$$evens == \{\, x : \mathbb{N} \mid x \bmod 2 = 0 \,\}$$

A set comprehension omitting both of p and t is fairly pointless, since

$$\{\, x : X;\, y : Y \,\} = X \times Y$$

page 64: Word count: constructing term in *lexicon*
page 67: Word count: constructing term in *line*
page 162: Be abstract (greatest common divisor): constructing term
page 172: Sets, quantifiers, toolkit (primes): constructing term
page 175: Sets, quantifiers, toolkit (square root): omitting the constructing term
page 175: Sets, quantifiers, toolkit (square root): using schemas in the declaration
page 297: Schemas: complicated constructing term in *swap*

set difference

Also known as 'set subtraction'.

$s \setminus t$ contains those elements of s that are not in t. For example

$$\{a, b, c\} \setminus \{c, d, e\} = \{a, b\}$$

page 120: Snakes and Ladders: in *square*, but not a slide or last square
page 167: Sets or functions: in *member* but not in *done*

set intersection

$s \cap t$ contains those of elements of s that are also in t. For example

$$\{a, b, c\} \cap \{c, d, e\} = \{c\}$$

See also *generalised intersection*.

set union

$s \cup t$ contains all the elements of s and of t. For example

$$\{a, b, c\} \cup \{c, d, e\} = \{a, b, c, d, e\}$$

See also *generalised union*.

signature

A schema can be considered as composed of its signature and its *property*. The signature introduces the schema variables and associates them with their types. A *declaration* is a signature along with implicit predicates. The signature of a schema S is sometimes written σS.

$$\sigma S = S \vee \neg S$$

page 287: Schemas: use in normalisation

source set

The name sometimes given to the set from which the elements of the *domain* of a binary *relation* are drawn.

See also *target set*.

specification, undefined

A specification may be undefined in those cases where there are no values to meet the specification. In such cases an implementation may do anything.

See section 22.5.3 for further discussion.

squash

squash is an operation that compacts a function from $\mathbb{N}_1$ to X into a sequence of X. For example

$$squash\{4 \mapsto c, 2 \mapsto b, 42 \mapsto e\} = \langle b, c, e \rangle$$

See sections 24.6.1 and 24.6.2 for further discussion.

page 70: Word count: use in definition of *upperseq*

successor function

The successor function, written *succ*, adds 1 to any natural number.

page 310: Language (mu): *squash*

suffix

A *relation* between *sequences*: s suffix t holds if s is a final contiguous subsequence of t, that is, if $u \frown s = t$.

See also *prefix, in*.

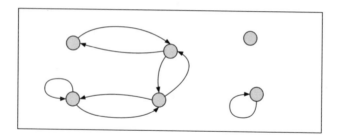

Figure B.3 A symmetric relation.

surjection

A surjection is a function that is 'onto'; its range is the whole of its *target set*. This may be partial ($\nrightarrow\!\!\!\!\rightarrow$), finite ($\nrightarrow\!\!\!\!\!\rightarrow$), or total ($\rightarrow\!\!\!\!\rightarrow$). An example of a surjection is shown in figure 17.7.

See section 17.5 for a discussion of the different kinds of functions and how they are related.

page 193: Sequences are sets (telephone directory): all users

symmetric relation

A symmetric relation r is one in which $(a \, r \, b) \Rightarrow (b \, r \, a)$. This is illustrated in figure B.3.

target set

The name sometimes given to the set from which the elements of the *range* of a binary *relation* are drawn.

See also *source set*.

tautology

A tautology is a predicate which is *true* under every possible interpretation.

See also *contingent*.

theorem

A specification should contain theorems that make important statements about the system. All theorems should be proved, else they are mere conjectures. A theorem is presented in the text as, for example

$$d \mid p \vdash q$$

where $d \mid p$ is a *schema text* and q is a predicate. It is equivalent to $d \vdash p \Rightarrow q$. The schema text on the left of the proof turnstile $\vdash$ is the 'hypothesis'; it declares the variables used in the theorem, and its predicate part p may be assumed when trying to prove the right hand side q.

page 85: Space flights: existence of initial state of *Venus*

page 215: Promotion: length of *pad*

page 291: Schemas: use of the turnstile

thinking ahead

It often pays to think ahead to requirements that a client or users may need even if these are not currently stated, and make provision for them. This is different from a *design decision*, which tends to restrict what the system can offer.

page 83: Space flights: extending for many users

•page 83: Space flights: putting variables into a schema

page 190: Sequences are sets (telephone directory): adding unnecessary detail

page 251: Bags (Scrabble): using *TILE*, not *CHAR*

tool support

There are a variety of tools available to support writing Z specifications, including formatters, syntax and type checkers, and proof assistants. [Parker 1991] catalogues available tools.

page 241: Free types (detail): declaration before use

toolkit

Many mathematical constructs may be defined in Z; it is often useful to define these within a toolkit. The sample toolkit defined in [Spivey 1992, Chapter 4] is assumed throughout this book, and we do not repeat the definitions here. Your own project might well need extra definitions, with a number of relevant laws, the validity of which you have to demonstrate.

Chapter 25 describes a real number toolkit. Appendix A defines some toolkit operations, used in the text of this book as an extension to the sample toolkit.

page 65: Word count: *wordFreq* using *sizebag*

page 65: Word count: *wordSeq* using anti-filter

page 69: Word count: using *monoSeq*

page 85: Space flights: distributed bag union in *alloc*

page 90: Space flights: *sizebag* used to check bookings

page 136: Tower of Hanoi: *sdecr* used to define *pole*

page 137: Tower of Hanoi: non-empty injective sequence

page 160: Be abstract (blue pencil): *bleep* using *uniqseq*

page 173: Sets, quantifiers, toolkit (primes): *consecutivePrimes* using *sincr*

page 215: Promotion: *pad* using *uniqseq*

page 251: Bags (Scrabble): *player* using *sizebag*

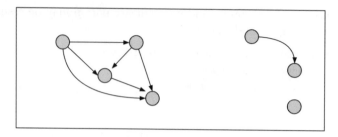

Figure B.4 A transitive relation.

page 254: Bags (Scrabble): distributed bag union
page 302: Language (red tape): *servesOn* using finite relation

total function

A function is total if the domain is the whole of its *source set*. It is written $\longrightarrow$. An example of a total function is shown in figure 17.6.

See section 17.5 for a discussion of the different kinds of functions and how they are related.

page 64: Word count: demonstrate that it it total
page 193: Sequences are sets (telephone directory): all telephones allocated

transitive closure

The transitive closure of a binary *relation*, written r^+, is the smallest *transitive relation* containing r. If r is considered as defining the places that can be reached in one 'hop', then r^+ defines all the places that can be reached in one or more hops.

See also *reflexive transitive closure.*

page 226: Free types (pack of cards): definition of *higherFace*
page 229: Free types (file system tree): definition of *isin*
page 234: Free types (file system tree): use in *dag*
page 295: Schemas: defining a partial order

transitive relation

A relation r is transitive if $(a\,r\,b) \wedge (b\,r\,c) \Rightarrow (a\,r\,c)$. If it is possible to go from a to b by multiple hops, then it is also possible to go by a single hop. This is illustrated in figure B.4.

page 175: Sets, quantifiers, toolkit (square root): abbreviating chains of relations
page 204: Error handling: linking expressions

use before declaration

A variable may be used before it has been declared in a Z specification, provided that it is possible to re-order the specification such that all variables are declared before being used. In general it is helpful to the reader to declare an item before using it, but occasionally it makes the specification more readable to do it the other way around.

Note that tools often enforce declaration before use, so you may not be permitted this luxury.

Ξ convention

By convention, if no other definition of ΞS is given, it is taken to be

$$\Xi S \;\widehat{=}\; [\, S;\, S' \mid \theta S = \theta S'\,]$$

The Ξ is part of the name of the schema and is used to indicate 'no change' on the state. If ΞS is defined explicitly, for example to include other variables and predicates, it overrides the default convention.

See also Δ *convention*.

page 107: Video shop: definition of Δ *VideoShopHire*

discussion

Throughout this book, discussion points appear.

page 138: Tower of Hanoi: state versus operation
page 190: Sequences are sets (telephone directory): use of power sets
page 250: Bags: sets versus quantifiers
page 254: Bags (Scrabble): stating that the size of a set is constant
page 256: Bags (Scrabble): framing schema in the game of Scrabble
page 257: Bags (Scrabble): how next player is modelled
page 258: Bags (poker): supplying parameters to a function
page 263: Calculator: no need to formalise well understood topics
page 277: Schemas: care needed with bag difference
page 308: Language (disjoint and partition): definition of distributed bag sum

Symbols

To help you find the appropriate entries, we give here a list of symbols and their names. Where the glossary entry differs from the symbol name, the glossary entry is given in parentheses.

==	abbreviation definition	λ	lambda-expression
◁	anti-restriction, domain	$\mapsto$	maplet
▷	anti-restriction, range	*max*	maximum
∘	backward relational composition	*min*	minimum
		$\mathbb{N}$	natural numbers
⊎	bag difference (bag operations)	$a \mathbin{..} b$	number range
		$\oplus$	overriding
⋹	bag membership	$\mathbb{P}, \mathbb{P}_1$	power set
count	bag multiplicity (bag operations)	pre	(precondition calculation)
♯	bag multiplicity (bag operations)	$\exists$	quantifier, existential
		$\exists_1$	quantifier, unique existential
⊗	bag scaling (bag operations)	$\forall$	quantifier, universal
⊑	sub-bag (bag operations)	ran	range
⊎	bag union (bag operations)	r^*	reflexive transitive closure
⤖	bijection	$\leftrightarrow$	relation, binary
#	cardinality	$\_r\_$	relation, infix
×	Cartesian product	⨟	relational composition / schema composition
s.x	component selection		
⌢	concatenation	⦇ ⦈	relational image
⌢/	concatenation, distributed	$r^\sim$	relational inverse
∧	conjunction / schema conjunction	r^k	relational iteration
		◁	restriction, domain
', ?, !	(decoration convention) / (schema decoration)	▷	restriction, range
		θ	schema binding
μ	definite description	$S \setminus (\ldots)$	schema hiding
Δ	Δ convention	$s \setminus t$	set difference
∨	disjunction / schema disjunction	$s \cap t$	set intersection
		$s \cup t$	set union
dom	domain	$\neg$	(schema negation)
⇸	finite function	↾	schema projection / sequence, filtering
$\mathbb{F}, \mathbb{F}_1$	finite sets		
Φ	(framing schema)	seq	sequence
::=	free type	↿	sequence, extraction
⋂	generalised intersection	iseq	sequence, injective
⋃	generalised union	seq_1	sequence, non-empty
id	identity relation	*succ*	successor function
⇔	if and only if / schema iff	↠	surjection
⇒	implies / schema implication	→	surjection, total
↣	injection	⇻	surjection, finite
⤔	injection, finite	⊢	(theorem)
↣	injection, total	→	total function
$\mathbb{Z}$	integers	r^+	transitive closure
		Ξ	(Ξ convention)

Appendix C

Bibliography

[Barden *et al.* 1992]
>   Rosalind Barden, Susan Stepney, and David Cooper. The use of Z. In [Nicholls 1992], pages 99–124.

[Barrett 1989]
>   Geoff Barrett. Formal methods applied to a floating-point number system. *IEEE Transactions on Software Engineering*, SE-15(5):611–621, May 1989.

[Bentley *et al.* 1986]
>   Jon Bentley, Donald E. Knuth, and Doug McIlroy. Programming pearls: a literate program. *Communications of the ACM*, 29(6):471–483, 1986.

[Bjørner *et al.* 1990]
>   Dines Bjørner, C. A. R. Hoare, and H. Langmaack, editors. *VDM'90: VDM and Z—Formal Methods in Software Development, Kiel*, volume 428 of *Lecture Notes in Computer Science*. Springer Verlag, 1990.

[Blyth 1990]
>   David Blyth. The CICS application programming interface: Temporary storage. IBM Technical Report TR12.301, IBM UK, Hursley Park, December 1990.

[Booch 1994]
>   Grady Booch. *Object-Oriented Analysis and Design with Applications*. Benjamin-Cummings, 2nd edition, 1994.

[Bowen 1987a]
>   Jonathan P. Bowen. Formal specification and documentation of microprocessor instruction sets. In H. Schumny and J. Mølgaard, editors, *Proceedings of Euromicro '87, Microcomputers: Usage, Methods and Structures*, volume 21(1–5) of *Microprocessing and Microprogramming*, pages 223–230. Elsevier North-Holland, August 1987.

[Bowen 1987b]
>   Jonathan P. Bowen. The formal specification of a microprocessor instruction

set. Technical Monograph PRG-60, Programming Research Group, Oxford University Computing Laboratory, January 1987.

[Bowen 1989]

Jonathan P. Bowen. POS—formal specification of a UNIX tool. *IEE Software Engineering Journal*, 4(1):67–72, 1989.

[Bowen & Hall 1994]

Jonathan P. Bowen and J. Anthony Hall, editors. *Proceedings of the 8th Z User Meeting, Cambridge 1994*, Workshops in Computing. Springer Verlag, 1994.

[Bowen & Nicholls 1993]

Jonathan P. Bowen and John E. Nicholls, editors. *Proceedings of the 7th Annual Z User Meeting, London 1992*, Workshops in Computing. Springer Verlag, 1993.

[Brien & Nicholls 1992]

Stephen M. Brien and John E. Nicholls. Z base standard, version 1.0. ZIP document ZIP/PRG/92/121, SRC D-132, Oxford University PRG, November 1992.

[Brown *et al.* 1986]

A. W. Brown, D. S. Robinson, and R. Weedon. Managing software development. In P. J. Brown and D. J. Barnes, editors, *Software Engineering '86*, volume 6 of *IEE Computing Series*, pages 197–235. Peter Peregrinus, 1986.

[Bryant 1990]

A. Bryant. Structured methodologies and formal notations: Developing a framework for synthesis and investigation. In [Nicholls 1990], pages 229–241.

[Carrington *et al.* 1990]

David A. Carrington, David Duke, Roger Duke, Paul King, Gordon A. Rose, and Graeme Smith. Object-Z: An object-oriented extension to Z. In S. Vuong, editor, *Formal Description Techniques II, FORTE'89*, pages 281–296. North-Holland, 1990.

[CESG 1991]

CESG. A formal development methodology for high confidence systems. CESG Computer Security Manual F, Communications-Electronics Security Group (L7), Government Communications Headquarters, Cheltenham, UK, February 1991.

[Chambers 1972]

Chambers Twentieth Century Dictionary. W & R Chambers, new edition, 1972.

[Clocksin & Mellish 1987]

W. F. Clocksin and C. S. Mellish. *Programming in Prolog*. Springer Verlag, 3rd edition, 1987.

[Cohen *et al.* 1986]

Bernard Cohen, W. T. Harwood, and M. I. Jackson. *The Specification of Complex Systems*. Addison-Wesley, 1986.

[Cooper 1990]
  David Cooper. Educating management in Z. In [Nicholls 1990], pages 192–194.

[Delisle & Garlan 1990]
  Norman Delisle and David Garlan. A formal specification of an oscilloscope. *IEEE Software*, pages 29–36, September 1990.

[Dick *et al.* 1990]
  A. J. J. Dick, P. J. Krause, and J. Cozens. Computer aided transformation of Z into Prolog. In [Nicholls 1990], pages 71–85.

[Dijkstra 1979]
  Edsgar W. Dijkstra. Structured programming. In Edward Yourdon, editor, *Classics in Software Engineering*. Yourdon Press, 1979.

[Diller 1990]
  Antoni Diller. *Z: An Introduction to Formal Methods*. Wiley, 1990.

[Draper 1993]
  Christine Draper. Practical experiences of Z and SSADM. In [Bowen & Nicholls 1993].

[Duke & Duke 1990a]
  David Duke and Roger Duke. Towards a semantics for Object-Z. In [Bjørner *et al.* 1990], pages 244–261.

[Duke & Duke 1990b]
  Roger Duke and David Duke. Aspects of object-oriented formal specification. In *Australian Software Engineering Conference*, 1990.

[Duke *et al.* 1990]
  Roger Duke, Gordon A. Rose, and Anthony Lee. Object-oriented protocol specification. In L. Logrippoo, R. L. Probert, and H. Ural, editors, *Protocol Specification, Testing and Verification 10*, pages 325–338. North-Holland, 1990.

[Duke *et al.* 1991]
  Roger Duke, Paul King, Gordon A. Rose, and Graeme Smith. The Object-Z specification language version 1. Technical Report 91-1, Software Verification Research Centre, Department of Computer Science, University of Queensland, May 1991.

[Fagan 1986]
  M. E. Fagan. Advances in software inspections. *IEEE Transactions on Software Engineering*, SE-12(7):44–51, 1986.

[Gardner 1965]
  Martin Gardner. *Mathematical Puzzles and Diversions*. Pelican, 1965.

[Garlan & Delisle 1990]
  David Garlan and Norman Delisle. Formal specifications as reusable frameworks. In [Bjørner *et al.* 1990], pages 150–163.

[Gerhart 1990]

Susan L. Gerhart. Applications of formal methods: Developing virtuoso software. *IEEE Software*, pages 7–10, September 1990.

[Giovanni & Iachini 1990]

R. Di Giovanni and P. Luigi Iachini. HOOD and Z for the development of complex systems. In [Bjørner *et al.* 1990], pages 262–289.

[Goldberg & Robson 1983]

Adele Goldberg and David Robson. *Smalltalk-80: The Language and its Implementation*. Addison-Wesley, 1983.

[Goldberg 1984]

Adele Goldberg. *Smalltalk-80: The Interactive Programming Environment*. Addison-Wesley, 1984.

[Gravell 1991]

Andrew M. Gravell. What is a good formal specification? In [Nicholls 1991], pages 137–150.

[Guindon 1990]

Raymonde Guindon. The knowledge exploited by experts during software system design. *International Journal of Man–Machine Studies*, 33(3):279–304, 1990.

[Hall 1990]

J. Anthony Hall. Using Z as a specification calculus for object-oriented systems. In [Bjørner *et al.* 1990], pages 290–318.

[Hall 1994]

J. Anthony Hall. Specifying and interpreting class hierarchies in Z. In [Bowen & Hall 1994], pages 120–138.

[Halliwell 1985]

Leslie Halliwell. *Halliwell's Film Guide*. Granada Publishing, 5th edition, 1985.

[Hammond 1994]

Jonathan A. R. Hammond. Producing Z specifications from object-oriented analysis. In [Bowen & Hall 1994], pages 316–336.

[Hayes 1990]

Ian J. Hayes. A generalisation of bags in Z. In [Nicholls 1990], pages 113–127.

[Hayes 1991]

Ian J. Hayes. Interpretations of Z schema operators. In [Nicholls 1991], pages 12–26.

[Hayes 1993a]

Ian J. Hayes. Flexitime specification. In [Hayes 1993b].

[Hayes 1993b]

Ian J. Hayes, editor. *Specification Case Studies*. Prentice Hall, 2nd edition, 1993.

[Hayes & Jones 1991]
>   Ian J. Hayes and Cliff B. Jones. Specifications are not (necessarily) exe-
>   cutable. *IEE Software Engineering Journal*, pages 330–338, November 1991.

[Hee *et al.* 1991]
>   K. M. van Hee, L. J. Somers, and M. Voorhoeve. Z and high level Petri
>   nets. In [Prehn & Toetenel 1991], pages 204–219.

[Helm *et al.* 1990]
>   Richard Helm, Ian M. Holland, and Dipayan Gangopadhyay. Contracts:
>   Specifying behavioral compositions in object-oriented systems.   *OOP-
>   SLA/ECOOP'90 Proceedings, ACM SIGPLAN Notices*, 25(10):169–180,
>   1990.

[Houston & King 1991]
>   Iain S. C. Houston and Steve King. CICS project report: Experience and
>   results from the use of Z in IBM. In [Prehn & Toetenel 1991], pages 588–596.

[Houston & Wordsworth 1990]
>   Iain S. C. Houston and John B. Wordsworth. A Z specification of part of the
>   CICS file control API. IBM Technical Report TR12.272, IBM UK, Hursley
>   Park, February 1990.

[Imperato 1991]
>   Michael Imperato. *An Introduction to Z*. Chartwell-Bratt, 1991.

[inmos]
>   inmos. IMS T800 architecture. Technical Note 6.

[Jacob 1991]
>   Jeremy Jacob. The varieties of refinement. In [Morris & Shaw 1991], pages
>   441–455.

[Johnson 1992]
>   Ralph E. Johnson. Documenting frameworks using patterns. *OOPSLA '92
>   Proceedings, ACM SIGPLAN Notices*, 27(10):63–76, October 1992.

[Johnson & Sanders 1990]
>   M. Johnson and P. Sanders. From Z specifications to functional implemen-
>   tations. In [Nicholls 1990], pages 86–112.

[Jones 1980]
>   Cliff B. Jones. *Software Development: a rigorous approach*. Prentice Hall,
>   1980.

[Kemp 1988a]
>   Duncan H. Kemp. Specification of Viper1 in Z. RSRE Memorandum 4195,
>   Royal Signals and Radar Establishment, September 1988.

[Kemp 1988b]
>   Duncan H. Kemp. Specification of Viper2 in Z. RSRE Memorandum 4217,
>   Royal Signals and Radar Establishment, October 1988.

[King 1990a]
> Steve King. The CICS application programming interface: Program control. IBM Technical Report TR12.302, IBM UK, Hursley Park, December 1990.

[King 1990b]
> Steve King. Z and the refinement calculus. In [Bjørner *et al.* 1990], pages 164–188.

[King & Sørensen 1989]
> Steve King and Ib Holm Sørensen. Specification and design of a library system. In John A. McDermid, editor, *The Theory and Practice of Refinement: Approaches to the Formal Development of Large-Scale Software Systems.* Butterworths, 1989.

[King *et al.* 1988]
> Steve King, Ib Holm Sørenson, and James C. P. Woodcock. Z: Grammar and concrete and abstract syntaxes. Technical Monograph PRG-68, Programming Research Group, Oxford University Computing Laboratory, 1988.

[Lano & Haughton 1994]
> Kevin Lano and Howard Haughton, editors. *Object-Oriented Specification Case Studies.* The Object-Oriented series. Prentice Hall, 1994.

[Lightfoot 1991]
> David Lightfoot. *Formal Specification Using Z.* Computer Science series. Macmillan, 1991.

[Lucas 1884]
> Édouard Lucas. La tour d'hanoï. *Science et Nature*, 1(8):127–128, 1884.

[Lupton 1991]
> Peter J. Lupton. Promoting forward simulation. In [Nicholls 1991], pages 27–49.

[Macdonald 1991]
> Ruaridh Macdonald. Z usage and abusage. RSRE Memorandum 91003, Royal Signals and Radar Establishment, February 1991.

[MacLean *et al.* 1994]
> Roy MacLean, Susan Stepney, Simon Smith, Nick Tordoff, David Gradwell, Tim Hoverd, and Simon Katz. *Analysing Systems: determining requirements for object oriented development.* BCS Practitioners Series. Prentice Hall, 1994.

[Mahoney & Hayes 1991]
> Brendan Mahoney and Ian J. Hayes. A case study in timed refinement: A central heater. In [Morris & Shaw 1991], pages 138–149.

[Mander *et al.* 1994]
> Keith C. Mander, Fiona Polack, and Mark Whiston. Software quality assurance using the SAZ method. In [Bowen & Hall 1994].

[May 1990]

David May. Use of formal methods by a silicon manufacturer. In C. A. R. Hoare, editor, *Developments in Concurrency and Communication*, University of Texas at Austin Year of Programming series, pages 107–129. Addison-Wesley, 1990.

[McMorran & Powell 1993]

Mike A. McMorran and Steve Powell. *Z Guide for Beginners*. Blackwell Scientific, 1993.

[Meyer 1988]

Bertrand Meyer. *Object-oriented Software Construction*. Prentice Hall, 1988.

[Mitchell *et al.* 1991]

Richard Mitchell, Martin Loomes, and John Howse. Organising specifications: a case study. Technical Report BPC 91/1, Brighton Polytechnic, Department of Computing, January 1991.

[MoD 1991]

The procurement of safety critical software in defence equipment. Interim Defence Standard 00-55 / Issue 1, UK Ministry of Defence, April 1991.

[Morgan 1990]

C. Carroll Morgan. *Programming from Specifications*. Prentice Hall, 1990.

[Morgan & Sanders 1989]

C. Carroll Morgan and Jeff W. Sanders. Laws of the logical calculi. Technical Monograph PRG-78, Programming Research Group, Oxford University Computing Laboratory, September 1989.

[Morgan & Sufrin 1993]

C. Carroll Morgan and Bernard A. Sufrin. Specification of the Unix filing system. In [Hayes 1993b].

[Morris & Shaw 1991]

Joseph M. Morris and Roger C. Shaw, editors. *4th Refinement Workshop*. Workshops in Computing. Springer Verlag, 1991.

[Mundy & Wordsworth 1990]

P. Mundy and John B. Wordsworth. The CICS application programming interface: Transient data and storage control. IBM Technical Report TR12.299, IBM UK, Hursley Park, October 1990.

[Nash 1990]

Trevor C. Nash. Using Z to describe large systems. In [Nicholls 1990], pages 150–178.

[Nicholls 1990]

John E. Nicholls, editor. *Z User Workshop: Proceedings of the 4th Annual Z User Meeting, Oxford 1989*, Workshops in Computing. Springer Verlag, 1990.

[Nicholls 1991]
John E. Nicholls, editor. *Proceedings of the 5th Annual Z User Meeting, Oxford 1990*, Workshops in Computing. Springer Verlag, 1991.

[Nicholls 1992]
John E. Nicholls, editor. *Proceedings of the 6th Annual Z User Meeting, York 1991*, Workshops in Computing. Springer Verlag, 1992.

[Nix & Collins 1988]
Christopher J. Nix and B. Peter Collins. The use of software engineering, including the Z notation, in the development of CICS. *Quality Assurance*, 14(3):103–110, September 1988.

[Norman 1980]
Barry Norman. *The Hollywood Greats*. Arrow, 1980.

[Parker 1991]
Colin E. Parker. Z tools catalogue. ZIP document ZIP/BAe/90/020, British Aerospace, Warton, May 1991.

[Phillips 1960]
Hubert Phillips. *The Pan Book of Card Games*. Pan, 1960.

[Polack *et al.* 1993]
Fiona Polack, Mark Whiston, and Keith C. Mander. The SAZ project: Integrating SSADM and Z. In James C. P. Woodcock and P. G. Larson, editors, *FME'93: Industrial-Strength Formal Methods*, volume 670 of *Lecture Notes in Computer Science*. Springer Verlag, 1993.

[Polack *et al.* 1994]
Fiona Polack, Mark Whiston, and Keith C. Mander. The SAZ method version 1.1. Technical Report YCS 207, Department of Computer Science, University of York, 1994.

[Potter *et al.* 1991]
Ben Potter, Jane Sinclair, and David Till. *An Introduction to Formal Specification and Z*. Prentice Hall, 1991.

[Prehn & Toetenel 1991]
S. Prehn and W. J. Toetenel, editors. *VDM'91: Formal Software Development Methods, Noordwijkerhout, Volume 1: Conference Contributions*, volume 551 of *Lecture Notes in Computer Science*. Springer Verlag, 1991.

[Rose 1992]
Gordon A. Rose. Object-Z. In [Stepney *et al.* 1992], Chapter 6, pages 59–77.

[Semmens & Allen 1991]
Lesley Semmens and Pat Allen. Using Yourdon and Z: An approach to formal specification. In [Nicholls 1991], pages 228–253.

[Shepherd & Wilson 1989]
David Shepherd and Greg Wilson. Making chips that work. *New Scientist*, 1664:61–64, May 1989.

[Shipman 1982]
> David Shipman.   *The Story of the Cinema,* volume 1.   Hodder and Stoughton, 1982.

[Smith & Duke 1989]
> Graeme Smith and Roger Duke. Specification and verification of a cache coherence protocol. Technical Report 126, Department of Computer Science, University of Queensland, August 1989.

[Spivey 1988]
> J. Michael Spivey. *Understanding Z: a specification language and its formal semantics,* volume 3 of *Cambridge Tracts in Theoretical Computer Science.* Cambridge University Press, 1988.

[Spivey 1992]
> J. Michael Spivey. *The Z Notation: a Reference Manual.* Prentice Hall, 2nd edition, 1992.

[SSADM 1986]
> Manchester NCC. *SSADM Manual Version 3,* 1986.

[SSADM 1990]
> Manchester NCC. *SSADM Manual Version 4,* 1990.

[Steggles & Hulance 1994]
> Pete Steggles and Jason Hulance. Z tools survey. Technical report, Imperial Software Technology, Cambridge, UK, June 1994.

[Stepney & Lord 1987]
> Susan Stepney and Stephen P. Lord. Formal specification of an access control system. *Software—Practice and Experience,* 17(9):575–593, 1987.

[Stepney *et al.* 1992]
> Susan Stepney, Rosalind Barden, and David Cooper, editors. *Object Orientation in Z.* Workshops in Computing. Springer Verlag, 1992.

[Sterling & Shapiro 1986]
> Leon Sterling and Ehud Shapiro. *The Art of Prolog: Advanced Programming Techniques.* MIT Press, 1986.

[Stewart 1992]
> Ian Stewart. *Another Fine Math You've Got Me Into.* W. H. Freeman, 1992.

[Stewart & Tall 1977]
> Ian Stewart and David Tall. *The Foundations of Mathematics.* Oxford University Press, 1977.

[Turner 1986]
> David Turner.   An overview of Miranda.   *ACM SIGPLAN Notices,* 21(12):158–166, 1986.

[Valentine 1993]
> Sam Valentine. Putting numbers into the mathematical toolkit. In [Bowen & Nicholls 1993].

[Wegner 1987a]
> Peter Wegner. Dimensions of object-based language design. *OOPSLA '87 Proceedings, ACM SIGPLAN Notices*, 22(12):168–182, 1987.

[Wegner 1987b]
> Peter Wegner. The object-oriented classification paradigm. In Bruce Shriver and Peter Wegner, editors, *Research Directions in Object-Oriented Programming*. MIT Press, 1987.

[Wells 1987]
> David Wells. *The Penguin Dictionary of Curious and Interesting Numbers*. Penguin, revised edition, 1987.

[West & Eaglestone 1989]
> Margaret M. West and Barry M. Eaglestone. Software development: Two approaches to animation of Z specifications using Prolog. *IEE Software Engineering Journal*, pages 264–276, July 1989.

[West *et al.* 1992]
> Margaret M. West, T. F. Buckley, and P. H. Jesty. Pelican safety study. Research Report 92.4, University of Leeds, School of Computer Studies, March 1992.

[Wikström 1987]
> Å. Wikström. *Functional Programming using Standard ML*. Prentice Hall, 1987.

[Woodcock 1989]
> James C. P. Woodcock. Structuring specifications in Z. *IEE Software Engineering Journal*, 4(1):51–66, 1989.

[Woodcock 1991]
> James C. P. Woodcock. An introduction to refinement in Z. ZIP document ZIP/RAL/92/005, Rutherford Appleton Laboratories, October 1991.

[Woodcock & Brien 1992]
> James C. P. Woodcock and Stephen M. Brien. $\mathcal{W}$: A logic for Z. In [Nicholls 1992], pages 77–96.

[Woodcock & Davies 1994]
> James C. P. Woodcock and Jim Davies. *Using Z: specification, proof and refinement*. Prentice Hall, 1995. To appear.

[Woodcock & Loomes 1988]
> James C. P. Woodcock and Martin Loomes. *Software Engineering Mathematics*. Pitman, 1988.

[Worden 1991]
> Robert Worden. The process of refinement. In [Morris & Shaw 1991], pages 1–5.

[Wordsworth 1989a]
> John B. Wordsworth. Practical experience of formal specification: a pro-

gramming interface for communications. In *Proceedings of ESEC'89*, number 387 in Lecture Notes in Computer Science. Springer Verlag, 1989.

[Wordsworth 1989b]

John B. Wordsworth. A Z development method. Draft version 0.11, IBM UK, Hursley Park, January 1989.

[Wordsworth 1992]

John B. Wordsworth. *Software Development with Z.* Addison-Wesley, 1992.

Index